MODERN POLITICAL ECONOMY

Ideas and Issues

(with revisions)

Edited by

JAMES B. HERENDEEN
Assistant Professor of Economics
Center for Continuing Liberal Education
The Pennsylvania State University

PRENTICE-HALL, INC., *Englewood Cliffs, New Jersey*

Library of Congress Catalog Number: 68–14800

current printing (last number)

10 9 8 7 6 5 4 3 2 1

Prentice-Hall International, Inc., London
Prentice-Hall of Australia, Pty Ltd., Sydney
Prentice-Hall of Canada, Ltd., Toronto
Prentice-Hall of India Private Ltd., New Delhi
Prentice-Hall of Japan Inc., Tokyo

Printed in the United States of America

PREFACE

The purpose of this collection of readings is to give an introduction to the basic ideas of modern political economy and to discuss several current economic policy issues. Political economy studies the way in which society organizes its economic and political institutions to achieve its economic goals. In a modern economy, more and more economic decisions are made through the political process. Only if the public and the policy makers have a high degree of economic literacy can wise and rational economic decisions be expected.

The readings are divided into ten general topics: Part 1, *The Scope and Method of Economics;* Part 2, *The Productive Process;* Part 3, *Measurement and Determination of National Income;* Part 4, *Stabilization Policy;* Part 5, *The Distribution of Income;* Part 6, *Government Spending;* Part 7, *Business, Labor and Agriculture;* Part 8, *The Balance of International Payments;* Part 9, *Economics and Ideology;* Part 10, *The Role of Government.* A brief commentary on the ideas and issues in each part—and discussion questions for each part—are furnished by the editor.

The editor wishes to acknowledge his debt to: Cyril Hager, Director, Center for Continuing Liberal Education, The Pennsylvania State University, who originally suggested the preparation of this type of book; Grant N. Farr, Head, Department of Economics, for encouraging the author to undertake the project; the Center for Continuing Liberal Education for publishing the initial edition of this book; Peter Dooley, who read the original draft of all the introductory sections and the editor's article "The Farm Income Problem," and made numerous helpful suggestions; and Wayne Schutjer for his helpful comments on the editor's article, "The Farm Income Problem."

JAMES B. HERENDEEN

CONTENTS

PART 4

STABILIZATION POLICY 99

PART 5

THE DISTRIBUTION OF INCOME 153

PART 6

GOVERNMENT SPENDING 191

PART 7

BUSINESS, LABOR, AND AGRICULTURE 227

PART 8

THE BALANCE OF INTERNATIONAL PAYMENTS 269

PART 9

ECONOMICS AND IDEOLOGY 291

PART 10

THE ROLE OF GOVERNMENT 325

PART 1

THE SCOPE AND METHOD OF ECONOMICS

The first section of this book is aimed at giving the reader a general introduction to the scope and method of modern economics. Economics can be considered a science of choice. It tries to give us knowledge of how society makes choices about economic matters. Since resources are scarce and have alternative uses, we must have a method of allocating the scarce resources among these alternatives. This basic problem can be divided into two subproblems:

(1) Making choices about the level of employment of resources. Usually society prefers to have resources, especially labor, more or less fully employed. Choices in this area involve alternative levels of taxation, government spending, and interest rates that will stimulate economic activity. The results of the choices influence the mix between private and public consumption and private and public investment. Also, they affect income distribution by their influence on interest rates, profits, the level of government transfer payments, and the general price level. This type of study is called *macroeconomics*.

(2) Making choices about the allocation of resources among alternative uses. Here society must decide what to produce, how resources are to be used in production, how products will be allocated to consumers, and how incomes generated by production will be allocated to the participants in the production process. This type of study is called *microeconomics*.

There are two general ways that society makes choices in economic matters. The first is the market; here choices are made by individual decision makers such as consumers, workers, and business corporations, in response to changes in relative prices and incomes or changes in expectations about future prices and incomes. If the market is very competitive, these prices are determined by the interaction of all producers, consumers, and resource suppliers in the market with no one having any control over price. With less than perfect markets, individual producers, consumers, or resource suppliers may be able to influence the prices and incomes they receive from the market.

Second, there is the political process. Producers, consumers, and resource suppliers can also make collective choices through government that will influence the terms they face in the market. These groups can influence government to take action to affect the general level of economic activity through its spending policies, its taxing policies, and its regulation of the money and credit. Also, political choices are used to furnish many public services. These include provision of a police force, national defense, public education, and public health services. In addition, there may be social costs which must be met by government action. Such costs to society as soil erosion and stream pollution are not costs to the individual farmer or businessman who causes the soil erosion or the stream pollution, but are costs to society.

Economics can be conveniently broken down into three fields in terms of the approach to the subject. These are economic analysis, applied economics, and political economy. Economic analysis attempts to develop abstract generalizations about economic behavior by using the methods of deductive and inductive reasoning. Deductive reasoning often takes the form of mathematics. Certain general assumptions about economic behavior are made and then the logical consequences of these assumptions are developed. By using such methods economists can arrive at certain general principles. For example, it can be shown that profit will be maximized by expanding output to the point where additional (marginal) revenue is just equal to additional (marginal) cost.

Inductive reasoning is used to give empirical generalizations to economics and to verify, or reject, the theories developed by deductive reasoning. It may be observed that, as the price of a commodity rises, the amount produced will increase. It may then be concluded that the amount supplied will ordinarily be an increasing function of price. And it can be shown that this is the behavior we would expect from a producer behaving as a profit maximizer.

Applied economics consists primarily of using the methods of economic analysis to answer particular economic questions. One of the tools used by the applied economist is econometrics. Econometrics is used to test the abstract economic theories developed by economic analysis. It does this by using methods developed by modern mathematics and statistics. For example, it may be hypothesized that the quantity of pork consumed will be a function of the price of pork, the price of beef, the price of chickens, the price of other foods, the price of nonfoods, and consumer incomes. This relationship may be formulated in mathematical form and then tested by statistical methods using observed data on actual consumption of pork and actual prices of pork and other commodities and actual consumers' incomes. The results can give the researcher some idea whether he should have confidence in his theoretical formulation to explain the demand for pork. Also, the results can be used to predict consumption, given certain changes in prices or income. The labor economists may use economic analysis and econometrics to examine the effect of a wage increase on the level of employment. An agricultural economist may use these tools to determine the effect of a particular government program on farm incomes. An economist concerned with general economic policy might measure the expected change in national income from a given change in taxes or government spending. As a scientist, the economist cannot say what is the best policy for society to choose. He can only analyze the economic consequences of alternative policy proposals and estimate various dollar costs or benefits of such programs. To say what is the best policy involves certain moral and ethical (value) judgments that cannot be resolved by the methods of economics. The economist attempts to develop theories that are generally true, that do not depend on particular economic or political systems, and that are independent of their own beliefs and values. When dealing with particular policy issues, he attempts to take goals as given by society rather than impose his own views on his analysis. Avoiding value judgments is, however, a goal, not reality. The economist can never completely divorce himself from his own preconceived ideas. He should, however, make the attempt. As Joan Robinson has said, "The objectivity of the social science arises, not because the individual is impartial, but because many individuals are continually testing each others' theories."*

This leads to the final field of economics, that of political economy. During the nineteenth century, what is today called economics was called "political economy." The term has fallen into disuse in the twentieth century. However, it seems that a large part of modern economics could be better described by this term. *Political economy* as used in this book will refer to society's political choices about how to organize its economic life—that is what are the basic economic goals of society and how can society organize its economic, social,

---

* Joan Robinson, *Economic Philosophy* (London: C. A. Watts and Co., Ltd., 1962), p. 23.

and political institutions to achieve these goals. Here, of course, economics becomes closely tied with sociology, and also with political and moral philosophy. Political economy cannot avoid the study of value judgments. This does not mean that the political economist can decide what are the best values for society to hold. Instead it is his job to analyze these values, test their consistency with the basic goals of society, and analyze how alternative economic organizations may achieve or impede these goals. Thus political economy puts economics into an institutional setting and recognizes that the means to various economic ends must come through adjustments of the institutional setting in which the economy operates.

The great economists—Adam Smith, Alfred Marshall, J. M. Keynes, and many more—were all of the above. They were seeking answers to pressing current policy questions; they advanced economic analysis by developing analytical tools with which to attempt to answer these questions; and they all had a vision of how society could best organize its economic institutions.

The article by Professor Knight traces the development of economic thought, summarizes the theories of the classical tradition in economics, discusses the methods of economics, and poses some of the problems of present-day economics. He stresses that each stage in the development of economic thought corresponds to a distinctive political order and a distinctive conception of man and society.

The article by Professor Boulding discusses the development of economic thought and the contributions of economic analysis to a better understanding of the economy and to increased ability to resolve important economic policy issues. In addition, he points out some of the unresolved problems in economic theory and policy.

Selection 1

Economics

FRANK H. KNIGHT

From "Economics," *Encyclopaedia Britannica, 1951 edition, Vol. 7. Reprinted by permission of Encyclopaedia Britannica, Chicago, Illinois.*

The term "economics" has come into general use since the early years of the present century, replacing the older "political economy" as the name of a somewhat vaguely defined branch of social science. The change of name reflected changes in the discipline itself, which had become subdivided into a number of specialties. A separation had been made between a pure science and the treatment of public—and to some extent of private—problems of policy, more or less explicitly "application;" another separation has been made between empirical fact—historical or statistical—and theory. The word "economy" comes from two Greek roots referring to the management of a household or estate. But in the past two centuries or so, the meaning has become generalized to cover all use of means in such a way as to "husband" them, to make them go as far as possible. "Political economy" itself is a modern term. It was introduced about the beginning of the seventeenth century (in French—corresponding to the German *Kameralwissenschaft*) to describe the study of the problems of the princely states which at the close of the Middle Ages in Europe replaced the feudal-ecclesiastical political order. It referred to the "economic" affairs of the state or principality—the raising and use of revenue and increase of resources—treating the state as the estate of the ruler. But this study never was generally known by this name. After the nationalistic epoch gave way to individualism or liberalism at the time of the Enlightenment in the late eighteenth century, "political economy" was adopted as the name of a science based on the new moral and political worker view, and the older literature came to be designated as "mercantilism."

Epochs in the Development of Economic Thought

The sketch above suggests four main periods or epochs in the evolution of modern economics, corresponding to those usually recognized in European history. They are the Greek (or "classical" in the meaning of general history, but the Roman contribution was minor), the medieval, the early modern (sixteenth to late eighteenth century), and the modern, roughly the nineteenth century. Each corresponds to a distinctive political order and to distinctive conceptions of man and society; and it is an important fact that books were written by and for different social classes in the different periods. The Greek literature was written by aristocratic philosophers and publicists and related to the problems of the city-state, nominally democratic but based on slave labor and with further exclusion of the merchant and financier from civic life. Such writers as Plato and Aristotle commented on many of the obvious facts and principles, such as the importance of division of labor and the use of money. But their interest centered in such moralistic and metaphysical notions as the condemnation of lending at interest as unnatural. Modern knowledge of the economic and industrial life of ancient Greece is derived mainly from other sources, incidental references in literature, and archeological remains. Many of the ideas were in fact survivals of primitive attitudes; they are found also in the older parts of the Bible and survive as a strong influence even today.

Medieval economic thought is still more moralistic and alien to the modern outlook. The literature was produced chiefly by and for monks, at a time when the monastic life was accepted as the ideal, when worldly interests were denounced in favor of salvation in a future world as the one serious concern of man. The dominant social organization was the Church, and recorded thought was more of the nature of preaching than of science, as words are now used. For this world, the accepted ideal was a static or customary society and civilization, every man working out his lot in the situation to which he had been "called." Trade was frowned upon, beyond limited routine exchange at "fair"—meaning customary—prices, corresponding with a customary standard of living for each social class, and interest-taking was condemned outright. In the later Middle Ages, however, the canon law and the Church courts played a large role in everyday affairs, and the monasteries themselves were the spearhead in great advances in both industry and trade. Numerous evasions of the prohibition against interest-taking, achieving the same result through other contractual arrangements, came into use and were recognized as legitimate. Men's interests were shifting to the concerns of earthly life, cultural, aesthetic, and scientific as well as material, that is, political and economic. The evolution of economics must be seen as integral with that of economic life and of European civilization as a whole.

The third period is best designated as that of economic nationalism, but the economic thought is usually called *mercantilism*. It dealt with the economic policies of the national monarchic states which displaced the feudal order at the close of the Middle Ages and in general dominated the Church, whether or not the states established national churches following the Reformation. Vast changes came over social life and men's conceptions and interests. A great cultural renaissance spread from Italy to northern Europe, and technological advances were made in all fields. Paper and printing, and especially the modern Arabic system of notation, the foundation of both science and business, were even more important than gunpowder and the compass and greatly improved methods in mining and metallurgy. The distinctive writings on economic matters were produced by political pamphleteers. It was the age of the "commercial revolution;" the monarchical states saw wealth through foreign trade as the basis of their power and money as the embodiment of wealth (*pecunia nervus belli*). Europe was flooded with silver and gold (especially from the New World) which came in chiefly by way of Spain and the northern countries. These countries, having no mines at home or in the colonies, centered attention on sharing the treasure through a favorable balance of trade—an excess of exports over imports. A quasi-alliance was formed between the governments and the wealthy merchant and financier class against the ecclesiastical power and the higher nobility. Meanwhile, social, moral, and intellectual as well as economic forces had tended, especially in the towns, to the emancipation of labor from slavery and serfdom. But men were not ready for the ideal of individual freedom; the state took the place of the Church, and the town oligarchies that grew out of the guilds as the supreme regulative authority, and their aggrandizement, became the accepted end of policy, with control over economic life as the means.

Mercantilism flourished from the sixteenth century down to the nineteenth century and was exemplified in innumerable writings and in the restrictive and regulative policies of such statesmen and rulers as Colbert, Burleigh, Cromwell, and Frederick the Great. Besides attempting to secure a favorable balance of trade (an excess of exports, bringing in money or bullion), other aims were low interest rates, low wages, and encouragement of population growth and colonies. Mercantilism has been interpreted as "nation-building" and as an advance toward free trade, which was promoted within the national domain, in contrast with the application of similar policies by smaller units in the medieval towns. Whether the measures advocated met the immediate needs of the times is still a disputed question. In economic terms the fallacies have long since been exposed, but the general attitude survives today, as the reader will observe in "protectionism." Contrary to the admitted advantages of international specialization, this is favored and practiced not only by the national states but by smaller units, such as the American states and municipalities.

Transition to Modern Political Economy or Economics

Modern economics is an aspect of modern thought and of the individualistic or "liberal" outlook on life, of which "capitalism," or the competitive system, or free business enterprise, is the expression on the economic side, as democracy is on the political. Our fourth epoch takes its rise in a second great cultural revolution in western Europe, in which the period of the Renaissance moved into that of the Enlightenment or Age of Reason. In this development leadership shifted, in the early modern period, from Mediterranean Europe to the northern countries and especially to England, with the British colonies in North America playing an important role. England escaped the wars of religion which devastated western continental Europe for over a century after the Reformation, and here especially religious toleration eased the tension between church and state. England was predominant in the great scientific movement of the seventeenth century, and the great Civil War and the Revolution of 1688 established representative government at the same time that the treaties ending the Thirty Years War fastened political absolutism on the major Continental states. In England, science was inspired with a "practical" philosophy, formulated by Francis Bacon, a contemporary of Galileo, the heir of Copernicus. This movement led naturally to the technological revolution of the later eighteenth and the early nineteenth century which involved the triumph of free enterprise; and modern economics is essentially the theory of free enterprise. It is interesting to observe that the great mercantilist writers of the later seventeenth century in England (contemporaries of John Locke in political philosophy) were in substance free traders, as Sir William Ashley has pointed out in detail. Thomas Mun's famous booklet, *England's Treasure by Forraign Trade* (published posthumously in 1664 but in circulation earlier), sophistically used the balance of trade argument in favor of freedom to export specie. Other writers, such as D'Avenant, Barbon, Child, and especially Sir Dudley North, worked out the theoretical argument for freedom in foreign trade about as explicitly and clearly as did Adam Smith himself nearly a century later. North argued that the wealth of a nation is that of its citizens and that the businessmen, traders, and producers are the best judges of when trade involves a net gain. It remained for someone to apply the same reasoning to internal policy, against the surviving guild restrictions or national control of apprenticeship, wages, and interest, grants of monopolies, and the like.

All through the later mercantilist period, economic relations were gradually becoming more free—controls were falling into disuse, particularly in England. The process, like the earlier disappearance of serfdom, is one of social development, to be explained by the sociologist and culture historian; the formulation of a general theory lagged behind the factual change, at least until the latter was far along. In notable respects the statement of free-trade doctrine came earlier in France, where the movement itself was much slower. It was here, of course, that the phrase "laissez faire" (earlier associated with *laissez passer*) originated, in the first half of the eighteenth century. The kingdom of France was subdivided into many districts with customs frontiers until the Great Revolution. About the same time appeared one of the most notable of the books anticipating the liberal point of view, the somewhat mysterious *Essai sur la nature du commerce en général* by Richard Cantillon. It is apparently a translation, perhaps by the author himself, of an English manuscript which has disappeared. Cantillon showed a fairly clear insight into the mechanism by which a free market will direct resources into the production of the goods in most demand. Similar insights were conspicuous in the nearly contemporary essays of David Hume, though he wrote no systematic treatise. Early in the second half of the century much attention was attracted by the writings of a French school, who called themselves *les économistes* but are now referred to as the Physiocrats. The word is practically equivalent to law (or rule) of nature. The leader was the court physician, François Quesnay. Like many of the mercantilists, these writers used rather absurd if ingenious arguments; and it has been pointed out that the position was connected with the self-interest of certain groups that had achieved wealth and power in the disturbed conditions in France after the death of Louis XIV, especially in consequence of the ambitious schemes of John Law and the famous "Mississippi Bubble." (A similar wave of speculative fury in England at the same time is known as the "South Sea Bubble," from the name of the most spectacular of many companies that were organized.) But the Physiocrats are to be credited with an attempt to see and analyze a national economy as a whole. Their most characteristic doctrine was the view that only agriculture yields a "surplus" beyond what is required for the support of the workers; hence land rent alone is available for the support of the state or the increase of wealth and is the only proper subject for taxation. These ideas survived in the work of Adam Smith and the British "classical" economists. The pre-Revolutionary statesman, A. R. J. Turgot, renowned for his courageous but abortive economic and fiscal reforms, was to some extent a disciple; his work, *Réflexions sur la formation et la distribution des richesses* (1766), is an exceedingly able treatise.

Classical Political Economy

In 1776 Adam Smith published *An Inquiry into the Nature and the Causes of the Wealth of Nations,* a work in which wisdom, learning, and the power of analysis are joined to an extraordinary degree. As already noted, Smith shared many of the popular prejudices that were evident in the writings of the Physiocrats. He held that "in agriculture nature works with man"—as though this were not true of all other pursuits—and that only labor is productive, and indeed only that labor is productive which at least reproduces the capital which supports it. Also, that the interests of businessmen, as a class, are more often opposed to the interests of the community than are those of landowners. Nevertheless, Smith gave the world a new view of the advantages of trade as a mechanism for working out the "division of labor" and a new "philosophy of commerce." But he saw in commerce, as well as in internal trade, a means to welfare—not merely to the aggrandizement of the state. His book was, in one leading aspect, a formidable tract directed against mercantilism. Money, from the communal point of view, he held to be merely an instrument, a "wheel of trade." The real source of a country's wealth, he said, is its "annual labor," and its wealth or well-being could be increased only by making its labor more effective, particularly by extending specialization and accumulating product in the form of capital. (For "labor" we should now say "productive resources.") That "the division of labor is limited by the extent of the market" is one of his most famous sayings.

These were Adam Smith's fundamental principles. He elaborated them with great skill in relation to concrete problems, showing unusual powers of fresh observation in his selection and use of illustrative material, and passing large sections of economic history and the whole range of the contemporary commercial and fiscal problems of Britain under survey. Although the book is the most influential brief ever formulated for unimpeded trade, neither hampered nor coddled by governments, its greatest importance lies not in that circumstance but in the general picture, at once simple and comprehensive, which it gives of the economic life of a nation. The apparent chaos of competition, the welter of buying and selling, are resolved or transmuted into an orderly system of economic cooperation by means of which, under individual freedom in contrast with central direction, the community's wants are supplied and its wealth increased. This general picture has been in the minds of economists ever since, whatever their opinions with respect to the efficiency or morality of the competitive system, and its general outline is admitted even by collectivists to be valid for their systems. Despite some sweeping phrases which invite another interpretation, Smith was no doctrinaire advocate of a hands-off policy by governments in respect of economic matters. His treatment must be understood against the background of conditions of his day, in which so much was a holdover from the period of mercantilism and even from the Middle Ages. He was opposed to monopoly, exclusive combinations, and special privileges of all kinds quite as much as to the type of legislation which aims at fostering a country's prosperity by restricting its trade. He is often styled the "apostle of self-interest," but he took no pains to conceal his dislike for some of the forms in which self-interest manifests itself in trade and industry, and he had no aversion to legal measures wherever they actually promised to be beneficial. What his attitude would have been under the later conditions of the nineteenth and twentieth centuries, toward the factory acts, toward social insurance, and, particularly, toward measures intended to foster equality of opportunity we cannot tell. But there is nothing in the aims of these newer types of legislation which runs counter to his principal contentions or which is inconsistent with his general economic philosophy.

Adam Smith's work had a profound influence, not in Britain alone, but in almost every part of the Western world. It was partly responsible for some radical changes in the commercial policies of governments, although its influence cannot be measured, since the current of the times was moving in the direction of his contentions. Its effect upon scientific thought and upon the character and quality of public discussions of economic questions cannot be questioned. Men like J. B. Say in France and K. H. Rau in Germany based their work very largely on Smith's and helped to diffuse his influence. Say, however, was more than a mere popularizer. He had some clear-cut views of his own and developed Smith's work in directions other than those it took in the hands of Smith's British successors. In the United States, Say's work came to be about as widely read as Smith's.

The particular trend which the development of economics took in Great Britain after Smith was largely determined by the character of the economic problems which confronted the nation, partly by reason of rapid changes in its own industrial structure (the Industrial Revolution) and partly in consequence of the French Revolutionary and Napoleonic Wars. Population increased rapidly, and in particular there was a "mushroom" growth of new industrial towns; foreign trade expanded, especially the export of industrial products and import of agricultural products, reversing the previous situation; yet agricultural cultivation was extended with the commercialization of farming and vast improvements of methods both of tillage and of stock-breeding. The changes were accentuated by interference with trade through the wars and governmental effort to maintain self-sufficiency in food (or to benefit the landed interest which controlled the government); land rents rose with the increase in agricultural prices relative to industrial prices; the currency was depreciated (a practically universal accompaniment of a major war); rates of interest and of profits were disturbed, and, after the peace, both industry and agriculture experienced depression conditions. Some of these conspicuous and important phenomena engaged the attention of Parliamentary committees; all of them attracted the interest of thoughtful men who, with Adam Smith's picture of the mechanism of organized economic life in their minds, thought of them as interrelated and attempted to explain them in some consistent and comparatively simple way. Out of the discussions of the period, in pamphlets and controversial tracts, there emerged a formal system of political economy. It owed much to Smith, but it stressed matters to which he had given little or no attention and emended his views at a number of important points. This newer political economy was concerned more largely with abstract general relations, but it dealt with real problems and dealt with them in what was intended to be a practical way. There is an appearance of paradox, but only an appearance, in the fact that the type of economics which grew out of attempts to deal intelligently with the problems of a period of economic storm and stress was one which gave particular attention to "normal tendencies" and to the conditions of "economic equilibrium" rather than to the immediate causes of economic maladjustments. A parallel may be found in the way in which the study of pathology has contributed to men's knowledge of normal physiology.

For convenience, the period of which we are now speaking may be taken as definitely beginning with the publication of David Ricardo's *Principles of Political Economy and Taxation* in 1817 and as culminating with the publication of John Stuart Mill's *Principles of Political Economy* in 1848. One who compares the economic tracts and the systematic treatises of that period with *The Wealth of Nations* will be impressed with the increased importance given to a group of problems which have continued to be principal concerns of economics—problems now commonly grouped under the head of "theory of value and distribution." These problems of price-mechanics unfortunately tend to get separated from the real issues of the way in which the price system organizes production and distributes the result. The theory of value, of course, attempts to explain why goods exchange at particular ratios—why some are relatively expensive and others cheap. (Absolute money prices are, of course, a matter of the value or purchasing power of money, a distinct problem.) The modern theory of distribution is really a part of value theory, dealing with the prices of "productive services," with a view to explaining the sharing of the national income or "social dividend." But the classical economists (from Smith to J. S. Mill) did not look at the problem in this way; they held a more metaphysical theory of the division of the total product into the three traditional shares: wages of labor, profits of capital, and rent of land. This theory will be considered presently. Later on, the conception of a fourth share, the profits of enterprise, or of the successful direction of production, was taken over from the French economists (Say and his followers); the earnings of capital, separated from the entrepreneurial functions of management and responsible risk-taking, were called "interest" (whether actually paid out for borrowed money or "imputed" to that of the owner, an individual, or a group). This has been more true in the United States than in Britain, where economists still rather typically speak of the "profits of capital" in the language of business and of everyday life. And the treatment of enterprise or risk-taking (better called uncertainty-bearing, since there can be no measurement of the risk as in gambling or insurance) raises problems on which there is no agreement among economists anywhere.

The threefold (or fourfold) classification of "factors" is clearly in part arbitrary. Some economists use a twofold classification, treating land as a particular form of capital; others point out that a logical classification would recognize many different kinds of capital, of labor, and of natural resources, with some kinds under one head economically less similar to others in the same class than to some in other classes. And it must also be recognized that, in the long run, all productive agents largely represent a cost of production, an investment of resources in the past (with wide variation in the relation between such cost and present value because of "uncertainty"), and that this investment is more or less subject to recovery and reinvestment in other types of productive agent. Yet the three forms of income are very real to ordinary thinking, which does not distinguish, for example, between the four or five elements obviously present in most personal earnings. One part is based on natural capacity, one on the "pain" or irksomeness of the work, one on the investment in training; and there is the factor of risk or imperfect foresight, which so profoundly affects the return on any investment for return in a fairly remote future; and, finally, noneconomic motives affect in special ways the investment in human capacity. A somewhat similar analysis could be made of the payments for the use of what are commonly classed as either natural resources or capital goods.

The classical theory of value stressed chiefly the tendency for the prices of goods produced and sold under competitive conditions to be proportionate to the respective costs of producing them. However, costs meant not the money outlays of the producers (entrepreneurs) but the "real" costs, human sacrifice or pain. For Ricardo in particular this in turn meant "quantity of labor;" that labor alone is really productive—other "factors" only "assisting"—was basic to the "labor theory of value," which was taken over and exploited for propaganda purposes by the various schools of socialists and economic radicals. Later, the notion that the "abstinence" involved in saving and accumulation of capital was also a pain cost was introduced by N. W. Senior (*An Outline of the Science of Political Economy* [1836]). The socialists of course scornfully rejected this innovation. The classical economists did not see, at least not at all clearly, that what is "economized" is the use of resources, both human and nonhuman, and that the ultimate meaning of the cost of any product is the nonuse of resources for some other end. This fact is now known as the "alternative cost" principle. But the alternative end sacrificed is not always and entirely a quantity of another marketable product but may be the leisure use of time and labor or some direct (nonmarket) use of any other resource. Interpreted in this way, the notion of pain cost has some validity. It should be noted, as all modern economists have recognized, that the cost explanation of value applies only in a long-run view, over time sufficient to adjust production to demand. The classical economists freely recognized that over short periods price depends on "demand and supply," that is, the demand for the existing supply already produced or for which irreversible commitments have been made.

A similar division between short- and long-run views was inevitable in connection with the theory of distribution. Neither theory has stood up well under later criticism, although many important facts and principles were recognized. In a general way, the short-run theory held that labor gets as wages its "means of subsistence" and the capitalist, the excess of the product (of labor or labor-plus-capital) on "marginal" land—or at the "intensive" margin on better land, in any case where no rent was deducted—*after* payment of a subsistence wage. Land (of a quality above that barely worth using) received as rent the excess ("surplus") product above that of the same amount of labor-and-capital on no-rent land. The foundation of the position is the subsistence theory of wages; but it is hard to make out whether this limitation was due to the power of the employer over the worker (Adam Smith sometimes comes near to stating the exploitation theory of the later socialists) or to a tendency of the working population to multiply up to the means of subsistence. The latter view (more conspicuous in Smith's treatment) would clearly operate only in the long run. And somehow another theory must be fitted into the picture—that of the famous wages fund. In its simplest version, this meant that the capital (the annual product of an economy or some ill-defined part of it) was supposed to be advanced to laborers each year, making the average wage simply the total capital divided by the total working population. Ricardo and later members of the school recognized that the period of production or turnover is longer than a year in industries employing a fixed capital, but they failed to see that capital is never produced by labor alone but rather reproduces itself (unless it is disinvested) so that no determinate period or cycle in production can be found.

In the long-run theory of distribution, the notion of cost played a part—though not as large a one as it logically should have in view of the fact that all productive agents, human or other, are in a general sense products. In the long-run interpretation, the idea that the standard of living determines wages is in effect a cost-of-production theory of the price of labor. This doctrine rested upon the theory of population associated with the name of T. R. Malthus, although it was clearly stated in general terms by Adam Smith and by still earlier writers. In the later form, the notion of "subsistence," as a physiological minimum, was replaced by, or interpreted to mean, a "standard of living," a scale or level which laborers think of as necessary for family life. If wages fall below that level, it was thought, the rate of growth of the working population will be negative (births fewer than deaths) and the decline in the labor supply will raise wages. If wages are above this level, population will increase and wages will fall—unless a higher standard of living becomes effective. Somewhat similar reasoning was applied to profit, the rate of return on capital. The supply tends to increase as long as the return is above what savers generally consider sufficient to compensate for the abstinence required to save and will decrease when it is below such a level; hence the rate of profit "tends toward" this level as a position of equilibrium.

The rent of land, however, was held not to be affected by the principle of cost. Land was thought to be permanently fixed in supply; it was defined by Ricardo as "the original and indestructible powers of the soil." Hence a rise in rent will not tend to counteract itself by bringing forth an additional supply—or reciprocally for a decline. Correspondingly, as already noted, rent was not supposed to be a part of, or to influence the price of, its produce, which in this view is determined by production costs (wages plus profit) on land barely worth using and yielding no rent—or by the cost at the "intensive margin." Changes in rent were thus the effect, not the cause, of changes in product prices. This doctrine rested on a sharp separation between land and capital (capital goods) which later economists have tended to view as unrealistic. It also rested on an assumption that land is used only to produce a single distinctive product and hence is not, like labor and capital, transferred from one use to another in response to changes in relative prices. This view has also given place to recognition that raw produce is less a product than a stage in the production of all final products. But there is an important element of truth in the older views. In the classical system of distribution as a whole a very important place was ascribed to the "law of diminishing returns," in a particular long-run or historical interpretation. As the theory ran, the growth of population, itself dependent on growth of capital, requires resort to poorer land and also to more intensive cultivation of land already in use. In either case, the increase of product would not be proportionate to the increased amount of labor and capital. Manufactures, in contrast, were thought to be subject to increasing returns, because of larger opportunities for the economies of the division of labor and for invention and the application of the fruits of scientific progress to industry. Agriculture also benefits by technical progress, but here the possibility of improvement was thought to be smaller and to be more than counterbalanced by the increasingly disadvantageous proportioning of labor and capital to land. Since laborers must always get the same real wages—the means of subsistence—the profits of capital must decline, until the growth of population and wealth would come to an end in a "stationary economy." Taken as a prophecy, this doctrine has so far been disproved by the course of events. The possibilities of improvement in agricultural technique were underestimated; new lands of good quality have been brought under cultivation and their produce brought to market by cheap transportation; and the Malthusian "law" has been partly falsified by declining birth rates accompanying the general progress of civilization—the rise in the effective standard of living already referred to.

Any general system of value theory must have something to say about the measure of value, hence the "value of money" or the general price level in contrast with relative prices. This problem was of especial concern to Adam Smith because of the price revolution and of its startling effects which had swept over Europe after the discovery of America. And this interest was nourished by the monetary and price changes of the period of the great wars of the French Revolution and of Napoleon. On this point, the classical school held to the doctrine later known as the "quantity theory of money:" other things being equal, the value of money (and reciprocally the price level) depends on its quantity in relation to the volume of production and trade. Allowance would also be made for the use of money substitutes, such as bank credit, already familiar in Europe. As a long-run view, this was supplemented by the notion that the quantity of money is determined by the costs of mining the precious metals. Among different countries, especially those with and those without mines, prices would tend to be equalized by a flow of money or bullion from countries in which it would buy less to those in which it would buy more. This part of classical value theory has in general stood up better than the views on values and distribution. It would be an error to think of these earlier economists as altogether preoccupied with abstract theories or not to recognize that their interest in these was born of an interest in practical problems. And in general, they were not such uncompromising opponents of any sort of interference by government in industry as some later critics and pretended expounders of their views have made them out to be.

The Critical Schools

Before reviewing the later progress of economics, especially the revolutionary developments of the later nineteenth century, it will be helpful to look at the principal types of criticism which have been directed against the older political economy, and in part are still maintained against the later developments, and at the conceptions which have been proposed as replacements. In the first place, "romanticists," like Adam Müller in Germany and John Ruskin in England, intensely disliked the new individualistic economic mechanism into the workings of which the economists were trying to probe. And, consequently, they particularly disliked the defense of this mechanism of economic laissez faire, which the economists in general did defend, by statement or implication. They preferred an ordered society, with economic subordinated to moral or religious or aesthetic values, such as they typically thought had been more or less fully embodied in the social structure of the Middle Ages. Work, they inclined to insist, is not merely a means to an end, particularly what are called economic ends, but good work is worth doing for its own sake and for its effect upon character. They did not impugn the fitness of economics as an instrument of attack upon its special problems but they belittled these problems.

Another group of writers, for whom there is no better descriptive name than "the critical school," come much closer to meeting the orthodox economists upon their own ground. One of the earliest, and much the most influential, of them was Sismonde de Sismondi (*Nouveaux principes d'économie politique* [1817] and other works). Other able writers, often without any conscious discipleship, have taken a similar position. These critics urge that more attention be given to the defects of the competitive economic mechanism, even viewed merely as a means of providing for material needs. They contend that the economists, contemplating the long-run or normal tendencies and the theoretical beauties of the automatic processes by which the pursuit of individual economic interests becomes organized into a vast scheme of economic cooperation, forget how often the mechanism breaks down and normal economic life is interrupted by crises and depression; how unemployment, chronic as well as epidemic, is a disease of this economic order; how equally the aggregate product is distributed among individuals or families; and how many of the things men do for their own economic advantage are in fact inimical to the interests of the community. As later critics have put it, businessmen are interested primarily in making money, which does not always mean making more goods. The picture of the "economic harmonies" (the title of a mid-nineteenth-century French apologetic work) requires, it is urged, rationalizing of the facts to an unwarranted degree. These criticisms also undoubtedly go too far. They unduly play down the role of the abstract principles stressed by the older economics in the general view of the economic activities of the community. And no economist of the first rank has ever been a devotee of the pure automatism of the market. But the critical school has had a wholesome influence on the progress of economic science. It should be observed that this school occupies a position between that of the orthodox school and that of the socialists who denounce the works of the latter as mere apologetic, a product of the existing economic order and prompted by the interest of those who benefit by its iniquities.

Another line of attack was adopted by the "historical school," or more accurately, "schools," since the term covers several different groups. This position has been represented in all countries, but it has been most influential in Germany. The most important of its early exponents were Friedrich List (*Nationales System der politischen Ökonomie* [1841]) and Wilhelm Roscher (*Grundlagen der Nationalökonomie* [1854] and other works). The form of a nation's economic life, said these critics, is a "historical category," peculiar to a given nation at a given time, a product of its past and therefore only to be understood by a study of that past. The wisdom of particular economic policies is relative to conditions of a place and time, and the supposedly universal laws of abstract economics need to be supplemented by or even subordinated to study of concrete facts of the national situation. If they had gone no further, the "historicists" would have found many to agree with them. But they tended to make of the historical method something arbitrary and doctrinaire. (Karl Knies, whose work, *Die politische Ökonomie vom Standpunkte der geschichtlichen Methode,* appeared in 1853, is a notable exception.) Not content with looking to history for the causes of these concrete differences of economic structure in which they were interested, they proposed to derive from history itself universal and binding laws, akin to those of physical sciences. They were fond of schemes of "stages" of economic development through which they thought every nation must pass. In these speculations they were really elaborating suggestions found not in historical research but in the Greek speculative historians. They regarded the forms taken by economic life, past and present, as inevitable products of historical forces; and at the same time, unconscious of the inconsistency, they advocated a rather heavy-handed control of economic activities by the state.

The British and French economists had looked upon the organization of economic life as being shaped and determined by the interplay of the interests and rational activities of individual men and had viewed the state as an instrument of individual purposes—well-being as judged, in the main, by each person for himself. The spokesmen of the historical school, in contrast, were strongly influenced by the philosopher Hegel, who ascribed a prior and independent value to the state, with individuals somewhat in the role of means, on the analogy of cells or organs in the human body, a view related to that of the mercantilists though more sophisticated. Although they pushed their views to extremes, they gave a needed emphasis to what has come to be called the "institutional" view of economic activities, as contrasted with the individualistic or contractual aspect. But both the older historicists and the later institutionalists (largely an American movement of the early twentieth century) slurred over the contrast between two kinds or meanings of "institution," that is, patterns of action moving in predestined grooves under the influence of relatively unconscious social forces, versus those embodying deliberate organization and control, such as the political organs of the state. The state, in turn, was conceived by the older schools in what would now be called "totalitarian" terms, while the institutionalists, like the socialists (in contrast with the Communists), thought of it as democratic. Historical economists have also been more ready to think of change, as contrasted with finality, in the pattern of economic organization, and they gave a useful impulse to the study of economic history, which is valuable both in itself and as a complement to economic theory. Under the influence of historical study the old dogmatism of the historical economists gradually gave way to a realization of the variety and complexity of the fabric of economic history; and the newer schools of historical economics, under the leadership of such scholars as Gustav Schmoller in Germany and Ashley and Unwin in Great Britain (to name only men no longer living), are, as they should be, devoted to historical research. The movement has also broadened out, particularly in Germany, under such leaders as Max Weber and Werner Sombart, into what is often called *sociological economics,* a position also well presented in France (Simiand, Halbwachs, Bouglé).

THE PROGRESS OF ECONOMIC THEORY

"Economic theory" is the name now commonly given to the more general and abstract parts of economics, to the "principles." These parts are no less practical than concrete-descriptive or applied economics but are less directly related to immediate problems. The mechanics of price relations or of markets affords a general explanation of the organization of production and distribution in so far as this is actually worked out and controlled through competitive buying and selling—which would largely be true even in a planned or socialistic economy that stopped short of complete military regimentation. This branch of the study bears somewhat the same relation to economic politics that pure physics bears to the engineering sciences. Hence the problems of values and distribution have continued to hold their place among the central concerns of economists. However, there has been a notable—one might say, revolutionary—change in the general character of the analysis. The older classical economists, as we have seen, centered their attention on the long-run relations between value and costs and were generally content to dispose of short-run variations of price by merely invoking the formula of demand and supply. This was used without careful analysis of the short-run situation, particularly of the role of demand. Work directed toward filling in this gap had important effects in changing the whole conceptual picture. Similar steps introducing the new analysis were taken independently and almost simultaneously, in the early seventies of the nineteenth century, by W. S. Jevons in England, Carl Menger in Austria, and Léon Walras in France and Switzerland. (It presently became known that they had been in part anticipated by earlier writers who were ignored and forgotten.)

Adam Smith, in a famous passage, had contrasted "value in use" with "value in exchange," noting that the former is high for water and low for diamonds, and conversely for the latter. The new discovery was that there is nonetheless a definite relation between value in use (or "utility") and exchange value, hence price. The value in use is not properly measured by the difference between having the normal supply of a good and having none at all, but by the difference it makes to have a little more or a little less; that is, things are actually valued by increments in consumption. Water, for example, has a wide variety of uses, all progressively satiable; and its exchange value at a particular time and place depends on its "marginal" use, the use and the degree of importance in that use which would have to be foregone if the supply were just a little smaller. From the standpoint of action, since a buyer has the choice of how much he will take, all units are alike and the use value as well as the exchange value of any total supply is the product of the value of the unit (increment) in the least important use by the number of units. Thus, where water is scarce its value—both use and exchange value—is exceedingly high because the marginal use is an intense desire or need; and if diamonds were abundant enough, their value would be small. And goods, however important, that are superabundant, the supply unlimited by any cost, have no economic utility or economic value, though to common sense this seems a paradox. The earlier utility or subjective-value theorists tended to think of the consumption of any quantity of a particular good as representing or causing a definite quantity of pleasure, and of rational economic behavior as that which yields a maximum of pleasure or happiness. It is now generally agreed that this is dubious psychology, and that the economic theories had better use the notion of a maximum without trying to say exactly what is maximized—much as the physicist speaks of matter or mass in terms of the way it is measured without trying to define its nature. Perhaps the most important feature of the new views, considered as theories of demand and of price, was not the psychological explanation but the clarification of the nature of what Adam Smith called the "effective demand." It was seen that the demand for a commodity by any consumer or in any market is not a definite magnitude but a functional relation (most commonly represented in textbooks by a descending curve) showing a whole schedule of decreasing amounts that will be purchased as the price is higher. The actual quantities depend on both the desires and tastes of the consumer or consumers, on their purchasing power, and, in addition, on the availability of other products competing for the expenditure of income and the prices of these. This idea served to clarify the relation that Smith and his followers had crudely expounded between "market price" and "natural price," now more generally referred to as price in the short run versus the long run. In the former case, the supply is typically the amount already on the market, and the price is the "marginal demand price" for this amount. But in the longer run, production itself responds to price and price to supply, so that the long-run or normal or "equilibrium" price is that at which the amount consumers will take is equal to the amount which producers find it profitable to produce. This advance is largely to be credited to Alfred Marshall (*Principles of Economics* [1890] and numerous later editions, considerably revised).

Still more important were indirect consequences of the new theories in connection with supply and cost. One such consequence was a gradual shift of emphasis from wealth to income as the primary fact in economic life and the center of attention in the science. With respect to price analysis, the earlier economists had recognized—though not clearly or consistently, with N. W. Senior an exception for clarity—that even in the long run, cost affects price only indirectly, by influencing production and supply, and hence, as it was now seen, "marginal utility," which is the direct determinant. But the cost of which producers take account is the payments they must make for the productive services they require, and the value of these is derived from, or merely reflects, the value of final products. But with respect to any single product, the costs that must be incurred reflect the value of resources in other uses, giving rise to the principle now generally known as "alternative cost," in contrast with the older theory of "real cost" or pain cost. Subjective sacrifices do play some role, but the correspondence between such cost and the money cost to the producer is very imperfect and the relation may be inverse. (J. S. Mill pointed out that higher-paid labor typically involves less pain than lower-paid, not more; but he proposed no satisfactory way of meeting this difficulty.) It was also gradually recognized that the costs of production consist of the payments which at the same time constitute the shares in the distribution of the product among the different "productive agents." Thus a rational conception of production in terms of the allocation of productive capacity among alternative modes of use, through the competitive bidding of business units (or their managers or entrepreneurs), explains at the same time the prices of final products, the costs of production, and "functional" distribution. "Personal" distribution depends, in addition, on the amount as well as the value of the productive services of all kinds that are owned or controlled by the various participants in economic activity.

Goods are typically produced by the cooperation of various kinds of productive services, and the special problem of distribution, in modern terms, is that of the division of this joint product among the different kinds of cooperating productive services or agents. If only one kind were employed, or even if a number of kinds were always used in fixed proportions, the problem would be simple; the value of the productive service (or combination) would obviously be the value of the product. But the fact that goods can be produced by combinations in variable proportions sets the problem and also affords the solution. One type of agent can be substituted for another, or the product can be increased or diminished a definite amount by varying the amount of one "factor," all others being held constant. This will be clear if one thinks of a farm producing, say, wheat, and assumes that the manager uses the three traditional factors, land, labor, and capital (embodied in capital goods). But using increasing amounts of any one factor involves "diminishing returns." It follows that under effective competition the joint product—of a whole economy as well as of each single enterprise—tends to be divided up in the proportions which measure the efficacy of each factor in increasing the product, when the available supplies of all the factors in the economy are used in the way that yields the maximum total product, measured by the economic demand. Around the end of the nineteenth century a number of writers (especially P. H. Wicksteed) pointed out that the principle of diminishing returns, previously applied only to the use of more labor and capital on a given amount of land, is reversible and quite general in application. It governs the competition of different industries and enterprises for given amounts of all the factors; and the historical question whether labor and capital really increase faster than the supply of land is a separate issue and is to be answered only by observing the facts. Hence, under given conditions, and under free and frictionless competition, the amount of product assigned (in technical terms, "imputed") to any particular laborer or other agent or unit is the amount which really depends upon the use of that particular agent. A laborer or other agent counts for more and in effect produces more when there is a larger supply of other agents to work with him or it. The amount earned will of course depend on effort and skill and the quality of management; and the "real" wage or other share will also depend on the prices of the final products for which the laborer or property owner spends the money income he receives. The effort of managers (entrepreneurs) to secure maximum return for their expenditures for productive resources will lead them to buy these in such proportions that "at the margin" equal expenditures secure equal increments to total product. Any resource will tend to move toward employments where the yield—of a "dollar's worth"—is highest. And the tendency, again in so far as competition is free and frictionless, is to establish such prices that all dollars' worths of each are of the same value to all employers.

This theory or principle that every agent tends to get what it "produces" does not mean that each person gets what he deserves and in fact tells us little about the ethical quality or social desirability of the result. It must be remembered that differences in respect of training and opportunity greatly affect men's productive capacities as workers and that institutions, especially inheritance, enter into this picture as well as into the ownership of property and the opportunity to accumulate. The swift process of change in technology and demand often robs men of the fruits of skill acquired at great cost and also of the fruits of investment committed to particular industries. In particular, such innovative activities as invention and exploration for minerals may yield anything from zero to a reward quite disproportionate to the outlay in effort or money. These facts set the general problem of profit and its ethical significance. Finally, even when a venture is not undertaken on a gambling chance, various impediments, including the antisocial activities of monopolists, prevent the free mobility of capital and labor from uses of lower to those of higher yield. The doctrine that "rewards tend to be proportionate to products" is true only as a tendency, but it is highly important as a corrective to the belief that there is little or no connection, and "product" itself, to repeat, is no measure of moral desert. The social problems raised must be examined on their merits, in terms of ethical principles and the pros and cons of the expediency of political measures. Enforcement of equality may reduce incentive and production, most especially the incentive to take the large risks or chances that always affect innovations. With respect to profit in particular—properly separated analytically from both wages of management and the yield of investment in fairly safe forms—it must be remembered that a prospect of disproportionate gain if successful is necessary if men are to assume voluntarily the risks of loss. The final judgment as to ideal right and the balance between that and expediency, where they seem to conflict, must be left to "that insidious and crafty animal vulgarly called a statesman or politician," to use a famous phrase of Adam Smith. Experience seems to show, however, that considerable taxation of exceptional gains is possible without demonstrably affecting incentives. As just suggested, profit, in realistic business usage, is a mixed form of income, containing elements of interest and of wages for that vaguely distinguishable part of management activity which may be treated as labor; and both the amount of the owner's capital and the proper rate of interest to allow are also uncertain. The distinguishing mark of profit is that its amount is not stipulated in any agreement or fixed in an exchange but is contingent upon the success of an enterprise or undertaking. In general, profit arises from error, or imperfect foresight, on the part of the responsible entrepreneur, in making policy decisions or in delegating these to salaried managers as his agents (in a corporation, managers are the agents of the voting stockholders as a group). "Pure profit" is the amount left over after making all stipulated payments for productive services, raw materials, etc., and after deduction of the going rate of payment for the entrepreneur's own capital and services. It is as likely to be a negative as a positive sum, and it is impossible to say conclusively whether the gains are greater or less than the losses in the aggregate for a whole economy. Pure profit is of course increased in any individual case by greater accuracy in the ultimate managerial decisions and tends to be decreased in particular by excessive optimism.

The rate of interest has also received much attention in modern discussion. Controversy was stimulated in particular by the publication, in the 1880's, of two books by E. von Böhm-Bawerk, a disciple of Carl Menger. He propounded two views of interest, both adumbrated a half-century earlier in the work of N. W. Senior. One is a reworking of the abstinence theory into one of postponement or "waiting" or discount of the future. Interest is viewed as the reward or necessary inducement for waiting, as the measure of the superior attraction of near over remote enjoyment. The other view regards interest as the yield or productivity of investment due to the greater efficacy of more roundabout processes. Böhm-Bawerk followed the Ricardian notion that capital goods are produced by labor, or labor and land; it has been pointed out that cooperation of previously existing capital is also involved and that in terms of values capital reproduces itself and in addition yields a surplus for consumption or further investment. The interest rate on loans tends to equal the ratio of the yield obtainable on investments to their amount, that is, the ratio of the net rental on capital goods (after provision for maintenance and eventual replacement) to their cost, and the cost is the value of consumable goods sacrificed in using productive capacity to create them. When conditions change after an investment is made, the capital which the good represents is the least cost of producing an item of the same earning power. The psychology of postponement operates by affecting the supply of savings for investment. Interest is a form in which the yield of a capital good (or some part of it) is paid and received, rather than a distinct share in distribution coming from a distinct source; the lease of a farm or building or other piece of property for a rental achieves the same general result as its sale coupled with a loan, and under perfect competition the choice would be a matter of indifference to both parties. The theory of interest is of the greatest importance in the general system of value theory, since the value of all durable goods bought and sold is immediately determined by the "capitalization" of the expected future income. This tends to be the same as their cost, since no such good will be produced unless it is expected to yield at least the going rate on its costs. But errors and unexpected changes in conditions often cause capital goods to be worth more or less than cost (to yield less or more than interest on cost), the difference being a profit or loss.

Methods of Economics

Reference has already been made to the controversy between the critics and the expounders of analytical or theoretical economics—allied in its methods and aims to the older political economy, even when different in content. It is essentially abstract and deductive, proceeding from a few general principles, such as those of diminishing returns and diminishing utility and the uniformity of price to all buyers and sellers in an effective or competitive market. Most of its conclusions can be viewed as "cases" under a general principle of economic behavior. The principle is that resources tend to be allocated among alternative modes of use in such a way that they will be equally remunerative in all and so will yield the maximum total return. In another form of statement, it posits an "economic man," whose behavior under given circumstances is completely rational. A free economic order must assume that men actually tend to be rational in the use of means, that they try to be and tend to succeed. The given circumstances include the wants to be satisfied, the resources themselves, and the modes of use or technology extant in the society at the time. These must be explained or treated mainly by other disciplines than economics. Any science which explains phenomena in terms of measured cause and effect must be abstract; economics (by this method) is often compared with theoretical mechanics based on "frictionless conditions"; and the concept of adaptive behavior in biology is a similar principle, since in fact adaptation is always more or less imperfect. The careful economic theorist does not confuse the abstraction of perfectly economic behavior, or the economic man, with the actual behavior of real men, any more than the physicist or engineer assumes that friction is absent in real machines. Applied economics must try to take account of the role in business life of error and of motives (good or bad), such as prejudice, curiosity, and the various forms of the play interest, which do not conform to the pattern of economic rationality. Competition itself, in the psychological meaning, is a noneconomic interest. The economic interest is merely a striving for efficiency in the use of means, whatever means are available and whatever ends are pursued. It does operate, at least in modern civilization, in a peculiarly regular and predictable fashion, and a community whose policies disregard its principles will suffer loss if not disaster. But these principles alone do not make it possible to predict the course of real events or the results of action. They must be filled in with data secured by inductive investigation, as well as qualified to allow for various departures from the behavior pattern of economic rationality.

Hence it will be evident that the other methods or approaches to economic data, notably historical research and statistical investigation, are not to be thought of as substitutes for sound theory, along the traditional lines, but as complementary to it. This is true also of social sciences other than history and statistics, notably psychology, with or without such qualifiers as social, political, analytic, etc. All are needed to supply data and interpretation, to put content and definiteness into the valid but highly abstract "laws" of economic choice and of market phenomena. Without such supplementation, economic laws have little value for prediction, since the essential factor of wants is not open to sense observation and any course of events that occurs can be fitted into the theoretical pattern. The growing accumulation of numerical information covering a wide variety of economic facts, coupled with the advance of statistical technique, has been working a notable change in the character and content of economics as a whole; without nullifying any of its established principles, it has given more knowledge of the actual degree of stability or variability in the relationships in real life. Interpretation of records covering averages and aggregates and their movements can add much to what can be inferred from commonsense principles or observation of particular cases. This does not mean, however, that economics will be or can be purely statistical, a new kind of "political arithmetic." The broader the average or aggregate, the more heterogeneous the data it covers, and these magnitudes become subject to limitations similar to those of abstract principles. If statistical magnitudes and correlations are to be understood and intelligently used—in guiding such measures as taxation and the regulation of business in the public interest—they must be understood through weaving them into the general structure of our knowledge and relating them to other things we know.

On the other hand, any brief statement of general principles is bound to make abstract economic theories appear thinner and more remote from the concrete facts of economic life than they are. There is a place and a need for all degrees of generality. In recent decades this need has found increasing expression in the developing and spreading study of mathematical economics, in which exposition is made accurate and compact by the use of graphs and of algebraic formulas. In the form of "econometrics" this movement also brings analytical theory into close alliance with concrete facts, statistically presented. Only by the use of mathematics is it possible to bring together into a single comprehensible picture the variety, the complexity, and most of all the interdependence, of the factors which determine prices, costs, output, and demand and the wages or hire of productive agents. The mathematical treatment of economic principles was the first successfully undertaken by the French economist, mathematician, and philosopher, A. A. Cournot (*Recherches sur les principes mathématiques de la théorie des richesses* [1838]). Elaborate mathematical formulations of the conditions of general economic equilibrium have been worked out, notably by Léon Walras (*Éléments d'économie politique pure* [1874 and later editions]) and his follower, Vilfredo Pareto (*Manuel d'économie politique* [1909] and other works). The principal value of such elaborate and abstract systems lies in forcibly reminding the inquirer that a change in practically any economic variable has direct or indirect effects on innumerable other magnitudes, thus preventing him from fatally oversimplifying conceptions of economic cause and effect. Other writers, notably Alfred Marshall, have adopted an intermediate position. Marshall was a competent mathematician but used and advocated the "literary" form of exposition (contemptuously so named by Pareto), relegating the mathematics to footnotes and appendixes in his monumental work. He also emphasized the interdependence of economic phenomena but centered his attention on the relations between the more closely related factors, the relations of greatest practical import, in contrast with system building. But his successors, of the Cambridge or "neoclassical" school (notably A. C. Pigou), were impelled to make more direct use of mathematics in their exposition, and the study and use of algebra has of late spread rapidly among economists in all countries. And, in line with the older classical tradition, the science places increasing emphasis upon factors which make for change and "disequilibrium," as well as those making for stability.

The Problems of Present-Day Economics

Since all general principles are necessarily abstract, the more theoretical parts of economics cannot be taken to be a complete and adequate account of the mechanism of modern economic life. They afford serviceable approximations to partial, but important, aspects of the truth; the study of history and factual data yields other true and important generalizations. Even in their present imperfect and incomplete state the generalizations an economist has at hand constitute an organon of proved effectiveness, an instrument by means of which some of the results of economic changes, whether planned or not planned, may be predicted with a fair degree of certainty. New problems constantly appear and challenge attention as facts change and new interests emerge, and different groups of problems have their special literature and engage the attention of corps of specialists. The most striking and possibly the most important characteristic of recent work in economics, as contrasted with the older, is its greater realism. It does not attempt to do without abstract conceptions, but it does attempt to take these from the world of affairs or bring them into line with facts.

This trait is conspicuous in the treatment of the two great practical problems or groups of problems which have particularly forced themselves on the attention of the public and of statesmen and economists in roughly the past two generations. These problems center respectively in the growth of large-scale corporate business and associations of firms which concentrate power and tend to exploit the public through monopoly and high finance (and labor problems are related to these) and in the mechanism of money and credit, commonly held responsible for the recurring phenomena of industrial fluctuations or business cycles, with their attendant wastes and hardships. Depressions and the measures taken by different countries for dealing with them, in connection with the impact of two world wars, have also intensified interest in international economic relations affecting money and capital movements and in trade in general and in tariff duties and other controlling devices. The depression of the 1930's and World War II generated a world-wide movement toward state control or planning of economic life, and particularly toward use of quotas on imports and strict control of foreign exchange, and even governmental conduct of foreign trade. In none of these fields is the ground completely explored or all the issues settled, but findings have been reached which appear to have permanent value. The outcome of the various fiscal and monetary measures to which governments have resorted, and the results of the restrictions imposed upon trade and industry, have in general been about what competent economists predicted, and this is true of the experience with reparations and monetary stabilization after World War I. The tendency has been to confirm long-established principles, though political considerations have made it difficult for governments to learn, or at least for them to apply, the lessons taught. This fact is especially prominent in connection with the perennial issues of protection in international trade and of inflation through cheap money or credit. Inflation is tempting as an easy way to finance a government at war, or under special financial stress from any cause, and as a way to achieve a bogus prosperity, not to mention the fallacy of making capital cheap and lightening the burdens of debtors through an abundance of money. (But inflationary measures may be justified to counteract deflation and relieve depression.)

The general form given to economics by the early classical writers was determined very largely by preoccupation with certain special types of problems, notably problems of national commercial policy. Recent events have brought this group of problems again to the fore, and later experience and discussion, while confirming earlier views in a general way, have led to some modification. The older economists, in their efforts to dig beneath that surface view of economic life which had deceived the mercantilists, held that money is merely an instrument or tool. They carried this idea to extremes, though in some types of "pure economic theory" today it is found convenient to go still further and assume that trade is conducted by barter, without the use of any special medium of exchange (all commodities having equally the character of money). But the phenomena of inflation and deflation, and of boom and depression, have forced modern economists to recognize that the use of money and credit has important effects on the character of effective demand and on production and distribution. Quite naturally, the Great Depression of the 1930's gave a tremendous impetus to discussion in this field, and its importance was further enhanced by the fear of depression, or boom and then depression, which might follow World War II, and by measures taken or proposed in this connection. A landmark in this discussion was the publication, in 1936, of a book, *The General Theory of Employment, Interest and Money,* by J. M. Keynes, of Cambridge University. It must suffice here to note that the discussion has at least called attention to one fact: The famous "law of the market" (often called "Say's Law" from its formulation by the great French economist) stating that the demand for any good is the supply of other goods, and the supply of any one is the demand for others, while a truism for a barter system, is not valid in the short run in a complex monetary economy. And further, the short run may be both longer and more important than is likely to be inferred from the orthodox or neoclassical exposition of economic theory. In emphasizing the nature and conditions of a theoretical equilibrium, these writers have tended to undue neglect of changes in monetary circulation (hoarding and dishoarding, or changes in the quantity of money or its velocity of circulation) and their often serious and protracted consequences. In particular, it cannot be assumed that monetary saving will be followed automatically and immediately by investment. The "funds" need not be offered on the loan market, and if they are offered they may not cause a sufficient decline in the long-run interest rate to cause real investment, since this depends largely on speculative anticipations and these in turn often depend more on conjuncture and mass psychology than on definite knowledge and rational calculation of future prospects. In consequence, production of capital goods, particularly the more lasting forms, including durable consumption goods, may decline heavily; and unemployment in these industries will cause shrinkage even in the industries producing for immediate consumption.

Even if it is admitted, as it doubtless must be, that if all prices were immediately and uniformly responsive to monetary changes, unemployment could not occur, this is not what happens in reality. In particular, monetary wages are "sticky" and are especially resistant to downward movement. And wages are the largest factor in production costs and notably in the variable and "marginal" costs which are most influential in producers' planning. Thus wage policy becomes a crucial factor in the problem. There is a real danger, even a probability, that reduction of wage rates may reduce total disbursement of purchasing power in the field of consumption, which may react seriously on the effective investment demand. Drastic action in the direction of inflation (or "reflation," a word that came into use in the early years of the Great Depression) may be the only feasible way of counteracting the tendency to a downward spiral. The appropriate methods and instruments of such action came to occupy a large place in the discussion and controversy set in motion by the distress of the thirties and particularly by Keynes and his followers and opponents. Accentuation of issues in international economic policy was another result, which can only be mentioned here; the need for any country to protect itself against economic repercussions abroad runs into measures open to the accusation of "exporting unemployment," and in the absence of wise concerted international action they certainly tend to aggravate the situation.

One of the conspicuous phenomena in recent economics has been intensified activity in the field of labor problems, already mentioned as a development consequent upon the labor movement of the nineteenth century and after and connected with the growth of large corporations and other forms of unified action among business interests. Up to the last quarter of that century there was little careful analysis of those problems, apart from discussion of the general theory of wages under some approximation to free competition. Now, however, there is hardly a field of economic inquiry which is more thoroughly cultivated or in which there is more controversy: it runs into the general problems of economic planning and socialism. The labor union movement and its significance, the pros and cons of collective bargaining, the length of the working day, factory legislation, profit-sharing, the organization of control within the enterprise, labor turnover, the legal minimum wage, the prevention and settlement of industrial disputes, compulsory arbitration, and social insurance in its various forms, as well as the causes of unemployment and its possible remedies, are all burning issues in both economic science and practical politics.

It is important to observe that all these practical problems have been brought into the scope of economics by the course of change in economic and business life; the attention now given to them does not mark a change of attitude or general social position among economists. The earlier thinkers, in response to the conditions and needs of their times, at the beginning of the modern industrial era, were primarily concerned with exploding popular fallacies with respect to the ways in which the prosperity of the community can best be secured and, with that end in view, in showing how the economic activities of individuals may work together, through the open market, and be so interrelated as to constitute a great communal economic mechanism. Under the circumstances, they were more concerned with what governments could not or should not do than with that they could wisely attempt. Thus they often gave the impression—an impression which careful study of the writings of the ablest of them will dispel—that they regarded that mechanism as all-sufficient, needing neither interference nor direction on the part of the community. While the need for a better understanding of the theory of the open-market organization and better appreciation of its merits is still present, modern economics tends to strike a different note. Its tone is less negative; it is more insistent in its search for and scrutiny of possible ways of altering for the better the organization of the community's economic life, while remaining on guard against the dangers of disaster from unforeseen results of wrong lines of action. Since almost every gain has its cost, most of the problems resolve themselves into a question of a balance of advantage. But the advantages and disadvantages are hardly ever purely economic, and therefore no analysis in terms of purely scientific economics can completely dispose of such questions. Political, social, and ethical ideals and issues must also be taken into account, and economists are showing an increased awareness of these broader considerations. The economist, however, may gauge the general character of the probable effects of a specific measure upon production and distribution and so make it possible to discuss the wisdom of any proposed action in the light of its probable consequences.

In connection with this shift of emphasis an important factor is the vast accumulation of more and more reliable factual data. Reliable records of economic activities, or at any rate of their results, are now brought together and published by governments and by business and other private organizations, on a scale which would have excited the envy of the older economists. A much wider range of economic experience is now available for study and analysis. In dealing with this new material—in a sense a by-product of the activities which it records—economics is impelled toward a more realistic and concrete view. It has to deal with economic events in the forms in which they actually occur and to search for the systematic relations which run through the mass of real events. But although the interests of economics have become more varied and concrete, and although its conceptions have become better adapted to handling the facts of economic life as those facts present themselves, economics remains a political or social science and also, in the old sense as well as new senses, a "theoretical" discipline. Particular findings or tenets have been discarded and replaced or fundamentally restated, and sweeping additions have been made. But the general picture of a scheme of communal economic life remains a picture sufficiently ordered to be useful for analysis and prediction, though imperfect enough to give point and purpose to its continued study, elaboration, and refinement, in spite of changes of viewpoint and of method.

Selection 2

Economics and the Economy

KENNETH E. BOULDING

From The Impact of the Social Sciences, *(New Brunswick, N.J.: Rutgers University Press, 1966). Reprinted by permission of the Rutgers University Press.*

The social sciences sometimes excuse themselves for their inadequacies by the plea of youth. In the case of economics this plea can hardly be sustained, for economics has good claims to be regarded as the second oldest of the sciences, younger than physics but older than chemistry. If we regard the date of founding of a science as the moment when it acquires a theoretical model sufficiently integrated and powerful so that inferences can be drawn from it which can be tested, then classical physics certainly dates from Newton and economics from Adam Smith, whose *Wealth of Nations* in 1776 set up an internally consistent framework of equilibrium theory, especially in regard to relative prices, which all subsequent work has modified only in detail rather than in essence. Furthermore, Adam Smith had a better theory of economic development than most economists have today. By contrast, chemistry was floundering in the phlogiston theory at that time and did not achieve a real theoretical integration until Dalton, in the 1820's. Darwin, in biology, comes still a generation later, psychology and sociology later still; indeed it can be argued that the biological sciences have still not really reached their Newtonian synthesis.

In spite of the fact that its basic theoretical formulations came rather early, it is only in the last thirty or forty years that economics has developed anything like an adequate system for the collection and processing of information about the economy. At the time of Adam Smith very little systematic information was available, and under the circumstances it is all the more astonishing that his theoretical formulation was as profound and insightful as it was. Many of the theoretical discussions at the time of David Ricardo in the first quarter of the nineteenth century were vitiated by the absence of any adequate statistics, economic information, or indexing. Even such a simple device as the index number of prices did not come into general use until 1870, though time series of individual prices and wages had been collected for a long time. Statistics of national income and its distribution, however, were virtually unknown before the twentieth century. Thus, Malthus was unable to confirm or to test the profound theoretical insights of his later work, *The Principles of Political Economy,* in which he largely anticipated the Keynesian system, and by virtue of sheer forensic ability Ricardo won the day. A hundred years later Keynes dramatically reversed the judgment of history. But even the success of the Keynesian theory depended to a considerable extent on the parallel developments in national income statistics, by which, for instance, the inner structure of a great depression in terms of the virtual disappearance of investment and the failure of consumption or government expenditures to rise in a compensating manner was clearly revealed.

Considering now in greater detail the impact of economics and especially of economists on the economy, one thinks of five names or groups of names as having had a major impact. I am excluding the mercantilists and the physiocrats, the first, because they represented as it were the distillation of popular wisdom rather than any great new theoretical insights, with the possible exception of Thomas Mun; and the latter because they did not have very much impact on anybody except perhaps on Adam Smith. The first great name, therefore, is Adam Smith, and his impact on the development of free trade is well known.

The free-trade argument, which is actually very subtle in *The Wealth of Nations* itself, can only be appreciated in the presence of a level of analysis of the economic system which clearly goes beyond what might be called a "folk economics." There has to be a concept of the economic system as a whole, of the problem of allocation of resources, an understanding of the way in which the price system in fact serves to allocate resources, an understanding of the fact that trade is a positive-sum game, as we would call it nowadays, in which both parties benefit, and an understanding of the advantages of specialization in the division of labor. By contrast the arguments of vulgar protectionism are derived substantially from folk images of economic processes, images which overweight the advantages to the few, which are concentrated, and underweight the disadvantages to the many, which are diffuse. Protection furthermore appeals to that hatred of the foreigner which is an unfortunate characteristic of the mass of mankind, and there may even be subtle psychoanalytic reasons behind the feeling that export is good and import is bad.

Adam Smith's demolition of the mercantilists was almost too complete, for as Keynes pointed out in what was a return to a kind of neo-mercantilism, a favorable balance of payments by increasing the money supply might well increase employment and output if a society were operating at less than full capacity. This, however, is a still more subtle argument, one which neither Adam Smith nor his opponents could possibly have used. It is an extraordinary tribute to the clarity and the forensic power of *The Wealth of Nations* that it did in fact have such an impact on the economic policies not only of Great Britain but also for a time of other countries. After 1860, it is true, rising nationalism and perhaps a not wholly unreasonable desire to use the tariff to foster growth industries led to a gradual retreat from the Smithian principles. Nevertheless, the strong pressure in the last twenty or thirty years towards the relaxation of trade barriers and even the relative economic success in development of countries like Malaya, which have taken advantage of successful trade opportunities and have not been afraid to specialize, indicates that Adam Smith is still a very live force in the world.

Furthermore, one can see the impact of Adam Smith on the economic ideology of the United States, especially in regard to internal economic policy, in such matters as the antitrust legislation, the regulation of monopoly, and a long prejudice against even such relatively mild interventions into the price system as the minimum wage. In the last thirty or forty years, it is true, we have largely lost our prejudices against intervening in the price system, though it is by no means certain that we have always intervened very successfully or intelligently. The voices of the so-called Chicago School of economists—notably Milton Friedman and George Stigler—with their frequently trenchant criticism of the kind of intervention which we have actually had is a tribute to the persisting vitality of Adam Smith's frame of thought.

In the generation after Adam Smith we find Ricardo and Malthus, each of whom exercised a substantial influence on the social system though in rather different ways. Malthus gave his name to a whole doctrine, Malthusianism, and as a result has perhaps received a good deal of unmerited abuse and even praise. His first *Essay on Population,* published in 1798, can certainly claim to be one of the most influential books of the last two hundred years, and it is even more relevant today than it was then. His great contribution is what might be called a "miserific vision" of long-run equilibrium in which the only really effective means of eventually bringing the growth of population to a halt is starvation and misery.

In this respect Malthus as a thinker was premature. He was successful in influencing the policies of his day largely for the wrong reasons, because his doctrine provided what looked like a good excuse for a highly restrictive and punitive poor law. With the wisdom of hindsight we can now see that for his own day, Malthus was quite wrong. He wrote at the beginning of an enormous expansion of the food supply, both through the occupancy of virgin lands and through substantial increases in yield per acre through scientific technology. Consequently, even though there has been an enormous increase in population since Malthus's day, the food supply until very recently has increased roughly in proportion, and indeed in the developed part of the world in a greater proportion.

Nevertheless, Malthus was right in pointing out that the food supply eventually could never keep up with the exponential growth of population, and today the Malthusian devil looms larger than ever. Even the socialists, who have always hated Malthus—not perhaps altogether unreasonably, in the light of the use which was made of his theories to beat down social change—are now being forced to admit that rapid population growth can undermine economic development and that the problem of a long-run equilibrium of population must eventually be faced. And "eventually" now means fairly soon.

It can be argued, therefore, that the immediate results of Malthus were rather disastrous. The English Poor Law of 1934, for instance, which is largely attributed to his influence, in fact may just have made poor old people a little more miserable than they otherwise would have been and may have had very little influence even on the growth of the English population. If the "Speenhamland" system of outdoor relief had continued, the poor would have been happier and the rate of economic development would not have been much affected. It is in our own day, however, that Malthus has really come into his own, and recognition of the desperate necessity for means of population-control, of which, incidentally, he would certainly not have approved, has become almost a commonplace.

If Malthus came too early, in a certain sense Ricardo came too late. He codified and clarified the insights of Adam Smith into a body of abstract doctrine, and it can be argued forcibly that the very success of this body of doctrine repressed the growth of knowledge in economics for almost a century and had substantially adverse effects on economic policy. Malthus again, with the genius he seemed to have for being premature, developed in his *Principles of Political Economy* in 1836 a remarkable body of insights into what we now think of as macroeconomics and anticipated the Keynesian revolution by a hundred years. Ricardo won his argument with him, however, and it was Ricardian thought that dominated the next century, with its orthodoxy of the gold standard, low government activity, balanced budgets, and a punitive poor law.

The fact that the nineteenth century in both Britain and America was as successful as it was certainly indicated that as a long-run formula for development the Ricardian model made some sort of sense and was certainly more successful than, shall we say, the profligate and insecure systems of Latin America. Nevertheless, many costs may have been unnecessarily high—the hungry forties, the depressed seventies and eighties, the excessive swing in the business cycle, and so on. Perhaps the very success of the Ricardian framework was its undoing. By the 1920's and still more the 1930's it had become very clear that this framework was inadequate to deal with the problems of the day. It may well be, therefore, as Keynes has suggested, that if Ricardo had written a generation earlier and Malthus had been more systematic and successful in debate the nineteenth century would have been just as successful in development and a good deal happier in terms of social costs. Like all the "ifs" of history, however, this is something we can never really know.

If economics is willing to claim Karl Marx, then from the point of view of the sheer magnitude of one man's influence on human history the impact of economics can well claim to be enormous. Probably no man in human history to date has had such an enormous impact on the world social system, for good or for ill. It is true that the impact of Marx depends not so much on the fact that he was an economist, for his contributions to economics are neither very good nor very original, but on the fact that he was a prophet and an ideologist whose vision of the world seemed to meet the needs of a great many in the succeeding century who were committed to social change. A good deal of the power of Marxian thought rises out of its synthetic and systematic nature, the fact that it represents what I would describe as a premature synthesis of the social sciences into a total vision of society. For minds which are intolerant of intellectual ambiguities, which want to know all the answers, a total system like Marxism is very attractive. Whatever the reasons for the impact, however, its magnitude can hardly be denied, for a third of the world's population now lives under regimes which owe their inspiration to Marx.

It is certainly beyond the scope of this essay to attempt to draw up a balance sheet on Marxism, and indeed it is still too early to do this. Both the costs and the benefits are very large, and under these circumstances it is hard to determine whether one exceeds the other. On the benefit side, Marxism has undoubtedly provided the excuse for the transformation of stagnant societies and for the spread of education, science, and technology into parts of the world where it had previously made little impact. It has produced a positive and reasonably high rate of economic development in virtually all the countries that it has touched. It has done this, however, at a very high social cost arising mainly out of the inadequacies of Marxism as a social theory. It represents, indeed, a highly special case which has relevance to some places and periods but not to all. The ideology of class war and revolution, furthermore, has been extremely costly in terms of human suffering, and even in terms of development, and countries which have achieved development without revolution, like Japan, have achieved the benefits with only a fraction of the costs. Both intellectually and aesthetically Marxism has also been costly in the sense that it has frozen the societies which it has dominated in a mid-nineteenth century complex of ideas and even tastes. What strikes one about the socialist countries today is their extraordinary Victorianism, and perhaps one of the costs of ideology is that it always imprints on the society it dominates the patterns of a dead past.

Oddly enough, it could easily be argued that the benefits of Marxism on the whole have been enjoyed mainly by the non-Marxist societies. The main significance of Marx was that he challenged the legitimacy of private property, the market as a social organizer, bourgeois ideals, and the bourgeois state. To any challenge to legitimacy there has to be a response, and the response to this challenge in the West has been quite profound. In Toynbeean terms, one could argue that Marxism provided almost an optimum degree of challenge to those societies which were already fairly well developed, whereas the challenge was simply too great for those societies of northeastern Eurasia which had not yet reached the point in development where the challenge could be met without catastrophe. Certainly the capitalist world today is far different from what it was in 1848, and some of the difference at any rate is a result of the response to the Marxist challenge, though how much is hard to evaluate.

The main reason why Marxism has not been successful in the West is that the dynamics of distribution followed an entirely different course from that which the Marxist theory predicted. Marx thought that the total amount of the product going to the worker would be fairly stable and that hence, the increase in the product would all go to the capitalist. What has happened in fact is that a very large increase in the product in Western societies has been achieved while the proportional shares have been fairly stable; actually, the proportion going to labor has been increasing. Instead of surplus value concentrating in the hands of the capitalists, therefore, it has been widely distributed throughout the whole population without the abolition of private property and without the development of centrally planned economies. Indeed it is in the centrally planned economies that the exploitation of labor—in the supposed interest of posterity, it is true—has been most severe. The failure of the Marxist prediction in the West is clear; what is not clear is how much of this was due to the inherent dynamics of a market-oriented society and how much of it was due to specific reactions in terms of economic policy arising out of the Marxist criticism. One can certainly argue that the change in the status of the labor movement, the rise of social security, the development of the progressive income tax, and so on, were in part at any rate responses to the Marxist challenge which produced a lot of benefit at a pretty low social cost.

Perhaps the great tragedy of Marxism as an ideology is that it was formulated before the great developments in mathematical economics, econometrics, and economic information collection and processing which have characterized the last hundred years and which have particularly flowered in the last third of a century. It is hard to associate this change with any single person, though Keynes certainly represents its prophet and visionary, even though he was not a very good mathematician or statistician. The impact of this "sophisticating" of economics has been very large in the last twenty years and promises to be even larger in the future. This sophisticating process has exhibited many of the characteristics of what might be called the middle stage in the development of a science, such as, for instance, characterized astronomy from Copernicus to Newton. There are shifts in fundamental vision, and in this regard it is not wholly unfair to compare Keynes with Copernicus, for the Keynesian revolution, like the Copernican revolution, represents a shift from a man-centered, behind-the-eyeball view of the universe to what might be called the system-oriented view.

There have also been a number of false starts and blind alleys. It is at least questionable, for instance, whether the mathematizations due to A. A. Cournot (1834), Léon Walras (1870), and V. Pareto (1896) have done much more than refine and make explicit the fundamental system which is implied in the classical economics of Adam Smith and Ricardo, even though that was not written in explicit mathematical language. Similarly, the empirical work of Wesley Mitchell in the 1920s on the business cycle seems to have been something of a blind alley, though one with a good many useful exits along the way.

The really powerful combination has been that of Keynesian theory with the collection and processing of national income statistics. National income statistics have done for Keynes what the telescope did for Copernicus. It has enabled us to watch the motions of the system and its component parts almost from month to month, certainly from quarter to quarter, and hence has given us a system of information feedback that we did not possess before. This combination of econometric models of the total economy with an information system which enables us to make reasonable estimates of the parameters has given us a sense of "steersmanship" of the economy which was quite foreign to the world before 1930. This is a change which has crept up on us rather slowly, so that we are apt to be unaware of its magnitude. There are many indications, however, that we have passed a subtle watershed and that we have achieved, as it were, revolutionary change without revolution, which is the most desirable way to do it.

If one is looking for a date of passing the watershed (though, as in Chicago, it is hard to tell where the watershed is), one might seize on 1946, with the passage of the Full Employment Act creating the Council of Economic Advisors and the Joint Economic Committee in Congress. This represented, as it were, the legitimation of economics as a profession and the establishment of economists as "lords spiritual" in the precincts of both the White House and Congress. The process has had its ups and downs. The success of the 1964 tax cut, however, with the relatively high rates of development of the 1960s, is perhaps the first conscious breakthrough in the United States of what might be called "national income economics." In Europe and in Japan the success of this kind of economics has been even greater, and in the last twenty years there have been rates of development which have been quite unprecedented.

The sense that the Second World War represented something of a watershed is enhanced if we draw the comparison between the twenty years which followed the First World War, from 1919–1939, with the twenty years following the Second World War, 1945–1965. The first twenty years were a total failure; they saw the fiasco of reparations, the economic collapse of the Great Depression, and the rise of Hitler, and they ended in the Second World War. In the socialist world, the period was even more disastrous; the economic collapse in Russia in 1921 and the disaster of the First Collectivization represented enormous breakdowns of the social system. In the "Third World" hardly any progress was made towards the abolition of the colonial system, and the international economy stagnated or even declined. It is hard, indeed, to avoid awarding these years an "F−" from the point of view of human welfare and decency. By contrast, the years from 1945–1965 at least seem to deserve a "C." We have not had any great depression; unemployment in the United States has rarely risen above 6 per cent of the labor force; reasonable rates of economic growth have been maintained; and in Europe and Japan and even some other countries, extraordinary rates of growth have been achieved, as much as 8 per cent per annum per capita in Japan, over 7 per cent in West Germany, and 5 or 6 per cent in a good many other countries. The colonial system has largely been disbanded, and even though the cold war and the world war industry represent an enormous burden on mankind of about $120 billion a year, at least there has been some progress towards international organization and peaceful coexistence, and we are certainly further from the Third World War in 1966 than we were from the Second World War in 1940, when it was actually under way.

One certainly would not wish to credit economics with all these achievements. Even if we only credit it with 10 per cent of the difference, however, this is very sizable. If, for instance, we had had a great depression in the United States in the 1950's instead of a mild stagnation, it would unquestionably have cost us $500 billion and an enormous worsening of the international climate. We certainly do not put much more than $100 million a year into economics, so that the rate of return on this investment could easily be of the order of thousands of a per cent per annum. It is not surprising, therefore, that the economics profession finds itself today in a rather self-congratulatory mood. Professor Schumpeter once said to me, "How nice economics was before anybody knew anything!" meaning, of course, that in the days before national income statistics, economists could spin any theories they wanted to and nobody could check up on them. Today the feedback from reality is great enough that it may cramp the artistic style of the theorist, but it unquestionably increases the power of the discipline.

The impact of economics is by no means confined to stabilization policy and the cure of unemployment. In the last twenty years we have seen the development of something called variously "management science," "operations research," and "decision theory." This is a body of theory, information collection, processing, and practice which in a sense emerged out of economics but which has now established itself as a fairly independent discipline, still, of course, within the social sciences.

Decision theory is a set of mathematical variations on the theme that everybody does what he thinks is best at the time, and management science consists essentially of a variety of techniques for defining and identifying the "best" out of a set of possible choices. The first step is to define the field of choice itself, which might be called the "agenda"; the second step is to define a function which enables us to order the elements of the field of choice and then select the one which stands at the top of the list. When the number of elements in the field of choice is small and valuation procedures are simple, folk knowledge is quite adequate to deal with the problem. When, however, the number of elements in the field of choice becomes very large, sophisticated procedures have to be devised if rational choices are to be made. Development in the fields of applied mathematics such as linear or non-linear programming consists essentially in devices for ordering large fields of choice through orderly mathematical procedures. The practitioners of management science now number several thousand, and they have unquestionably made a substantial contribution to the development of more realistic and sophisticated decisions in organizations of all kinds, both public and private.

At the moment it is virtually impossible to evaluate the impact of this movement, for it has not really been in existence a long enough time. As with everything else, one has to balance the gains against possible losses. The gains represent decisions made with the aid of these sophisticated procedures which are more profitable to the decision-maker or perhaps to the society at large than those which would be made without them. The gain here is the difference between our evaluation of those elements of the set of choices which would be selected in the presence of sophisticated procedures and those elements which would be selected without them. Here a great deal depends on the nature of the utility function, as it is called, that is, the evaluations of the various elements in the set of choice. If these are only a few elements in the set which are very highly valued, with all the other elements having a very low valuation, mistakes in decision can be very important. If on the other hand there are a large number of elements, as it were, bracketed at the top of the list, and all of about equal value, then a decision is unimportant; anything we decide will be all right. Unfortunately, we do not know enough about the value functions of our society to know how far one or the other of these patterns prevails. If it is the second, then refined decision-making processes do not add much to our total welfare; if the first condition prevails, they may add a great deal.

There are also possibilities of certain costs of sophisticated decision-making procedures. They may, for instance, give an illusion of certainty to the decision-maker in situations which have objective uncertainty, and uncertain situations require a very different kind of behavior and different decision procedures from certain ones. In an uncertain situation, for instance, he who hesitates is frequently saved; and an important aspect of decision-making consists of the capacity not to pre-empt the future but to leave decisions open. Sophisticated decision procedures may lead to premature closure, to too little emphasis on liquidity and hesitation, and hence perhaps to disastrous mistakes. One worries about this especially in the international system, where pseudosophistication could easily lead to greater instability. The only remedy for that little learning which is a dangerous thing is, however, more of the same, or perhaps more of a different kind of learning. There is never any way back to ignorance, even when ignorance is bliss. Consequently we may expect that the decision-making process will become more and more sophisticated and that as a result fewer mistakes in decision will be made.

The long-run consequences of a substantial improvement in decision-making processes may be rather unexpected. There might, for instance, be some sacrifice of long-run development for short-run stability. The capacity to make mistakes and suffer the consequences is certainly an important aspect of the evolutionary process, and sophisticated decision procedures may easily introduce a diminution of the rate both of social mutation and selection. Improved decision procedures, for instance, could result in increasing the duration of life of organizations of all kinds. What this would do to the long-run rate of social evolution is not clear, but this perhaps is something that we can leave the future to worry about.

It is clear that economics as a social science has now reached a degree of sophistication where its impact on the economy is very substantial and is likely to be even greater in the future. It can hardly be denied as far as economics is concerned that we now know something and that this knowledge can be applied. Knowing something, however, is not knowing everything, and we still have a long way to go. I would not like to give the impression that economics has reached its summit of achievement and that there are no more problems to be solved. In fact there is a great deal yet to be done, both in theory and in the development of information collection and processing, and the mood of the economist should not be that of resting on his oars and enjoying his laurels but rather pulling up his sleeves and getting about a number of very urgent jobs.

One of the biggest unsolved problems, in economic policy certainly, is that of the intelligent use of the price system. This problem has two aspects. One is the problem of the general level of prices and money wages. The other is the problem of the relative price structure. Even the problem of the general level is still quite unsolved, and it remains the Achilles' heel of national income economics. It is fairly easy to stabilize or do anything we want with the national income in dollar terms. If we want this, for instance, to grow at 5 per cent per annum, suitable adjustments of the fiscal and monetary system would easily permit this, and we are certainly within sight of devising a social-cybernetic apparatus which would keep the rate of growth of the gross national product in dollar terms within easily tolerable limits.

The dollar value of the national product, however, is a product of two aggregates or indices, and is equal to the quantity of output in real terms multiplied by the money price level of this output. Within a stable or controlled total dollar value of the national output, it would be quite possible to have substantial fluctuations in opposite directions of the quantity level and the price level. What we really want to control, however, is the quantity level. It is the fluctuations in this or the failure of this to grow which causes trouble, and the ideal of aggregative economic policy would be a steady growth of the total quantity of output at some reasonable figure. The dollar value we know how to control fairly well; the price level we do not know how to control. The great dilemma of stabilization policy is that before we reach the ideal output or full employment, the market forces of the economy seem to create an unacceptable rate of increase in the level of prices and money wages.

Up to now, the only institutional device we have discovered to deal with this is Presidential anger, institutionalized in the form of guidelines, and this is a system that would not stand very much strain. It may be, as Gardner Means has suggested, that we shall find a solution to this problem through certain modifications of the tax system which will discriminate against increases in income due to increased prices or money wages, but this still seems to be fairly far in the future.

When we come to the problem of the ideal structure of relative prices, the situation both in theory and in practice can only be described as deplorable. In the United States, for instance, we are only just beginning to realize that a great deal of our intervention in the relative price structure, which was motivated at least in part by a desire to redistribute income towards the poor, has in fact redistributed income towards the rich. This is certainly true of agricultural policy, for instance, where trying to solve the problem of agricultural poverty by raising the relative prices of agricultural commodities has resulted in subsidizing the rich farmers, who after all have a lot to sell, and doing very little for the poor farmers except chasing them out of agriculture altogether—which, as a matter of fact, may not be a bad solution. In terms of economic development and rate of technological change, agricultural policy has in fact been an uproarious success, but in terms of the objectives of social justice which originally gave rise to it, it is open to very severe criticism.

One could give a great many examples of cases in which governmental distortion of the price system has had a very dubious result. Even in the case of public education, where we have supposedly subsidized education by making it either cheap or free, a considerable amount of the subsidy has gone to the rich or middle classes. The local tax system which supports these educational subsidies is frequently extremely regressive, so that actually it taxes the poor to educate the middle classes and the rich. It is not surprising under the circumstances that human resources are wasted and that we have a problem of self-perpetuating pockets of poverty which the system of public education completely fails to touch. If we were willing to use the price system more, to charge full-cost fees and to use public funds to provide scholarships, many of the present economic problems of the educational system might be solved. The state universities are an even more flagrant case of subsidizing the rich by a regressive tax system in the interest of what is supposed to be equal opportunity, which in fact is nothing of the sort. Even social security is open to charges that it is a much heavier burden on the poor than on the rich and that it actually represents very little in the way of redistribution. It also involves a substantial tax on the present generation of young people, who in effect are buying insurance and annuities at very poor rates in order to subsidize their improvident grandparents.

When we look at things like antitrust policy, the confusion about what we ought to do about the relative price structure becomes all the more patent. While the antitrust legislation in the United States can be defended on the grounds that it has created a mild irritant for decision-makers of the business community which has prevented them taking certain easy ways out and hence has pushed them in the direction of fostering technological improvement, it cannot be defended on the grounds of any logical consistency or on the grounds of any theory about ideal prices or even ideal forms of economic organization. When we turn to the regulated industries, we see a considerable success with the American Telephone and Telegraph Company and a disastrous failure with the railroads, so here again it is clear that the solutions of the past do not necessarily apply to the present.

At the root of a great deal of the failure of what we might call microeconomic policy lies a serious defect in economic theory itself—its inability to deal with the larger problems of the distribution of income. There are still many unsolved problems, for instance, even in the question of the incidence of taxation on the distribution of income. We still do not really know the extent to which manipulation of the price system, for instance through minimum wages or subsidies, affects the overall distribution. We also do not have any adequate theory of the long-run distribution of property, on which the distribution of income in part rests. These are technical problems which we cannot go into now, but they deserve to be noted in case economists get a little intoxicated with their present success.

Another problem of enormous importance where the contribution of economics is at the least ambiguous is that of economic development. The demand for rapid economic development on the part of the poor countries is now so insistent that the economics of development has become extremely fashionable and has a large market. Nevertheless, the economic models of development leave much to be desired and have by no means always been helpful. Partly this is because the developmental process goes far beyond economics in the narrow sense and involves a unified social dynamics which still exists only in embryo. Hence it is perhaps unfair to blame economics for what is really a failure of general social science. Economists, however, are not altogether guiltless of presuming to know more than they do and of giving advice when they should have been doing research. It is clear that economic development involves profound cultural change as well as economic change in the narrow sense, and though we do have the beginnings of a general developmental theory, for instance in the works of Everett E. Hagan and David C. McClelland, we may need to wait another twenty years before we see in terms of success and failure how some of these principles work out.

In conclusion, one may note that the problem of what might be called comparative economic systems still remains to be solved in a scientific, as opposed to an ideological, manner. The cold war, even ideologically, has certainly diminished in intensity in the last ten years, and economics can take some credit for this. The careful analytical study of socialist economies on the part of Western economists and of capitalist economies on the part of socialist economists have produced, if not agreement, at least a substantial area of professional discourse and mutual understanding. It can be recognized, of course, that the choice between a centrally planned economy and a market-based economy depends on non-economic factors more than it does on strictly economic ones. Nevertheless, a good deal remains to be done in what might be called the cost-benefit analysis of economic institutions, especially now that substantial modifications in both socialist and capitalist institutions have proceeded to the point where different countries provide a very wide spectrum of overall economic institutions. I would hesitate to suggest at this stage that we could do a cost-benefit analysis, shall we say, of the American financial system and compare this with Yugoslav investment planning; but at least some more or less rational comparisons might be in order. The conclusion of such a study might well be that the differences between the various systems are not significant enough to warrant putting much effort into changing them except by a succession of incremental changes, which would make the outlook look rather bad for revolution. However, it should also be possible to do a cost-benefit analysis on revolution, at least in a rough way, which might easily produce rather radical changes in the popularity of various ideologies. All this, of course, is very speculative. It suggests, however, that there is a large field of research here for the future, which might have a substantial effect in reconciling the present world split.

The general conclusion of this chapter, then, would seem to be that, as far as economics is concerned, we look to the past with modest satisfaction and to the future with hope. I trust that it is not merely the fact that I am a professional economist which gives rise to the optimism of this conclusion, but at least in a day of constant bemoaning it is nice to be able to take at least a modest satisfaction in something. In the next chapter, I fear, not even that small pleasure will be granted.

DISCUSSION QUESTIONS

1. Relying on the selections by Professors Knight and Boulding discuss some of the major contributions of economic analysis to our understanding of the economic system and to our ability to resolve policy conflicts.
2. Distinguish between macroeconomics and microeconomics.
3. Discuss the market and the political process as means by which society makes economic choices. What are some advantages and disadvantages of each system? What types of economic decisions might be best handled by each system?
4. If economists knew all the relevant facts about a particular economic problem and agreed completely on the economic relations involved, there would still not likely be general agreement among them as to the appropriate policy action for resolving the problem. Explain why.

SELECTED REFERENCES

Bach, George Leland, *An Introduction to Economic Analysis and Policy,* 5th ed., Englewood Cliffs, N.J.: Prentice-Hall, Inc., 1966, chaps. 1, 2.

Boulding, Kenneth E., *The Skills of the Economist,* Toronto: Clarke, Irwin & Co., Ltd., 1958, chap. 1.

Friedman, Milton, "The Methodology of Positive Economics," in *Essays in Positive Economics,* Chicago: The University of Chicago Press, 1953.

Hutcheson, T. W., *Positive Economics and Policy Objectives,* London: George Allen and Unwin, Ltd., 1964.

Krupp, Sherman Roy (ed.), *The Structure of Economic Science: Essays on Methodology,* Englewood Cliffs, N.J.: Prentice-Hall, Inc., 1966.

Mrydal, Gunnar, *Value in Social Theory,* New York: Harper and Row, Publishers, Inc., 1958.

Robinson, Joan, *Economic Philosophy,* London: C. A. Watts & Co., Ltd., 1962. See especially chap. 1.

PART 2

THE PRODUCTIVE PROCESS

"Economic life is an organization of producers to satisfy the wants of consumers."* Goods and services are produced because other people are willing to pay for them. In turn consumers are able to pay for the goods and services because of the incomes they earn from production. Not everyone has to work in order to have a claim against income generated by production. Some people earn a return because they own a scarce item of production (such as land) or the means of obtaining a scarce item of production (such as financial capital) which they are willing to make available to producers rather than to engage in production themselves. Likewise, the person drawing a veteran's pension is getting a transfer income. Someone earning income from current production is paying taxes which the government in turn pays to the veteran. He is being compensated for his services to society in some past war. There are many other private and public transfers of similar nature.

Not all goods are produced for immediate consumption. Producer goods are sold to other producers to enter another stage of production. Steel sold to an auto company is an example. Some producer goods are used in current production, such as the steel for auto production; some may be added to inventories; and some may be used to build new plant and equipment, such as steel used to build a new

---

* J. R. Hicks, A. G. Hart, and J. W. Ford, *The Social Framework of the American Economy*, 2nd ed. (New York: Oxford University Press, 1955), p. 20.

lathe for a factory. Consumer goods, on the other hand, satisfy consumer wants directly. Some consumer goods can only be used once. Examples are food and gasoline. Durable consumer goods render their services over a period of time. These include automobiles, refrigerators, and furniture.

Not all of current output is consumed. Part is used to replace, repair, and maintain capital equipment that is wearing out. In addition, part of current output is used to expand the present stock of capital so that future production and income can be larger than current production and income. Thus, current production is equal to production of consumers' goods and net additions to the stock of capital.

A primary problem of economics deals with the social organization of production and exchange. There are many ways that society can organize its economic activity. The article by Heilbroner describes three general ways that this can be done. None of these methods—tradition, command, and the market—is mutually exclusive. Even in the modern market economy of the United States there are important elements of command and tradition. Government power is used to direct and regulate much economic activity: production is channeled into military purposes, public utilities are regulated, farm prices and incomes are supported, and tariffs are enacted to protect particular industries. Also, custom and tradition are of great importance: businessmen follow customary pricing practices, and individuals from certain social positions are limited by custom to certain professions. The whole market system presupposes an institutional framework of law and custom built up over centuries.

Within this institutional framework, how does a market economy operate to solve the problems of production and distribution? The individuals in the economy can be conveniently classed as producers, consumers, and resource suppliers. These groups interact through two types of markets: the product market, where consumer goods and services are sold to consumers; and the resource market, where land, labor, and capital are sold or rented to producers. The producers combine these resources and intermediate goods purchased from other firms to produce final products. Prices in product markets are determined by the interaction of consumer decisions about purchases and producer decisions about what to offer for sale. Prices in the resource market are determined by interactions of business decisions about what resources to purchase or hire and by decisions of resource suppliers about what resources to furnish to the productive process. Thus producers, consumers, and resource suppliers, within the institutional setting of a capitalist system, each pursuing his own interest, determine for society what goods will be produced, how these goods will be allocated to consumers, what resources will be employed, and what incomes the resource suppliers will receive. In practice, however, the system does not work as smoothly as the theory implies. It is an ethical question which cannot be answered on purely economic grounds whether the solution given by the market is in the best interest of society. Some people do very well under the system; others come off very badly. But the system does work; production, consumption, distribution, accumulation, and investment continue indefinitely. However, it is not a very smooth process; the market, if left to itself, may produce periods of boom and inflation followed by periods of stagnation and unemployment.

Selection 3

The Productive Process

J. R. HICKS, ALBERT GAILORD HART, and JAMES W. FORD

From The Social Framework of the American Economy *(New York: Oxford University Press, 1955), pp. 17–44. Reprinted by permission of Oxford University Press.*

Production and Exchange

1. Worker, Employer, and Consumer

Economic affairs enter into the life of every one of us, the most important economic activity in the life of the ordinary man being the way he earns his living. People earn their living in all sorts of different ways—by manual work, by brainwork, in factories, in offices, and on farms; in dull ways, in interesting ways. But the thing common to all ways of earning one's living is doing work and being paid for doing it. In most countries the majority of people earn their living by working "for" some particular employer; they receive their payment in the form of a wage or salary (the latter is only a word of Latin origin meaning "wage," used instead of *wage* so as to sound grander). But there are some people (it happens with musicians, gardeners, and journalists, for example) who may divide their time between two or three employers. And there are others (shopkeepers, doctors, farmers who deliver milk directly, and so on) who serve quite large numbers of different employers or *customers*—for it is really very much the same thing. Whatever sort of work it is that is done, whatever form the payment for doing it takes, the common element is always there. In order to earn his living a man has to work, and there has to be someone—an employer, or customer, or client—who is prepared to pay him for doing it.

Now why should the employer be prepared to pay? There are in fact several distinct cases. In the first place, an employer may be prepared to pay to have work done for him because the work is directly useful to him personally. A sick man goes to (that is employs) a doctor because he hopes as a result to feel better in health. A householder hires a collector to keep trash from accumulating. A woman patronizes a hairdresser for the sake of "beauty." In these instances, and in many others of similar character, the work performed provides something the employer or customer directly wants. Whatever the nature of the want to be satisfied, the fact that he is to get something he wants explains why he is prepared to pay for the work to be performed.

In many other cases the employer is prepared to pay not because the work done is of any use to him personally, but because he expects it to result in something useful to a third person (the consumer) who will be willing to pay for it. The immediate employer is here nothing but an intermediary; he pays his employee, and the consumer pays him. The wants which are to be satisfied are the consumer's wants; the employer is willing to pay because he expects to be paid by the consumer.

The necessity of having some sort of employer-intermediary is made evident when one reflects how many workers there are whose work is in itself absolutely useless, though it becomes very useful when it is combined with the work of other people. The typical factory worker, nowadays, is engaged on some small, specialized operation, which is only a stage in the making of some part of a useful article, a part like the lace of a shoe or the chain of a bicycle. Unless there are other workers to perform the other stages and make the other parts, his work is utterly useless. There is no point in doing work of this kind unless there is someone to organize the different operations into a unity. To do this is the work of the employer-intermediary, the business manager or director, the professional employer who brings together the different people with the different skills needed to produce the complete article. Such an employer is not a consumer like the man who employs a doctor or a furnace cleaner; he is a worker or producer, contributing his own very important share to the process of producing goods which consumers want. Employer and employed are in fact cooperating together in the production of something useful to consumers. They each of them derive their earnings from the payments made by the consumers, who purchase the finished articles they have produced.

Every firm or business consists in essence of a cooperation of workers, organized in some way or other to produce salable products. But the products are not always sold directly to consumers. Very often the product of one firm is sold to another firm, which performs some further operation upon it before it reaches the consumer's hands. Even when a firm has turned out the precise material product which the consumer wants—the jam, the toothpaste, or the newspaper—there is still the further stage of providing it at the place and time where and when it is wanted. To do this is the function of the trader and the shopkeeper, who assist in satisfying people's wants just as much as other workers do. It often happens, on the other hand, that the product turned out by a firm has not yet reached the material form in which the consumer will finally want it. The products of steelworks and spinning mills are only the raw materials of useful articles; they are usually sold to other firms, which use them as ingredients in further production. But even in these cases the chain connecting the particular firm with the ultimate consumer, although it may be quite a long one, is still there. If we take the trouble we can see for ourselves that the ultimate object of the work which is done is to assist in making something some consumer will want and will be willing to pay for. That consumer may be near at hand, or he may be at the other end of the earth; still he can always be found if we look for him. It is only because there is a prospect of finding a consumer at the end of the whole process, who will be prepared to pay for something he finds useful or desirable, that people can find employment in industry or in any sort of production at all.

Specialization and Mutual Exchange

Thus it appears that the whole of the economic activity of humanity (that vast complex of activities which we call the Economic System) consists of nothing else but an immense cooperation of workers or producers to make things and do things that consumers want. When it is described in this way, the economic system may sound quite an admirable thing—perhaps too admirable to agree with our experience of it. But in fact there is nothing necessarily admirable about a cooperation to satisfy the wants of consumers. The wants are usually harmless, but they may be deplorable; the methods of cooperating to satisfy even the most respectable wants are sometimes inefficient and stupid. Yet whether the wants are good or bad, whether production is organized efficiently or not, the description still holds. Economic life is an organization of producers to satisfy the wants of consumers.

Who are these consumers for whom the world is working? To a very large extent they are the workers and producers themselves. People are workers and producers (or dependents of workers and producers) in one capacity and consumers in another. The consumer who spends his money on the product of one industry (a bicycle or a suit of clothes) has earned that money by working in another occupation (say, printing or market gardening). The bicycle makers and the clothing and textile workers spend their earnings in turn on the products of other industries, the workers in these spend their earnings on other products, and so on. Among the various classes of workers and producers who come into the picture at one or another of these stages, there will be some who will spend some part of their earnings on the books and newspapers, the vegetables and flowers, which were the products of the printers and market gardeners we started with.

The organization of production and consumption in the modern world is an immensely complicated affair; but if we turn our minds to the way it would be worked out in a simpler state of society, the general nature of the organization is at once apparent. Before the improvements in transportation which have taken place in the last two centuries, the vast majority of the human race lived in fairly self-contained villages, villages which traded with one another in a few kinds of goods but were in the main self-supporting. In such a village the principle upon which production has to be organized becomes clear at once. The whole thing is a system of exchanges. The farmer uses some part of his produce to satisfy his own wants but sells some part to his neighbors. With the proceeds of that sale he buys other things which he needs—clothes from the weaver, woodwork from the carpenter, pottery from the potter. The weaver, in his turn, spends some of his time making his own clothes; but he sells most of his produce, using the proceeds to purchase the farmer's milk or the potter's pots. And so on. "You do this for me, and I will do that for you." It is on bargains of this sort that the whole organization rests.

The advantage of organizing economic life in this way arises from the increased efficiency which comes from each person having a job, and sticking to it. "The jack of all trades is master of none." Although excessive specialization results in monotonous work, some degree of specialization is needed before any skill can be acquired. Instead of each person working so as to satisfy his own wants alone, which would mean wasting a great deal of time in continually shifting over from one job to another, everyone becomes to some extent a specialist, concentrating on one particular job or small range of jobs. The other things he wants done are done for him by other people, and in exchange for these services he uses his skill in serving them.

The main difference, from this point of view, between the primitive village organization and the economic system of the modern world is that in the modern world specialization has been carried immensely further. The wants of the ordinary person in the twentieth century are catered to by a system of exchanges in which an immensely larger number of people take part. The ordinary worker does not do more than assist in the production of some useful article. He joins together with a large number of other workers in producing something which will be useful to others, or perhaps to some of those he joins with; the things he gets in exchange are themselves the result of extensive, even world-wide, cooperation among producers. The reason for the adoption of this complicated system is still the technical advantage of specialization; subdividing productive processes has increased the efficiency of labor, enabling all sorts of more efficient methods (particularly mechanical methods) to be introduced into production. Nevertheless, in spite of the greater complexity of the specialization involved, the principle remains the same, "You do this for me, and I will do that for you."

Complications to the System of Exchange

Money. We have now discovered two different ways of looking at the economic system. On the one hand, we can look upon it as a cooperation of producers to satisfy the wants of consumers; on the other hand, remembering that the producers and consumers are largely the same people, we can look upon it as a system of mutual exchanges. We shall find, as we go on, that it is very useful to have these two different points of view from which to approach our subject. Some things will be clearer from one of these standpoints, some from the other; and we can use one as a check against the other. It will be particularly useful when we come to making the fundamental classifications, which will occupy us in the next two chapters, to be able to check them up from each of these points of view. But before we proceed to that, we ought to satisfy ourselves that our treatment of the system as one of mutual exchanges is really correct, and not subject to qualifications. There are certain difficulties which do undoubtedly present themselves, and of which we ought to take proper account.

First of all, there is the question of money. Although the ultimate object of anyone who works or produces is to acquire useful things in exchange for his work, the immediate way he gets paid is not in the form of directly useful things but in the form of money. The printer and journalist do not supply their customers with newspapers, getting bread and meat and clothes in direct exchange; they sell their newspapers for money, and then spend money upon the things they want to buy as consumers. There is an obvious convenience in this arrangement. It must often happen that the people who supply the printers with clothes do not want to take newspapers to the full value of the clothes. If they had to take payment in newspapers, they would be obliged to resell the newspapers to another set of people; this would take time to arrange and would obviously be extremely inconvenient. To replace these complicated resales by a simple handing on of tickets—for that is really what it amounts to—saves an immense amount of trouble. The people who sell clothes to the printers do not take payment for them in newspapers but in tickets—that is, money. If they like, they can spend some of the money on newspapers, but if they prefer to spend it on bread and cheese, there is nothing to stop them. If they pass on the money to makers of bread and cheese, these people can spend it on newspapers, or they can hand it on to someone else to spend on newspapers, or it can be handed on again. The use of money enables indirect or roundabout exchanges to take place, without the goods which are exchanged having to be passed on unnecessarily from one person to another. That is the advantage we get from the use of money; it increases the flexibility of the system of exchanges to an extraordinary extent. But it does not make much difference to the essence of the system. Instead of newspapers being exchanged for clothes directly, the exchange takes place in two stages—the newspapers are sold for money, the money is spent on clothes. And so long as the money is only acquired to be disposed of again without abnormal delay, the division into the two stages proceeds quite smoothly. But sometimes the second stage of the exchange is unduly delayed; goods are sold for money, and yet the money is not spent again until a considerable time has elapsed. When this happens on an unusual scale, the result may be that the system of exchanges gets clogged. The world has had some bad experiences of this sort during the last generation; the economic system has shown itself capable of developing monetary diseases of several different kinds. The Theory of Money, which is a special department of economics, is particularly concerned with studying these diseases. Most of it lies outside the field which we shall study in the present volume. But it is impossible to study economic problems at all realistically without paying some attention to these matters, so that we shall be bound to encounter some aspects of these monetary diseases even here.

Private property. Another complication comes from the ownership of property. Most useful goods cannot be produced by human effort alone; the workers need tools to work with and materials to work on. The products of agriculture are produced from the land. The products of mechanical industry are produced with machines. If agricultural land and industrial plant are in private ownership, the owners of these useful resources may be able to exact a price for their use. That is to say, people may acquire tickets which entitle them to purchase other people's products, not by contributing their labor to the productive process, but by allowing the use of their property. This is a matter of the most profound social significance, since some of the deepest divisions in society turn on the distinction between capitalist and worker. As we go on, we shall find that economics has to concern itself with these divisions to a very considerable extent. All the same, our double description of the economic system does not appear to be affected by the private ownership of property. The owner of property contributes to the productive process by allowing the use of his property in production; to that extent he has to be reckoned as a producer. He exchanges the use of his property for a share in the products of industry and in this way enters into the system of exchanges. It is quite true that he gets these advantages much more easily than the worker does. Or if (as is usually the case) he is also a worker, he gets larger advantages than other workers do from the performance of similar work. If we decide, on the ground of convenience, to reckon the owner of property as producer, we must not allow ourselves, in consequence of this decision, to beg any questions about the desirability of private property as an institution. The institution of private property has to be tried by more searching tests. But we shall find it easier to apply those tests if we begin by getting a clear idea about the working of the system in which private property functions.

Government. The only real qualification to the rule that the economic system can be looked on as a system of exchanges comes from the economic activities of governments, national and local. Some part of the money which people receive, in return for the labor they have performed, or for the property they have allowed to be used, is taken away from them by public authorities in taxes, social security contributions, and the like. In order to see how these taxes fit into the system, we must consider the purposes for which they are raised. Governments sometimes raise taxes in order to make presents to some of their own citizens or to foreigners; under this heading would come such things as tribute to a foreign power, pensions to the ex-soldiers of past wars, relief to the unemployed. All these things are just compulsory gifts from one set of persons to another. Some of them are very sensible and desirable, some very undesirable. But some of the taxes which are raised by governments are raised for another purpose—in order to pay for the employment of people to do work for the good of the community in general, as, for example, soldiers or policemen or highway maintenance workers. These people's work is part of the productive process; but it does not result in the production of such things as can be bought by individual consumers, though consumers in general do undoubtedly desire that they be provided. The wants satisfied by work of this sort are social wants, not individual wants. During wartime a very large proportion of a nation's productive power is turned over to the satisfaction of social wants, for the whole of the armed forces and of the munition industries must be reckoned as working to that end. Even in time of peace, the number of people whose work has to be reckoned as being directed to the satisfaction of social wants is usually quite considerable.

It might be supposed, at first sight, that the proportion of its population working for the satisfaction of social wants would be a measure of the degree of socialization reached by a particular nation. But that is not so. Even in a completely socialized state, like Communist Russia, where the government is very nearly the only employer of labor, the proportion of persons working to satisfy social wants need not be abnormally high. For in a socialist state, the government does not only control the production of those things that are wanted socially, it also controls the production of things wanted individually. (There are, of course, little bits of socialism in this sense even in nonsocialist countries—nationalized railways, municipal gasworks, and so on.) In a socialist state, people work for the government, whether they are producing social goods, like roads and parks and military airplanes, or individual goods, like food and clothing. The roads and military airplanes are paid for by the public out of taxes. But the food and clothing are bought from the government, just as they would be bought from private producers in a community which was not organized in a socialist manner. Over the greater part of the field, the socialist government merely acts as an intermediary, in the same way as the private employer. Thus there is nothing in socialism, as such, to prevent us from regarding the economic system as a system of exchanges. Indeed, most of the economic theory in this volume can be applied to a socialist state, just as much as to one which is based on a system of private enterprise. In either case we can look upon the economic system as a cooperation of producers to satisfy consumers' wants (including social wants); or alternatively (apart from the qualification about taxation) we can look upon it as a system of mutual exchanges.

Goods and Services

The Definition of Production

As soon as we have understood the double nature of the economic system, as it was explained in the previous chapter, we can see that it will be convenient to shape our further classifications in ways which will fit in with each of the two aspects. Henceforward we shall mean by *production* any activity directed to the satisfaction of other people's wants through exchange; we shall use a *producer* to mean a person engaging in production in this sense. A person whose wants are satisfied by such production we shall call a *consumer*. Previously we have used these terms in a looser manner. From now on we shall try to confine them to these precise senses.

Let us see what we are committed to by these definitions. The words *producer* and *consumer* are widely used in ordinary speech and in business. But in practical life they do not need to be used very precisely or uniformly, so that they are often used in senses which do not square with our definitions. Farmers, for instance, are fond of drawing a contrast between their own activities as "producers" of foodstuffs, and those of the traders or retailers, who merely sell or "distribute" them. On our definition the retailer is a producer just as much as the farmer. The work done by the retailer is a part of the process of satisfying consumers' wants, just as much as the work of the farmer. Milk on the farm and tobacco at the factory are of little use to anyone except the farmer and manufacturer themselves; milk on the doorstep and tobacco in the shop are provided, more or less, where and when the consumer wants them.

The reason why people have been able to persuade themselves that farmers are producers while retailers are not is of course that the word *production,* used in other senses than the economic, suggests the making of something material, something you can touch or handle, something you can cart about on a truck or bring home in a paper bag. A very great part of economic production does consist in the making of material goods, but quite a large part does not. The trader and retailer deal with material goods, but they do not make them. Their part is to take goods already made and to make them more useful by supplying them at the places and times at which they are wanted. But there are many sorts of workers who are not concerned with the production of material goods at all; doctors, teachers, civil servants and administrators, passenger transport workers, entertainers, domestic servants—all of these are producers in our sense, though they do not produce material products. They do useful work and are paid for it, consequently they count as producers. The things they produce are useful services, not material goods. It is convenient to say that the things produced by producers and consumed by consumers are of two kinds—material "goods" and immaterial "services."

The performance of such services as these is included in production. But if we are to be faithful to our definition, we may not say that all performance of services for other people counts as production. Production is activity directed to the satisfaction of other people's wants through exchange; thus it is only those services which are paid for that have to be included. The most important kind of services which, on this test, have to be left out are the services performed within the family—the work done by wives for their husbands, by parents in looking after their children, and so on. These services are not to be reckoned as productive, because they are not paid for. It is of course not very convenient that we have to exclude this essential work from our definition of production, but there does not seem to be any help for it, if we are to have the advantage of using words in precise and well-defined ways.[1] The fact that we have excluded it from our definition does not absolve us from keeping the fundamental economic importance of this sort of work very much in our minds.

The Case of Immaterial Services

There was a stage in the development of economic thought when the inclusion in the definition of production of those direct services which are paid for was not

[1] A further discussion of this, and of some related subjects, will be found in Appendix, Note A [of Hicks, Hart, and Ford].

accepted even by economists. Adam Smith himself confined the term "productive labor" to that labor which is devoted to the production of material goods. In a famous passage,[2] he gave a list of such occupations as must be reckoned to be "unproductive." Beginning with "menial servants," he goes on:

> *The sovereign, for example, with all the officers both of justice and of war who serve under him, the whole army and navy, are unproductive laborers. . . . In the same class must be ranked, some both of the gravest and most important, and some of the most frivolous professions; churchmen, lawyers, physicians, men of letters of all kinds; players, buffoons, musicians, opera-singers, opera-dancers, etc.*

This looks like the same fallacious, or at least uneconomic, way of thinking that is common among those who approach economic affairs from the standpoint of the technical processes of manufacture; it is strange to find it in the most famous of all economists. The manufacturer and the farmer naturally think of production as *making* something. We have seen that economics has to have a wider definition. Why did Adam Smith suppose the contrary? It was not because he supposed the distinction between material and immaterial products to have any economic significance; his reason was more subtle. Later economists have not been prepared to allow their definition of production to be influenced by it, but they have had to pay much attention to it in other parts of their economic theory. Adam Smith put it in this way:

> *The labor of the menial servant does not fix or realize itself in any particular subject or vendible commodity. His services generally perish in the very instant of their performance. . . . Like the declamation of the actor, the harangue of the orator, or the tune of the musician, the work of all of them perishes in the very instant of its production.*

The reason why Smith adopted his odd definition of production was because he was impressed by the fact that the production of most goods takes time, often a very long time, and the consumption of these goods comes afterward. The significant thing about direct services is that the acts of performing the labor and of enjoying the results of the labor are contemporaneous and inseparable. Goods, on the other hand, have to be produced first and consumed afterward. The production and consumption of goods form a process. The further classifications, which will concern us in the rest of this chapter and in the next, are all concerned with the economic system considered as a process.

The Time Taken in Production
Consumers' Goods and Producers' Goods

On a certain day (say, in the spring of 1950) the reader of this book probably ate a piece of bread for lunch. Behind that piece of bread was a considerable history. A day or two earlier it was baked by a baker, who for his stage

---

2 *Wealth of Nations,* Book II, chap. 3 (Vol. 1, p. 314 in Cannan's edition.)

in the process of breadmaking used various ingredients, notably flour. Some weeks earlier the flour was milled out of wheat, various kinds of wheat being very probably mixed together. This wheat was harvested, probably during the year 1949, the precise date depending on the part of the world from which it came. Some months before the time of harvesting the wheat must have been sown, and before the sowing the land on which it was grown must have been plowed. With this simple line of operations, from the plowing of the land to the bread on the table, not much less than a year elapsed between the start and the finish. Often it would be a good deal more than a year. But this is by no means the whole of the history behind that piece of bread.

At every stage in the process described—plowing, sowing, harvesting, threshing, milling, baking—power or fuel was needed. The power used for plowing may have been nothing more modern than the traditional horse. If so, that horse had to be fed, its feeding stuffs had to be grown, and the growth of the feeding stuffs extends the production process backward for another series of months. Or the power may have been provided by a tractor; tractors use oil, so that the getting of the oil and its transport to the farm (another stage involving at least a month or two) also have to be reckoned into the process of production of the bread. The same will hold for the power (of whatever kind) used in harvesting, threshing, and milling, also for the coal or electricity used at the bakery. Of course many of these latter processes will be going on simultaneously, so that they do not lengthen the total time taken by production. Nevertheless, when we have taken the power into account, the whole period looks more like two years than one.

Even this is not all. The tractor, the threshing machine, the ships and railways used to transport the grain, the elevator used for storing it, the milling machinery used for making the flour, even the baker's oven—all these had to be made at some time or other, and the reason why they were made was because they would be useful in the manufacture of bread. Not of course this single piece of bread, which is far too humble an article to be able to claim for itself alone such mighty antecedents; but this piece of bread and millions like it are the reasons why the tractors and elevators and ovens and the rest of them were brought into being. All this elaborate equipment was in fact constructed as part of the process of manufacturing bread.

If at some date, three months or six months or a year before the bread appeared upon the table, we had examined how the process of producing it was getting on, we should have found that most of the equipment was already made and in use, while the raw material of the bread was still in the form of growing crops, or threshed wheat, or bags of flour. These things can all be looked upon as stages in the manufacture of the bread. Whatever stage has been reached, even if it is only the making of a tractor, or the building of a railroad tank car to transport the oil to feed the tractor, something has been done which will prove useful and help toward the final production of bread. The products which result from these early stages are useful products, but not products which are directly useful for satisfying the wants of consumers. Their use is to be found in their employment in the further stages, at the end of which a product which is directly wanted by consumers will emerge. It is convenient to use the term *goods* to cover the products of these earlier stages, as well as the final product which the consumer purchases. But the products of the earlier stages are called *producers' goods,* to distinguish them from the *consumers' goods,* which do satisfy the consumer's wants directly.

In our illustration, the bread is a consumers' good; the wheat, the flour, the tractor, the ship, the oven (and so on) are producers' goods. A producers' good may be technically finished, in the sense that the particular operation needed to produce it is completed (the wheat has been harvested, or the tractor ready for use). Or it may not be technically finished, but still in process, even so far as its own stage is concerned (the grain may be standing in the field, or the flour mill under construction). In either case it is a producers' good, because further stages are needed before the result of the whole process can pass into the consumers' hands. The consumers' good is the end of the whole process; producers' goods are stages on the road toward it.

The Time Taken in Consumption— Durable-Use and Single-Use Consumers' Goods

The production of any consumers' good one cared to select could be similarly shown to consist of a process, occupying in all quite a considerable time, and involving the production of a number of producers' goods on the way. It has next to be noticed that with some consumers' goods, but only with some, consumption is also a process taking an appreciable time. Consumers' goods can be divided, from this point of view, into two classes.

In the first class we have goods, like the bread of our example (and foodstuffs generally), which are used and used up in a single act. The careful housewife may make a loaf of bread last two or three days, but only by dividing it into slices, and consuming the slices at intervals. Each piece of bread is used up as soon as it is used at all. Other consumers' goods that are of the same type are fuel, tobacco, matches, and writing paper. I shall call these goods *single-use goods.* From the point of view of the consumer, services are similar in character to the single-use goods; but, as we have noticed, they are different on the production side.

The other goods I shall call *durable-use goods.* Houses, furniture, clothes, radios, bicycles, and automobiles are examples of this second class. Their common characteristic is that they can go on being used for considerable periods. The fact that they have been used on one day does not prevent them from being used again on the next. The lengths of time for which they can go on being used vary of course a good deal. A pencil is probably to be reckoned as a durable-use good, in spite of the fact that it is bound to wear out after a few months of use. At the other extreme are such things as old furniture, which can go on being used almost indefinitely (apart from accidents), so long as it is properly looked after and kept in good repair.

The widely used terms *perishable goods* and *durable goods* do not quite express the distinction between single-use and durable-use goods. Single-use goods —raw cotton, for example—may be extremely durable in storage but cannot be used without being used up. Many users of the term "perishable" use it to cover such storable single-use goods as fibers, grains, canned foods, and liquors. But in doing so, they slur over the fact that the durability of these goods—like that of durable-use goods—makes flexible the relation between date of purchase and date of use. It seems better, therefore, to use the terms so that durable goods are a broader class including durable-use goods.

Every consumer buys both single-use and durable-use goods. Most of the single-use goods which are purchased have to go on being purchased, week after week, day after day. To have had a good meal yesterday does not prevent one from wanting another good meal today; to have been warm last night does not prevent one from needing to be warmed again this afternoon. Durable-use goods, on the other hand, go on being useful for long periods after they have been bought. Thus they do not need to be bought continuously, but only when the want for them first appears, or when an old one has broken down or become impossibly shabby. It follows that while the purchase of most sorts of single-use goods will take place at fairly regular intervals, purchases of durable-use goods may be very irregular. This is a matter of considerable importance for the running of the productive process. If all the goods consumers wanted were single-use goods, it would be comparatively easy to organize the economic system so as to keep it running continuously at the same level of activity. The production of durable-use goods is much harder to stabilize, just because the need to purchase such goods is so much less regular. Nevertheless, durable-use goods are of great importance to the consumer. Although food and warmth, the most urgent necessities, are single-use goods, some durable-use goods are essential at any standard of living; at a higher standard of living they provide more solid satisfaction than single-use goods can do. Most luxury single-use goods are related to entertainment; luxury durable-use goods range from good housing and good clothing to books, pictures, musical instruments, garden plants, and other typical ingredients of a civilized life. People who buy these things can satisfy their wants for them without buying them so regularly as they would buy food. In consequence it is hard to arrange for their production in ways that will not involve economic disturbances. Very much the most difficult case is that of housing; we shall discuss it in more detail in another connection.[3]

A Similar Distinction among Producers' Goods

A similar distinction between single-use and durable-use varieties can be made for producers' goods. Some producers' goods are used up—though this may only mean that they have passed on to the next stage in their production—as soon as they are used at all. Others can go on being used in the same way for long periods. In the illustration we gave, the wheat, the flour, and also the oil and the electricity were single-use goods in this sense; the tractor, the ship, and

---

[3] See below, chap. VIII [of Hicks, Hart, and Ford].

the baker's oven were durable-use goods. Generally speaking, single-use producers' goods are the materials used in industry, though half-finished products ought also to be reckoned as single-use goods at another stage. Durable-use producers' goods are the instruments of production—tools, machinery, industrial plant of all kinds. The production of durable-use producers' goods is perhaps even harder to stabilize than the production of durable-use consumers' goods—for roughly the same reasons. But we are not yet in a position to deal with such questions.

Consumption and Investment

The Annual Period

We have now got a general idea of the productive process; but before we can turn to the facts, and try to make sense of them, we need yet another set of definitions. The processes of production and exchange which we have been describing go on more or less indefinitely; they have gone on since the dawn of history and will go on as long as the human race exists. Although it is true in one sense that particular processes come to an end every day with the completion and sale of finished consumers' goods, these goods have usually been produced along with many others (the durable-use producers' goods used in making them are for the most part still in existence, and being used again). Thus it is very difficult to find a self-contained process which can ever be said to be really over, just as we have seen that it is very difficult to find a date on which it can really be said to begin. The only way in which we can limit our investigations, so as not to have to deal with the whole of human history at once, is to select a particular period of time and to confine our attention to the working of the productive process during that period. Usually (though not always) the period it is most convenient to take is a year.

The statistics of production referred to in the introductory chapter of this book[4] are usually for annual periods. They must, of course, always refer to some period. There is no point in saying that the number of planes produced is 1,000 without stating the time to which this output refers. An output of 1,000 planes, spread over two months, is the same rate of output as 500 planes in one month. If we are to use our definitions so as to square with measurements of the quantity of production, our definitions, too, must refer to a particular period of time.

Let us therefore fix our minds on the working of the productive process during a particular year—say, 1950. We must think of the whole stream of time as being spread out before us, like a film which has been unwound. We take our scissors and cut out a particular section of the film. Or we may say that we put a spotlight upon this particular year, leaving everything before it and after it in the dark. What is the effect of this limitation upon the classifications we have given?

---

[4] [The reference is to Hicks, Hart, and Ford].

The Productive Process during the Annual Period

During the year producers will be turning out services and goods of all kinds, single-use goods, durable-use goods, producers' goods, consumers' goods. Most of the single-use goods will be used up in the course of the year, the consumers' goods in the direct satisfaction of consumers' wants, the producers' goods in the making of consumers' goods. It is fairly evident that single-use producers' goods, produced and used up during the year, ought not to be reckoned as part of the total production or output of the year. If we were to include both the bread and the flour out of which it is made, we should be reckoning the same productive effort twice; if we did this, there would be no reason why we should not include the wheat as well, and even the wheat standing in the field as well as the threshed wheat after harvest. Once we allowed ourselves to reckon in both the single-use consumers' goods and the single-use producers' goods out of which they are made, there would be nothing to stop us from dividing the process of production into a large number of stages and counting what is essentially the same product as many times as we like. This would make the result of our calculation completely arbitrary. "Double counting" of this sort has clearly got to be avoided.

Those single-use producers' goods produced and used up during the year must not be counted as part of the year's production. But does this mean that all producers' goods have got to be excluded? At first sight one might suppose so, but that is not the case. For the production we are concerned with is the production of the year 1950, and some of the durable producers' goods produced during 1950 will outlast 1950. We have to pay special attention to the carry-over from one year to another.

At the beginning of the year (the morning of 1 January 1950) there exists in the community a particular stock of goods, including some from all our four types, but among which the durable-use goods are no doubt predominant. These goods are inherited from the previous year; for the most part they are the result of production in that and in earlier years. The durable-use consumers' goods inherited from the previous year include the houses people are living in, the furniture they are using, the clothes they are wearing, and so on. The durable-use producers' goods will include the factories, the machinery standing in the factories, the railways, ships, trucks, tools, and so on, which are available for use in production during the coming year. The single-use producers' goods which are inherited will include stocks of materials waiting to be sold. The single-use consumers' goods (not so many of these) will include such things as foodstuffs already in the larder; remembering that the retailer is also a producer, foodstuffs in the shops ought to be reckoned as producers' goods.

This is the position at the beginning of the year. Then the wheel of time rolls on and the wheels of production begin to turn. The goods in the larder are used up and replaced by new goods out of the shops—that is to say, producers' goods become consumers' goods. At the same time, the vacant places in the shops are filled by new producers' goods coming forward—that is to say, the materials existing on 1 January are worked on by labor, with the help of durable-use producers' goods, and turned by degrees into finished products. At the same time, other workers using other durable-use producers' goods are preparing new materials. And other workers are making new durable-use goods. So the process goes on, with a continual stream of new consumers' goods passing into consumption, and new single-use producers' goods poking their heads out of the productive process, only to be tucked in again.

Those producers' goods that are produced during the year, and used up in further production within the year, do not count as part of the year's output. They are taken to be included in the consumers' goods of which they are the materials. If we were allowed to extend our gaze into the indefinite future, we should presumably find all the producers' goods incorporating themselves in consumers' goods in this way; but we are not allowed to look forward indefinitely. The year has an end as well as a beginning; many of the consumers' goods in which the producers' goods of this year will be incorporated belong to future years, not to this year. There will be producers' goods left over at the end of this year, just as there were producers' goods left over to this year from the year before.

There is no reason why the quantity of producers' goods bequeathed to 1951 should be the same as that inherited from 1949. The single-use producers' goods inherited from 1949 will, for the most part, have been used up in the production of 1950; new goods will have been produced to replace them, but these new goods may be greater or less in amount than the goods that have been used up. Some of the durable-use producers' goods inherited from 1949 will also have been used up, or worn out, during 1950; and even those that are not worn out will be a year older in January 1951 than they were in January 1950; this will often mean that they have a year's less "life" left in them. Against this *wear-and-tear* or *depreciation* of the durable-use goods already in existence has to be set the production of new durable-use goods; but the wear-and-tear may or may not be completely offset by the new production. If it is not completely offset, the quantity of such goods at the disposal of the community will be less at the end of the year than it was at the beginning; if it is more than offset, the quantity at the end of the year will be greater.

The same process of using up and replacing will occur with consumers' goods as well. The year 1950 will have inherited from its predecessors certain quantities of consumers' goods (mainly durable-use goods, houses, and so on); it will hand on certain quantities to its successors. One of the tests of successful productive activity during the year is to be got by comparing the quantities at the end with those at the beginning.

The Factors of Production and the Social Output

The process of production during the year can therefore be described in summary fashion in the following way. At the beginning of the year, there exists a certain stock of goods (all our four kinds) which we may call the Initial Equipment. During the year the initial equipment is worked upon by labor, and there is produced from it a stream of goods. Some of these goods are producers' goods used up within the year, so that (to avoid double counting) they are not included among the final products from whose value the year's product is estimated.

The goods that are included consist partly of consumers' goods, consumed within the year, partly of new equipment, added to the initial equipment as a result of the year's production. The equipment that exists at the end of the year becomes the initial equipment of the next year; it equals the Initial Equipment of the first year *plus* the New Equipment which has been added *minus* the using up of equipment (single-use goods used up *plus* wear-and-tear on durable-use goods) which has taken place within the year. This is the scheme of the productive process which we need to have in our minds.

All the product or output of the year comes from Labor and the Initial Equipment; these are therefore called the Factors of Production. The output of goods consists either of consumers' goods consumed within the year (Consumption) or of New Equipment. We can therefore set out our scheme in the form of a table:

Factors of Production = Labor *plus* Initial Equipment
They Yield:
Product (or Output) = Consumption *plus* New Equipment

And for the effect on equipment of the year's production:

Initial Equipment 1951 = Initial Equipment 1950 *minus* using up of Equipment during 1950 *plus* New Equipment produced in 1950

The classification set out in this table is of fundamental importance for the whole of that part of economics which we shall study in this book. Everything further we have to say is nothing but elaboration of it and application of it to practical problems. For when theory has reached this point, it does begin to be capable of being applied.

Complications—Labor Services and Use of House-Room

Before we can proceed to these applications, it should first be noticed, however, that the table as it stands is not quite complete. In the first place, services have been left out of account, as Adam Smith left them out of account—and for what turns out to be substantially the same reason. Just as we have been learning to do, Adam Smith thought of the productive process as consisting of labor working on initial equipment and making it grow into consumption goods and new equipment. And services did not fit into the picture properly; consequently he excluded them as "unproductive." We have decided not to take that way out, and so we must find some way of fitting services into our picture. We can really do so quite easily, if we include the services produced in the year as part of the consumption of the year, and allow for the possibility that these services may have been produced by labor alone, without making use of initial equipment to any important extent. (Of course—and this is even more true today than it was in Smith's time—services may require the assistance of durable-use goods from the initial equipment if they are to be produced. For instance, passenger transport workers provide direct services, but they use a great deal of equipment in providing these services.) This, then, is one of the adjustments which have to be made.

The other adjustment concerns the durable-use consumers' goods, which are included in the initial equipment and do in fact form an important part of it. Take, for example, houses. The houses that exist at the beginning of the year do for the most part go on being used during the year. The use of a house is a thing for which people are prepared to pay; a man pays rent for the right to live in a particular house, just as he pays for the goods he or his wife purchases in the shops. We reckon the goods purchased in the shops as part of the consumption of the year, and since house-room is purchased by consumers in the same sort of way, it is convenient (even if it means some stretching of terms) to reckon the use of house-room as part of the consumption of the year, and consequently also to reckon it as part of the production or output of the year. Strictly speaking, we ought to do the same for all the durable-use consumers' goods contained in the initial equipment (automobiles, for example). But, largely because houses are very frequently rented by their occupiers, while automobiles are usually bought outright, it is usual (even if it is not very logical) to include in this way only the use of houses.[5] Houses are in any case the most important type of durable-use consumers' goods.

Our revised table may therefore be written as follows:

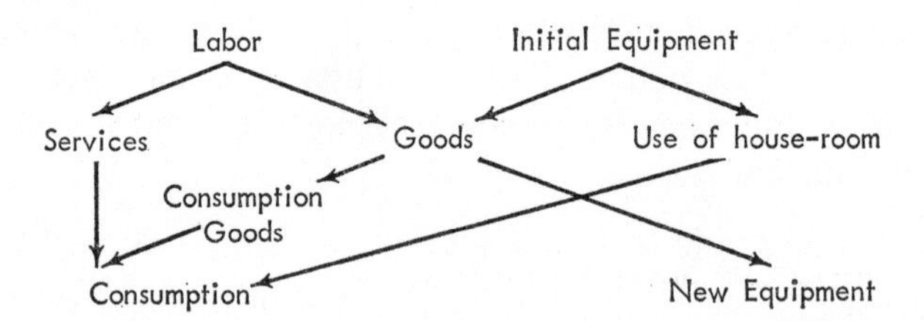

The new houses produced during the year are of course included in the new equipment.

Definitions of Capital and Investment

Our table is now complete, but before we can use it we must introduce two new terms. Instead of our phrase 'initial equipment," economists usually employ

[5] See Appendix, Note A [of Hicks, Hart, and Ford].

the term "Capital" (or Wealth); instead of our phrase "new equipment" the term "Investment" (or Capital Formation) is now generally used. We had better familiarize ourselves with these important words.

So far I have avoided talking about capital and investment because these are such outstanding instances of the way in which economists have taken words used by businessmen and given new meanings to them, meanings which are not (at least on the surface) the same as business meanings. There is a relation between the meanings of capital and investment in economics and their meanings in business practice; we shall try to get that relation cleared up before we are done. But for the moment it is only the economic meanings that concern us.

In economics, the Capital (or Wealth) of a community consists in the stock of goods of all sorts possessed by the community (either by its individual members, or by associations of its members, such as governments) at a particular moment of time. Thus our "initial equipment" is the capital possessed by our community on 1 January. In economics, investment is the making of additions to capital. Thus the making of our new equipment is Investment (or Capital Formation).

In this terminology, the Factors of Production are Labor and Capital.[6] The goods and services produced by the factors of production are partly consumed within the year (consumption), partly used to make additions to capital (investment). In order to produce these goods and services, some part of the capital possessed at the beginning of the year is used up (Wear-and-Tear or Depreciation of Capital). The net addition to capital within the year is therefore the total production of additions to capital, with depreciation deducted. This net addition to Capital is called Net Investment. Consumption *plus* Net Investment *equals* Net Product.

The definitions given in this last paragraph will become familiar enough as we go on. For the whole program which lies before us is involved in these definitions. In the next two parts of this book we shall study the factors of production—labor and capital. In the last part we shall study the Net Product of the economic system; we shall discuss how it is measured, we shall examine some of the reasons for variations in its size, and we shall examine how it is divided up among different people, so that some are rich and some poor. All these things are developments of the fundamental classifications we have been giving.

Let us pass on to discuss the factor of production labor. The first problem to be considered under that head is the problem of Population. For although not all the people living in a country are producers, it is the total population of the country that mainly governs the number of the workers available to take part in the process of production.

---

[6] Land, which nineteenth-century economics used to reckon as a third factor of production, is here included in "capital." For the justification of this arrangement, see below, chap. VIII [of Hicks, Hart, and Ford].

Selection 4

The Economic Problem

ROBERT L. HEILBRONER

From The Making of Economic Society *(Englewood Cliffs, N.J.: Prentice-Hall, Inc., © 1962), pp. 1–17. Reprinted by permission of Prentice-Hall, Inc.*

Man, it is repeatedly said, does not live by bread alone. Indeed, when we look back over the pageant of what is usually called "history," the humble matter of bread hardly strikes the eye at all. Power and glory, faith and fanaticism, ideas and ideologies are the aspects of the human chronicle that crowd the pages of history books. If the simple quest for bread is a moving force in human destiny, it is well concealed behind what one philosopher-historian has called "that history of international crime and mass murder which has been advertised as the history of mankind."[1]

Obviously, man cannot live without bread. Like every other living thing, as the imperious first rule of continued existence, the human being must eat. And this first prerequisite is less to be taken for granted than at first appears, for the human organism is not, in itself, a highly efficient mechanism for survival. From each one hundred calories of food it consumes, it can deliver only about twenty calories of mechanical energy. On a decent diet, man can produce just about one horsepower-hour of work daily, and with that he must replenish his exhausted body. With what is left over, he is free to build a civilization.

In many countries, the basic expectation of human continuity is far from assured. In the vast continents of Asia and Africa, in the Near East, even in some countries of South America, brute survival is the problem which stares humanity in the face. Millions of human beings have died of starvation or malnutrition in our present era, as countless hundreds of millions have died over the long past. Whole nations are acutely aware of what it means to face hunger as a condition of ordinary life: it has been said, for example, that the Egyptian *fellah,* from the day he is born to the day he dies, never knows what it is to have a full stomach. In many of the so-called underdeveloped nations, the life span of the average person is less than half of ours. Not many years ago, an

---

[1] Karl Popper, *The Open Society and Its Enemies,* 3rd ed. (London: Routledge & Kegan Paul, Ltd., 1957), Vol. II, 270.

Indian demographer made the chilling calculation that of one hundred Asian and one hundred American infants, more Americans would be alive at sixty-five than Indians at *five!* The statistics, not of life, but of premature death throughout most of the world are overwhelming and crushing.

THE INDIVIDUAL AND SOCIETY

For most Americans, these considerations are apt to seem tragic but remote. None of us is conscious of a struggle for existence to anything resembling a life-or-death degree. That it might be possible for us to experience severe want, that we might ever know in our own bodies the pangs of hunger experienced by an Indian villager or a Bolivian peon is a thought which it is nearly impossible for us to entertain seriously.

Short of a catastrophic war, it is highly unlikely that any of us ever will know the full meaning of the struggle for existence. Nonetheless, even in our prosperous and secure society, there remains, however unnoticed, an aspect of life's precariousness, a reminder of the underlying problem of survival. *This is our helplessness as economic individuals.*

It is a curious fact that as we leave the most impoverished peoples of the world, where the human being with his too few calories of energy scratches out for himself a bare subsistence, we find the economic insecurity of the individual many times multiplied. The solitary Eskimo, Bushman, Indonesian, Nigerian, left to his own devices, will survive a considerable time. Living close to the soil or to their animal prey, the peoples with the lowest standards of living in the world can sustain their own lives, at least for a while, almost single-handed. With a community numbering only a few hundred, they can live indefinitely. Indeed, a very large percentage of the human race today lives in precisely such fashion—in small, virtually self-contained peasant communities which provide for their own survival with a minimum of contact with the outside world. This large majority of mankind suffers great poverty, but it also knows a certain economic independence. If it did not, it would have been wiped out centuries ago.

When we turn to the New Yorker or the Chicagoan, on the other hand, we are struck exactly by the opposite condition, by a prevailing ease of material life, coupled at the same time by an extreme *dependence* of the individual in his search for the means of existence. In the great metropolitan areas where most Americans live, we can no longer envisage the solitary individual or the small community surviving, short of looting warehouses or stores for food and necessities. The overwhelming majority of Americans have never grown food, caught game, raised meat, ground grain into flour, or even fashioned flour into bread. Faced with the challenge of clothing themselves or building their own homes, they would be hopelessly untrained and unprepared. Even to make minor repairs in the machines which surround them, they must call on other members of the community whose business it is to fix cars, or repair plumbing, or whatever. Paradoxically, perhaps, the richer the nation, the more apparent is this inability of its average inhabitant to survive unaided and alone.

We survive in rich nations because the tasks we cannot do ourselves are done for us by an army of others on whom we can call for help. If we cannot grow food, we can buy it; if we cannot provide for our needs ourselves, we can hire the services of someone who can. This enormous *division of labor* enhances our capacity a thousandfold, for it enables us to benefit from other men's skills as well as our own.

Along with this invaluable gain comes a certain risk. It is a sobering thought, for example, that we depend on the services of only 180,000 men—fewer than one out of every three hundred people working in the nation—to provide us with that basic commodity, coal. An even smaller number of workers—less than 75,000—are responsible for running the locomotives which haul all the nation's rail freight and passenger service. A still smaller number—under 15,000—comprises our total commercial aircraft pilot and navigator crew. A failure of any one of these very small groups to perform its functions would cripple us: in the case of airplane pilots, slightly; in the case of locomotive engineers, badly; in the case of coal miners, perhaps disastrously. As we know, when from time to time we face a bad strike, our entire economic machine may falter because a strategic group ceases to perform its accustomed tasks.

Along with the abundance of material existence as we know it goes a hidden vulnerability: our abundance is assured only insofar as the organized cooperation of huge armies of people is to be counted upon. Indeed, our continuing existence as a rich nation hinges on the tacit precondition that the mechanism of social organization will continue to function effectively. *We are rich, not as individuals, but as members of a rich society, and our easy assumption of material sufficiency is actually only as reliable as the bonds which forge us into a social whole.*

Economics, Scarcity, and Social Organization

The problem of how societies forge and maintain the bonds which guarantee their material survival is the basic problem of economics.

We know very little of how those bonds may have been originally constituted. Man appears on the scroll of history as a member of a group, and as such, the beneficiary of a rudimentary division of labor. Yet it is noteworthy that even his simplest familial cooperation is not achieved instinctually as is the case with communities of insects or of animals, but must be buttressed with magic and taboo and maintained by more or less repressive laws and traditions.

Strangely enough, then, we find that man, not nature, is the source of most of our economic problems. To be sure, the economic problem itself—that is, the need to struggle for existence—derives ultimately from the scarcity of nature. If there were no scarcity, goods would be as free as air, and economics, at least in one sense of the word, would cease to exist as a social preoccupation.

And yet if the scarcity of nature sets the stage for the economic problem, it does not impose the only strictures against which men must struggle. For scarcity, as a felt condition, is not solely the fault of nature. If Americans today, for instance, were content to live at the level of Mexican peasants, all our material wants could be fully satisfied with but an hour or two of daily labor. We would experience little or no scarcity, and our economic problems would virtually disappear. Instead, we find in America—and indeed in all industrial societies—that as the ability to increase nature's yield has risen, so has the reach of human wants. In fact, in societies such as ours, where relative social status is importantly connected with the possession of material goods, we often find that "scarcity" as a psychological experience and goad becomes more pronounced as we grow wealthier: our desires to possess the fruits of nature race out ahead of our mounting ability to produce goods.

Thus the "wants" that nature must satisfy are by no means fixed—while, for that matter, nature's yield itself is not a constant, but varies over a wide range, depending on the social application of human energy and skill. Scarcity is therefore not attributable to nature alone but to "human nature" as well; and economics is ultimately concerned not merely with the stinginess of the physical environment, but equally with the appetite of the human temperament.

Hence we must begin a systematic analysis of economics by singling out the functions which social organization must perform to bring human nature into social harness. And when we turn our attention to this fundamental problem, we can quickly see that it involves the solution of two related and yet separate elemental tasks:

1. A society must organize a system for producing the goods and services it needs for its own perpetuation.
2. It must arrange a distribution of the fruits of its production among its own members, so that more production can take place.

These two tasks of economic continuity are, at first look, very simple. But it is a deceptive simplicity. Much of economic history, as we shall see, is concerned with the manner in which various societies have sought to cope with these elementary problems; and what strikes us in surveying their attempts is that most of them were partial failures. (They could not have been total failures, or society would not have survived.) Hence it behooves us to look more carefully into the two main economic tasks to see what hidden difficulties they may conceal.

The Production Problem

What is the difficulty which the production problem poses? What are the obstacles which a society encounters in organizing a system to produce the goods and services it needs?

Since nature is usually stingy, it would seem that the production problem must be essentially one of engineering, or technical efficiency. It would seem to revolve around the effort to economize, to avoid waste and apply social effort as efficaciously as possible.

This is indeed an important task for any society, and a great deal of formal economic thought, as the word itself suggests, is devoted to economizing. Yet this is not the core of the production problem. Long before a society can even concern itself about using its energies "economically," it must first marshal the energies to carry out the productive process itself. That is, *the basic problem of production is to devise social institutions which will mobilize human energy for productive purposes.*

This basic requirement is not always so easily accomplished. For example, in the United States in 1933, the energies of nearly thirteen million people—one quarter of our work force—were not directed into the production process. Although these unemployed men and women were eager to work, although empty factories were available for them to work in, despite the existence of pressing wants, somehow a terrible and mystifying breakdown short-circuited the production process, with the result that an entire third of our previous annual output of goods and services simply disappeared.

We are by no means the only nation which has, on occasion, failed to find work for willing workers. In the very poorest nations, where production is most desperately needed, we frequently find that unemployment is a chronic condition. The streets of the Asian cities are thronged with people who cannot find work. But this, too, is not a condition imposed by the scarcity of nature. There is, after all, an endless amount of work to be done, if only in cleaning the filthy streets or patching up the homes of the poor, building roads, or planting forests. Yet, what seems to be lacking is a social mechanism to put the unemployed to work.

Both these examples point out to us that the production problem is not solely, or perhaps even primarily, a physical and technical struggle with nature. On these "scarcity" aspects of the problem will depend the speed with which a nation may forge ahead and the level of well-being it can reach with a given effort. But the original mobilization of productive effort itself is a challenge to its social organization, and on the success or failure of that social organization will depend the volume of the human effort which can be directed to nature.

Putting men to work is only the first step in the solution of the production problem. Men must not only be put to work; they must be put to work *in the right places.* They must produce the goods and services which society needs. In addition to assuring a large enough quantity of social effort, the economic institutions of society must also assure the *proper allocation of that social effort.*

In a nation such as India or Brazil, where the great majority of the population is born in peasant villages and grows up to be peasant cultivators, the solution to this problem offers little to vex our understanding. The basic demands of society—food and fiber—are precisely the goods which its peasant population "naturally" produces. But in an industrial society, the proper allocation of effort becomes an enormously complicated task. People in the United States demand much more than bread and cotton. They need, for instance, such things as automobiles. Yet no one "naturally" produces an automobile. On the contrary, in order to produce one, an extraordinary spectrum of special tasks must be performed. Some people must make steel. Others must make rubber. Still others must coordinate the assembly process itself. And this is but a tiny sampling of the far from "natural" tasks which must be performed if an automobile is to be produced.

As with the mobilization of its total production effort, society does not always succeed in the proper allocation of its effort. It may, for instance, turn out too many cars or too few. Of greater importance, it may devote its energies to the production of luxuries while the majority of its people are starving. Or it may even court disaster by an inability to channel its productive effort into areas of critical importance. In the early 1950's, for instance, the British suffered a near economic collapse because they were unable to get enough of their workers to mine coal.

Such allocative failures may affect the production problem quite as seriously as a failure to mobilize an adequate quantity of effort, for a viable society must produce not only goods, but the *right* goods. And the allocative question alerts us to a still broader conclusion. It shows us that the act of production, in and of itself, does not fully answer the requirements for survival. Having produced enough of the right goods, society must now *distribute* those goods so that the production process can go on.

The Distribution Problem

Once again, in the case of the peasant who feeds himself and his family from his own crop, this requirement of adequate distribution may seem simple enough. But when we go beyond the most primitive society, the problem is not always so readily solved. In many of the poorest nations of the East and South, urban workers have often be unable to deliver their daily horsepower-hour of work because they have not been given enough of society's output to run their human engines to capacity. Worse yet, they have often languished on the job while granaries bulged with grain and the well-to-do complained of the ineradicable "laziness" of the masses. At the other side of the picture, the distribution mechanism may fail because the rewards it hands out do not succeed in persuading people to perform their necessary tasks. Shortly after the Russian Revolution some factories were organized into communes in which managers and janitors pooled their pay, and from which all drew equal allotments. The result was a rash of absenteeism on the part of the previously better-paid workers and a threatened breakdown in industrial production. Not until the old unequal wage payments were reinstituted did production resume its former course.

As was the case with failures in the production process, distributive failures need not entail a total economic collapse. Societies can exist—and indeed, in the majority of cases, do exist—with badly distorted productive and distributive efforts. It is only rarely, as in the instances above, that maldistribution actively interferes with the actual ability of a society to staff its production posts. More frequently, an inadequate solution to the distribution problem reveals itself in social and political unrest or even in revolution.

Yet this, too, is an aspect of the total economic problem. For if society is to insure its steady material replenishment, it must parcel out its production in a fashion that will maintain not only the capacity but the willingness to go on working. And thus again we find the focus of economic inquiry directed to the study of human institutions. For a viable economic society, we can now see, is not only one which can overcome the stringencies of nature, but one which can contain and control the intransigence of human nature.

THE THREE SOLUTIONS TO THE ECONOMIC PROBLEM

Thus to the economist, society presents itself in an unaccustomed aspect. He sees it essentially as an elaborate mechanism for survival, a mechanism for accomplishing the complicated tasks of production and distribution necessary for social continuity.

But the economist sees something else as well, something which at first seems quite astonishing. Looking not only over the diversity of contemporary societies, but back over the sweep of all history, he sees that man has succeeded in solving the production and distribution problems in but three ways. That is, within the enormous diversity of the actual social institutions which guide and shape the economic process, the economist divines but three overarching *types* of systems which separately or in combination enable humankind to solve its economic challenge. These great systemic types can be called economies run by Tradition, economies run by Command, and economies run by the Market. Let us briefly see what is characteristic of each.

Tradition

Perhaps the oldest and, until a very few years ago, by far the most generally prevalent way of solving the economic challenge has been tradition. It has been a mode of social organization in which both production and distribution were based on procedures devised in the distant past, rigidified by a long process of historic trial and error, and maintained by heavy sanctions of law, custom, and belief.

Societies based on tradition solve the economic problems very manageably. First, they deal with the production problem—the problem of assuring that the needful tasks will be done—by assigning the jobs of fathers to their sons. Thus a hereditary chain assures that skills will be passed along and that the ongoing jobs will be staffed from generation to generation. In ancient Egypt, wrote Adam Smith, the first great economist, "every man was bound by a principle of religion to follow the occupation of his father and was supposed to commit the most horrible sacrilege if he changed it for another."[2] And it was not merely in antiquity that tradition preserved a productive orderliness within society. In our own Western culture, until the fifteenth or sixteenth centuries, the hereditary allocation of tasks was also the main stabilizing force within society.

---

[2] *The Wealth of Nations* (New York: Modern Library, Inc., 1937), p. 62.

Although there was some movement from country to town and from occupation to occupation, birth usually determined one's role in life. One was born to the soil or to a trade; and on the soil or within the trade, one followed in the footsteps of one's forebears.

Thus tradition has been the stabilizing and impelling force behind a great repetitive cycle of society, assuring that society's work would be done each day very much as it had been done in the past. Even today, among the less industrialized nations of the world, tradition continues to play this immense organizing role. In India, until very recently at least, one was born to a caste which had its own occupation. "Better thine own work is, though done with fault," preached the *Bhagavad-Gita,* the great philosophic moral poem of India, "than doing other's work, even excellently."

Tradition not only provides a solution to the production problem of society, but it also regulates the distribution problem. Take, for example, the Bushmen of the Kalahari Desert in South Africa who depend for their livelihood on hunting prowess. Elizabeth Marshall Thomas, a sensitive observer of these peoples, reports on the manner in which tradition solves the problem of distributing their kill.

> *The gemsbok has vanished . . . . Gai owned two hind legs and a front leg, Tsetchwe had meat from the back, Ukwane had the other front leg, his wife had one of the feet and the stomach, the young boys had lengths of intestine. Twikwe had received the head and Dasina the udder.*
> *It seems very unequal when you watch Bushmen divide the kill, yet it is their system, and in the end no person eats more than any other. That day Ukwane gave Gai still another piece because Gai was his relation, Gai gave meat to Dasina because she was his wife's mother . . . . No one, of course, contested Gai's large share, because he had been the hunter and by their law that much belonged to him. No one doubted that he would share his large amount with others, and they were not wrong, of course; he did.*[3]

The manner in which tradition can divide a social product may be, as the illustration shows, very subtle and ingenious. It may also be very crude and, by our standards, harsh. Tradition has often allocated to women, in nonindustrial societies, the most meager portion of the social product. But however much tradition may accord with or depart from our accustomed moral views, we must see that it is a workable method of dividing society's production.

Traditional solutions to the economic problems of production and distribution are most commonly encountered in primitive agrarian or nonindustrial societies, where in addition to serving an economic function, the unquestioning acceptance of the past provides the necessary perseverance and endurance to confront harsh destinies. Yet even in our own society, tradition continues to play a role in solving the economic problem. It plays its smallest role in determining the distribution of our own social output, although the persistence of such traditional payments as tips to waiters, allowances to minors, or bonuses based on length of

---

[3] *The Harmless People* (New York: Alfred A. Knopf, Inc., 1959), pp. 49–50.

service are all vestiges of old traditional ways of distributing goods, as is the differential between men's and women's pay for equal work.

More important is the place which tradition continues to hold, even in America, as a means of solving the production problem—that is, in allocating the performance of tasks. Much of the actual process of selecting an employment in our society is heavily influenced by tradition. We are all familiar with families in which sons follow their fathers into a profession or a business. On a somewhat broader scale, tradition also dissuades us from certain employments. Sons of American middle-class families, for example, do not usually seek factory work, even though factory jobs may pay better than office jobs, because "blue-collar employment" is not in the middle-class tradition.

Even in our society, which is clearly not a "traditional" one, custom provides an important mechanism for solving the economic problem. But now we must note one very important consequence of the mechanism of tradition. *Its solution to production and distribution is a static one.* A society which follows the path of tradition in its regulation of economic affairs does so at the expense of large-scale rapid social and economic change.

Thus the economy of a Bedouin tribe or a Burmese village is in few essential respects changed today from what it was a hundred or even a thousand years ago. The bulk of the peoples living in tradition-bound societies repeat, in the daily patterns of their economic life, much of the routines which characterized them in the distant past. Such societies may rise and fall, wax and wane, but external events—war, climate, political adventures and misadventures—are mainly responsible for their changing fortunes. Internal, self-generated economic change is but a small factor in the history of most tradition-bound states. Tradition solves the economic problem, but it does so at the cost of economic progress.

Command

A second manner of solving the problem of economic continuity also displays an ancient lineage. This is the method of imposed authority, of economic command. It is a solution based not so much on the perpetuation of a viable system by the changeless reproduction of its ways, as on the organization of a system according to the orders of an economic commander-in-chief.

Not infrequently we find this authoritarian method of economic control superimposed upon a traditional social base. Thus the Pharaohs of Egypt exerted their economic dictates above the timeless cycle of traditional agricultural practice on which the Egyptian economy was based. By their orders, the supreme rulers of Egypt brought into being the enormous economic effort which built the pyramids, the temples, the roads. Herodotus, the Greek historian, tells us how the Pharaoh Cheops organized the task.

> [*He*] *ordered all Egyptians to work for himself. Some, accordingly, were appointed to draw stones from the quarries in the Arabian mountains down to the Nile, others he ordered to receive the stones when transported in vessels across the river. . . . And they worked to the number of a*

> *hundred thousand men at one time, each party during three months. The time during which the people were thus harassed by toil lasted ten years on the road which they constructed, and along which they drew the stones; a work, in my opinion, not much less than the Pyramid.*[4]

The mode of authoritarian economic organization was by no means confined to ancient Egypt. We encounter it in the despotisms of medieval and classical China, which produced, among other things, the colossal Great Wall, or in the slave labor by which many of the great public works of ancient Rome were built. Of course, we find it today in the dictates of the communist economic authorities. In less drastic form, we find it also in our own society, for example, in the form of *taxes*—that is, in the preemption of part of our income by the public authorities for public purposes.

Economic command, like tradition, offers solutions to the twin problems of production and distribution. In times of crises, such as war or famine, it may be the only way in which a society can organize its manpower or distribute its goods effectively. Even in America, we commonly declare martial law when an area has been devastated by a great natural disaster. On such occasions we may press people into service, requisition homes, impose curbs on the use of private property such as cars, or even limit the amount of food a family may consume.

Quite aside from its obvious utility in meeting emergencies, command has a further usefulness in solving the economic problem. Unlike tradition, the exercise of command has no inherent effect of slowing down economic change. Indeed, the exercise of authority is the most powerful instrument society has for *enforcing economic change*. One example is, of course, the radical alterations in the systems of production and distribution which authority has effected in modern China or Russia. But again, even in our own society, it is sometimes necessary for economic authority to intervene into the normal flow of economic life to speed up or bring about change. The government may, for instance, utilize its tax receipts to lay down a network of roads which brings a backwater community into the flux of active economic life. It may undertake an irrigation system which will dramatically change the economic life of a vast region. It may very considerably affect the distribution of income among social classes.

To be sure, economic command which is exercised within the framework of a democratic political process is very different from that which is exercised by strong-arm methods: there is an immense social distance between a tax system controlled by Congress and outright expropriation or labor impressment by a supreme and unchallengeable ruler. Yet, whilst the means may be much milder, the *mechanism* is the same. In both cases, command diverts economic effort toward goals chosen by a higher authority. In both cases it interferes with the existing order of production and distribution, to create a new order ordained from "above."

This does not in itself serve to commend or condemn the exercise of command. The new order imposed by the authorities may offend or please our sense of social justice, just as it may improve or lessen the economic efficiency of

---

[4] *Histories,* trans. Cary (London: G. Bell & Sons, 1904), Book II, 124.

society. Clearly, command can be an instrument of a democratic as well as of a totalitarian will. There is no implicit moral judgment to be passed on this second of the great mechanisms of economic control. Rather, it is important to note that no society—certainly no modern society—is without its elements of command, just as none is devoid of the influence of tradition. If tradition is the great brake on social and economic change, so economic command can be the great spur to change. As mechanisms for assuring the successful solution to the economic problem, both serve their purposes, both have their uses and their drawbacks. Between them, tradition and command have accounted for most of the long history of man's economic efforts to cope with his environment and with himself. The fact that human society *has* survived is testimony to their effectiveness.

The Market

There is also a third solution to the economic problem—that is, a third solution to the problem of maintaining socially viable patterns of production and distribution. This is the *market organization of society,* an organization which, in truly remarkable fashion, allows society to insure its own provisioning with a minimum of recourse either to tradition or command.

Because we live in a market-run society, we are apt to take for granted the puzzling—indeed, almost paradoxical—nature of the market solution to the economic problem. But assume for a moment that we could act as economic advisers to a society which had not yet decided on its mode of economic organization. Suppose, for instance, that we were called on to act as consultants to one of the new nations emerging from the continent of Africa.

We could imagine the leaders of such a nation saying, "We have always experienced a highly tradition-bound way of life. Our men hunt and cultivate the fields and perform their tasks as they are brought up to do by the force of example and the instruction of their elders. We know, too, something of what can be done by economic command. We are prepared, if necessary, to sign an edict making it compulsory for many of our men to work on community projects for our national development. Tell us, is there any other way we can organize our society so that it will function successfully—or better yet, more successfully?"

Suppose we answered, "Yes, there is another way. Organize your society along the lines of a market economy."

"Very well," say the leaders. "What do we then tell people to do? How do we assign them to their various tasks?"

"That's the very point," we would answer. "In a market economy no one is assigned to any task. The very idea of a market society is that each person is allowed to decide for himself what to do."

There is consternation among the leaders. "You mean there is *no* assignment of some men to mining and others to cattle raising? No manner of selecting some for transportation and others for cloth weaving? You leave this to people to decide for themselves? But what happens if they do not decide correctly? What happens if no one volunteers to go into the mines, or if no one offers himself as a railway engineer?"

"You may rest assured," we tell the leaders, "none of that will happen. In a market society, all the jobs will be filled because it will be to people's advantage to fill them."

Our respondents accept this with uncertain expressions. "Now, look," one of them finally says, "let us suppose that we take your advice and let our people do as they please. Now let's talk about something important, like cloth production. Just how do we fix the right level of cloth output in this 'market society' of yours?"

"But you don't," we reply.

"We don't! Then how do we know there will be enough cloth produced?"

"There will be," we tell him. "The market will see to that."

"Then how do we know there won't be *too much* cloth produced?" he asks triumphantly.

"Ah, but the market will see to that, too!"

"But what *is* this market that will do all these wonderful things? Who runs it?"

"Oh, nobody runs the market," we answer. "It runs itself. In fact, there really isn't any such *thing* as 'the market.' It's just a word we use to describe the way people behave."

"But I thought people behaved the way they wanted to!"

"And so they do," we say. "But never fear. They will want to behave the way you want them to behave."

"I am afraid," says the chief of the delegation, "that we are wasting our time. We thought you had in mind a serious proposal. But what you suggest is madness. It is inconceivable. Good day, sir." And with great dignity the delegation takes its leave.

Could we seriously suggest to such an emergent nation that it entrust itself to a market solution of the economic problem? That will be a problem to which we shall return. But the very perplexity which the market idea would rouse in the mind of someone unacquainted with it may serve to increase our own wonderment at this most sophisticated and interesting of all economic mechanisms. How *does* the market system assure us that our mines will find miners, our factories workers? How does it take care of cloth production? How does it happen that in a market-run nation each person can indeed do as he wishes and, withal, fulfill the needs which society as a whole presents?

Economics and the Market System

Economics, as we commonly conceive it and as we shall study it in much of this book, is primarily concerned with these very problems. Societies which rely primarily on tradition to solve their economic problems are of less interest to the professional economist than to the cultural anthropologist or the sociologist. Societies which solve their economic problems primarily by the exercise of command present interesting economic questions, but here the study of economics is necessarily subservient to the study of politics and the exercise of power.

It is a society which solves its economic problems by the market process that presents an aspect especially interesting to the economist. For here, as we shall see, economics truly plays a unique role. Unlike the case with tradition and command, where we quickly grasp the nature of the economic mechanism of society, when we turn to a market society we are lost without a knowledge of economics. For in a market society it is not at all clear that the problems of production and distribution will be solved by the free interplay of individuals without guidance from tradition or command.

In subsequent chapters of this book we shall analyze these puzzling questions in more detail. But first there is a problem which has surely occurred to the reader. As our hypothetical interview with the leaders of an emergent nation must have suggested, the market solution appears very strange to someone brought up in the ways of tradition or command. Hence the question arises: how did the market solution itself evolve? Was it imposed, full-blown, on our society at some earlier date? Or did it arise spontaneously and without forethought? These are the questions to which we must first turn, as we retrace the evolution of our own market system out of the tradition- and authority-dominated societies of the past.

DISCUSSION QUESTIONS

1. What are the three methods of organizing production which are discussed by Robert Heilbroner? What role does each play in the American economy?
2. Discuss how money, government, and private property complicate the simple system of exchange discussed by Hicks, Hart, and Ford.
3. Distinguish between consumer goods and producer goods. Why are producer goods that are used up in current production not counted as part of current output?
4. The basic questions to be answered by an economic system are what goods and services to produce, how to produce them, and for whom to produce them. How would these questions be answered in a purely competitive market economy?

SELECTED REFERENCES

Brennen, Michael J., *The Theory of Economic Statics,* Englewood Cliffs, N.J.: Prentice-Hall, Inc., 1965.

Dooly, Peter C., *Elementary Price Theory,* New York: Appleton-Century-Crofts, 1967.

Knight, Frank H., *The Economic Organization,* Harper Torchbook ed., New York: Harper and Row, Publishers, 1965. (Copyright, 1933 and 1951, by Frank Knight.)

Scitovsky, Tibor, *Welfare and Competition,* Homewood, Ill.: Richard D. Irwin, Inc., 1951.

PART 3

MEASUREMENT AND DETERMINATION OF NATIONAL INCOME

National income can be measured in terms of the total value of production or in terms of the value of income earned from that production. On the product side, output can be broken down into personal consumption, gross private domestic investment, net exports, and government purchases of goods and services. This breakdown is useful because each reflects a different type of decision-making unit. The consumer is purchasing goods for his individual satisfaction, and his total purchases will depend largely on the level of his income and his preference between consumption and saving. Private domestic investment reflects primarily decisions of business units to purchase new plant and equipment. These decisions depend on the level of retained earnings, interest rates, and future profit expectations. In addition, private domestic investment includes changes in business inventories. Government spending is determined by current and past government decisions with respect to public consumption of such items as military equipment, roads, and schools. The difference between exports and imports is net exports, that is, net foreign demand for our output. The total of consumption, gross investment, government spending, and net exports gives gross national product, the value of national output at current prices. If an allowance for capital consumption (annual depreciation of plant and equipment) is deducted, the total becomes net national product.

Included in the income side are wages and salaries, proprietors' incomes, corporate profits, and net interest received by households. This total is national income, or income earned from current production. To this total must be added indirect business taxes to obtain net national product from the income side. These are excise, sales, and real estate taxes that enter the market value of goods but do not show up as a payment to a resource because business accounting deducts these as an expense item before profits are calculated. Thus they reflect a claim by government against final output.

Receipts and expenditures for the total economy must be equal, but this is not true for individual sectors. Ordinarily households spend less than they receive, the difference being personal savings. In most years the business sector spends more than it receives in order to be able to invest in new plant and equipment to increase its future earning power. It pledges part of these future earnings in order to be able to borrow savings from households. Households may also use their savings to accumulate securities of government or foreigners.

The next step is to see what determines the level of national income. Prior to the publication of *The General Theory of Employment, Interest, and Money* by John Maynard Keynes in 1936, most economists thought that income was determined by productive capacity. It depended on the current labor force, current stock of capital equipment and land, and the current level of skills and technique. Production, it was thought, would automatically adjust to the level necessary to keep these resources fully employed. Output would grow over time as the stock of resources increased and as skills and technique changed to allow greater output per unit of input. Unemployment could only be a temporary phenomenon caused by changes in demand for particular skills to which workers had not yet adjusted or to unwillingness of workers to accept lower wages. However, during the Great Depression, millions of workers were unemployed for several years and a steady cutting of wages appeared to do nothing to alleviate the situation. The *General Theory* explained chronic unemployment and radically changed the way in which economists, and later the public, viewed the operation of the economic system.

The Keynesian system may be summarized as follows:

(1) The level of skills and stock of labor and capital define the level of full employment.

(2) Whether or not the economy is actually at full employment depends on the level of aggregate demand.

(3) Aggregate demand depends on total expenditures by households (consumption), by business (private domestic investment), by government (government purchases), and by foreigners (net exports).

(4) Consumption depends on the level of income, investment depends on interest rates and profit expectations, government spending is dependent on policy decisions of the government, and net exports depend on our demand for foreign goods and foreign demand for our goods.

(5) A change in expenditure for any of the components of aggregate demand will lead to a larger change in income. If the government decides to increase expenditures for armaments by 10 billion dollars, this 10 billion becomes income for people in the armaments industry. However, they do not leave the money in their pocket; instead they spend most of it for food, clothing, new cars, or business investment in new plant and equipment. The people who receive this new income in turn spend a large portion of it. The magnitude of the expansion depends on the rate at which individuals and businesses save out of the additional income they receive and the rate at which government taxes the additional income. If, however, the economy is already at or near full employment, little additional output will be forthcoming and the increased expenditure will be dissipated on rising prices.

The Keynesian system gives an explanation of the aggregate level of economic activity and how this level of activity can be regulated. In a free market system it is generally considered undesirable for government to interfere with the decisions of individual consumers or of businessmen. However, Keynes argued that these decisions could still be left primarily to the market and the basic framework of a capitalist system could be preserved. Government need only regulate the total level of spending by its taxing decisions, its spending decisions, and its decisions about interest rates and the availability of credit.

In addition to the ideas about the aggregate level of spending, Keynes' theories also had important implications about the distribution of income. Keynes was unsympathetic to people who live off interest and dividends. He favored the businessman who engages directly in production. Prior to the *General Theory,* it was thought that high interest rates and large inequalities of wealth were necessary to generate saving. Only the rich did much saving, and they would save only if generously rewarded. Keynes argued that the rich will save anyway, the problem being to channel their saving into investment or consumption. High interest rates would increase inequality, as the rich received most of the interest income. In addition, high interest rates would increase costs to the businessman and consumer and therefore deter investment and consumption.

Selection 5

National Income and Product

EDWARD C. BUDD

From "National Income and Product", *prepared for the Grolier Encyclopedia 1962. Reprinted by permission of the publishers, Grolier, Inc., New York.*

While concepts of national income were formulated by writers on economics as early as the seventeenth century, and crude attempts at statistical measurement are almost as old, comprehensive estimates of national income and product are of relatively recent origin in almost all countries. In the United States it was not until after World War I that a private research organization, the National Bureau of Economic Research, began its monumental work on national income estimates. The first governmentally sponsored estimates appeared during the 1930's. Since that time considerable improvement has been made in both the theoretical and statistical bases of the series, and today the United States national income and product statistics constitute perhaps the most comprehensive measures available of American economic activity.

At the basis of national income accounting is the concept of production: the creation of goods and services for satisfying human wants through the use of the services of economic resources (land, labor, and capital). From the truism that the value of incomes earned from production is identically equal to the value of output itself, it follows that income can be estimated by measuring either the value of goods and services produced, or the value of incomes earned in their production. Both methods are used in preparing the estimates.

In the first or "product" approach, the value of output can be obtained as the sum of the end or *final* products of the economy. Care must be taken to exclude the value of those goods which are used up in the production of other goods and hence already reflected in the value of the latter. For example, adding the value of flour used in making bread to the value of the bread itself would result in double-counting the flour, since the selling price of the bread already includes the value of the flour used.

In practice, the distinction between final and intermediate products is not so simple as the above example might imply. All goods and services purchased by ultimate consumers or "households" are clearly final products, since they are designed for the ultimate satisfaction of human wants. All purchases by governmental units can also be considered as final products. While the government is not itself an ultimate consumer, it can be viewed simply as furnishing to the community as a whole without charge the goods it purchases from business, together with the results of its own productive activity.

At first sight it might appear that all goods and services purchased by businesses should be classified as intermediate, since they will ultimately be used up in the production of other goods. Bakery ovens and delivery trucks, for example, are required for the manufacture and sale of bread. Nevertheless, part of the goods acquired by businesses will contribute to future rather than to current production. A newly produced oven or truck is part of current output, but its value will be reflected in the value of bread sold to consumers only in future years. Hence the value of newly produced durable or capital goods (producers' durable equipment and new construction) must be counted as final products in measuring current output. Any increase in producers' inventories of goods which are not used up in the current period must also be included, under increases in business inventories; the flour which the baker has purchased but not yet baked into bread is part of current production. Similarly, any reduction in inventories must be subtracted from the measure of current output: the flour taken from the baker's inventory for the current output of bread and not replaced is the result of past production and must be deducted.

Finally, part of our production is sold abroad as exports. From this must be deducted the value of the goods and services we import from abroad, since imports, which are the results of other countries' production, are already reflected in the value of this country's final products. The total of these four components —consumption (purchases of goods and services by households), investment (construction, purchases of producers' durables, and changes in inventories), government purchases of goods and services, and net exports (exports minus imports)—is called gross national product (GNP).

It would be a mistake to suppose that only production which is reflected in explicit market transactions should be included in income estimates. The concept of productive activity is almost as broad as life itself, since people are almost continually engaged in activities which contribute in one way or another to their satisfaction and well-being. Practical considerations have of necessity, however, limited the measure of output to those goods and services which either are exchanged on markets or easily could be should their owners or producers so desire. The value of food and fuel produced and consumed on farms, for example, is included in GNP even though no market transaction occurs, whereas the value of housewives' services to households is not (even though paid domestic service is). Other imputed values included in the United States estimates are the rental value of dwellings occupied by their owners, the value of food and housing furnished to employees by their employers with no charge, and the value of certain services of financial intermediaries (such as banks and insurance companies) which are not reflected in explicit market transactions.

The second method of estimating income and product is through incomes earned in the various producing units of the economy, since the income generated by any unit is necessarily equal to the value it adds to production. The most important producing unit in the American economy is the business firm. The value it adds to production is equal to the sum of its sales and additions to its inventories less its purchases of intermediate goods and services from other firms. Failure to deduct purchases would lead to overstating income in much the same way that the inclusion of both intermediate and final products would lead to an overstatement of GNP when viewed from the product side; the purchases will be counted as the production of the selling firms and must not be included in the value added by the purchasing firm. Income claims on the firm's value added include the compensation of its employees, interest paid its creditors (less any interest it receives), and indirect taxes (excise, sales, and property taxes) levied by government. The difference between the sum of these claims and the firm's value added is its gross income; its net income is obtained after deducting an allowance for the value of the firm's capital which has been used up in producing its value added (depreciation or capital consumption). This net income may take the form of corporate profits if the business unit is a corporation; proprietor's income, if an unincorporated enterprise (including farmers and independent professional practitioners); or rental income of persons, if a landlord or an owner-occupant. Combining estimates for all firms yields income originating in business enterprises (employee compensation, net interest, and net business income) and other charges against business gross product (indirect taxes and capital consumption allowances).

Value added or income originating in other productive units is measured in a somewhat different way. Since most governmental units, unlike business firms, do not sell their output, income originating in government is measured by factor cost incurred, in particular, by the compensation of government employees. For households, it is equal to the wages of domestic help and interest on consumer debt. Income originating from abroad is equal to the difference between receipts of and payments to foreign countries of interest, dividends, and corporate profits. The sum of incomes originating in business firms, government, households, and from abroad is called *national income*. Adding indirect taxes paid by business to national income gives net national product.

When business capital consumption allowances are added to net national product, the resulting total (gross national product) should be the same as that obtained when measured from the product side. Because the measurement of the income and of the product side of GNP are largely independent of each other, however, the two totals usually differ by a small sum, called the *statistical discrepancy*. The size of this figure does not necessarily indicate the accuracy of the estimates. Gross national product as measured from both the income and product sides is shown for 1960 for the United States in Table 1. The product side is allocated by type of purchaser as explained above. An allocation by type of product (durable goods, nondurable goods, and services) is also available for the United States estimates.

Table 1
UNITED STATES NATIONAL INCOME AND PRODUCT, 1960
(in billions of dollars)

Income or earnings side	
Compensation of employees	293.7
Proprietors' income	48.2
Rental income of persons	11.7
Corporate profits	45.1
Net interest	18.4
NATIONAL INCOME	417.1
Indirect business taxes	45.6
Other adjustments	1.2
NET NATIONAL PRODUCT (measured from income side)	463.9
Capital consumption allowances	43.1
GROSS NATIONAL PRODUCT measured from income side)	507.0
Statistical discrepancy	—2.6
GROSS NATIONAL PRODUCT	504.4

Product or expenditure side		
Personal consumption expenditure		328.9
Durable goods	44.3	
Nondurable goods	152.4	
Services	132.2	
Gross domestic investment		72.4
New construction	40.7	
Producers' durable equipment	27.5	
Change in business inventories	4.2	
Net exports of goods and services		3.0
Exports	26.6	
Imports	23.6	
Government purchases of goods and services		100.1
GROSS NATIONAL PRODUCT		504.4

Source: *Survey of Current Business,* July 1961.

If Table 1 had been presented in terms of net national product (NNP) rather than GNP, capital consumption allowances would have been subtracted from gross domestic investment to show net domestic investment on the product side and would not have been shown separately on the income side. While GNP is perhaps the most widely used income accounting concept, it does involve a certain amount of duplication in measuring production. GNP counts goods at their market value, which includes the cost or value of existing durable capital goods used up in production; in addition, GNP includes the value of all newly produced capital goods, even though part of these are necessary in order to make good such consumption of the existing capital stock as results from production. While NNP on this account is a superior measure of production, present statistical estimates of capital consumption allowances do not provide a satisfactory measure of capital used up, since they are based largely on accounting depreciation allowances made by business.

A measure of total production which is not shown in Table 1 is gross domestic product, which can be obtained from gross national product by subtracting income originating from abroad (net factor earnings originating in the rest of the world). While this latter item does represent income accruing to United States residents, it is not the result of productive activity occurring within the boundaries of the United States. The difference between gross domestic product and gross national product is trivial for the United States, but quite significant for many other countries.

In Table 1, the components of national income have been shown in terms of the distributive shares or types of factor costs incurred to product output. In Table 2, national income is presented in terms of the sectors or industries in which it originates. Such industrial allocations of income cannot be given for GNP or NNP, since data on the industrial distribution of indirect taxes are not available.

Table 2
UNITED STATES NATIONAL INCOME ORIGINATING BY INDUSTRY, 1960
(in billions of dollars)

Agriculture, forestry, and fisheries	17.2
Mining	5.5
Contract construction	22.5
Manufacturing	121.6
Wholesale and retail trade	68.8
Finance, insurance, and real estate	42.3
Transportation	17.8
Communications and public utilities	16.6
Services	30.5
Households and institutions	19.5
Government	52.5
Abroad (Rest of the world)	2.3
NATIONAL INCOME	417.1

Source: *Survey of Current Business,* July 1961.

One important aspect of national income estimates which serves to underline the usefulness of the approach in giving a statistical picture of the economy is the set of national income accounts. The economy is divided into major economic groups or sectors, with all of economic activity summarized in transactions that occur between sectors. The current United States system contains a producer account, which is identical with the national income and product account shown in Table 1; a consumer or household account, which shows the sources of personal income and its allocation among consumption, tax payments, and personal saving; the government account, giving its tax receipts, its transfer payments, its expenditures on goods and services, and its surplus (or deficit) on income and product transactions; a foreign account, which summarizes United States transactions with the rest of the world, and a saving-investment account, which reconciles the saving of the four major groups (producer, consumer, government, foreign) with domestic and foreign investment.

An even simpler version of a national accounting system can be developed in terms of sector receipts and expenditures, where each sector's receipts are shown as the algebraic sum of its earnings from production and its net receipts (positive or negative) of transfer income. Since income transfers are not claims or earnings arising from productive activity, but simply redistributions of income within the economy, they cancel out for the economy as a whole, leaving the sum of all sectors' receipts equal to their income earned from production, that is, equal to GNP. Government, for example, swells its receipts by collecting taxes (a positive transfer); since, however, business and household receipts are reduced by the amount of taxes they pay, taxes do not enlarge the economy's spendable receipts. The business sector's receipts (gross retained earnings) include capital consumption allowances and undistributed corporate profits. Net government receipts are the difference between the government's tax collections and its transfer payments to households (for example, social security benefit payments). Households' earnings from production (national income less corporate profits) as adjusted for such receipts as dividends, government interest and transfer payments, and for payments of personal tax is called *disposable income* and is useful as a measure of consumer purchasing power. The system is summarized in Table 3, with the estimates for 1960. Expenditures are the same as those shown in Table 1. While receipts for any sector need not equal its expenditures, for the economy as a whole receipts and expenditures are identical. Gross national product can therefore be viewed in three ways: as expenditures on final products, as income earned from production, and as income receipts of households, business, government, and the foreign sector.

Table 3

RECEIPTS AND EXPENDITURES BY MAJOR ECONOMIC GROUPS, UNITED STATES, 1960
(in billions of dollars)

	Receipts	*Expenditures*
Households or persons:		
Disposable income	351.8	
Consumption expenditure		328.9
Business:		
Gross retained earnings	51.7	
Gross domestic investment		72.4
Government:		
Net government receipts	102.0	
Purchases of goods and services		100.1
Foreign:		
Net governmental transfers	1.6	
Net exports		3.0
Statistical discrepancy	—2.6	—
GROSS NATIONAL PRODUCT	504.4	504.4

Source: *Survey of Current Business,* July 1961.

Selection 6

The Economics of John Maynard Keynes

DUDLEY DILLARD

From: The Economics of John Maynard Keynes (*Englewood Cliffs, N.J. Prentice-Hall, Inc., 1948*), *pp. 1–12, 51–55. Reprinted by permission of Prentice-Hall, Inc.*

Introduction and Fundamental Ideas

I am more attached to the comparatively simple fundamental ideas which underlie my theory than to the particular forms in which I have embodied them . . . .[1]

Within the first dozen years following its publication, John Maynard Keynes's *The General Theory of Employment, Interest and Money* (1936) has had more influence upon the thinking of professional economists and public policy makers than any other book in the whole history of economic thought in a comparable number of years. Like Adam Smith's *Wealth of Nations* in the eighteenth century and Karl Marx's *Capital* in the nineteenth century, Keynes's *General Theory* has been the center of controversy among both professional and nonprofessional writers. Smith's book is a ringing challenge to mercantilism, Marx's book is a searching criticism of capitalism, and Keynes's book is a repudiation of the foundations of laissez faire. Many economists who were at first highly critical of Keynes have deserted their old position for the Keynesian camp. In book after book, leading economists acknowledge a heavy debt to the stimulating thought of Lord Keynes.

If the influence of Lord Keynes were limited to the field of technical economic doctrine, it would be of little interest to the world at large. However, practical economic policy bears even more deeply than economic theory the imprint of Keynes's thought. A few examples of the wide and growing acceptance of Keynes's philosophy of governmental intervention, public investment, and other forms of economic policy designed to fill the gaps in the private enterprise economy are: the economic policies of the New Deal, the special economic message

---

[1] J. M. Keynes, *The Quarterly Journal of Economics,* February, 1937, p. 211.

of President Truman to Congress at the close of the Second World War, the English, Canadian, and Australian "White Papers" on unemployment policy, the Murray Full Employment Bill of 1945 and the Employment Act of 1946 in the United States, the provision in the new French Constitution which requires an annual employment budget, the newer thinking in the field of fiscal policy, the International Monetary Fund, and the International Bank for Reconstruction and Development. It appears that the trend in economic policy in those countries where private enterprise is still vigorous will be in the direction which Lord Keynes charted. Many of his ideas and most of his theoretical apparatus can be useful in socialist economies even though his fundamental social philosophy is anti-Marxian.

During his lifetime Keynes wrote numerous books, many of which are outstanding contributions to special fields of economics. Clearly, however, *The General Theory of Employment, Interest and Money* contains the essence of his contribution to general economic theory. This work, published when he was fifty-two years of age (he lived to be sixty-two), is a product of his mature thought. It seems appropriate that a book on the economics of Keynes should begin with a discussion of the fundamentals of his thinking as outlined in the *General Theory*. The fundamental ideas are to be distinguished from the form in which these ideas are expressed. In the first restatement of his position after publication of the *General Theory,* Keynes wrote: "I am more attached to the comparatively simple fundamental ideas which underlie my theory than to the particular forms in which I have embodied them. . . ."[2] The theory stands or falls on these basic ideas. The forms in which the ideas are presented, on the other hand, allow for compromise. It is mainly these forms which have been the subject of debate subsequent to the publication of the *General Theory*. Once the fundamental ideas are clear, the rest falls easily into place. A full statement of the underlying ideas involves, of course, an explanation of the framework upon which they are built, but for the purpose of a general introduction the framework can be temporarily neglected. These fundamental ideas center around the following: (1) the *general* nature of Keynes's theory, (2) the role of money, (3) the relation of interest to money, (4) investment, and (5) uncertainty about the future.

A General Theory

In the title of his book *The General Theory of Employment, Interest and Money,*[3] Keynes's emphasis is on the word *general.* His theory deals with *all* levels of employment in contrast with what he calls "classical" economics, which is concerned with the special case of full employment. The purpose of Keynes's general theory is to explain what determines the volume of employment at any

[2] "The General Theory of Employment," *The Quarterly Journal of Economics,* Vol. LI, February, 1937, No. 2, 211.

[3] J. M. Keynes, *The General Theory of Employment, Interest and Money*. New York: Harcourt, Brace & World, Inc., 1936.

given time, whether it happens to be full employment, widespread unemployment, or some intermediate level. For reasons to be explained in the following chapter, the classical school assumes there is a tendency for the economic system based on private property in the means of production to be self-adjusting at full employment. Keynes challenges this assumption and calls the classical theory which is based on it a *special* theory, applicable only to one of the limiting cases of his *general* theory. Keynes attempts to show that the normal situation under laissez-faire capitalism in its present stage of development is a fluctuating state of economic activity which may range all the way from full employment to widespread unemployment, with the characteristic level far short of full employment. Although unemployment is characteristic, it is by no means inevitable. Another "general" aspect of the general theory is that it explains inflation as readily as it does unemployment since both are primarily a matter of the volume of effective demand. When demand is deficient, unemployment results, and when demand is excessive, inflation results. If Keynes' more general theory is correct, then the special theory is at fault not only in being the theory of a limiting case, but also in being largely irrelevant to the actual world in which unemployment is obviously one of the gravest problems. Most of the significant differences between the classical theory and Keynes' theory stem from the difference between the assumption that full employment is normal and the assumption that less than full employment is normal. The one is a theory of a stationary equilibrium and the other a theory of a shifting equilibrium.

There is another equally important meaning associated with the term "general" as it appears in the title of Keynes's book. His theory relates to changes in employment and output in the *economic system as a whole* in contrast with traditional theory which relates primarily, but not entirely, to the economics of the individual business firm and the individual industry. The basic concepts of Keynes's over-all theory are the aggregates of employment, national income, national output, aggregate supply, aggregate demand, total social consumption, total social investment, and total social saving. The relationships between individual commodities expressed in terms of individual prices and values, which constitute the chief subject matter of traditional economics, are important in Keynes's general theory, but they are subsidiary to the aggregate or over-all concepts of employment, income, et cetera. A little reflection will reveal that conclusions which are valid for the individual unit may not be valid when applied to the economic system as a whole. For example, some people may get rich by stealing from others, but obviously a whole community cannot enrich itself merely by its members plundering each other.

The Theory of a Monetary Economy

During his early career, Keynes was primarily a specialist in monetary theory and monetary policy. His greatest work prior to his *General Theory* was a two-volume *Treatise on Money*. When he moved from the narrower field of monetary theory to the broader field of general economic theory, Keynes took money along with him and gave it a place of tremendous importance in the determination of employment and production in the economic system as a whole. He refers to his analysis as "the theory of a monetary economy" (pp. vii, 239, 293). Money serves three functions: as a medium of exchange, as a unit of account, and as a store of value. Of these three, the store-of-value function is most important in defining Keynes's "monetary economy." People with more income and wealth than they currently consume may store the surplus in several forms, including hoarding money, lending money, and investing in some type of capital asset. If they choose to store their wealth in the form of money, they receive no income; if they lend their money, they receive interest; and if they purchase an investment asset, they expect to receive profits. Since money as a store of wealth is barren and other forms of wealth yield returns in the form of interest or profit, there must be a special explanation why people sometimes prefer to store wealth in the barren money form. Keynes gives as an answer the fact that money may be the safest form in which to store wealth. In lending money and in buying income property, there are uncertainties which do not exist as long as one's wealth is kept in the money form. Owners of money have a type of security which owners of other kinds of wealth do not enjoy.

When wealth-holders generally express a preference for hoarding money rather than lending or investing it, the production of real social wealth is handicapped. This preference for owning money rather than owning income-yielding wealth exists to a significant degree only in a world in which the economic future is uncertain. If the world were one in which the economic future could be predicted with mathematical certainty, there would be no sense in storing wealth in the barren money form. Only the highly uncertain nature of the economic future explains why there is a preference for storing wealth in the form of non-income-yielding money. As Keynes says, the desire to store wealth in the form of money is "a barometer of the degree of our distrust of our own calculations and conventions concerning the future. . . . The possession of actual money lulls our disquietude; and the premium which we require to make us part with money is the measure of the degree of our disquietude."[4]

Interest a Premium for Not Hoarding Money

The desire of wealth-holders to store wealth in the form of money against the risks of lending is not an absolute desire. It may be overcome by paying a premium in the form of interest. Interest is the reward for parting with control over wealth in its liquid form. The *rate* of interest depends on the intensity of the desire to hoard, or on what Keynes calls "liquidity preference," for speculative purposes. The stronger the liquidity preference, the higher the rate of interest which must be paid. An increase in the desire of the public to hold money increases the rate of interest, although it is possible for the banking and monetary authorities to meet this increased desire by increasing the quantity of money.

---

[4] "The General Theory of Employment," *op. cit.*, page 216.

Keynes's emphasis is not on the actual hoarding of money but on the *desire* to hoard. "Hoarding" is one of those phenomena which appear quite different when looked at from the individual, as compared with the economy-wide, point of view. An individual wealth-holder can increase the amount of money he holds only at the expense of someone else as long as the total supply of money does not increase. Therefore when the public as a whole wants more money, it cannot get it, and the increased desire for money results in the necessity of paying a higher premium to those who do part with their money. But when the price that must be paid for money increases, many types of new business activity that might be carried out at lower rates of interest will not be carried out at all. Therefore, an increase in interest rates tends to reduce effective demand and, in normal times, to cause unemployment.

Although the notion that interest is a reward for not-hoarding money may seem very ordinary from the layman's point of view, it is most unusual from the point of view of traditional economic theory. Interest has been looked upon by economists as a reward for saving, that is, a reward for postponing consumption rather than as a premium for surrendering liquidity. The importance of interest and money in Keynes' theory is indicated by their inclusion in the title *The General Theory of Employment, Interest and Money*. As further discussion will indicate, the ultimate theoretical explanation of unemployment in Keynes's theory is found in the peculiar properties of money and interest. In the absence of money or of any form of wealth with the properties of conventional money, Keynes contends the economic system would tend to be self-adjusting at the point of full employment (p. 235). Although the title indicates a theoretical emphasis on money and interest as the basis of the ultimate explanation of unemployment, from the point of view of practical policy Keynes places even greater stress on the instability of demand for capital assets arising from the irrationality of the private investment market.

Investment the Important Determinant of Employment

In a society characterized by great inequality of wealth and income, the economic ability of the community to consume is limited. The rich have more income than they wish to consume currently and the poor have so little income that their ability to consume is narrowly restricted. As a consequence, there is a sizable potential surplus of resources in excess of what is needed to produce consumers' goods. This surplus, if it is to be used at all, must be devoted to producing things that are not to be currently consumed. This production in excess of what is currently consumed is called *investment*. Investment includes such activity as building new factories, new houses, new railroads, and all other types of goods which are not to be consumed as fast as they are produced. The distinction between consumption and investment is fundamental to Keynes's entire analysis. His theory reduced to its simplest terms states that employment depends upon the amount of investment, or that unemployment is caused by an insufficiency of investment. This, of course, is a great simplification. Nevertheless, it indicates the emphasis on investment. Not only do some workers receive employment directly in building new factories, houses, railroads, et cetera, but the workers so employed spend their money for the products of factories already built, pay rent on houses already built, ride railroads already built, et cetera. In brief, employment in investment activity helps to maintain demand for the consumption output of existing facilities. In order to make full use of the factories already in existence, we must always be building new factories. Otherwise, in our society with its characteristic widespread inequality of income, there will not be enough money spent to keep the old factories going. If investment falls off, unemployment results. Clearly, it is very important to understand what determines the amount of investment that actually takes place. The most important section of Keynes's *General Theory* is Book IV, entitled "The Inducement to Invest." If we mean by a "cause" that factor in a complex combination of factors which fluctuates most widely and suddenly, we may say that investment is the determinant of employment. Employment fluctuates primarily because investment fluctuates. Unemployment results primarily from an inadequacy of investment. If investment can be controlled, total employment can be controlled. A high level of employment depends upon a high level of investment. The clue to understanding the general theory of employment is found in the answer to the question: What causes investment to fluctuate and characteristically to be less than the amount required for full employment?

Psychological Irrationality a Cause of Instability

Investment fluctuates because present knowledge about the future rests on a precarious basis and therefore decisions which relate to the uncertain future also are precarious and subject to sudden and sweeping revision. Since investment is production other than for present consumption, it is connected with the future in a direct manner. Although investment may take the form of producing more consumers' goods than are currently consumed, the more important form is investment in durable producers' goods, like factories, houses, railroads, apartment houses, et cetera.[5] A decision to build a factory depends on what is expected to happen in the future. However, the outstanding fact about the future, so far as economic life is concerned at least, is that we know very little about it. The potential investor must be guided by his *expectations* in reaching his decision to build or not to build a new factory. The vague and uncertain state of our knowledge rules out the possibility that these expectations can be reduced to a rational, scientific basis. Yet, as practical people living in a society whose pro-

[5] Houses might be included in durable consumers' goods, but income statistics classify them under investment. They are of such obvious importance that they have been used for illustrative purposes here even though they are not strictly a producers' good.

ductivity depends upon large-scale investment in durable assets, we must make and do make decisions concerning the long-term future, even though they rest on a foundation of shifting sand. Since those who make these dollars-and-cents decisions have very little confidence in the correctness of the judgment which leads to any particular investment, the prevailing attitudes which affect investment and employment so seriously are easily provoked to sudden change. If wealth-accumulation were a matter of secondary importance, the vague and uncertain state of our knowledge of the future would not matter so greatly. But under modern industrial capitalism, wealth-accumulation (investment) is the basis of the successful functioning of the entire economic system.

In the market place, entrepreneurs and other prospective investors shelter themselves from the turbulent stream of coming events that flows out of a dimly lit future by adopting protective attitudes that give the appearance of rational conduct. These attitudes include the assumption that the present is a much better guide to the future than a candid examination of the past would warrant. There is, in other words, a tendency to abstract from the fact that we know very little about the long-term future. The further assumption is made that existing opinions as reflected in the stock market, bond market, and other organized markets are based on a correct summing up of future prospects. Finally, because investors have so little confidence in their own opinions, they tend to rely upon the judgment of the majority or average. What Keynes calls "conventional judgments" become the basis of market-place behavior. They are conventional because they involve a general concurrence of opinion or the acceptance of a convention as a substitute for genuine knowledge which does not exist. Although investors have grave doubts concerning the soundness of action based on mass psychology, they accept it as correct behavior in the absence of any positive evidence that it is incorrect. When something new does turn up to indicate that past behavior has been incorrect, a violent shift takes place. Conventional judgments lend some stability as long as the convention is accepted, but when the convention breaks down, instability becomes the order of the day. Thus the state of expectations rests on a razor's edge and investment markets are charged with potential panic. When one conventional judgment gives way to another, all new judgments tend to move in the same direction. The sweeping nature of changes in conventional judgments stands in contrast with the classical theory of the market which assumes that the pessimistic decisions of some strong-minded individuals will offset the optimistic decisions of other strong-minded individuals.

By assuming that investors possess present knowledge about the future quite different from that which they actually possess, the classical theory underestimates "the concealed factors of utter doubt, precariousness, hope and fear."[6] The over-rationalistic psychology of the classical economists leads to a misinterpretation of behavior in the investment market, and to a neglect of the strategic role of money as a protective link between the present and the uncertain future.

[6] "The General Theory of Employment," *op. cit.*, page 222.

For, as we have seen, the uncertain future which makes real investment hazardous also lends enchantment to money as a store of value.

Despite these important differences between the psychological assumptions of Keynes and those of the classical school, there is one respect in which their psychological theory is similar. The classicists assume rational behavior on the part of individuals. The individual behavior posited by Keynes is also rational, within the limitations of the given situation. It is quite rational for a bewildered investor to want to hold money during a depression-created crisis, even though this behavior brings results that are highly irrational from the point of view of the economic system as a whole. Whereas the classical economists are concerned with rational behavior in a rational world, Keynes is concerned with rational behavior in an irrational world.

Under five separate headings we have outlined the fundamental ideas of Keynes's *General Theory*. It is a general theory that pertains to all levels of employment for the economic system as a whole. It is a theory of a monetary economy in the sense that money is an important form in which to store wealth, and interest is the premium paid for not-hoarding wealth in this form. It is a theory in which fluctuations in the volume of investment account for fluctuations in employment. Fluctuations in the volume of investment are largely accounted for by the fluctuating and uncertain nature of expectations regarding the future returns from capital assets and the future terms on which money may be lent at interest. From the presentation of these basic ideas, it is apparent that they are closely related to each other. One idea cannot be discussed without bringing in the others. The theory of interest and money is really one theory. Investment involves consideration of money as an alternative form of storing wealth. Investment in real capital assets occurs only if the expectations of profits are in excess of the premium that must be paid for borrowing money. The uncertain nature of knowledge about the future accounts both for the existence of money as a store of value and the precariousness of investment in real capital assets. These related ideas are all brought together into one theory of employment, which is the essence of the *General Theory* and may be stated as follows: In a world in which the economic future is highly uncertain and in which money is an important form for storing wealth, the general level of employment depends upon the relation between the expected profits from investment in capital assets and the interest premium which must be paid to induce wealth-holders to surrender control of their money. If there is confidence in the future, real investment will occur and employment will be at a high level. Although interest will continue to be paid for not-hoarding, this premium can be paid and still enable entrepreneurs to carry out real investment on terms which they expect to be profitable. When confidence in the future is lacking and the expectations for profits are dim, the premium required to get wealth-holders to part with their money will exceed the expected rate of return. Investment and employment will fall to a low level. A depression is a period in which the premium that must be paid for not-hoarding money exceeds the rate of return expected from building new capital assets of almost every type. Therefore, men are not employed to build new factories, and lacking income, they have little money with which to buy the output of existing factories. While the economic storm is raging, no one is able to pay the premium necessary to lure away from wealth-holders their highly preferred cash. Wealth-accumulation dwindles, workers lose their jobs, and the storm grows worse.

Practical Meaning of the Main Concepts

Among all the terms and concepts used by Keynes in *The General Theory of Employment, Interest and Money,* the three which stand out above all the rest as the strategic, independent variables are the propensity to consume (consumption schedule), the marginal efficiency of capital (investment-demand schedule), and the rate of interest (liquidity-preference schedule). The choice of these three independent variables or strategic factors arises from the nature of Keynes's interest in practical policy. The ultimate purpose of his theory is to explain what determines the volume of employment, or in terms of the practical problems involved, what causes unemployment. To explain the cause means, in a significant sense, to point to those factors or to a course of action which, if changed or followed, will remedy the malady. Thus when we say a common cold is caused by sitting in a draft, we usually mean that by not sitting in a draft a cold will not occur or is less likely to occur. To explain unemployment means to indicate those aspects of the economic system which need to be changed or subjected to social control in order to assure a high level of employment. Keynes says: "Our final task might be to select those variables which can be deliberately controlled or managed by central authority in the kind of system in which we actually live."[7]

Realistic theory is necessarily conditioned by the theorist's sense of values and by his ideas as to what is practicable policy. The realistic nature of Keynes's theory may be attributed largely to his vital concern with a specific type of economic program. This does not mean that Keynes's theoretical concepts are worthless in relation to policies other than those advocated by him, nor does it mean that his policies or any other policies necessarily follow from his abstract, theoretical concepts. However, a recognition of the social values and practical aims of a pioneering theorist like Keynes gives a richer insight into the meaning of his abstract theoretical concepts and propositions. A concept like the propensity to consume, or consumption function, is a formal, mathematical relationship between amounts of consumption corresponding to amounts of income for the community as a whole. But this is only the bare bones. The full meaning of this formal concept as used by Keynes emerges in terms of the use to which he puts it. He uses it to show the necessity of a high rate of consumer expenditure, which, perhaps, can be obtained by a more equal distribution of income and wealth. He uses it to indicate the desirability of steeply progressive taxation and large government outlays for social services. The propensity to consume is further

---

[7] Keynes, *The General Theory of Employment, Interest and Money*. New York: Harcourt, Brace & World, Inc., 1936, p. 247.

refined in the form of the marginal propensity to consume, which is used to derive the concept of the investment multiplier. The commonsense meaning of the investment multiplier is that in times of depression when private investment lags, government investment in public works will increase the national income not only by the amount of the public outlay but by some multiple of it.

In these terms Keynes makes a case for public works and becomes an advocate of public spending. His theory is referred to as a "spending" theory. To call a theory a spending theory has no meaning except in relation to some fairly specific steps or policies that may be followed to increase aggregate demand above what it would be in the absence of such policies. When we trace the concepts to their practical consequences, the lifeless forms of abstraction begin to take on definite shape and meaning. We see them emerging as plans of action, altered behavior, policies. The theory is put into practice. Only when theory is put into practice—that is, only when we trace the theory to its practical consequences—can we hope to test its validity by an appeal to facts and thus arrive at an evaluation of its probable workability in the actual world.

The operational or practical meaning of Keynes's theory will be referred to often in this book in the belief that this method will facilitate the understanding of what is likely to appear to be an intrinsically difficult body of doctrine. At this juncture we allude briefly to the operational significance of Keynes's theories of the rate of interest and the marginal efficiency of capital, the two independent variables which, along with the propensity to consume referred to in the preceding paragraph, determine the level of employment. The uniqueness of Keynes's theory of the rate of interest runs in terms of the importance of controlling the quantity of money. The novel concept is liquidity preference for the speculative motive. Wealth-holders have a preference for keeping their assets in a liquid form, the form of money, and it is this desire to hoard which determines the level of interest rates. An easy-money policy under a strong monetary authority can keep down the interest rates and thus stimulate investment and employment. However, Keynes's practical sense is too strong to lead him to attach sole importance to interest rates and so we find a parallel stress on the marginal efficiency of capital. The chief characteristic of the marginal efficiency of capital is its great instability. It may fall so low in depression that no reduction in interest rates will induce private investment. To alleviate the consequences of instability in the marginal efficiency of private capital, Keynes advocates government direction of total investment, including public investment, to compensate for the inevitable fluctuations in private investment. A low rate of interest and a high marginal efficiency of capital are the conditions favorable to investment and employment. Since the natural tendency is for the rate of interest to stay up and the marginal efficiency of capital to come down, laissez-faire policies will leave the volume of investment short of what is necessary for full employment. Both of these determinates of investment involve psychological attitudes toward the future which cause investment to be much less stable than the volume of consumption. The instability of these factors determining investment leads Keynes to say that employment is determined by investment.

The Paradox of Poverty and Potential Plenty

Keynes's principle of effective demand furnishes an explanation of the paradox of poverty in the midst of potential plenty, one of the grave contradictions of modern capitalism. A poor community will have little difficulty employing all its resources because it will tend to spend on consumption a large proportion of its total income. Only a small gap needs to be filled by investment, and since the stock of accumulated capital assets will be slight in the poor community, the demand for investment will be brisk. A wealthy community, on the contrary, will have great difficulty maintaining full employment because the gap between income and consumption will be large. Its investment outlets must be great if there are to be enough jobs for all. Failing to find these outlets, the potentially wealthy community will be forced to reduce its actual output until it becomes so poor that the excess of output over consumption will be reduced to the actual amount of investment. To make matters worse, the very fact that a community is rich in accumulated capital assets weakens the inducement to invest because every new investment must compete with an already large supply of old investments. The inadequacy of demand for investment reacts in a cumulative fashion on the demand for consumption. The factories that are already built cannot be used because more factories are not being built. Unemployment on a mass scale exists in the midst of potential plenty. Thus, as Keynes says, "the richer the community . . . the more obvious and outrageous the defects of the economic system." Keynes finds no reason to assume that the growing gap between income and consumption at high levels of employment will be filled automatically, that is, without conscious social action, except under special historical circumstances like those existing in the nineteenth century or in time of war. War has a distinct if ironical advantage over peaceful industry in that it calls for the production of things which are to be exploded and shot away and do not remain to compete with more production of the same type at a later date. If war and threat of war are banished from the world, the capitalist countries will once more be confronted with the tasks of finding sufficient outlets for new investment to provide employment for all of its millions of workers who cannot be employed in consumption industries.

DISCUSSION QUESTIONS

1. Distinguish between the income and product approaches to measuring national income. Explain why, if errors in measurement are ignored, both approaches must give the same answer.
2. How does the Keynesian system of economics explain the determination of national income? How does this view differ from the classical view that preceded it?
3. Explain why many economists and business leaders have been highly reluc

tant to accept the Keynesian conclusion that a capitalist market economy will not automatically adjust to full employment.

4. Explain the paradox of thrift, that is, the idea that an increased desire to save by the community as a whole might cause falling output, unemployment, and a reduction of actual saving.

SELECTED REFERENCES

Dernberg, Thomas, and Duncan McDougall, *Macro-Economics,* 2nd ed., New York: McGraw-Hill Book Co., 1963.

Hansen, Alvin, "Keynesian Thinking and the Problems of Our Time," in *The American Economy,* New York: McGraw-Hill Book Co., 1957, pp. 152–175.

Heilbroner, Robert L., *Understanding Macroeconomics,* Englewood Cliffs, N.J.: Prentice-Hall, Inc., 1965.

Keynes, J. M., *The General Theory of Employment, Interest and Money,* New York: Harcourt Brace & World, Inc., 1965. (Originally published 1936.)

Klein, Lawrence R., *The Keynesian Revolution,* 2nd ed., New York: The Macmillan Company, 1966. See especially chap. 3.

Smith, Warren L., and Ronald L. Teigen (eds.), *Readings in Money, National Income and Stabilization Policy,* Homewood, Ill.: Richard D. Irwin, Inc., 1965.

PART 4

STABILIZATION POLICY

Since the passage of the Employment Act of 1946, the Federal Government has been committed to promoting economic stability at high levels of employment. Although price stability was not specifically mentioned in the act, it has come to be included as part of stabilization policy. Stabilization policy developed from a desire to avoid a major depression after the war; from the experience of government during the war in directing economic activity; and from the ideas of the Keynesian economists which gave a theoretical justification for this type of government activity. The act did not, however, spell out how stabilization was to be achieved. Twenty years later, the ideas behind stabilization policy came to be accepted by Congress, and stabilization policy, with the passage of the 1964 tax cut bill, became reality.

There are two general types of stabilization policy: monetary policy and fiscal policy. Monetary policy involves regulating the quantity of money in circulation, and therefore, the availability of credit and the level of interest rates. Fiscal policy deals with government spending or taxing policies. The aim of both is to maintain a high level of economic activity at reasonably low levels of unemployment and with a relatively stable price level.

Monetary policy has long been accepted as a legitimate role for the Federal Reserve System, a relatively independent government agency which does not necessarily follow the lead of the administration. The Federal Reserve can regulate, within limits, the amount of money in circulation and, thus, the ease of credit and level of interest rates. Money is generally defined as currency in circulation plus demand deposits (checking account balances) at commercial banks. The Federal Reserve System has three main tools for influencing the quantity of money in circulation:

(1) The reserve ratio. This is the ratio of reserves to deposits that member banks must maintain. If, for example, the reserve ratio is 20 per cent, this means that member banks must have one dollar either on deposit with their Federal Reserve Bank or in vault cash for every five dollars of total deposits. Or, of the five dollars of deposits, four dollars could be used for loans or the purchase of securities and one dollar must be kept as reserve cash. If the ratio is lowered to 16⅔ per cent, only one dollar for every six dollars of deposits is needed for reserves. The one dollar of cash could now support five dollars in loans or securities rather than four. By expanding its loans the banking system can increase its deposits (other customers will redeposit most of the proceeds of any new loans, either with the loaning bank or some other bank in the system) and thereby increase the amount of money in circulation. An increase in the reserve ratio forces banks to restrict their loans and convert some of their securities to cash, reducing the amount of money in circulation.

(2) The discount rate. This is the interest rate charged to banks which borrow from the Federal Reserve. An increase in the rate may discourage banks from borrowing to get additional cash reserves. Also, it means that banks will likely increase the rate they charge their customers and therefore discourage borrowing. However, borrowing by businessmen is relatively unresponsive to small changes in the interest rates, so that this, by itself, is relatively ineffective as a control of credit.

(3) Open market operations. The Federal Reserve may also engage in buying and selling of government securities in the open market. If the Federal Reserve buys securities, new funds will be injected into the system. If securities are bought directly from banks, the cash shows up directly as increased reserves for the banking system. If the securities are purchased from individuals or nonbank institutions, they will in turn deposit it and the cash still ends up as new reserves. With these new reserves, loans and deposits can be expanded, so that the amount of money in circulation is thus increased. The sale of government securities by the central bank will soak up cash and have a restricting effect on money and credit.

However, monetary policy by itself may not be sufficient to stabilize economic activity. During a period of falling prices and incomes, excess reserves may only be added to idle balances. Bankers may be unwilling to lend during a depression and businessmen may be unwilling to invest no matter what the interest rate. Also, low interest rates may encourage the flow of funds out of the country if foreign interest rates are higher than domestic rates. Tight money policies during inflation may restrict long-term investment projects, thereby hindering future growth.

There are two types of fiscal policy: automatic stabilizers and discretionary stabilizers. Automatic stabilizers are mechanisms built into the economic system (also called built-in flexibility) which tend to dampen the effect of an upswing or a downswing. The two most important automatic stabilizers are income taxes and unemployment compensation. As total expenditure falls (say, from a reduction of private investment) tax receipts of the government will fall by a larger percentage. Therefore, disposable income and consumption will fall by a smaller percentage than expenditures. In addition, as expenditures fall, unemployment compensation will increase as people are laid off. This will also tend to keep consumption from falling by as large a percentage as expenditures. Thus, an initial fall in expenditure will bring forth a smaller total change in income than would be the case if consumption varied directly with expenditures. However, built-in flexibility also applies to upswings. A given increase in expenditure will generate a smaller total change in income, because tax receipts will increase by a larger percentage than income and because unemployment compensation will be reduced. Automatic stabilizers do not prevent booms or recessions—they only dampen the effect that a change in expenditure, from whatever source, will have on economic activity.

Discretionary fiscal policy involves direct government action to change its spending or taxing policies in order to influence the total level of demand. Prior to the tax cut of 1964, changes in taxation or expenditures were primarily for other goals: to finance wars, to implement new government programs, and so on. Although these all had important effects on economic activity, this was not the primary goal: sometimes the effect was good; sometimes it was bad.

The rationale behind discretionary fiscal policy is that sufficient aggregate demand should be generated to ensure full employment. If full employment is not being achieved, this implies that current investment plans of business and expenditure plans of government are insufficient to offset savings plans of households and tax plans of government. Fiscal policy calls for a reduction in taxes—which will increase private consumption and investment—or an increase in government spending—which increases public consumption and investment and also induces additional private spending.

The idea behind the 1964 tax cut was that tax rates were too high and acted as a "fiscal drag" on economic activity. Government economists pointed out that from 1956 to 1963 the government had a deficit during five out of eight years. However, the economy had been at much less than full employment during these years. If the economy had been at full employment, at existing tax rates additional tax receipts would have been sufficient to cause a surplus in each of these years. It was argued that high taxes were restricting private spending and keeping full employment from being achieved. Thus, paradoxically, the way to solve a government deficit was to reduce taxes, not increase taxes. This would stimulate additional private consumption and investment and generate additional income. At higher levels of income, despite lower tax rates, higher tax receipts would be forthcoming. By adding to this the increased tax receipts resulting from normal growth in income over time without a tax cut, there would be sufficient tax receipts to balance the budget in three or four years if government expenditures were held in line.

In order to use fiscal policy for stabilization purposes, the traditional goal of annual balanced budgets must be abandoned. During slack times, if expenditures are increased or taxes reduced to stimulate demand, the government must cover the difference between its expenditures and tax receipts by borrowing. During inflationary periods the government would increase taxes or reduce expenditures and run a surplus to dampen total demand. Is there reason for concern over the size of the government debt? Should government attempt to balance its annual budget or run a surplus so that it can pay off its outstanding debt? Usually it is argued that government deficits will be inflationary. This, however, depends on the circumstances. If a government deficit is financed by selling bonds to the public, no new money is created. If the bonds are sold to the Federal Reserve, then new money is created. However, an increase in the money supply does not necessarily mean inflation. As the economy grows, additional funds are needed each year to finance larger volumes of transactions. If the economy is at less than full employment, additional expenditures can generate additional output with little or no rise in prices.

Most of the government debt is held within the country. Thus, for every dollar of debt, there is a corresponding dollar of assets held by an American. As a country, we owe the debt to ourselves. In the future, if the government decides to pay off the debt, it will merely tax its citizens to pay its citizens. Whether borrowing or repaying, the debt involves a transfer of assets within the present or a future generation. The government is not passing a burden to future generations without also passing them a like asset.

There may, however, be real costs of a government deficit. If the economy is at or near full employment, borrowing to finance additional expenditures will likely be inflationary. This has been the case in all major wars. With inflation, holders of money or bonds and people living on fixed dollar incomes are handicapped. In addition, increasing the government debt may have undesirable effects on the distribution of income. Most government securities are held by relatively wealthy individuals or institutions. Thus the government is taxing the public to make payments to a relatively well-off sector of the economy. However, people who hold these government securities no doubt pay higher taxes also, so that the redistribution effects may not be too important. If the economy could be stimulated by increased private spending, a similar transfer would take place. Businesses and households would have to borrow to finance these expenditures. Again, the interest payments would go to the relatively wealthy people, who receive most of the interest income.

The primary problem of stabilization policy in the late 1950's and early 1960's was how to stimulate the economy to higher levels of economic activity. This concern culminated in the tax cut of 1964. More recently the concern of policy makers has been with inflation. To the stimulus of the tax cut in 1964 was added, during 1965 and 1966, the increased government spending of the Vietnam war and a high level of business investment spending. During 1966 the consumer price index increased by 3.3 per cent. From 1960 to 1965 the average increase was 1.36 per cent per year. The article by W. Carl Biven discusses demand-pull, cost-push, and structural inflation. Although the rising prices of the late 1950's when unemployment levels were relatively high may have been mainly of the structural and cost-push varieties, the more recent inflation during 1966 was probably primarily of the demand-pull type. The wage-price guidelines adopted by the Kennedy and Johnson administrations were designed primarily to cope with structural and cost-push inflationary forces. Their purpose was to attempt to improve the trade-off between unemployment and inflation, that is, to lower the amount of inflation resulting from any given reduction in the level of unemployment. These voluntary guidelines were unable to restrain the heavy demand pressures of 1965–1966.

Selection 7

Economic Stability

LESTER V. CHANDLER

From E. O. Edwards (ed.), The Nation's Economic Objectives *(Chicago:*

In February, 1946, Congress enacted a law that was to be a landmark in the history of American economic policy—the Employment Act of 1946. That this was one of the first major pieces of legislation after World War II was no coincidence; it symbolized the high priority of economic stability as a goal of our society. How highly Americans prized economic stability at that time can hardly be appreciated by those who have not experienced economic instability in its most extreme and painful forms. Memories of the Great Depression were then still vivid, and fears of its resumption widespread.

Economic instability had, of course, been a matter of concern long before the fateful 1930's. We have had cyclical fluctuations, with alternating periods of prosperity and depression, almost from the beginning of our industrialization. Many had come to believe that such instability is an almost inevitable characteristic of our free enterprise system, which relies largely on free markets to organize and direct its economic activities and on large numbers of private business firms to employ its resources and produce its output. The achievements of the free-enterprise system have been great indeed. Offering freedom of choice of occupation, freedom to establish and operate enterprises, and freedom of scope for ability and ambition, it is consistent with our general desire for freedom. Under this system we have developed the most productive economy the world has ever seen and achieved the world's highest living standards. Yet none can deny that this performance has been marred by recurring periods of recession and depression, with their huge waste of productive power and their severe hardships for the unemployed and others.

Though the Great Depression was not our first, it was certainly our worst. Beginning in 1929, it dragged on for a dozen years until it was finally ended by our accelerating rearmament program. At the bottom of the depression in 1932 and 1933, when our total labor force included only about 51 million persons, the number of unemployed averaged over 12 millions. Of those in the labor force nearly one out of four was unemployed. Even after the upturn, the situation remained serious. From 1933 until 1941 there was no year in which the number of unemployed fell as low as 7 millions or the percentage of unemployed fell as low as 14 per cent. For the last half of the 1930's, unemployment averaged 8.5 millions, or more than 16 per cent of the labor force.

If we wished to deal with the matter statistically, we could put dollar values on the huge amounts of output that could have been produced but were not—on the consumer goods that were not turned out and on the factories, equipment, homes, hospitals, schools, and churches that were not built. But there is no satisfactory way of measuring the accompanying hardships and frustrations—the plight of the unemployed who lost both income and status and of those who lost their homes, farms, and savings. Amidst such frustrations, economic, political, and social conflicts became embittered and sharpened. In some other countries facing similar situations, millions seeking economic security turned to totalitarians of the left or right, even at the cost of their liberties. Similar dangers were not absent here. And most tragic of all, the frustrations and conflicts generated by the Great Depression played an important, and perhaps a vital, role in bringing on World War II.

Such were the roots of the full-employment bill which was introduced in both houses of the Congress at the beginning of 1945, some months before VE Day. It grew out of the extreme economic instability of the 1930's and reflected widespread fears that similar conditions would reappear at the end of the war as government expenditures fell from their wartime peak, orders for munitions and military supplies were canceled, and millions of men and women were mustered out of the armed forces.

The Employment Act of 1946, which gained the unanimous approval of the Senate and passed the House with an overwhelming majority, ranks as a landmark in the history of American economic policy, primarily as a symbol of our aspirations and of the new responsibilities of government for promoting economic stability at high levels of employment. Now a large majority of both Democrats and Republicans of both liberal and conservative persuasion joined in stating that "the Congress hereby declares that it is the continuing policy and responsibility of the Federal government to use all practicable means . . . to promote conditions under which there will be afforded useful employment for those able, willing, and seeking to work, and to promote maximum employment, production and purchasing power."

But however important the Employment Act was as a general statement of policy and responsibility, it certainly was not a blueprint for action. In the process of getting a bill that would be acceptable to all factions, Congress retreated into broad generalities and provided neither the specific definition of goals nor the specific methods of implementation that are required for policy actions. The Act did not even define clearly its employment goals. It was recognized then, as it is today, that various types of frictions and immobilities in labor markets make it impossible to achieve and maintain "full employment" in the literal sense of zero unemployment. But there were then, as now, wide differences of opinion as to how ambitious the goal should be. Some insisted that we should strive for a situation in which the number of job vacancies would always exceed the number of unemployed. Others insisted on less ambitious goals. The Act, by using the general term "maximum employment," left this issue undecided.

The Act provided even less guidance on another set of issues that have in practice presented equally thorny problems—the relationship of employment goals to our other objectives of national policy. It did recognize that such problems would arise, for it stated that the government's actions to promote maximum employment should be "consistent with its needs and obligations and other essential considerations of national policy." Yet it did not even identify these "needs, obligations and other essential considerations"; it did not indicate how they should be ranked relative to employment goals; and it was silent as to what should be done if other considerations came into at least apparent conflict with the promotion of employment objectives.

The Act was no more specific as to the methods to be used to promote its objectives. It did provide for the creation of two new agencies—the Council of Economic Advisers in the Executive Office of the President and the Joint Economic Committee of the Congress. These agencies received power only to study, report, and recommend; power to act remained with the Congress and the Executive Office. The Act did not specify the particular instruments to be used, to say nothing of the relative roles that they should play. However, a study of the legislative history of the Act brings out clearly at least three points of general agreement. First, the purpose was not to supersede or weaken our predominantly free-enterprise system, but rather to strengthen it and improve its stability. In the words of the Act, its objectives were to be promoted "in a manner calculated to foster and promote free competitive enterprise and the general welfare." Second, there was to be a minimum reliance on direct, detailed controls over the policies and actions of consumers and business firms. Few indeed would have voted for the Act if it had contemplated continuing far into the peacetime period of wartime types of controls over prices, wages, allocations, and production. Third, it was generally agreed that the objectives of the Act were to be promoted predominantly through regulation of the aggregate demand for output—the rate of total spending for consumption, investment, and government purposes. This prescription followed from diagnosis of the proximate cause of instability in the past—the instability and self-reinforcing fluctuations of total demand for output. For example, the widespread unemployment and waste of other resources in the 1930's did not reflect any lack of desire on the part of businessmen to hire workers and produce. Rather, it reflected the gross inadequacy of aggregate demand for output—levels of demand so low that business could not find a market for its capacity output at prices high enough to cover costs, to say nothing of yielding profits. The appropriate remedy, therefore, was to achieve and maintain aggregate demand for output at levels which would at all times make it profitable for business to provide maximum employment and production. Many, including business leaders, pointed out that this was essentially a conservative policy. The government's role could be largely limited to that of maintaining aggregate demand at such levels as to induce business to make its maximum contribution to the general economic welfare, and this would not involve direct or detailed government intervention in the market processes determining prices, wages, and production.

What specific instruments should be used to maintain aggregate demand at appropriate levels? Here again the Employment Act itself provides no answer. However, both its legislative history and the thinking of the times indicate primary reliance on two sets of instruments—monetary policy and the government's fiscal policy. To this end, the Federal Reserve System was to use its instruments of general monetary and credit management—its discount policy, open market operations, and control over the legal reserve requirements of banks. If aggregate demand became, or threatened to become, inadequate, the Federal Reserve should increase the supply of money and credit and lower interest rates, thereby stimulating investment spending, which would indirectly stimulate consumption spending as well. If, on the other hand, aggregate demand became so great as to induce price inflation, the Federal Reserve should seek to curb it by restricting the supply of money and credit and raising interest rates.

The general principle that the Federal Reserve should use its monetary policy to promote economic stability is not very controversial, though there is no lack of controversy over the specific policies to be followed. Monetary management has long been a function of the government and the central bank, and most agree that it can be useful. Yet in the postwar period there has been widespread doubt that monetary policy alone can assure the maintenance of appropriate levels of aggregate demand. From the experience of the 1930's, many concluded that monetary policy used alone is incapable of restoring prosperity. My own opinion is that they go too far when they conclude that the episode of the 1930's proves that monetary policy is incapable of bringing recovery. Instead I would conclude that expansionary policies were so long delayed and so weak that we have no way of knowing how effective a timely and aggressive expansionary monetary policy might have been. Yet I would insist that there are indeed depressed situations in which monetary policy alone will be insufficient to bring full recovery and still more situations in which other measures alone or in conjunction with monetary policy will bring recovery sooner and with less undesirable side effects. There is, indeed, an important and even essential role for fiscal policies.

By the government's fiscal policy we mean, of course, its policies relative to its taxes and expenditures; we shall not discuss here related policies concerning government lending, loan insurance, and debt management. The government obviously must have fiscal policies of some sort, and with government taxing and spending equal to about a quarter of our gross national product these policies inevitably exert an important influence, whether favorable or unfavorable, on aggregate demand for output. The achievement and maintenance of maximum employment and production require that these powers be used to promote an appropriate behavior of aggregate demand. I shall not review here the details of the theory of stabilizing fiscal policy. However, the general principles are relatively simple. The government can support or increase aggregate demand by cutting taxes or by increasing its rate of expenditures. By decreasing taxes, it leaves a larger part of the national income in the hands of families and business firms and enables them to spend more for output. As those enjoying the tax cut spend more, they create more income for others and enable them to demand more output. An increase in government expenditures for output both increases directly the demand for output and creates income for those who supply the government, thereby enabling them to spend more and create more income for others. The government may also increase its expenditures in the form of transfer payments—in such forms as unemployment benefits and relief payments. An increase in government expenditures of these types enables the recipients to spend more, thereby creating more income for others and enhancing their demand for output. Note that in all these cases the total increase in the aggregate demand for output may be expected to be much larger than the initial tax reduction or the initial rise in government expenditures.

Similarly, the government may restrict a rise in aggregate demand for output or actually reduce that demand by raising taxes or by decreasing its rate of expenditures. Here again, the total restrictive effect on aggregate demand may be expected to be considerably larger than the initial rise of taxes or the initial decrease in government expenditures.

It should be clear that the deliberate use of fiscal policy to maintain aggregate demand at levels which will induce maximum employment will frequently, if not usually, be inconsistent with the maintenance of an unusually balanced budget or the maintenance of any other fixed relationship between the government's total revenues and total expenditures. Consider first the case of a business recession with falling incomes and rising unemployment. The very decline of national income will reduce the size of tax bases, reduce total tax yields, and tend to turn a budget surplus into a deficit or a deficit into a larger deficit. Yet this is the type of period in which a stabilizing type of fiscal policy calls for tax reduction or an increase of government expenditures. Consider next the case in which aggregate demand is rising to inflationary levels. The very rise of national money income increases the size of tax bases and total tax yields and tends to turn budget deficits into surpluses or to enlarge surpluses. Yet the appropriate fiscal policy for stabilization purposes at such times is likely to call for an increase in effective tax rates or a reduction in government expenditures.

In short, fiscal policy will in case after case be successful in maintaining aggregate demand at appropriate levels only by destabilizing the relationship between the government's total revenues and total expenditures. We shall see later that this type of fiscal policy has run into strong controversy and opposition, that this opposition has decreased both the frequency and aggressiveness of its use, and that this in turn has militated against the success of our program to promote continuous economic stability.

We find, then, that the Employment Act, despite its importance as a statement of intention and of national responsibility, did not provide a blueprint for action, for it did not define in operational terms either its objectives or its methods of implementation. These problems were left to be worked out later. We are still trying to solve these problems and cannot truthfully say that we have found fully satisfactory solutions. The results to date may be called a qualified success. With World War II now more than seventeen years behind us, we have not yet experienced a serious depression like that of the 1930's or even one like that following World War I. The percentage of the labor force unemployed has at no time exceeded 7.5 per cent, and in no year has it averaged above 7 per cent. This represents a real improvement over the performance of the economy in the prewar period, and this has not, I believe, been accidental. Yet the record has been far from perfect. In this postwar period we have had four recessions—those of 1949–1950, 1953–1954, 1957–1958, and 1960–1961. Moreover, the last two recoveries have been quite weak, with unemployment remaining considerably above the minimum levels reached in earlier prosperity periods and also well above the minimum unemployment necessitated by imperfections and immobilities in labor markets. It has now been five years since unemployment was as low as 5 per cent, and during most of the time unemployment has been well above this level. There are ominous signs that the maintenance of high levels of employment and output may present even more difficult and challenging problems in the future.

I want to deal now with some of the major problems that have been encountered and that may continue to bedevil us as we seek to promote maximum employment and production. The first set of problems relates to the general topic of this series of lectures: the multiplicity of the nation's economic objectives. And, one should also add, the multiplicity of its political and social objectives.

At the end of World War II, when memories of the Great Depression were still painfully vivid, many would have said that the objective of promoting maximum employment and production should take precedence over all others. But we know now that we also want many other things involving the economy. We want economic freedom for consumers, workers, and businessmen; stability of price levels; rapid economic growth; a large foreign aid program for both humanitarian and national security reasons; a large program for national defense; an equitable distribution of income; equilibrium in our balance of international payments; and so on. The list could be extended almost indefinitely.

It would be too pessimistic to conclude that these numerous objectives must inevitably come into conflict with each other and that to promote any one we must sacrifice some of the others. Yet it is clear that where objectives are so numerous, the probability of conflict is increased, and it becomes likely that no one of them will be promoted to the utmost.

Let us look at some relationships among four of these objectives: the promotion of maximum employment, promotion of the rate of economic growth, maintenance of stability of price levels, and promotion of equilibrium in our balance of international payments.

The Employment Act does not mention explicitly the objective of promoting economic growth. Nor could the framers of that Act foresee the unprecedented importance that would come to be attached to this objective in the postwar world. Never before have so many countries been so conscious of the possibility of economic growth or so determined to use national policies to promote it. In the United States we want a higher rate of economic growth for many reasons: to provide more employment opportunities; to raise our standards of living; to support on a larger scale our national security program, including foreign aid; and to symbolize the superiority of our economic and social system over that of the Iron Curtain countries. This last objective has received increasing attention as our growth rate has come to lag behind that of many other countries.

Some economists would argue that though the Employment Act did not mention economic growth explicitly, this objective is implicitly included in that of promoting maximum employment, production, and purchasing power. There is much validity in this view. It is clear that the economic stability we seek is not stability on a horizontal or stagnant level. Rather, it is stability on our growth-possibility curve. We can have maximum employment in the sense of minimum unemployment only if actual output rises with our total productive capacity. Unemployment will grow if actual output fails to rise as much as is made possible by the growth of our labor force and of productivity per man-hour. To this degree the objective of promoting economic growth is included in that of promoting maximum employment.

Nevertheless, I contend that the emergent postwar emphasis on economic growth gave at least a new emphasis and even a new dimension to our economic objectives. It seemed to provide an almost independent reason for increasing aggregate demand fast enough to elicit maximum production. It directed attention not only to the rate of total output but also to the composition of output, with a new emphasis on those types of output which would increase productive capacity. If maximum employment were our only objective, we might achieve it with an output composed largely of consumer goods and with little capital formation. The growth objective placed a new emphasis on capital formation. It also became a strong force against the adoption of restrictive monetary and fiscal policies which would be useful in curbing inflation but might inhibit growth. For example, it was cited in opposition to restrictive monetary policies which would raise interest rates and make investment more expensive and against tax policies that might reduce abilities or incentives to save, invest, take risks, or promote technological innovation.

This brings us to another type of economic stability—stability of price levels, or of the purchasing power of the dollar. The Employment Act made no mention of price levels, and repeated proposals that the Act be amended to include price-level stability as an explicit objective of national policy have all failed of adoption. But the fact that this objective is not stated in any law does not mean that it has been an unimportant consideration in national policy. On many occasions the actions of the Federal Reserve and the fiscal authorities have been strongly influenced by their desire to reduce the pace of price increases, if not to achieve complete stability of price levels. Their actions have been more restrictive and less liberal than would have been dictated by considerations relating to employment and growth.

Public and official concern for price-level stability has been greatly enhanced by the large rise of prices during the past two decades. Since 1941 the consumer price index has doubled; the dollar has lost half of its purchasing power over consumer goods. It is important to note, however, that only a small fraction of this increase in the price level can be attributed to peacetime policies of promoting employment and growth. Most of it resulted from World War II and the Korean conflict. Two-thirds of the total price increase since 1941 had occurred by August, 1948, when the wartime and postwar surge of prices had reached its peak. Another one-tenth of it occurred in the ten months following the outbreak in Korea in June, 1950. Only a quarter of it has occurred since March, 1951. Thus in the twelve and a half years since March, 1951, consumer prices have risen only about 18 per cent, or less than 1.5 per cent a year. Such a rate of price increase is hardly frightening in itself and would not have created so much public protest and official concern if it had not been superimposed on the large increases growing out of World War II and the Korean conflict.

Nevertheless, the price increases of the past decade or so have posed serious problems for our policies of promoting maximum employment and growth, primarily because they have so often occurred while unemployment was still considerably above the minimum levels necessitated by frictions and immobilities in labor markets. It had, of course, been recognized that an excessive growth of the aggregate demand for output could create a "demand-pull" inflation of money wage rates and prices. But it had been hoped and expected that this would occur only after unemployment had approached its irreducible minimum and that up to that point increases in aggregate demand would induce an increase in the supply of real output, rather than increases in wages and prices.

Now it appeared that these expectations were too optimistic. We even began to hear that we were experiencing a new type of inflation—not "demand-pull," but "wage-push," "cost-push," "sellers' inflation," or "markup inflation." The general idea was that we had become victims of the monopoly power of big unions and big business—that even in the midst of substantial unemployment the unions demand wage increases in excess of average increases in productivity per man-hour, this raises costs, and business marks up prices. A few economists have even gone so far as to argue that this wage-push, markup process of price inflation is largely independent of the levels of aggregate demand and unemployment and cannot be halted by restricting aggregate demand. Surely this is going too far; surely there is some level of aggregate demand and unemployment that will stop the process. But this is little consolation to a nation desiring both price stability and maximum employment, for the level of unemployment required for price stability may well be excessive in view of our employment and growth objectives.

Thus by the time the prosperity of 1955–1957 gave way to the recession of 1958, we were engaged in a serious national debate concerning our objectives relative to employment, growth, and price levels. And there was a growing opinion that these objectives could be reconciled satisfactorily only if we could somehow improve the market processes which determined wages and prices. This debate is not yet ended. But in the meantime, since the end of 1959, the problem has been made much more complex by the intrusion of a new set of considerations—considerations relating to the deficit in our balance of international payments and the shrinkage of our net international reserves. Now, for the first time in over thirty years, our freedom to pursue expansionary monetary and fiscal policies to promote employment and growth is jeopardized by the state of our international payments and reserves.

The deficit in our balance of payments did not originate suddenly and dramatically in 1960. Rather, it started as early as 1950. The general pattern during the period has been something like this. Our exports of goods and services have exceeded our imports almost every year, usually by considerable amounts. But our foreign investment and grants to other countries have exceeded our net export balance, and we have paid the difference by giving them gold and short-term claims against dollars. In both ways we have increased the international reserves of other countries. Until about 1960 this process was, on the whole, beneficial to the world and without immediate threat to the international position of the dollar. The continued deficit in the United States balance of payments, which continuously increased the gold and dollar reserves of other countries, played a major role in enabling those countries to remove restrictions on international trade and payments and to reconstruct world trade on a liberal basis. At the same time, our gold reserves still seemed large enough to maintain confidence that the United States could meet all its international payments without reducing the value of the dollar in exchange markets and to do this without restricting our freedom to pursue domestic objectives.

In 1960, as the deficit in our balance of payments continued and our net international reserve position continued to deteriorate, the situation changed markedly. For the first time in more than a generation, fears arose that the United States would not be able to redeem in gold all of its short-term dollar liabilities to foreigners and that the dollar might depreciate in exchange markets. These fears were dramatized by large speculative increases in the dollar price of gold in the London market and by flights of short-term funds from the United States to European financial centers. Though the situation has since improved somewhat, confidence in the dollar exchange rate has not yet been fully restored.

Our experience since 1960 illustrates dramatically how considerations relating to the state of a nation's balance of payments and international reserves can inhibit its efforts to promote maximum employment and growth at home. Our problem has been made especially difficult because the deficit in our balance of payments has continued despite the fact that most of the rest of the world has been in a boom while we have been in recession or, at best, in a state of incomplete recovery. Throughout this period the economies of most of western Europe have been operating close to capacity levels. This has justified relatively high interest rates in several European financial centers. Moreover, the high levels of real income in Europe have supported high levels of demand for imports, including imports from the United States. In this country, however, conditions have been far different. First we had the recession of 1960–1961, and then a weak and incomplete recovery. At no time during this entire period has unemployment been as low as 5 per cent, and most of the time it has been much higher. This was clearly a period in which the domestic objectives of promoting employment and growth called for an expansionary monetary policy, and expansionary fiscal policy, or both. Yet any actions which would effectively promote these domestic objectives would tend to widen the deficit in our balance of payments and perhaps lower confidence in the dollar.

A really aggressive, expansionary monetary policy became doubly dangerous. To the extent that it lowered interest rates and especially short-term interest rates, it would widen the gap between rates here and in western European financial centers and stimulate further outflows of short-term funds. And what started as capital outflows induced by interest-rate differentials could generate lack of confidence in the stability of the dollar exchange rate and induce capital flights. Moreover, any expansionary policy, whether monetary or fiscal, that succeeded in raising our level of employment and output would tend to increase our balance-of-payments deficit by increasing our imports. With larger real output and income we would buy abroad both more raw materials to feed our production processes and more finished goods. The deficit would be further widened if our attempts to raise employment and output induced further increases of wages and prices. Such increases of domestic costs and prices would tend both to decrease our exports and increase our imports.

In short, our problems of promoting maximum employment and growth have become much more complex during the past three years. Before 1960, our efforts to promote growth and employment by increasing aggregate demand were inhibited only by our desire to avoid the domestic consequences of price inflation. Now we face, in addition, urgent and restrictive considerations relating to our balance of payments. There can be little doubt that this has been a major reason for our failure to take more aggressive expansionary actions to remedy the high rate of unemployment and the slow rate of growth during the past three years.

Is this perplexing situation merely temporary? Will our balance-of-payments and international reserve positions soon improve enough to restore in large measure our freedom to concentrate on domestic objectives? Perhaps so. Recalling that only a few years ago many were forecasting a chronic dollar shortage, one hesitates to forecast a chronic dollar glut. For example, the current inflationary pressures in western Europe may rescue us at least temporarily by enabling us to increase our exports and decrease our imports. But we cannot afford to be too optimistic. I think it more likely that it will be a long time before our balance-of-payments and international reserve positions will again be such as to give us the degree of freedom to pursue domestic objectives that we enjoyed for so many years before 1960.

There are, of course, many types of actions relative to balances of payments and international reserves that can be taken to increase our freedom to pursue domestic objectives. In a later paper my colleague, Professor Machlup, discusses various measures of international economic cooperation that would help us and other nations promote economic objectives. But many of these, as well as unilateral actions that we might take, involve choices among objectives, some highly important, others less so. For example, we might restrict imports by raising tariffs or imposing quantitative restrictions, but this would invite retaliation and conflict with our objective of expanding world trade and increasing the efficiency of the world's economy. We could reduce sharply, or even discontinue, our foreign aid program, but this would conflict with our humanitarian and national security objectives. We might restrict outflows of short-term capital, long-term capital, or both, but this would present serious enforcement problems and also conflict with our objective of promoting the free international flow of capital to increase the efficiency of the world's economy. We might also secure greater freedom to follow expansionary domestic policies by lowering the exchange rate on the dollar, which would make our exports less expensive to the rest of the world and our imports more expensive. However, one can confidently predict that this action will not be taken by the United States except as an almost last resort. Some of the objections to devaluation of the dollar are largely emotional and should not be weighed heavily. But there are also very substantial objections to such an action. To mention only one, devaluation of this great key currency, which is a major component of the international reserves of other countries, could do serious damage to the world's monetary system. For this and other reasons I hope that the present exchange rate on the dollar can be maintained. But the cost of maintaining a fixed exchange rate can be excessive, and the cost can be in the form of unemployment and a sluggish growth rate.

Such, in brief outline, is the history of our efforts since World War II to promote maximum employment and production. Let us now look to the future and try to identify some of the major problems that we are likely to encounter in our efforts to promote stability and growth. One thing is clear: aggregate demand and actual output will have to rise far above present levels if we are to avoid excessive and growing levels of unemployment. Output is at the present time considerably below capacity levels and unemployment considerably above the minimum levels necessitated by labor-market frictions. On top of this, our capacity to produce is rising rapidly. The size of our labor force will grow at a rapid pace, especially during the second half of this decade as the large numbers born in the early postwar years reach the working age. Moreover, continuing technological change and other forces increasing output per man-hour will continue to reduce the demand for labor relative to output. Thus we face the problem of creating enough new jobs to absorb those now unemployed, the large group of new additions to the labor force, and those who will become disemployed by continuing technological advances. To achieve this will require continuously large increases in aggregate demand and actual output.

As we attempt to solve this set of problems we shall almost certainly continue to concern ourselves with multiple objectives and conflicts among them. We shall continue to debate about maximum employment, economic growth, price-level stability, and considerations relating to our balance-of-payments and international reserve positions. To devise and administer a combination of policies that will reconcile these objectives in some optimum way will challenge our ingenuity.

I believe that one of the most difficult tasks, as well as one of the most crucial, is that of securing a more satisfactory response of real output to increases of aggregate demand. We must find some way to avoid price increases and excessive wage increases while unemployment is still above the minimum levels necessitated by frictions in labor markets. Even perfect control of the behavior of aggregate demand will not enable us to reconcile our objectives satisfactorily if average money wage rates rise more rapidly than average output per man-hour. With average output per man-hour rising only about 2 or 2.5 per cent a year, more rapid increases of average wage rates inevitably raise costs of production and induce price increases.

Will this problem bedevil us in the future? For about three years now, prices have been almost stable and wage rates have been rising less rapidly than before. Some observers are much encouraged by this recent experience and believe this problem is now behind us. Perhaps it is. But we should remember that this has been a period in which unemployment has been continuously far above minimum levels. I fear that if we raise aggregate demand enough to eradicate this excess unemployment, we shall see a resumption of the upward wage-cost-price movements.

What specifically should we do to make real output more responsive to increases in aggregate demand and to avoid excessive wage increases while unemployment is still above minimum levels? There are few of us indeed who think it either politically feasible or economically desirable to have formal government control of wages, which would almost inevitably lead to detailed controls of the structure, as well as the general level, of wages and also to controls of prices. At the other extreme, there is little reason to expect success from a series of general, vague admonitions to unions and employers to "be good," "show restraint," and "remember the public interest." Such vague exhortations without any guiding principles are likely to be ineffective; and if effective, to be arbitrary and harmful.

In its report in January of 1962 the Council of Economic Advisers made a proposal which, I believe, deserves favorable consideration. Briefly, the Council proposed that before the beginning of each year the Council or some other responsible body should present a projection of economic conditions for that year and a proposed set of guidelines for wage behavior. These guidelines would indicate the type of wage behavior that would be most conducive to promoting the nation's economic objectives. Both the data and the guidelines would then be subjected to close scrutiny and full discussion by outside economists and by employers, unions, and others. Out of this process should come a better understanding of the facts and issues involved, and some guidelines for those who engage in wage bargaining and for those who judge the process and results.

One cannot forecast how successful such a program would be. To evolve suitable guidelines is no easy task. Moreover, there is no assurance that the behavior of employers and unions would be much affected. But surely the results would not be worse than those of the present situation, in which we have no guidelines based on rational economic analysis and little public understanding of the facts and issues involved.

We should also recognize that there are some types of unemployment that will not respond satisfactorily to even the most precise control of aggregate demand. I refer to the unemployed left in regions abandoned by industries or those whose occupations have been made obsolete by decreased demand for their products or by changes in technology. These unemployed obviously cannot find employment if aggregate demand is insufficient to create enough job opportunities, but there may be no level of aggregate demand which is desirable on other grounds that would draw them into employment. More specific measures are required to inform them of job opportunities, to retrain them, and to assist in their relocation. Our efforts of this type have been far too limited, but such programs as have been instituted have demonstrated their value to the country as a whole, as well as to the unemployed. They can make both employment and output respond more favorably to increases in aggregate demand.

In presenting the last two points I have argued that even if we achieved the most accurate control of aggregate demand for output, we would still need to adopt other measures to promote more favorable responses of employment and output. But we still have far to go before achieving such an accurate control of aggregate demand. There are several reasons for this, but I shall concentrate on only one: an inadequate use of fiscal policy for stabilization uses. Like many others, I believe we have relied too heavily on monetary policy and that our fiscal policies have lacked flexibility, timeliness, and power. This was true even before 1960, when our pursuit of domestic objectives was unhindered by considerations relating to our balance of payments. It applies with special force to situations such as we have had during the past three years, when considerations relating to our balance-of-payments and international reserve positions have been in the forefront. This has inhibited our use of monetary policy to increase aggregate demand and eradicate excessive unemployment, for an expansionary monetary policy aggressive enough to achieve these purposes would lower our interest-rate structure markedly, encourage capital outflows, and perhaps seriously damage confidence in the stability of the dollar in exchange markets. It may well be true, as many have alleged, that the Federal Reserve has allowed itself to be too much inhibited by these international considerations. Yet these dangers are indeed real, and I am convinced that in this environment the Federal Reserve could not safely have adopted monetary policies expansionary enough to achieve its domestic objectives. What has been needed for some time now is an expansionary fiscal policy in the form of tax reduction, an increase in government expenditures, or both—measures that would increase aggregate demand without necessitating decreased interest rates. But we have not yet had a tax reduction, and such increases in government expenditures as have occurred were adopted largely for other reasons and have been too small to induce the necessary rise of aggregate demand. For all this, we have been paying and continue to pay a high price in terms of excessive unemployment and a gross national product tens of billions below capacity levels.

If fiscal policies are to contribute more toward promoting our economic stabilization objectives, we shall have to solve several difficult problems. One is to achieve more general agreement both within and outside the government that the promotion of economic stability should be a major objective of fiscal policy. This is not to say that economic stability should be the only objective of our tax and expenditure policies. We must continue to be concerned with equity in the distribution of tax burdens, the social usefulness of the government's substantive programs, the allocation of resources between the private and public sectors, efficiency in both sectors, and so on. But these other important objectives are not irreconcilable with that of promoting economic stability, and we need to make sure that our concern for them does not lead us to downgrade or neglect our stabilization goals.

We shall also have to achieve a better understanding, both within and outside the government, as to the types of fiscal policies required to promote economic stability. As indicated earlier, this involves repudiation of a fiscal rule that still commands the loyalty of many influential people—the rule of an annually balanced budget. Many still believe that the appearance of a large budget surplus should always be countered by a tax cut or an increase in government expenditures, and that a large budget deficit should always be eradicated by tax increases or decreased government expenditures.

One must respect the basic motivations of those who advocate an annually balanced budget; they seek to promote fiscal responsibility and efficiency in government. I only wish that this simple and easily understood rule of thumb would indeed give us the results we seek. But the fact is that it will often produce or accentuate economic instability. Deficits will often occur when aggregate demand for output is inadequate. Tax increases or decreases in government expenditures at such times will magnify the inadequacy of demand. Also, surpluses in the budget may often occur when aggregate demand is excessive. Tax cuts or increases in government expenditures at such times would accentuate inflationary pressures. Thus the simple rule of an annually balanced budget is unacceptable. However, as this rule is abandoned we shall have to develop and secure general understanding and acceptance of new principles to promote fiscal responsibility and efficiency. This will be difficult, but it is both possible and essential.

As we achieve greater understanding and more general agreement as to the types of fiscal policies that will best promote our objectives, the timeliness and flexibility of fiscal actions should be improved. Congress itself may be able to move more quickly and appropriately, with less delay and controversy. And it might delegate to the President, with appropriate instructions and safeguards, limited powers to change taxes, expenditures, or both.

Now for the summing up. Our attempts to promote economic stability in the period since World War II can, I think, be judged a qualified success. We have avoided a major depression; our recessions have been shallow and short; our real output has grown markedly; and since 1951 the rate of price increases has been kept within tolerable bounds. But we have no reason for complacency. The record to date has left much to be desired. We have not yet reached enduring solutions to basic problems relating both to objectives and to methods of implementation. We have not yet adjusted to our new international economic position that has emerged as the economies of other industrialized countries have recovered and prospered, freedom of international capital movements has been restored, and our balance-of-payments and international reserve positions have deteriorated. We cannot foresee other environmental changes that the future will bring, but it is safe to predict that they will be numerous and important. For example, technological changes will almost certainly continue to be rapid and important. The whole international monetary mechanism built around gold exchange standards may prove to be defective and to require far-reaching reforms, if it is not to interfere with our efforts to promote economic stability. And it may well turn out, as Per Jacobssen of the International Monetary Fund has warned us, that in the coming years economic forces will be predominantly toward deflation rather than inflation. We must be prepared for the possibility that the task of promoting economic stability will become more difficult rather than less so. This task is well begun, but it is far from finished.

Selection 8

The National Debt—Do We Owe It to Ourselves?

ABBA P. LERNER

From Everybody's Business, *by Abba Lerner (Michigan State University Press, 1961), pp. 104–114. Reprinted by permission of Michigan State University Press.*

When an editor of a newspaper or a cartoonist runs out of ideas, he can always call attention to the "national debt." The cartoonist can show the citizen being crushed by an enormous burden. The editorial writer will express himself arithmetically. Since nobody knows what is meant by a million dollars, let alone two hundred and ninety billions of dollars, the arithmetic can be very impressive. For example, he might ask how long you thought it would take you to pay off the national debt if you were given a full-time job of repaying it at the rate of one dollar every second. Years? Maybe hundreds of years? Not so easy. To pay out two hundred and ninety billion dollars at one dollar per second for seven hours a day working three hundred days a year would take about 40,000 years. And at the end of the 40,000 years would the national debt have disappeared? On the contrary, all this repayment would not even have begun to make a dent on the compounding of the debt into really astronomic trillions of trillions of dollars. It would take a *thousand* people each paying out a dollar a second just to pay off the interest so as to stop the debt from growing any bigger than the accumulated unpaid interest.

On Mondays, Wednesdays, and Fridays the editorials frighten us with these unimaginably large numbers and tell us that the country is being destroyed by the tremendous national debt. But on Tuesdays, Thursdays, and Saturdays the same editorial page will remind us that we are enjoying a higher standard of living and greater prosperity than ever before. If we remembered Monday's editorial on Tuesday, we might wonder how we are able to manage so well in spite of the national debt and whether this could possibly be because we owe it only to ourselves.

Editorials dismiss the notion that we owe the national debt to ourselves as too ridiculous to deserve further analysis, and continue their arithmetical exercises. But when the scoffing and the arithmetic are over, the question still remains, "If we do not owe the national debt to ourselves, to whom *do* we owe it?" To this there is no answer. There is *nobody else* to whom we owe the debt. The national debt is a debt which the people in the United States owe, through the government, to the holders of the government bonds who, with some insignificant exceptions, happen to be the people in the United States. No matter how funny it may seem to some, we don't owe it to Germany or Japan or Russia or any other country. We do, as a nation, owe the national debt to ourselves.

Our owing it to ourselves has important consequences. First, there is no analogy between the national debt and a private, personal, or business debt. If I have a personal debt, I am that much poorer. The man to whom I owe this debt can ask me to pay it at some time. If I pay him, it is a sacrifice on my part, and it may come at an extremely inconvenient time. The payment of my private debt means, for a time, consuming and enjoying less than I would otherwise be able to. I may have to tighten my belt.

But if part of the national debt is repaid, it is not true that the nation has to tighten its belt. The productive resources of the country are no less; the amount of goods produced is not diminished. What happens when a part of the national debt is repaid is that some money is taken from some of the inhabitants of the country and is given to others. The nation as a whole does not have to consume any less than before.

The analogy between personal debt and national debt is false because a personal debt is really an *interpersonal* debt—a debt of one person to another. The proper analogy to a personal debt is an *international* debt—a debt of one nation to another. The paying nation then does have to tighten its belt. But, it must be impressed upon the reader, a national debt is completely different, and repaying it does not involve any tightening of the national belt.

This would not sound so surprising if we remembered that there is the same difference when national and personal debts are *incurred*. When I incur a *personal* debt, the borrowed money enables me to consume more than I produce and earn myself. This is not true of *national* debt. Since the lenders are also inhabitants of the country, the borrowing of national debt only means a transfer among consumers and investors within the country (including the government as a consumer or investor on behalf of the public). The borrowing does not enable the nation to consume more than it produces. It does not allow the nation to loosen its belt in the first place, and that is why it does not force it to tighten it again when the debt is repaid.

Yet it would be false to give the impression that the national debt doesn't matter at all. It is important to distinguish between the imaginary effects and the real effects of the national debt and to deny only the imaginary effects. But to many people the denial of imaginary effects looks like a denial of *all* the effects. This is sometimes the fault of those who deny the imaginary effects in using unnecessarily strong language. They tend to speak rather like a person whose twisted ankle has been exaggerated by rumor into a near fatality. He is tempted to say, "Why, it's nothing at all!" He doesn't really mean it is nothing at all; a twisted ankle can be extremely painful. He merely means to say that the other story is quite false. In the same way, to deny the imaginary effects of national debt is not to imply that there are no real effects to be concerned about.

The first imaginary effect I want to deal with is the notion that national debt is a national impoverishment. People speak as if the United States is poorer by two hundred and ninety billion dollars, the size of its national debt, just as any individual is poorer by the amount of his personal debt. To show his "net worth" in his balance sheet, the individual must subtract his debts from his assets. The mistake in applying this procedure to the nation is in forgetting that every debit has a credit.

If anybody owes money, there is somebody to whom the money is owed. This is always the case; there are no exceptions. The wealth of the nation includes the net worth of all the individuals in it, yet the nation is never poorer on account of a private debt by one individual in the country to another. This is because although the debt must be subtracted to get the figure for the net worth of the debtor, it must be added to get the figure for the net worth of the creditor, and the two items cancel when they are added in to show the wealth of the nation. And when the debt is paid, again the nation is not impoverished because the creditor receives all the money that the debtor pays, and the two opposite aspects of the transfer are equally part of the account of the nation.

All this seems to be very well understood by almost everybody, *but only for private* debt. Yet it applies in exactly the same way to public debt. For every dollar which you and I as residents of the United States owe, through our government, to the owners of the national debt, there is a corresponding creditor who owns a United States debt certificate of one kind or another. When we total the debt, it is our duty, if we do not want to mislead, to total the credit, too. And if we count both, they cancel out.

While it is common for only the debit side of the national debt to be counted, I don't know of anybody who has counted only the credit side. But it could be said with equal logic, or rather illogic, that the United States is *richer* because among the things which Americans own are two hundred and ninety billions of national debt—in the form of first-class, gilt-edged securities guaranteed by the United States Government. You can repeat the arithmetical exercises of the editorialist and see how long it would take to count this part of our *wealth*. This, of course, would be just as silly as doing the opposite. The United States is not any richer on account of the national debt than it is poorer because of it. Against the credit there is a debit, just as against the debit there is a credit.

It is commonly stated that the national debt will lead the United States to bankruptcy. What does this mean? A person is bankrupt if he cannot meet the demands of his creditors, is brought into court, and declared bankrupt by a judge. He then knows that if he were to borrow any more money without warning the lender that he has been declared bankrupt, he could be sent to jail. It is perfectly clear that this couldn't be done by any judge to the United States. In the first place, the United States Government can always legally meet its obligations by creating legal-tender money—and it is not illegal for the government to do that, even though it is illegal for anybody else. And in the second place, if for any reason the United States should refuse to meet any of its obligations, nobody has the power to do anything about it.

At this point the argument is generally changed and bankruptcy is declared to mean not bankruptcy, but a decline of the purchasing power of the dollar, which is quite a different and very serious thing. The national debt can contribute to a rise in prices, which means a fall in the value of the dollar. It may do this to a large or to a small degree, or not at all, depending upon many other factors, but we can only deal with this problem if we are clear that we are talking about changes in prices, and not about bankruptcy. I shall discuss such effects on prices later in dealing with the possible *real* effects of the national debt.

Another bogey is the question of what will happen when the national debt has to be repaid. One answer to this we have already given. If and when the repayment is made, the repayment will be received by people in this country and there will be no net deprivation involved for the country as a whole. The other and perhaps more important answer is that there is no date when the national debt has to be repaid. It is, of course, true that government bonds fall due at certain dates, but this does not mean that new bonds cannot then be issued—often even to the very same people. Many owners of national debt would be very unhappy if they could not reinvest the money all over again in the same way and for the same reasons as before.

There is a possibility of a sudden loss of confidence in the government, and people may then want to cash in their government securities. It would be a very serious matter for any individual or corporation if it were suddenly called on to pay off its creditors in cash; but not for the government. This is because the government can create the money people want to hold instead of government bonds, and everybody can be happy. People who want cash can have cash, and as long as they only want to hold onto the cash, no harm is done; the government may also feel happier because it now does not have to pay so much interest. On the other hand, people may not want to hold the money, but may decide to spend it. This could cause some real troubles which will soon be considered.

Another argument—and this one is quite a tear-jerker—is that the national debt will be a burden on our grandchildren, and that it is immoral and heartless of us to allow posterity to pay for our profligacy. This is nothing but an echo of the original confusion. If the debt should be repaid by our grandchildren, it is hard to see who would be receiving the repayment except our grandchildren. There is, besides, the other question as to whether or not the debt would in fact ever need to be paid off, and this applies just as much in our grandchildren's time as in the present.

At this point in the argument, there usually comes a bothersome snag phrased something like this: "Well, the mere existence of the national debt may not be so dangerous, nor is it likely to be called on to be repaid, and if it is we can probably handle that all right, but what about the *interest* on the national debt?" This is perhaps the most curious of all the objections. The man who brings it up is like a woodsman miraculously still sitting up in the air on a tree branch which he has sawed off. If the mere existence of the national debt doesn't do any harm then there is no need for one to worry about the interest. One way of dealing with the interest is to borrow more money with which to pay it. All that would happen then is an increase in the national debt—which, it has been demonstrated, itself does no harm.

The apparent danger, or wickedness, or the profligacy of a person's spending more than his income—from which we get the false analogy to national debt—seems to apply doubly in the case of interest. I am not only failing to repay my debt, but I am actually getting deeper into debt meeting the interest. This is so doubly dangerous a course of behavior for any individual that it is twice as hard to remember that it is different for the nation. But the logic applied previously cannot be avoided here. The interest payments, just like national debt repayments, are paid by Americans to Americans. The nation as a whole is not impoverished by the interest payments any more than it is enriched by them.

Another objection we have to meet is that of the person who points to the physical destruction during the wars when most of our debt was incurred, and our failure to build houses or factories during these times. This lack is pointed to as constituting the real burden of the national debt on our children and grandchildren. The answer to this is that the destruction and failure to reconstruct will undoubtedly be a very real burden on our children and grandchildren. Many people in Europe and other parts of the world have suffered cruelly because of it. But the destruction would have been just as bad if no debt whatever had been contracted in connection with it. If all the money spent by governments during the wars had been raised by taxes, but there had been the same destruction and failure to replace factories, houses, and other useful things, there would be exactly the same real burden on our children and grandchildren. It is on the wars that we must blame the destruction, not on the debt.

A more respectable argument is made by certain accountants who say that we have a false picture of how rich we are. They have suggested that every person, in order to get an accurate picture of how well off he is, ought to subtract from his visible wealth his share of the national debt. This would be a sound corrective for people who are prone to underestimate the burden of that part of his taxes, present and future, which is due to the existence of the national debt. But taxpayers are more prone to exaggerate than to underestimate these burdens, and even for those who underestimate this burden, counting their share of the national debt as an *additional* burden (however they may compute what is their share) would constitute a preposterous overcorrecting unless (a) they had counted the expected taxes as zero and (b) it was in fact decided to impose enough in taxes to pay off the whole national debt. Such calculations would not, however, make many people believe that the wealth at their disposal is really curtailed, so that not much harm could be done apart from the political effects of exaggerating the debit side of the national debt. This would hamper the development of rational policies in the incurring and the repayment of national debt.

After all this, it may seem as though we should just forget about the national debt, and simply write it off. If we owe it to ourselves, why bother to keep an account? The reason why the national debt cannot be simply repudiated is that the "we" does not indicate exactly the same people as the "ourselves." Although, *as a nation,* we owe the national debt to ourselves, some people owe more than they are owed; other people are owed more than they owe. Those who have a larger part of their wealth in the form of government securities than others would be hurt by a cancellation or repudiation of the national debt. We have persuaded them in the name of patriotism (often with dubious arguments) to buy government securities. It would be bad faith not to honor the national obligations to those who responded to the appeal.

Certain left-wingers maintain that the existence of national debt makes the rich richer and the poor poorer. They point out that most of the national debt belongs to rich people. (This, of course, is not surprising; after all, that is one reason why they are rich.) But everybody, including the poor, is taxed to provide the interest payments to the rich. On the other hand, right-wingers and rich people point out that rich people are taxed much more heavily than the poor and that government bonds are owned by very large numbers of people most of whom are by no means rich.

Actually these two arguments more or less negate each other. The rich as a class would lose more than the poor from a repudiation of the bonds, but they would also gain more than the poor from the reduction in taxes that would accompany it. Just as a rich man gets much more in interest, he also pays much more in taxes than a poor man. All in all, it is doubtful whether the existence of the national debt has any appreciable effect on the relationship between the rich and the poor.

Now let us discuss the *real* effects of the national debt. The mere *existence* of the national debt has an effect on total spending. The people who own the national debt feel richer because of it and therefore they spend more money. Whether the extra spending is good or bad in its effect depends upon what the economy needs. If the economy is in a state of depression because there is not enough spending, then the extra spending brought about by the national debt is a good thing. It results in better business, more employment, and a higher national income. But if there is enough spending to begin with, so that there is no depression, or if there is already too much spending so that the economy is suffering from inflationary pressures, the extra spending brought about by the national debt is a bad thing. It creates inflationary pressures or it increases them.

One way to stop people from spending too much is to increase taxes so that they have less money left to spend. This would not *really* impoverish them, whatever the individual taxpayer may feel about it, because all that the extra taxes would do would be to take away the extra money with which people were bidding up prices in trying to buy more than was available. After they pay the taxes, although they would be *spending* less, they would still be *buying* just as much as before but at lower prices. Only the *inflation* would be reduced by the extra taxation, not the quantities of goods and services that the public could actually obtain.

Nowadays governments for various reasons have to undertake large expenditures. There is at the same time so much expenditure for private consumption and private investment that if it were not for heavy taxes there would be too much spending and inflation. Since the existence of the national debt causes

·xtra consumption, there must be more taxation to avoid inflation. Such addi-ional taxation, although it does not constitute a subtraction from real income, loes have harmful indirect effects which are discussed in Chapter XIV.[1]

Even though it would be immoral to repudiate the national debt now that we ıave it, would it not have been better if we had not incurred it in the first place ınd so avoided these harmful indirect effects? What if the government had not ;pent the money, or if it had raised the money by taxing instead of borrowing?

The answer is that our national income would have been less all throughout ıistory, and not only by the amount of the national debt but by a multiple of hat amount. Whenever the government (or any business or anybody else for hat matter) spends money, income is created for the producers of what is ›ought. The income thus created results in more spending by those who have ·eceived it, and this in turn creates extra income for still others, so that the total ncome is increased by several times the initial increase in spending. The $290 ›illion of government spending (which was financed by the borrowing that built ıp the national debt to its present size) has thus resulted in contributing several imes that amount to our total national income up to date—perhaps a thousand ›illion dollars. Without this two hundred and ninety billion dollars of government ;pending, and if no other spending had taken its place, we would have been in ı really bad way. Some of the spending we could very well have done without, ›ecause there was at certain periods too much spending, which resulted in nflation. But without the income created directly and indirectly by the $290 ›illion of government expenditure, we would have suffered from much longer ınd much deeper depressions throughout our history. Not only would we have :onsumed less over the period, but there would have been less investment, too. Ve would today have fewer and poorer factories and roads and houses than we ıave. In real terms we would be much poorer, not richer.

Let us now suppose that the national income had been maintained all through ıistory *without* creating any national debt—that private companies and corpora-ions had spent money instead of the government, with the same effect in main-aining income, consumption, and investment; so that the real wealth of the :ountry—its productive equipment—would be the same. We would then have no ıational debt. Would we be any better off?

Not at all. The expenditures by corporations and businesses and individuals vould have built up private claims to wealth in exactly the same way that they ıave been built up by the national debt. American citizens would now own an xtra two hundred and ninety billion dollars in shares of General Motors and ›ther corporations. These shares would make them feel just as rich as govern-nent securities do (or perhaps richer, inasmuch as dividend payments are gen-rally higher than interest payments on national debt). We would therefore have he same extra spending or more. There would be exactly the same inflationary ›ressures and it would be just as necessary for the government to levy heavy axes to prevent the inflation.

Our heavy taxes are made necessary by our great accumulation of private

[1] [The reference is to Lerner.]

claims to wealth. These have the same effects whether they are in the form of national debt or whether they are in the form of ownership of property in businesses and corporations and houses. It is the ownership of claims to wealth which makes people spend more, and if this would otherwise lead to too much spending, there has to be more taxation to protect us from inflation. The blame lies not with the existence of national debt as such but with the existence of *any* claims to wealth.

This is, of course, no argument against increasing our national wealth. The benefits from an increase in wealth are certainly very much greater than the difficulties that accompany the increase.

Our conclusion is that we *do* owe the national debt to ourselves, that it is not a terrible danger to our society as imagined by those who think it is the same kind of thing as personal or interpersonal debt, and that there are some real problems, but that these problems are due to the existence and growth of *any* private claims to national wealth rather than of that part of private claims to wealth that are the counterpart of the national debt. These difficulties are connected with taxation, which is the subject of the next chapter.[2]

---

[2] [The reference is to Lerner.]

Selection 9

Inflation

W. CARL BIVEN

From Economics and Public Policy *(Columbus, Ohio: Charles E. Merrill Books, Inc., 1966), pp. 148–177. Reprinted by permission of Charles E. Merrill Books, Inc.*

An important problem for public policy in the postwar years, and one that is likely to recur in the future, is the problem of inflation, our subject in this chapter.

Although there is not complete agreement among economists as to a precise definition of the term, it is sufficient for our purposes to begin with the understanding that we mean by *inflation* a rise in the general or average price level. We should emphasize the word "average" for we do not mean by price stability that all prices are constant. That the prices of some goods are rising while the prices of others are falling is to be expected. Changes in relative prices are a normal part of a well-functioning free enterprise system. It is the price mechanism that coordinates the intentions of producers and consumers in a competitive economic system and provides for the allocation of resources according to consumer desires. The mechanism is a vital part of the system. We are speaking here of fluctuations in the general price level.

Measurement of Inflation

While this definition of inflation is relatively simple, the problems of actual measurement of price-level variations are considerable. Furthermore, the difficulties are dramatized by the practical importance which price indexes assume in society today. "Monetary policy aimed at price stabilization may be considerably affected by monthly movements in the CPI [Consumer Price Index] or WPI [Wholesale Price Index]; similarly, wages affecting millions of employees are adjusted regularly on the basis of changes in the 'cost of living,' as reflected in the CPI, and many business purchase contracts, particularly for fixed capital assets, include provisions for escalation in line with the WPI or one of its segments. Society in general, as consumers, savers, or producers, make decisions based upon past and anticipated movements in the price level."[1]

---

[1] Harold M. Levinson, "The Postwar Inflation," in Joint Economic Committee, *Staff Report on Employment, Growth, and Price Levels,* 86th. Cong., 1st. sess., 1959 (Washington, D.C.: Government Printing Office, 1959), p. 106.

There are three main indexes used in the United States to measure changes in the price level: the Consumer Price Index, the Wholesale Price Index, and the GNP Implicit Price Deflator. The total bundle of output in the economy includes such a diverse range of goods and services that a measure of the movement of the over-all price of this bundle is, for some purposes, useless. It is necessary to develop an index that disaggregates, that applies to some portion of total output. The Consumer Price Index and the Wholesale Price Index are measures of this kind.

Consumer Price Index

The Consumer Price Index not only restricts itself to a measurement of variations in consumer prices, but also limits itself to variations in the cost of living for a particular class of consumers, as the official name of the index, "Consumer Price Index for Urban Wage Earners and Clerical Workers," suggests. The index was begun during World War I. "Despite many changes and improvements in statistical procedures, the revised CPI continues to be what it has always been —a measure of price change, and of price change only, in items purchased by urban wage and clerical workers for their own consumption. The major orientation of the index is toward its use in collective bargaining as a yardstick for measuring changes in real income of workers."[2] Since urban wage and clerical workers and their families comprised 56 per cent of the total urban population in 1960,[3] the index is broadly representative of changes in the cost of living for American families and, for this reason, it is widely used as representative of inflationary or deflationary trends in the economy.

The various consumer goods are obviously not of equal importance and an index which treated consumer goods in this way would be misleading. Variations in the price of thread do not affect consumer purchasing power to the same degree as do variations in the prices of housing and automobiles. Items in the consumer price index must be weighted, therefore, according to their importance in the consumer's budget. The mechanics of constructing the consumer price index involve the selection of a "market basket" of goods and services that is typical of the purchases of city wage earners and clerical workers during a specific base period, weighting the items in the basket, and computing the variations in the over-all price of this market basket over time. The most recently revised version of the Consumer Price Index which became effective in January, 1964, has about 400 items in the "market basket." The selection of the basket and the weighting of the items was based on surveys of consumer expenditures conducted in 66 metropolitan areas and urban places in 1960–1961. "Through December 1963, the index applied only to families of two persons or more. With the January 1964 index, the coverage has been extended to include single work-

[2] Sidney A. Jaffe, "The Statistical Structure of the Revised CPI," *Monthly Labor Review*, LXXXVII, No. 8 (1964), 916.

[3] *Ibid.*, p. 917, n. 5.

ers living alone. . . . The average size of families represented in the index is about 3.7 persons, and the average family income in 1960–1961 was about $6,230 after taxes. The average income after taxes of single persons represented in the index was about $3,560."[4] The base period for the index is 1957–1959.

There are several things that can lead to a bias in an index constructed in this way. First of all, the index does not take into consideration variations in quality. If the price of an item included in the basket remains unchanged while quality improves, the consumer obtains a larger amount of satisfaction for the same outlay, but this is not reflected in the index. Or, again, if the price of an item rises but quality improves in the same proportion, cost, relative to satisfaction, has remained constant but the index registers an increase in the cost of living. Failure to take quality changes into account introduces a bias into the index in an upward direction. A particularly important source of bias is a failure to adjust for a rise in the productivity of services. If the fees that doctors charge for office visits go up over time, for example, this is reflected in the index as an increase in the cost of living. Obviously, however, the benefits derived from such professional services also rise over time. Although the price of consultation may go up per visit, and be recorded in the index as a price increase, the cost of medical service in terms of benefits received may, in fact, be constant or even decline. Precisely how important the bias due to failure to allow for quality improvements is impossible to determine. Its existence suggests, however, that for a highly dynamic economy, in which rapid improvement is taking place in the quality of goods and the productivity of services, a constant CPI really means a falling price level and a gently rising CPI means a constant price level.

A second problem arises because the market basket, which is fixed in the computation of the index, may not be fixed in terms of consumers' actual market behavior. Even though the prices of goods and services in the basket of the base year increase, it may still be possible for the consumer to achieve the same level of satisfaction by switching his purchases to new products that have been developed or to old products, both of which may be available at a lower cost. Indifference among several options leaves the consumer with a method of circumventing or cushioning the effect of price rises as long as all items are not affected during a period of price increase to the same degree. This defect in the index can be removed by frequent adjustment of the composition of the market basket of the base period. As a matter of fact the basket is adjusted periodically. However, since the index was begun it has undergone only three major revisions and several interim adjustments. A comprehensively revised index was introduced in 1940, 1953, and 1964. Partial revisions were interspersed among these major revisions. "The recent revision, effective with publication of data for January 1964, is the first to be initiated by the Bureau of Labor Statistics on the principle that review and revision should be a regular part of the index program. In contrast, previous major revisions were carried through at long intervals and after

---

[4] Bureau of Labor Statistics, *The Consumer Price Index, a Short Description* (Washington, D.C.: Government Printing Office, 1964), p. 1.

drastic changes in the economy raised questions about the validity of the index measurement of price change. The Bureau hopes to review and revise the index at approximately decade intervals."[5]

WPI and GNP Deflator

The Wholesale Price Index is designed to measure the variation in prices of goods involved in the intermediate levels of the production process and excludes goods sold directly to government and consumers. It is heavily weighted in terms of raw materials, machinery, and equipment. A more comprehensive index than either the Consumer or the Wholesale Price Index is the GNP Deflator, whose coverage is comparable to that of the GNP. In addition to the items contained in the other two indexes, the GNP Deflator includes two additional and important segments of economic activity, construction and government. Both the Wholesale Price Index and the GNP Deflator, like the Consumer Price Index, suffer from the failure to allow properly for the complex pattern of quality changes. Furthermore, in the measurement of price change in the government sector, the GNP Deflator actually measures changes in the cost of inputs rather than changes in the prices of the services which the inputs provide. It does not take into account improvements in productivity of government workers. An increase in wages and salaries of government employees automatically means, therefore, an increase in prices as measured by the GNP Deflator. While it may be difficult to measure increases of productivity in the government sector, a failure to give any consideration to productivity improvements introduces an upward bias in the data.

The GNP Deflator is used, primarily, to deflate "money" GNP and provide data on the behavior of "real" GNP through time. Unlike the CPI and WPI, which are published on a monthly basis, the GNP Deflator is available only on a quarterly basis. For this reason the CPI and WPI are used more commonly even though the coverage of the GNP Deflator is more comprehensive.

The Historical Record

The three indexes are plotted for the years 1929–1964 in Figure 1. The three series move in a parallel fashion.

An examination of the figure is revealing with regard to the historical record of price fluctuation in the United States over the last three and a half decades. The beginning of World War II was the signal for an upward march in prices. From 1940 to 1945 the Wholesale Price Index rose by almost 35 per cent, the Consumer Price Index by almost 29 per cent, and the GNP Deflator by 39 per cent. This was to be expected. Modern nations do not fight wars without serious dislocations and, in comparison with previous experience, the World War II price rise was not unusual.

---

[5] Jaffe, *op. cit.*, p. 916.

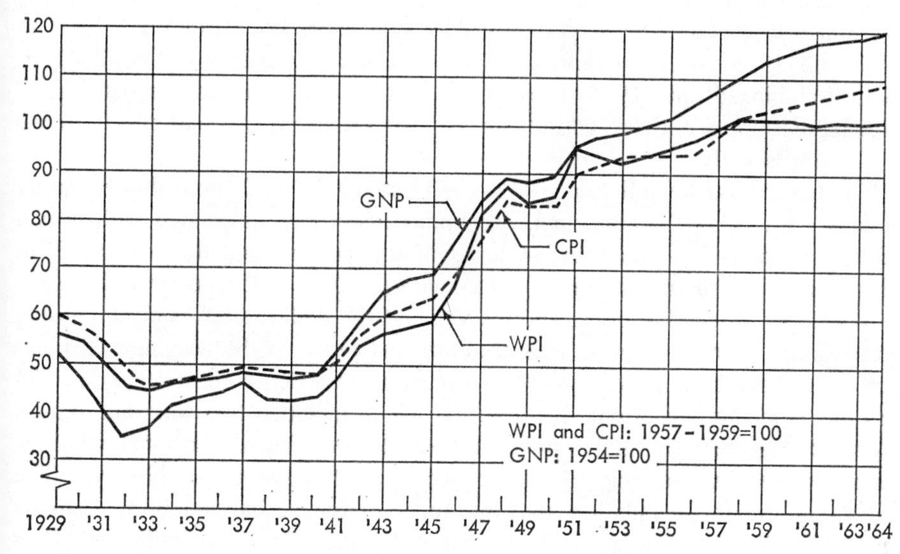

Source: Department of Commerce and Department of Labor.

Figure 1. CONSUMER PRICE INDEX, WHOLESALE PRICE INDEX, GNP IMPLICIT PRICE DEFLATOR, 1929–1964

In the postwar period the increase in prices is concentrated in three main periods: from the end of the war to 1948, from 1950 to 1953, and from 1955 to 1958. From 1958 to 1964, the Wholesale Price Index was stable. The Consumer Price Index and the GNP Deflator drifted upward gradually but at a slower rate than in previous postwar periods. In 1965 the Wholesale Price Index has started to rise, at a modest rate, for the first time in seven years. The Consumer Price Index has drifted upward at a rate slightly faster than that of the 1958–1964 period.

The increase in prices during the first two intervals cited is again traceable to causes associated with war periods. The 1945–1948 price rise is an aftermath of World War II. Due to the shortage of goods and the rationing imposed during the war, the nation accumulated a large amount of buying power in the form of liquid funds. At the same time the productive capacity of the nation, which had been drafted into the defense effort, had to be reconverted to peacetime production. The temporary imbalance between the spending power of the nation and its productive capacity caused prices to rise as soon as price controls were removed. From 1945 to 1948, the Wholesale Price Index rose by almost 52 per cent, the Consumer Price Index by almost 34 per cent, and the GNP Deflator by 30 per cent.

The first postwar recession began in the latter part of 1948. Both the Consumer Price Index and the Wholesale Price Index fell slightly in 1949; the former from 83.8 to 83.0 and the latter from 87.9 to 83.5.

With the start of the Korean War in mid-1950, prices started to rise again.

From 1950 to 1951 the Wholesale Price Index rose by over 11 per cent, the Consumer Price Index by 8 per cent. The Wholesale Price Index fell back in 1952 and 1953 but the Consumer Price Index continued to rise until 1953, when it stabilized until 1955. From 1955 to 1958 all three indexes rose again. This increase was not due entirely to excessive demand, a point to which we shall return shortly.

The two periods of inflation, 1945–1948 and 1950–1953, both due primarily to causes involving the abnormal, exogenous distortions associated with armed conflict, account for about three-fourths of the postwar inflation up to 1958. This point is worth emphasizing, for the understanding of the public with regard to what has happened to prices and the value of the dollar in terms of purchasing power is not always accurate. It is doubtful that much of the war-induced inflation could have been prevented. "The American experience from 1939 to 1953 was by no means exceptional for a period which included two wars and only a short interwar period; similar price movements have been associated with the dislocations and stresses of war and postwar years throughout our history."[6] The remaining amount of inflation, that due to other forces, has not been dramatic in amount. We are dealing here with what is called "creeping inflation." It is necessary to keep this in mind when discussing the effects of inflationary pressure if we are to have some sense of balance in discussing the problem. For the classic effects of inflation, such as the redistribution of income and wealth, are frequently dramatized by being placed in the context of the extreme case, hyperinflation. In such a condition confidence in money completely breaks down. A situation deteriorated to this degree occurs only with a rapid increase in prices. "Historical experience suggests that a marked 'flight from cash' does not usually begin unless prices are at least doubling every six months."[7] The entire war and postwar inflation is so far removed from this condition quantitatively as to involve a qualitative difference. This is even truer if the war-induced inflation is omitted. From 1955 to the present, a period closer to normal than the previous inflationary periods since the end of World War II, the Consumer Price Index has risen on the average less than 2 per cent a year. This is not a dangerous amount, particularly when upward bias in the index is taken into consideration.

It has already been said that the 1955–1958 inflation was partly due to vigorous demand but part was not.

> *Both 1955 and 1956 were boom years and there is nothing surprising about the behavior of the price indexes in this period. . . . The index of production reached its peak in December, 1956, but did not begin to decline definitively until October, 1957. Construction kept rising until December, 1957. Unemployment was in the neighborhood of 4 per cent for the first half of 1957 but started to climb in September. What is remarkable is that the price rise continued so long after the downturn. The indicators all be-*

---

[6] Levinson, *op. cit.*, p. 106.

[7] Martin Bronfenbrenner and Franklyn D. Holzman, "Survey of Inflation Theory," *American Economic Review,* Vol. LIII, No. 4 (1963), 644.

> *haved as in a normal recession, except the price indexes. Clearly, demand was falling but prices did not decline.*[8]

It is primarily because of this period, when, paradoxically, inflation persisted despite a lack of intensive, over-all demand pressure, that a substantial interest developed in reexamination of the causes of inflation. To this subject we now turn our attention.

Causes of Inflation

It is critical for purposes of public policy, of course, to understand the causes of inflation, for unless the causes are understood the proper solution cannot be applied. Three main types of inflation, differentiated in terms of what brings about the upward movement of prices, can be mentioned: demand-pull, cost-push, and structural inflation.

Demand-Pull Inflation

The traditional economic theory of inflation is of a demand-pull variety, a case of "too many dollars chasing too few goods." The particular form into which it developed in neoclassical thinking was in terms of the quantity theory of money. Allowing somewhat for oversimplification, the real and fundamental relationships in classical thinking, as we have seen in a previous chapter, are determined independently of the absolute level of prices. The absolute level of prices is determined by the quantity of money. Assuming in the equation, $P = \frac{V}{T} M$, full employment output and a constant velocity, for reasons already discussed in a previous chapter, there exists a proportional relationship between the supply of money, M, and the average price level, P. "By World War I, this particular, narrow version of demand-pull inflation had more or less triumphed. The wartime rise in prices was usually analyzed in terms of rises in the over-all money supply. And the postwar German inflation was understood by non-German economists in similar terms."[9] Some economists explained the inflationary process in other ways, but the prevailing thought was in terms of the quantity theory. "While most writers were too cautious to expect that the rise in prices would be exactly equal to the percentage excess of the increase in circulating media over available supplies of goods, surprisingly little attention was given to the underlying factors which would alter the velocity of monetary circulation in wartime."[10]

---

[8] Willard L. Thorp and Richard E. Quandt, *The New Inflation* (New York: McGraw-Hill Book Co., 1959), p. 96.

[9] P. A. Samuelson and Robert M. Solow, "Analytical Aspects of Anti-Inflation Policy," *American Economic Review*, Vol. L, No. 2 (1960), 178.

[10] John Lintner, "The Theory of Money and Prices," in Seymour E. Harris (ed.), *The New Economics* (London: Dennis Dobson, Ltd., 1947), pp. 504–505.

Instead of explaining an inflationary rise in prices in terms of a stock (the money supply), Keynesian theory explains it in terms of a flow (aggregate spending). The nucleus of the theory, essentially an extension of the model contained in *The General Theory,* was developed by Keynes in 1939 in *How to Pay for the War*. The argument simply states that if unemployed resources exist in the economy, an increase in spending will result, as a first reaction, in an increased utilization of factors and increased output. Once full employment is reached and bottlenecks appear, further expansion of aggregate demand leads to an increase in prices. In the phrase coined during the war, an "inflationary gap" appears.

In Figure 2 a total spending curve $(C + I + G)$ is presented. The quantities on the two axes are in real terms, that is, expressed in constant prices. Assume that the X_1 level of GNP is the level associated with full employment. At this full-employment level we have the maximum amount of goods available to consumers, investors, and government. The total spending curve shows, however, that the amount which all spenders wish to buy at the full-employment level of GNP exceeds the amount available. Buyers wish to purchase something in excess of 100 per cent of potential output. This situation easily develops in a war period when a large proportion of the nation's resources must be diverted to the production of war goods. The amount by which desired spending exceeds the value of potential output at current prices (*ab* in Figure 2) is called the "inflationary gap." Because desired spending exceeds capacity output, prices rise.

As we have presented the inflationary gap in Figure 2, the rise in prices will continue indefinitely unless something happens to reduce the excess spending. The gap will not close automatically unless the rise in prices in some way indirectly affects consumption, investment, or government and reduces the

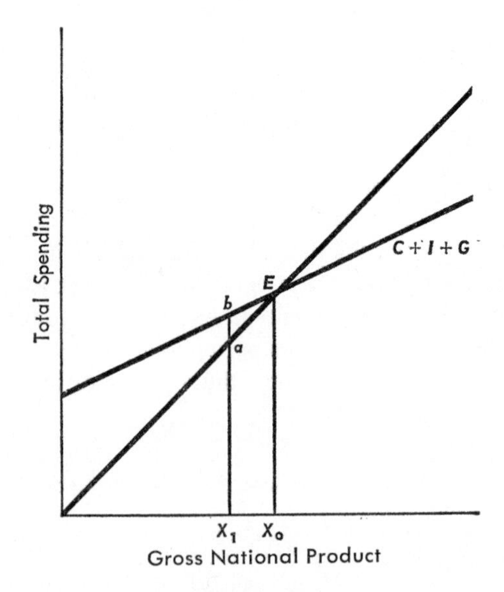

Figure 2

amount of desired spending to a level equal to output potential. It is possible for forces to go into operation, as a result of the price rise, to shift the $C + I + G$ curve downward. A progressive income tax, for example, may cause tax revenues to rise more rapidly than prices. This would result in less disposable income for all levels of real income and, in turn, reduce consumption spending. On the other hand, the indirect effects of the price rise could be to widen the gap. This would happen, for example, if consumers and investors attempted to anticipate price increases by intensifying consumption and investment spending. Whether or not the gap closes depends on the net indirect effect of the price rise on total spending.

The above explanation represents the simplest statement of the expenditures approach to inflation. While considerable work has been done on developing the model, such as recasting it in dynamic form, for our purposes the above is sufficient.[11] The method of closing an inflationary gap through public policy is to impose restraints on spending. This can be done through monetary and fiscal policy, or, in a critical situation, such as war, through a direct means such as rationing.

Cost-Push Inflation

Although the monetary theory of inflation and the expenditure approach differ considerably from one another, they both interpret inflationary pressure as generated on the side of demand, and they fall into the demand-pull variety of explanation. Another approach is to consider inflation as arising from the supply side due to pressure exerted by unions or firms independently of demand conditions. Cost theories of inflation have appeared at various times in economic history. "Cost inflation has been the layman's instinctive explanation of general prices increases since the dawn of the monetary system. We know of no inflationary movement that has not been blamed by some people on 'profiteers,' 'speculators,' 'hoarders,' or workers and peasants 'living beyond their station.' Cost-inflation reasoning underlay, for example, the various Statutes of Laborers which followed the medieval Black Death."[12] The cost theories that were developed in the postwar period are not totally new, therefore, but they represent an attempt to modify in a systematic way the demand-pull theory arising out of Keynesian analysis.

Wage Push

The more common version of cost inflation theory attributes inflation to union pressure for increased wages. The theory does not hold that all wage increases

---

[11] For a brief survey of postwar developments, see Bronfenbrenner and Holzman, *op. cit.*, pp. 602–607.

[12] *Ibid.*, p. 613.

are inflationary. If there is an increase in productivity, that is, an increase in output per man-hour, wages can rise without affecting unit cost of production. If a worker is paid $2.00 per hour, for example, and produces 20 units per hour, the unit labor cost is 10¢. If the wage increases to $3.00 an hour, but output also goes up to 30 units per hour, the unit labor cost remains constant. It is only when wage increases are not properly related to productivity increases that unit cost rises and the share of profits is reduced. It is not impossible that the relative share of labor and capital could be subject to adjustment so that the relative fall in profits would not set off a reaction on the part of management. Ordinarily, however, management would resort, when possible, to a price increase in an effort to protect profit's share of income.

The power of a union to push wages up is not unlimited but depends on the constraints which the economic conditions of the environment in which it operates impose. If the product demand curve which a firm faces, for example, is highly elastic—that is, the firm is involved in a highly competitive situation—the demand curve for labor, other things being equal, also tends to be elastic. In such a situation unusual wage demands are hard to satisfy without affecting the employment of workers and, possibly, the financial stability of the firm. When the firm's product demand curve is inelastic, on the other hand, increases in labor cost due to wage demands in excess of increases in productivity can be passed on to the customer more easily in the form of higher prices. It is generally agreed that firms in oligopolistic market structures provide a more favorable climate for wage demands since the relatively high degree of market control means less elasticity in the product demand curve.

The position of the union is again strengthened if bargaining is industry-wide rather than with the individual firm. This is true for competitive industries as well as those with a degree of market concentration. The aggregate demand curve for all firms together has a smaller degree of elasticity than the individual demand curve of the separate firms. An individual firm granting a wage increase in unison with other firms in the industry does not have the problem of incurring a competitive disadvantage as does a firm acting alone. The trend toward industry-wide bargaining, in whatever particular form it takes, has, generally speaking, strengthened the power of unions to exert pressure on wages in an upward direction.

Industry-wide bargaining not only means that unions are presented with less elastic product demand curves but also that the results obtained by one union in a certain industry can be more readily compared with those obtained in another. Rivalry among unions leads to attempts to emulate "neighboring strategic wage rates,"[13] and the result can be an upward push on cost. For example, an increase in wages in a "key" industry may be justified in terms of an increase in demand for the industry product—and a resulting increase in the demand for labor in that industry—or may be based on such factors as an above-average increase in productivity. In the first case an increase in wages would naturally reflect, then,

[13] A phrase used by Bronfenbrenner and Holzman, *Ibid.*, p. 618.

a relative shift in product demand in the economy; in the second case, the increase in wages could be made without an increase in labor cost. Unions bargaining with other industries may attempt to imitate the settlement obtained in the first industry in order to prevent "inequitable" differentials from arising. If these other industries have not experienced a relative increase in demand or have not had comparable increases in productivity, wage increases in these industries result in an upward push. Wages, in this case, are determined independently of demand or cost conditions in the particular industry but are based on the motive of removing differentials. Imitation of a key settlement leads to a "pattern" of agreements which have, in their total effect, an inflationary impact.

Identification Problem

It is difficult to distinguish cost from demand-pull in practice and it is easy to fall into a trap of identifying an inflation as cost-push when, in fact, excessive demand pressure is the cause. Just because wages are rising faster than increases in productivity does not necessarily mean that a given inflation is of a cost variety. In an intensive demand inflation, wages will eventually follow prices upward in a wage-price spiral as workers attempt to maintain their standard of living, but such an inflation does not originate with market power. It is sometimes suggested that identification can be made by reference to timing. If the price increase came first, it is a demand-pull inflation; if the wage increase preceded, it is a cost-push type.

> *The trouble is that we have no normal initial standard from which to measure, no price level which has always existed to which everyone has adjusted; so that a wage increase, if one occurs, must be autonomous and not a response to some prior change in the demand for labor. As an illustration of the difficulty of inference, consider average hourly earnings in the basic steel industry. They rose, relative to all manufacturing from 1950 on, including some periods when labor markets were not tight. Did this represent an autonomous wage-push? Or was it rather a delayed adjustment to the decline in steel wages relative to all manufacturing, which took place during the war, presumably as a consequence of the differential efficiency of wage control? And why should we take 1939 or 1941 as a standard for relative wages? And so on.*[14]

Because of the difficulty of gathering conclusive empirical evidence there is disagreement about the extent of cost-push inflation. While many economists feel that unions do have the power to cause inflationary pressure, others disagree or feel that the union pressure has been exaggerated. Albert Rees points out, for example, that for unions to be able to push up labor costs, which, in turn, are passed on by employers in the form of higher prices "assumes that customers will continue to take the same quantities of goods at higher prices. However, to the extent that employers meet customer resistance, they will tend both to reduce

---

[14] Samuelson and Solow, *op. cit.*, p. 183.

employment and to absorb cost increases; both of these reactions will check the spiral."[15] For unions to be able to obtain wage increases in excess of productivity would require action by monetary and fiscal authorities to maintain demand adequate to prevent unemployment. The cost-push phenomenon can exist, therefore, only in the context of inflationary monetary and fiscal policy. What appears to be a wage-push inflation, it is said, is, in the final analysis, a demand-pull inflation.

Sellers' Inflation

Some economists have argued that it is not only labor that can exert an upward pressure on the price level. Firms, it is said, can attempt to improve their share of the national income through price increases independently of union action. The terms "sellers' inflation" and "market power inflation" are broader terms than "cost inflation" and emphasize the efforts of all groups to increase price. In sellers' inflation, pressure originating in one industry can spread itself to other sectors. Higher price in one industry is higher cost to another, requiring a price increase in the second industry. The urge to imitate also acts as a transmission belt. In this process some industries are more important than others. In a controversial study of price increases from 1947 to 1958, Eckstein and Fromm found that steel had a key position in the upward movement. "The result is very striking: if steel prices had behaved like the rest of the index, the total rise from 1947 to 1958 would have been 14 points instead of the actual increase of 23 points, that is, the extraordinary behavior of steel accounted for 40 per cent of the rise over the 11 years."[16]

The argument that firms can originate inflationary pressure is related to the phenomenon of concentration of power in American industry. When prices are determined in a competitive market featuring a large number of buyers and sellers, the individual seller does not have much control, if any, over the price. The price, to the single firm, is given. A large proportion of production today, however, does not take place in purely competitive markets but rather in oligopolistic market structures consisting of a few, large firms. Such firms, because of their size and because they control a sizable proportion of output, do have the power to influence price. It is common to refer to prices determined in such an environment as "administered prices."

While much attention has been directed to the pricing policies of large firms in Congressional hearings and in popular discussion, it is quite difficult to develop a theoretical basis for the argument that large firms are, by themselves, a source of inflationary pressure. Traditional economic theory suggests that prices set by monopolists or oligopolists are higher, at any particular time, than prices determined under competitive conditions. It does not follow from this,

---

[15] "Do Unions Cause Inflation?" *Journal of Law and Economics,* Vol. II (1959), p. 89.

[16] Otto Eckstein and Gary Fromm, *Steel and the Postwar Inflation,* Joint Economic Committee, *Study of Employment, Growth, and Price Levels,* Study Paper No. 2, 86th Cong., 1st sess., 1959 (Washington: Government Printing Office, 1959), pp. 7–8.

however, that upward changes in price over time are necessarily different in the oligopoly case from what they are in competitive markets. In order to show a relationship between corporate bigness and a general price rise, one needs to show the precise mechanism through which size and inflationary pressure are related. One such attempt can be briefly summarized.

Surveys of pricing practices of large firms report that the most frequently mentioned objective in pricing on the part of large firms is to obtain a target return on investment.[17] The target return is looked upon as a long-run objective, that is, an average to be achieved over a number of periods, a rate of return on a "standard volume" of production. It has been held that target-return pricing lends itself to a pressure on prices in an upward direction.[18] The size of the target can be revised in an upward direction for reasons other than a change in demand. United States Steel, it is said, for example, justified its price increase of 1957 on the basis of a need for higher earnings to finance expansion and modernization.[19] Large firms may also raise the target, and the price, in order to protect declining profits during a recession when the firm operates at low levels of plant utilization.

It would seem illogical for firms to raise price in order to improve earnings in a period of constant demand and even more so in a period of declining demand when price decrease rather than increase has been the classical reaction. Given, however, the assumptions under which businessmen usually operate, it is said, such price behavior is not necessarily illogical at all. Businessmen apparently believe that the industry demand curve is inelastic. The mechanics of price elasticity suggest, of course, that when a demand curve is inelastic, a rise in price increases total revenue while a drop in price decreases it. For an elastic curve, the opposite is true. If the decision maker thinks that the demand is inelastic, an increase in price is a logically consistent type of behavior when an increased rate of return is felt to be necessary. An objection raised to this type of argument is that if profits in an industry can be improved by climbing up an inelastic demand curve, why had the option not been exercised before? If, on the other hand, the industry curve is not really inelastic, but businessmen only think it is, why do they not eventually learn the true condition in the market?

Galbraith has argued, in a frequently discussed article, that a price increase by oligopolistic firms in a period of slack demand may seem to represent market power inflationary pressure but, in reality, simply be a lagged response to a previous demand variation. A modern economy consists of firms operating in a variety of market structures. At one extreme are the cases of pure competition, such as agriculture; at the other are cases of oligopoly, such as the steel industry.

---

[17] See A. D. H. Kaplan, J. B. Dirlam, and R. F. Lanzillotti, *Pricing in Big Business: A Case Approach* (Washington: The Brookings Institution, 1958). See also R. F. Lanzillotti, "Pricing Objectives in Large Companies," *American Economic Review*, Vol. XLVIII, No. 5 (1958), 921–940.

[18] See John M. Blair, "Administered Prices: A Phenomenon in Search of a Theory," *American Economic Review*, Vol. XLIX, No. 2 (1959), 431–450.

[19] *Ibid.*, p. 442.

In competitive markets an increase in demand results immediately in a price increase. "The adaptation of prices to the increase in demand is automatic: in the nature of the competitive markets, no individual has the power to halt the adaptation."[20] In the case of oligopolistic markets the "response pattern" is different. An increase in demand first expresses itself as an increase in orders. "The price adaptation must come later and as a result of specific entrepreneurial decision."[21] If the oligopolistic firm was at a profit-maximizing position before the increase in demand, it is no longer in that position after the increase. In order to arrive at the new profit-maximizing position, it must raise the price. For oligopolistic firms, however, there is a time-lag in the response resulting temporarily in "unliquidated monopoly gains." One of the reasons for the imperfect adaptation is the fear that high profits will invite demands by unions for higher wages. Since wage increases are regarded as irreversible, the oligopoly delays the response to an increase in demand. When the union is able to press through a wage increase at the next round of wage negotiations, however, the oligopoly's reason for not raising price no longer exists. The wage increase followed by a price increase is interpreted by the general public as evidence of market power inflationary pressure when, in fact, what has actually occurred is a delayed response to a previous increase in demand.

Galbraith's hypothesis is consistent with the belief of many economists that large firms, because of changing price at infrequent intervals, slow down the rate of inflationary rise in a period of excessive demand.

Structural Inflation

A third type of inflation which associates price increases with causes involving a mixture of those identified in the first two types is called *structural* inflation. This type of inflation is associated with the name of Charles L. Schultze.[22] Schultze's hypothesis has several parts, but the most well known is his argument that inflation can arise even if there is not an excess of aggregate demand, relative to productive capacity, provided there is a shift in the pattern of demand. Schultze begins by pointing to the fact that price movements in our economy are not symmetrical; that is, prices move upward but are rigid in a downward direction. Should there be a shift in the composition of over-all demand, this could lead to a price increase in the industry or industries experiencing an

---

[20] J. K. Galbraith, "Market Structure and Stabilization Policy," *Review of Economics and Statistics,* Vol. XXXIX, No. 2 (1957), 126–127.

[21] *Ibid.,* p. 127.

[22] See C. L. Schultze, "Recent Inflation in the United States," Joint Economic Committee, *Study of Employment, Growth, and Price Levels,* Study Paper No. 1, 86th Cong., 1st. sess., 1959 (Washington: Government Printing Office, 1959). For an appraisal of Schultze's significant paper, see Hyman P. Minsky, "Employment, Growth and Price Levels: A Review Article," *Review of Economics and Statistics,* Vol. XLIII, No. 1 (1961), 1–12; and Romney Robinson, "Employment, Growth, and Price Levels, The Joint Economic Committee Report," *American Economic Review,* Vol. L, No. 5 (1960), 996–1010.

expansion of markets. Wages can also go up as the industries affected attempt to attract labor. If prices and wages were flexible in other parts of the economy, this shift in demand would not cause a problem. If prices fell in those industries from which demand has shifted, this downward movement of prices would counterbalance the rise in those sectors experiencing more intensive demand. Because of the downward rigidity of prices, however, this compensating movement does not take place. Prices rise in the expanding industries and remain constant, or approximately so, in others. The net effect is a rise in over-all prices.

In addition, the increase in prices can spread to industries experiencing constant or declining markets. Rising prices in one sector may mean rising input costs to the demand-deficient sectors. These sectors may, accordingly, raise price in order to protect profit margins. "When the composition of demand changes rapidly," as Schultze has said, "prices of semi-fabricated materials and components tend to rise, on the average, since price advances among materials in heavy demand are not balanced by price decreases for materials in excess supply. Wage rate gains in most industries tend to equal or almost equal those granted in the rapidly expanding industries. As a consequence, even those industries faced by sagging demand for their products experience a rise in costs. This intensifies the general price rise, since at least some of the higher costs are passed on in prices."[23]

The inflation that results from these changes in the composition of demand and the peculiar reaction of the economic structure to this pressure does not neatly fall into either the demand-pull or cost-push type of inflation previously discussed. "Rather it originates in excess demands in particular sectors and is spread to the rest of the economy by the cost mechanism. It is a characteristic of the resource allocation process in an economy with rigidities in its price structure. It is impossible to analyze such an inflation by looking only at aggregate data."[24] Schultze attributed much of the 1955–1957 inflation to pressure originating in the capital goods sector.

There is another strand to the Schultze hypothesis. Schultze argues that there has been in the postwar period an increase in the relative importance of overhead cost.[25] This increase is due to two factors. First of all, there has been an increase in technical and supervisory personnel at the expense of direct labor.

> *Between 1947 and 1957 total nonfarm employment rose by slightly more than 8 million. More than 6 million of this rise was accounted for by increased employment of overhead type personnel, and only 1½ million by direct labor. . . . Within manufacturing the shift to overhead labor has been even more radical. All of the postwar gain in employment has taken place among nonproduction workers. From 16 per cent of total employment in 1947 they have risen to 23 per cent in 1957. Between 1955 and 1957 the relative growth was even more rapid, as nonproduction worker*

---

[23] Schultze, *ibid.*, p. 1.
[24] *Ibid.*, p. 2.
[25] See particularly Chapter 4, *ibid.*, pp. 78–96.

employment rose 10 per cent while production worker employment was declining.[26]

A second reason for the rise in overhead cost has been that the ratio of relatively short-lived equipment to long-lived plant has risen substantially, with the result that depreciation as a proportion of total cost has tended to increase.

The effect of a rising proportion of fixed cost in the total cost mix is to make average cost more sensitive to variations in output. Had expansion in overhead cost been matched by expansion in output, average cost could have been held in line. However, this was not the case. "The distinguishing characteristic of the 1955–1957 period was a continued investment boom in the face of stable aggregate output; all industries were expanding their capacity and their employment of overhead personnel, yet only a select few were enjoying a concomitant rise in sales. Finding themselves faced with shrinking margins during a period of supposed prosperity, it is quite likely that producers attempted to recapture some part of their increasing costs in higher prices."[27]

The Phillips Curve

The alternative theories of inflation and their implications for public policy can be contrasted by reference to Figure 3, which contains the so-called "Phillips curve," named after the economist with whom it is primarily associated.[28] The curve relates per cent change in the money wage rate on the vertical axis with unemployment expressed as a per cent of the labor force on the horizontal axis. Examining data for the United Kingdom over the period 1861–1957, Phillips found a relationship between money wage changes and unemployment.

The curve in Figure 3 shows a relationship in which the percentage change in money wages rises with decreases in the amount of unemployment. Suppose that, in the figure, OM represents full employment, which in the United States would amount to 3 or 4 per cent. According to the curve depicted here, an OM rate of unemployment would be associated with an ON percentage increase in money wages. A money wage increase is not, as we know, necessarily inflationary. As long as wage increases are in line with productivity gains, unit labor cost is constant and there is no upward pressure on prices. Let us suppose, however, that the average increase in productivity amounts to OS. According to the United States experience, this would be about 2.5 to 3 per cent. If this were the case, the desired level of unemployment, OM, would be associated with a money wage increase that is in excess of productivity gains and, therefore, inflationary. In order to hold wage increases in line with increases in productivity, an unem-

---

[26] *Ibid.*, p. 80.

[27] *Ibid.*, p. 91.

[28] See A. W. Phillips, "The Relation Between Unemployment and the Rate of Change of Money Wage Rates in the United Kingdom, 1861–1957," *Economica,* Vol. XXV, No. 100 (1958), 283–299.

ployment level of *OT* would have to be tolerated. The cost of price stability would be, therefore, an excess of unemployment above the 3 to 4 per cent level of the amount *MT*.

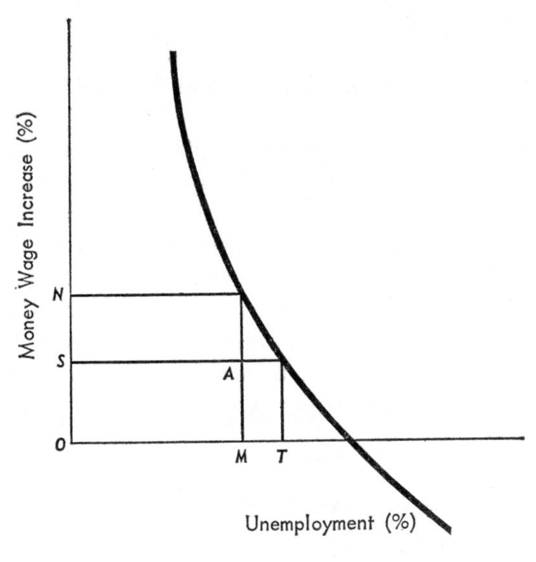

Figure 3

In terms of public policy it is important to know the position of the Phillips curve. If the curve intersected point *A*, both full employment and price stability would be possible. Full employment, *OM*, would be associated with a money wage increase of *OS*, a rate of change consistent with productivity improvement. If the curve lies to the left of point *A*, again full employment and price stability would be consistent objectives. It would be possible, through monetary and fiscal policy, to restrain inflation but without doing so at the cost of excess unemployment. If, on the other hand, the curve lies to the right of point *A*, as it does in the curve presented here, a trade-off problem exists. One would have to choose between price stability and some unemployment as a national goal or full employment with some inflationary pressure.

If unions and firms are not able to exert inflationary pressure and if inflation is due solely to excess demand, then the Phillips curve lies to the left of point *A*. The curve might, in fact, lie on the horizontal axis, or possibly below it, as unemployment decreases and you move from right to left for unemployment greater than *OM*. Only when you reach *OM*, and labor is in short supply, does the wage rate rise. If pressure on the wage rate appears as unemployment decreases because of bottlenecks due to imperfect mobility of labor and because of some limited capacity on the part of unions to exert pressure, the curve may lie above the horizontal axis but still to the left of *A*. If pressure groups, unions or large firms, have the power to exert strong influence on prices, however, the curve lies to the right of point *A*. The same thing is true if changes in the composition of demand occur and price increases in the demand-intensive sector are not offset by price declines in other parts of the economy.

We do not have enough information at the present time to determine the position of the Phillips curve precisely, but an attempt by Samuelson and Solow to fit a Phillips curve to American data is interesting. Using data going back to the beginning of the century, they found a consistent pattern. "Wage rates do tend to rise when the labor market is tight, and the tighter the faster."[29] However, the pattern was not the same for all periods. For the first two decades of the century, "manufacturing wages seem to stabilize absolutely when 4 or 5 per cent of the labor force is unemployed; and wage increases equal to the productivity increase of 2 to 3 per cent per year is the normal pattern at about 3 per cent unemployment."[30] From 1946 on, however, the pattern is different. "The annual unemployment rate ranged only narrowly, from 2.5 per cent in 1953 to 6.2 per cent in 1958. Within that range, as might be expected, wages rose faster the lower the unemployment rate. But one would judge now that it would take more like 8 per cent unemployment to keep money wages from rising. And they would rise at 2 to 3 per cent per year with 5 or 6 per cent of the labor force unemployed."[31]

Support by Monetary and Fiscal Authority

Even if the power of unions and large firms to cause inflationary pressure is conceded, it seems likely that, in order for undue pressure on the wage rate and the price level not to lead to unemployment and a slowdown in economic activity, some cooperation on the part of the monetary authority is necessary. A higher level of prices means that a larger supply of funds is needed to finance the increased money transactions. If the monetary authority refuses to ratify the higher level of prices by an expansion in the money supply, tightness in credit markets will eventually appear, with an adverse effect on the level of economic activity. An expansionary policy on the part of fiscal authorities may also be necessary. Some economists have argued that the Employment Act, reflecting a national policy of concern for full employment, in effect provides a guarantee for pressure groups that steps will be taken by the monetary and fiscal authorities to prevent cost pressure from leading to unfavorable results. "The crux of the matter," Bach has said, "is that the issue of income distribution (money and real) is shifted from the traditional textbook fragmented market place to a politico-economic arena in which the monetary-fiscal authority may be only one of several powerful groups. . . . Once the enormous potential power of monetary-fiscal expansion is widely recognized and its use generally accepted, the pressure groups will have little to lose from intermittent or con-

---

29 Samuelson and Solow, *op. cit.*, p. 189.

30 *Ibid.*

31 *Ibid.*

tinuous efforts to improve their individual income positions through wage-price pressures in the market place and through direct pressures on government for income-raising measures. . . . In a modern 'democratic' state, it would be a remarkably insulated and politically insensitive monetary-fiscal 'authority' indeed that would consistently permit the development of unemployment rather than expand purchasing power (and raise prices) to maintain total output and employment."[32] The fear that too strong a social guarantee of full employment may remove one of the important reasons for wage and price restraint has led to a variety of policy suggestions by some economists ranging from the rather extreme view that government ought not to guarantee full employment to the more moderate recommendation that the Employment Act ought to be amended to include explicitly the objective of price stability.

Implications for Public Policy

After reviewing the literature on the subject of inflation, one is left with the conclusion that there is not a well-formed consensus among economists about its causes. "Various theories of the inflationary process may preliminarily be thought of as constituting a spectrum," as Schultze has said. "The place of any particular theory in that spectrum depends on what it postulates about the likelihood of significant and sustained increases in prices without the prior and continuing stimulus of rising demands for commodities and factors of production. The greater the degree of 'independence' one assigns to price and wage decisions, the closer one is to the 'cost-push' end of the spectrum; and, of course, vice versa."[33] Perhaps no one theory is satisfactory for any given period of price rise but rather a mixture of forces is at work. Market pressure and the tensions caused by structural factors can both be operative at the same time. In addition, while aggregate demand may not be excessive during a period of price increase, inflation may still be due, in part, to congestion developed during a previous period of expansion, the impact of which, however, is delayed because of lags in reaction time.

Confusion about the causes of inflation hampers the policy maker, of course, since a rational solution cannot be applied unless one knows the source of the problem. A solution appropriate to one type of inflation may be inappropriate to another type. Since there is disagreement over the cause of inflation, there is also disagreement about its remedy.

Inflations which are caused by excessive aggregate demand are susceptible to control by the standard application of monetary and fiscal techniques. If an inflation is caused, however, by dramatic shifts in the composition of demand, even though aggregate demand is not excessive, general monetary and fiscal controls are obviously not appropriate. To apply restrictive pressures to the entire econ-

---

[32] Reprinted from G. L. Bach, "Monetary-Fiscal Policy Reconsidered," *Journal of Political Economy,* Vol. LVII, No. 5 (1949), 388, by permission of the University of Chicago Press.

[33] Schultze, *op. cit.,* p. 18.

omy when demand is not generally excessive is like firing a shotgun blast when a precisely directed rifle shot is needed. The penalty for such misdirected action is to reduce the growth rate for the entire economy just to lessen price pressures in a particular sector. The proper solution is selective monetary or fiscal control aimed at the specific pressure point; that is, credit restraint or budget action directed toward specific industries.

This solution, on the other hand, is filled with difficulties. In the first place, to restrict deliberately the pressure in a sector of the economy reacting to changes in the composition of demand is to interfere with the normal behavior of the allocation process. Shifts in the pattern of demand are supposed to lead to price and wage increases as a normal way of drawing the factors of production into an expanding industry. It is not the price increase in the expanding sector that is the problem; it is the failure of prices to drop in those sectors which are experiencing a decrease in relative demand that causes the rise in the average price level. In the second place, the application of monetary and fiscal controls in a selective way gets us involved in detailed and discriminatory regulation by administrative action that has implications for economic freedom which make many people uncomfortable. The Federal Reserve has, at present, regulatory power over credit used in the stock market and has had in the past, during the war emergencies, selective power over the control of consumer credit. But the Board, under the leadership of Chairman Martin, has resisted receiving the power of selective control in more normal times on the basis that this involves more control than is consistent with the operation of a free enterprise system.

If, again, inflation in the 1955–1957 period can be explained, in part, as Schultze has suggested, by an increase in the ratio of fixed to total cost, an interesting question arises as to the proper way of dealing with such a situation. As fixed cost becomes more important in the cost structure, average total cost becomes more sensitive to variations in output. Average cost rises noticeably as output declines and falls as output increases. It would be interesting to know whether or not this phenomenon is really important. "If it is, then over-all monetary-fiscal policies are effective as price regulators—except that they work in reverse."[34] An expansionary monetary-fiscal policy would increase output, lower average cost, and, paradoxically, relieve pressure on prices. A restrictive policy, on the other hand, would aggravate an inflationary situation by preventing firms from reaching the higher levels of output where average costs are lower.

If inflation is caused by market pressure exerted by unions and large firms, several alternative approaches could be taken. Monetary and fiscal controls cannot touch the source of the trouble directly but, as has already been pointed out, some economists hold that these controls can provide a climate within which market pressure can be exerted only at the penalty of unemployment. Defendants of this position argue that government guarantees of full employment help to fix the Phillips curve in a position to the right, and that if such guarantees were removed, the curve would shift to the left as labor came to realize that

[34] Robinson, *op. cit.*, p. 1006.

excessive wage demands are penalized by unemployment. That such a result would follow cannot be guaranteed. It is possible that organized labor would not react in the expected manner. It is also possible that a low-pressure economy would develop other complications that would counteract the effects due to a lessening of labor militance. As Samuelson and Solow have pointed out, "a deliberate low-pressure policy to stabilize the price level may have a certain self-defeating aspect. It is clear from experience that interregional and inter-industrial mobility of labor depends heavily on the pull of job opportunities elsewhere, more so than on the push of local unemployment. . . . A low-pressure economy might build up within itself over the years larger and larger amounts of structural unemployment. . . . The result would be an upward shift of our menu of choice, with more and more unemployment being needed just to keep prices stable."[35] Even if it were certain, however, that doses of unemployment would reduce union pressure on prices, the question arises as to how politically feasible such a policy is. Galbraith is probably correct when he says that "no policy designed to promote the stabilization of prices has any chance of permanent success if it depends, either directly or indirectly, on deliberately continued unemployment."[36] In addition, it could easily be that the opportunity cost of preventing inflation in this way is considerably more burdensome than the harmful effects of a creeping inflation.

If the use of monetary and fiscal control as a constraint on market power inflation is ruled out, then the number of economists who would agree that inflation of this type is possible is considerably increased. In such a situation, we are left with some type of administrative action as the only alternative, if the price rise is, in fact, to be controlled. Direct control of wages and prices involves too much government involvement to be feasible politically and administrative problems too enormous to be acceptable in practical terms. A variety of milder forms of government involvement has been suggested.[37] One approach, labeled by cynics as "jawbone policy," involves simply an appeal by government to unions and business for restraint in bargaining and price setting. A more formalized approach would require large firms to give notice of an intention to increase price to a public commission created for the purpose. Such a notice would generally be followed up by hearings on the matter of whether or not the price increase is justified and is in harmony with the public interest. This could be accompanied by a fact finding by the commission concerning the need for the increase and the effect on the over-all economy. The purpose of such an approach is, of course, to rally public opinion. Public opinion can be focused on the problem through simple publication of the findings or, in a more vigorous approach, the findings can be accompanied by an advisory opinion. This ap-

---

[35] Samuelson and Solow, *op. cit.*, pp. 190 and 193.

[36] J. K. Galbraith, "Administered Prices and Monetary-Fiscal Policy," in Lawrence S. Ritter (ed.), *Money and Economic Activity* (2nd ed.; Boston: Houghton Mifflin Company, 1961), p. 366.

[37] See the discussion in Emmette S. Redford, *Potential Public Policies to Deal with Inflation Caused by Market Power,* Joint Economic Committee, *Study of Employment, Growth, and Price Levels,* Study Paper No. 10, 86th Cong., 1st sess., 1959 (Washington, D.C.: Government Printing Office, 1959), pp. 8–29.

proach differs from direct regulation only in a matter of degree. Government does not itself regulate but through its instrumentality creates a pressure designed to achieve the same result.

Aside from the problem of the relation of such involvement to economic freedom, there are many administrative problems arising out of this approach. Should both wages and prices be subject to such scrutiny, and, if so, precisely what wages and prices should be included? The rise of the price of chocolate malts at a corner drugstore obviously should not be processed through such a screening procedure, but what is the standard for determining what industries or firms are important enough to be included? If increases in prices are to be considered, should failure to reduce price also be a matter of consideration? This would be a much more difficult problem, for it would extend the range of coercion from a purely negative type—telling people they cannot do something—to a positive type—telling people they should do something. Also, if the prevention of price increases were the sole responsibility of such a commission, the commission would be activated only when cases were brought to it; if exerting pressure for downward adjustments were also its responsibility, the commission would have to actively seek out cases at issue. The increased complexity of the problem is obvious. Yet if Schultze is right in his analysis of recent inflation in the United States, inflation is caused ultimately by the fact that as demand shifts, the average price level rises because price increases in the demand-intensive sector are not matched by decreases in the demand-scarce sector.

Another administrative problem of major proportions would be the difficulty of selecting criteria for judging price and wage increases. Something as formal as the precedents established historically in the case of public utilities would seem to be too cumbersome to administer on a wider basis. But less precise criteria, such as historical earnings, are bound to involve a commission in arbitrary judgment that leads to intensive controversy. This, in fact, is the main problem of public regulation; it inevitably involves, in the end, arbitrary judgment. Again, how would the problem of shifting demand be handled? Price increases in industries experiencing more intensive demand are a normal part of resource allocation. To prevent them is to interfere with this basic process. On the other hand, judging just how much increase is called for requires a rather sophisticated knowledge about the intensity of the shift which our present tools of analysis do not provide.

In addition to these administrative problems there is the further difficulty that the government would become a punching bag for pressure groups from all sides. The creation of a formal procedure for processing notices of price increase would make the matter of income distribution, of determining the relative shares to go to various groups, a political matter as well as an economic one.

The Wage-price Guidelines

Probably because a formal approach to supervision of wage and price increases is filled with so many difficulties, attempts to deal with the problem have been rather informal and *ad hoc* in character. A word should be said about the wage-price "guidelines" approach initiated by the Kennedy Administration and continued by the Johnson Administration. The guidelines were first proposed in the 1962 *Economic Report of the President*[38] and reaffirmed in subsequent reports. The introductory statement of the guidelines rejected mandatory controls and attempted to tread lightly over the sensitive area of private and public interest.

> *Mandatory controls in peacetime over the outcome of wage negotiations and over individual price decisions are neither desirable in the American tradition nor practical in a diffuse and decentralized continental economy. Free collective bargining is the vehicle for the achievement of contractual agreements on wages, fringes, and working conditions . . . . Similarly, final price decisions lie and should continue to lie in the hands of individual firms. It is, however, both desirable and practical that discretionary decisions on wages and prices recognize the national interest in the results.*[39]

The method for getting recognition of the national interest is the opinion of an informed public which "can help to create an atmosphere in which the parties to such decisions will exercise their powers responsibly."[40] The guidelines are developed to provide the public with a basis for judging whether a particular wage-price decision is in the national interest.

The basic criteria for noninflationary wage increases center around the productivity measure. If wage increases are not in excess of increases in productivity, labor costs do not rise and prices can remain constant without the relative share of wages and profits being affected. Increases in productivity are not, however, uniform across an economy. The experiences of industries and firms during any time period are not the same. In order to obtain a rule applicable to all industries, the guidelines appeal to the trend rate of over-all productivity increases.

> *The general guide for noninflationary wage behavior is that the rate of increase in wage rates (including fringe benefits) in each industry be equal to the trend rate of over-all productivity increase. General acceptance of this guide would maintain stability of labor cost per unit of output for the economy as a whole—though not of course for individual industries.*
>
> *The general guide for noninflationary price behavior calls for price reduction if the industry's rate of productivity increase exceeds the over-all rate—for this would mean declining unit labor costs; it calls for an appropriate increase in price if the opposite relationship prevails; and it calls for stable prices if the two rates of productivity increase are equal.*[41]

Wage increases, then, would be uniformly related to an average increase in productivity, but differences in productivity experience would be adjusted for by price variation.

---

[38] See *Economic Report of the President, 1962,* pp. 185–190.
[39] *Ibid.,* p. 185.
[40] *Ibid.*
[41] *Ibid.,* p. 189.

Productivity gains would serve as a guide but must be modified by other considerations. The rule must be flexible enough to allow wage and price to serve their function as resource allocators and to allow for adjustment of historical inequities. The *Economic Report* specifically mentions four modifications of the general rule:

> *(1) Wage rate increases would exceed the general guide rate in an industry which would otherwise be unable to attract sufficient labor; or in which wage rates are exceptionally low compared with the range of wages earned elsewhere by similar labor, because the bargaining position of workers has been weak in particular local labor markets.*
>
> *(2) Wage rate increases would fall short of the general guide rate in an industry which could not provide jobs for its entire labor force even in times of generally full employment; or in which wage rates are exceptionally high compared with the range of wages earned elsewhere by similar labor, because the bargaining position of workers has been especially strong.*
>
> *(3) Prices would rise more rapidly, or fall more slowly, than indicated by the general guide rate in an industry in which the level of profits was insufficient to attract the capital required to finance a needed expansion in capacity; or in which costs other than labor costs had risen.*
>
> *(4) Prices would rise more slowly, or fall more rapidly, than indicated by the general guide in an industry in which the relation of productive capacity to full employment demand shows the desirability of an outflow of capital from the industry; or in which costs other than labor costs have fallen; or in which excessive market power has resulted in rates of profit substantially higher than those earned elsewhere on investments of comparable risks.*[42]

The problem of getting adherence to the guidelines has been left, for the most part, to the prestige of the Presidential office and the public support that this office can rally.

There are obviously a number of problems associated with the guidelines. Although the pressure on participating parties is less than would result from direct wage and price control, yet, in the final analysis, the individual right to make decisions and the demands of the public good are still brought into direct confrontation if the guidelines are effective at all. But beyond this basic problem the administrative complications are sizable. Expecting firms to drop price, when the rules of the game call for such action, without any further pressure than informed public opinion seems unrealistic. Public opinion can be awakened when a crisis is provoked by the threat of inflationary increases in crucial industries, but it seems far-fetched to expect public opinion to be activated in all the innumerable cases where firms refuse to lower price. The 1964 *Report* itself says, in reporting on two years' experience with the guidelines, that "it is fair to say that large industrial enterprises thus far have not widely heeded this advice."[43]

The four modifications of the basic guidelines are certainly appropriate. An

---

[42] *Ibid.*

[43] *Economic Report of the President, 1964,* p. 120.

inflexible rule would be unworkable. But the problem of finding a factual basis for deciding when changing patterns of demand call for an exception and by how much or when historical inequities justify a modification are considerable.[44] Since the criteria for justifying exceptions to the rule are hard to express in an exact way, any decision can be rationalized in terms of the exceptions and the general rule is thereby endangered.

For all the difficulties associated with the guidelines, however, it will be interesting to follow the developments of this approach. As the Council of Economic Advisers has said: "It is desirable that labor and management should bargain explicitly about the distribution of the income of particular firms or industries. It is, however, undesirable that they should bargain implicitly about the general price level."[45] Whether or not the guidelines will make a genuine contribution toward constraining labor-management negotiations in such a way as to prevent inflationary pressure from resulting is yet to be determined.

Accepting Inflation

The fact that inflation is so difficult to control and that the alternative cost in terms of freedom, growth, and employment is so high has led some economists to the conclusion that we simply ought to accept it as a fact of life and learn to live with it. Sumner Schlichter represents this type of viewpoint. He suggests that in a dynamic economy instability of prices is natural.

> *It would be strange if growth could occur without pronounced effects upon the price level. As a matter of fact, sometimes rapid growth has been accompanied by falling prices; at other times rapid growth has been accompanied by rising prices. Periods when the price level was stable have been exceptional. If one examines the decade changes in the wholesale price level beginning with 1798 and ending with 1958, one finds only four decades out of sixteen in which the net movement of the wholesale price level, up and down, was less than 10%. One finds eight decades in which the net movement was more than 20%. In eight decades the movement of the price level was upward, and in eight decades it was downward. . . . The economy has demonstrated rather impressively that it has been capable of operating satisfactorily under rising, falling, or stable prices.*[46]

In the present period, with the existence of strong unions, inflation may have to be accepted if the goals of full employment and adequate growth are to be fulfilled. "Inflation may or may not *cause* the benefits, but, in the present state of our knowledge, it is an inseparable by-product of the processes that produce important benefits."[47]

---

[44] For a discussion of the guidelines, see "Those Perplexing Guideposts," *Fortune,* September 1962, pp. 219–224.

[45] *Economic Report of the President, 1962,* p. 188.

[46] "Slow Inflation: An Inescapable Cost of Maximum Growth Rate," *The Commercial and Financial Chronicle,* March 26, 1959, p. 36.

[47] "On the Side of Inflation," *Harvard Business Review,* Sept.–Oct. 1957, pp. 28 and 30. (Emphasis in original.)

In addition, Schlicter argues, the bad effects of inflation are frequently overstated. For example, the idea that creeping inflation inevitably leads to galloping inflation, he says, "is a widely disseminated bit of nonsense. All of the important industrial countries of the free world have had creeping inflation during the last few years, yet in every case except Switzerland and Belgium the rise in the consumer price index was less in the period 1953–1957 than in the period 1948–1953."[48] Furthermore, he argues, the effects of inflation are partly beneficial. Some upward flexibility provides a safety valve for the strain that inevitably develops in the intense bargaining over relative shares by labor and capital and so contributes to industrial peace and the avoidance of strikes.

There is great appeal to this line of thought. If one were to speculate about the way in which the United States will handle inflation in the future, however, the very complexity of the problem and the level of success of our past experience in dealing with it suggest that Americans will resist recognizing the possibility that we have a dilemma involving a trade-off problem, alternate between attacks on inflation and attacks on unemployment, and end up with an in-between solution, recurring departures from full-employment, and, on the average, mild inflationary price behavior.

DISCUSSION QUESTIONS

1. Distinguish between monetary policy and fiscal policy. Under what conditions might monetary policy be ineffective as a stabilization mechanism?
2. Explain why the goal of an annually balanced federal budget is inconsistent with the use of discretionary fiscal policy for stabilization purposes.
3. Discuss some of the possible real costs of federal deficit financing. How relevant are these arguments if the economy is operating much below full employment?
4. Explain how, during the late 1950's and early 1960's, domestic stabilization policy was constrained by the chronic balance of payments deficit.
5. Distinguish between demand-pull, cost-push, and structural inflation. What policy actions might be appropriate to combat each type of inflation?

SELECTED REFERENCES

Bator, Francis M., "Money and Government," *Atlantic Monthly,* April 1962.

Heller, Walter W., *New Dimensions of Political Economy,* New York: W. W. Norton & Co., Inc., 1967.

Schultz, George P. and Robert Z. Aliber (eds.), *Guidelines: Informal Controls and the Market Place,* Chicago: The University of Chicago Press, 1966.

Smith, Warren L. and Ronald L. Teigen (eds.), *Readings in Money, National Income and Stabilization Policy,* Homewood, Illinois: Richard D. Irwin, Inc., 1965.

---

[48] *The Commercial and Financial Chronicle,* March 26, 1959, p. 37.

PART 5

THE DISTRIBUTION OF INCOME

Economic theory tells us that, with pure competition and fully employed resources, each unit of resource will be paid a price equal to the value of the additional output produced by using that unit of resource. Thus, the prices which land, labor, or capital will bring in the market depend on two things: productivity and scarcity. The income of a resource supplier will depend on the amount of resources he owns and offers for hire and the price these resources bring in the market. However, the prices of resources are often not competitively determined. Some professions may be able to restrict entry to their ranks and therefore make their services scarce. Others may be able to establish a price in the market that will limit the amount hired. Also, the hirer of resources may have sufficient market power to hold down the resource price. Some resources, such as land in the center of a city, may be naturally scarce and receive a high reward; others, such as the labor services of small-scale tenant farmers in the South, are found in excess supply and therefore receive only a meager reward.

For the total economy, income distribution is strongly influenced by government activity. An increase in government spending will spur economic activity and increase profits relative to wages. A policy of high interest rates gives a windfall gain to people who earn interest income. An inflationary policy redistributes income from creditor to debtor and from receivers of fixed incomes to receivers of flexible incomes. A decision to grant a government contract to a particular firm in a particular region affects interindustry and interregional income distribution. In addition, many types of government and private transfers have important effects on income distribution. These include social security benefits, unemployment compensation, veterans' benefits, farm program payments, gifts and endowments by individuals and corporations, retirement programs, and many more. Also, government taxation policies have similar effects. Allowable deductions to certain industries or groups of individuals will significantly affect their income.

In addition, income distribution is affected by inheritance, education, and luck. The person who inherits property is assured an income whether he works or not; in addition, he is assured a good education and access to the best jobs. A person born into a middle-income family may not inherit much wealth but is assured of receiving a good education and access to a good job. A person born into a low-income family has no assurance of an adequate education or of access to a good job. Because of his environment, background, and training, he may not aspire to acquire them.

In some very general way the average level of wages, salaries, rent, and interest may reflect marginal productivity. But the income received by any individual or group in society is strongly influenced by social position, education, market power, political power, the level of economic activity, and the amount of private or public transfers received. Profit is what is left over after all other claims against output are paid. It, too, depends on management or entrepreneurial skill and the level of economic activity.

The article by R. H. Tawney gives the arguments for a more equitable distribution of wealth. Liberty is meaningless if the individual does not have the power to act on his own behalf and to resist unwarranted actions of others. A person cannot be free if he is subject to the arbitrary authority of a few who control wealth. Thus, he argues, freedom and liberty will be increased with a more equal distribution of wealth because wealth confers power on the individual which allows him to act and to resist.

A concentration of political power is greatly feared. The Constitution provides many safeguards to keep political power widely dispersed and to guard against the arbitrary use of such power. At the time the Constitution was established, economic power was not a major problem. This was a nation of farmers, shopkeepers, and small manufacturers. Traditional economic theory was based on an economy of small firms. In such an economy the power of any one firm would be small. In our present economic system large firms are the rule, not the exception, and a large amount of the country's wealth is controlled by a small proportion of the population.

The article by Robert J. Lampman explains how income is distributed and redistributed in the United States, gives recent figures on income distribution, distinguishes between poverty and inequality, and looks at recent trends in both. He concludes that inequality has not changed much in recent years but that poverty has been retreating. The article by Theodore W. Schultz discusses various policy approaches to the poverty problem.

Selection 10

The Conditions of Economic Freedom

R. H. TAWNEY

From R. H. Tawney, Equality, *4th ed. (London: George Allen and Unwin, Ltd., 1952), pp. 174–190. Reprinted by permission of George Allen and Unwin, Ltd. and Barnes & Noble, Inc.*

Power is the most obvious characteristic of organized society, but it is also the most ambiguous. The discussion of the problems which it presents has been prejudiced by the confusion of the reality with its forms, and by the concentration of interest upon certain of its manifestations to the exclusion of others. A realistic treatment of it has suffered, in particular, from the habit of considering it primarily, or even purely, in political terms. Power is identified with political power, and political power is treated as a category by itself. It is regarded as possessed by individuals as members of a state, or as exercised by a state on behalf of its members.

Political authority is a genuine form of power, and is, for both good and evil, an important form. But it is one form, not the only form. In reality it is one species of a larger genus. Recent political thinkers have shown that sovereignty is not merely the attribute of the State, but is shared, in different degrees, by other forms of association; and, if sovereignty is more extensive than the authority of the State, power is obviously more extensive than sovereignty and the rights conferred by it. The river exists before it is canalized so as to carry the barge and drive the mill. The fact of power exists independently of the right to power. Sometimes, indeed, it exists in spite of it.

The Definition of Power

Power may be defined as the capacity of an individual, or group of individuals, to modify the conduct of other individuals or groups in the manner which he desires, and to prevent his own conduct being modified in the manner in which he does not. Everyone, therefore, possesses some measure of power, and no one possesses more than a measure of it. Men exercise only the power that they are allowed to exercise by other men, whom, when their clothes are off, they much resemble; so that the strong are rarely as powerful as they are thought by the weak, or the weak as powerless as they are thought by themselves. Its ultimate seat is—to use an unfashionable word—the soul. It rests on hope and fear, the belief of those who submit to it that its agents can confer upon them benefits, from food to spiritual peace, and inflict evils, from hunger to misery of mind. Hence its foundations vary from age to age, with the interests which move men, and the aspects of life to which they attach a preponderant importance. It has had its source in religion, in military prowess and prestige, in the strength of professional organization, in the exclusive control of certain forms of knowledge and skill, such as those of the magician, the medicine-man, and the lawyer. It is thus both awful and fragile, and can dominate a continent, only in the end to be blown down by a whisper. To destroy it, nothing more is required than to be indifferent to its threats, and to prefer other goods to those which it promises. Nothing less, however, is required also.

The Concentration of Economic Power

It is not the case, therefore, as is sometimes suggested, that all forms of power are, in the last resort, economic, for men are so constituted as to desire other than temporal goods and to fear other than economic evils. It is true, however, that, since economic interests, if not the most intense, are the most generally operative and continuous in their operation, most forms of power have economic roots and produce, in turn, economic consequences. There are certain natural resources, certain kinds of property, certain types of economic organization, on the use of which the mass of mankind depend for their well-being. The masters of these resources, therefore, are in a position, in the absence of countervailing measures, to secure exceptionally favorable terms for themselves, and to exercise an unusual degree of control over the lives of their fellows.

Naturally, the class which, for the time being, is economically preponderant tends normally to be that which discharges the most conspicuous public obligations. Naturally, it often displays the graces of civilization in an exceptional degree. Naturally, again, the relations of cause and effect are commonly reversed, so that it is said to exercise power because it is educated and fit to govern, not to possess culture and influence because its economic position has brought exceptional opportunities of both within its reach. Such phenomena may be inevitable, but they deserve to be scrutinized. The sage who defined his Utopia as a society in which any man can say to any other, "Go to hell," but no man wants to say it, and no man need go when it is said, may have been crude in expression, but he was sound in substance. Pride and fear are the attitudes least becoming human beings, and a people which is a people, not a mob, will be intolerant of both. It will respect all men and feel awe of none. It will give short shrift to all forms of authority, whether political or economic, which breed arrogance in this class and servility in that.

POWER IN AN INDUSTRIAL SOCIETY

Economic power has a special significance in industrial societies, owing to the nature of the social structure that the great industry produces. In regions where the pattern of life is drawn by petty agriculture and small-scale industry, economic interests may be a consuming passion, as with the peasant who ruins his own and his family's health in order to add a few roods to his holding. But the force which they wield is small, since it is broken into fragments. It is dispersed in numerous small rivulets, each of which may irrigate a meadow but which cannot, till collected, generate the energy to drive an engine.

The influence of a spider is limited by the size of its web, and in such conditions economic power is feeble, because economic interdependence is slight. Its stature and role, in an industrial civilization, are obviously different. For the characteristic of modern industry, and of the financial arrangements associated with it, is not only that it increases, by its technological triumphs, man's power over nature, but that, in the absence of deliberate restraints imposed by society, it heightens that of some men over others, by organizing and concentrating it. It normally involves a concentration of ownership, and therefore of the rights which ownership confers. Its method is mass production, and mass production involves the control of large armies of workers, who execute, by small groups, who direct and plan. It makes all, or nearly all, types of economic activity interdependent, so that those who control a key service can impose their terms on the remainder. It increases the scale of enterprise, and thus increases both the number and length of the threads which can be manipulated by the staff-work of a single headquarters.

Hence, in an industrial society, the tendency of economic power is to be massed in blocks. The number of those who make the decisions upon which the conduct of economic affairs and, therefore, the lives of their fellowmen, depend is diminished; the number of those affected by each decision is increased. The late Dr. Rathenau once remarked that the economic life of Europe was controlled by three hundred individuals,[1] and his picture, if overdrawn, was not wholly unveracious. Lord Melchett smiles, and there is sunshine in ten thousand homes. Mr. Morgan frowns, and the population of two continents is plunged in gloom.[2]

---

[1] H. Kessler, *Walter Rathenau* (New York: Harcourt, Brace & World, Inc.), 1930, p. 121. [Walter Rathenau (1867–1922) was a German industrialist and politician, a power in numerous German firms, and deviser of the controls over the German economy in the first years of World War I.]

[2] [Lord Melchett (1868–1930), a British industrial leader and one-time associate of Lloyd George in the Liberal party, was a director in a large number of companies, a member of the British Cabinet, and leader in the movement to consolidate British industry and secure labor peace after the General Strike of 1926.]
[J. P. Morgan, Jr. (1867–1943) was the last of the Morgan dynasty of financiers, each of whom in his day was regarded by many as the epitome of American capitalism.]

This concentration of initiative is the most familiar commonplace of recent economic history. The increase in the scale of the business unit, which is the simplest illustration of it, can in some countries be observed from decade to decade, with the aid of statistics grouping firms according to the personnel which they employ. In Germany, for example, which grew in a generation from a nation of industrial dwarfs to one of the industrial giants, the percentage of workers employed in establishments with 1,000 employees or more almost doubled in the generation between 1882 and 1907; while in the industries most typical of the new order, such as chemicals, the metal industries, and electrical engineering, it underwent a threefold, thirteenfold, and, in the case of the last, which at the first date hardly existed, a fortyfold increase. The movement has continued since that date, the percentage of workers in establishments with 1,000 employees or more rising, for example, in mining from 52.4 in 1907 to 71.6 in 1925, in machine-making from 21.6 to 32.6, and in the chemical industry from 18.2 to 34.4. In the United States, where industrial concentration has attained the most imposing dimensions, the establishments with a capital of $1,000,000 or over formed, in 1914, 2.1 per cent of the total, employed 35.9 per cent of the wage earners, and produced 49.2 per cent of the value of the total output. In 1925 they formed 5.6 per cent of the total, employed 56.8 per cent of the wage earners, and produced annually 67.6 per cent of the value of the output.[3]

No comparable figures are available for Great Britain; but it is not open to question that development has proceeded, though at a slower pace, in the same direction. In the production of pig iron the capacity of each undertaking increased nearly threefold between 1882 and 1924, while between 1920 and 1928 the average output per furnace rose over 60 per cent and the output per man over 50 per cent. Even in the coal industry, which is notorious for its attachment to the organization of a bygone era, 84 per cent of the output was produced, as long ago as 1923, by 323 concerns employing over 1,000 workers each, and nearly one-fifth was produced by 57 firms.[4] In engineering and shipbuilding, iron and steel, chemicals and explosives, amalgamations have produced a small but rapidly increasing number of giants with a personnel ranging from 10,000 to 40,000. In the railway industry, since the Act of 1921, over half a million workers have been employed by four companies. Even in the traditional citadel of individualism, the cotton industry, the Lancashire Cotton Corporation now controls a substantial proportion of one section of the trade; while proposals for cutting out weak competitors and concentrating production are received with a favor not accorded them in the recent past.

---

[3] For the German figures for 1925, see *Wirtschaft und Statistik,* 1929, p. 36, and for the earlier years W. Sombart, *Die deutsche Volkswirtschaft im neunzehnten Jahrhundert,* 1921, Anlage 22, pp. 506–507. For the American figures see the *Biennial Census of Manufactures for 1925,* 1928, p. 1221.

[4] Committee on Industry and Trade, *Factors in Industrial and Commercial Efficiency,* 1927, p. 4; *Report of Royal Commission on the Coal Industry,* 1926, p. 47. (Published by the British Government.)

The Growth of Cartels

Thus, while the sentiment of the business world remains fixed in its aversion to bureaucracy, its own practice and organization are increasingly bureaucratic. Nor, of course, is the increase in the dimensions of individual firms an adequate index of the concentration of economic control. It has been accompanied by the growth of different forms of combination, which has as its effect that industries are, in an increasing measure, united in practice, even while the businesses composing them continue to retain their separate identities.

The importance of that movement on the Continent, and, in particular, in Germany, has long been a commonplace. "In the United Kingdom" stated the Committee on Trusts nearly twenty years ago, "there is at the present time in every important branch of industry an increasing tendency to the formation of trade associations and combinations, having for their purpose the restriction of competition and the control of prices." The same tendency is revealed in the growth of international organizations, such as the European Steel Cartel, allocating an output of some 25,000,000 tons between the producers of four countries; the British-American Tobacco Company, with a capital valued at approximately £100,000,000; and the International Match Corporation, with its 150 factories and 50,000 workers in twenty-eight different countries. The more imposing of them form, like the iron, steel, and coal interests of the Ruhr-Lorraine-Luxembourg region, or the undertakings formerly associated with Hugo Stinnes, or the "Big Five" of the American Meat Trust, with its 500 subsidiary companies in South America, Australia, and Europe, what are, in effect, extraterritorial economic states, with which few political states dare risk a fall.[5]

Even more significant is the control by small groups, whether of producers or mere speculators, of primary products, such as rubber, oil, tin, and coffee; the amalgamation of financial interests, which in England reduced the number of joint-stock banks from 104 in 1890 to 18 in 1924, 84 per cent of the aggregate deposit and current accounts being held, at the latter date, by five among them; and the control of the majority of the channels of public information by a handful of rich men, which resulted from the discovery that the trade of selling paper with advertisements on one side and news or nonsense on the other is the natural monopoly of the ambitious millionaire, since it requires a fortune to engage in it, and as far as the millionaire is concerned, requires nothing else. As the scale of organization increases, and one field of enterprise after another is conquered by combination, the lines of the structure necessarily tend to steepen. It is a pyramid in which power radiates downward, from a tiny knot of bankers at the top, through intermediate layers of industrialists and merchants, to the mass of common men, who are twitched this way and that by the masters of the show, like puppets on wires. The brisk little goddess Individual Enterprise must oc-

---

[5] *Report of Committee on Trusts,* 1919, pp. 2, 8–9; *Factors in Industrial and Commercial Efficiency,* 1927, pp. 110–114.

casionally look down from her seat on the summit with some qualms of perplexity as to the appropriateness of her temple.

Liberty and Equality

Liberty and equality have usually in England been considered antithetic; and, since fraternity has rarely been considered at all, the famous trilogy has been easily dismissed as a hybrid abortion. Equality implies the deliberate acceptance of social restraints upon individual expansion. It involves the prevention of sensational extremes of wealth and power by public action for the public good. If liberty means, therefore, that every individual shall be free, according to his opportunities, to indulge without limit his appetite for either, it is clearly incompatible, not only with economic and social, but with civil and political, equality, which also prevent the strong exploiting to the full the advantages of their strength, and, indeed, with any habit of life save that of the Cyclops. But freedom for the pike is death for the minnows. It is possible that equality is to be contrasted, not with liberty, but only with a particular interpretation of it.

The Purpose of Political and Economic Arrangements

The test of a principle is that it can be generalized, so that the advantages of applying it are not particular, but universal. Since it is impossible for every individual, as for every nation, simultaneously to be stronger than his neighbors, it is a truism that liberty, as distinct from the liberties of special persons and classes, can exist only in so far as it is limited by rules, which secure that freedom for some is not slavery for others. The spiritual energy of human beings, in all the wealth of their infinite diversities, is the end to which external arrangements, whether political or economic, are merely means. Hence institutions which guarantee to men the opportunity of becoming the best of which they are capable are the supreme political good, and liberty is rightly preferred to equality, when the two are in conflict. The question is whether, in the conditions of modern society, they conflict or not. It is whether the defined and limited freedom, which alone can be generally enjoyed, is most likely to be attained by a community which encourages violent inequalities, or by one which represses them.

Inequality of power is not necessarily inimical to liberty. On the contrary, it is the condition of it. Liberty implies the ability to act, not merely to resist. Neither society as a whole, nor any group within it, can carry out its will except through organs; and, in order that such organs may function with effect, they must be sufficiently differentiated to perform their varying tasks, of which direction is one and execution another. But while inequality of power is the condition of liberty, since it is the condition of any effective action, it is also a menace to it, for power which is sufficient to use is sufficient to abuse. Hence, in the political sphere, where the danger is familiar, all civilized communities have established safeguards, by which the advantages of differentiation of function, with the varying degrees of power which it involves, may be preserved, and the risk that power may be tyrannical, or perverted to private ends, averted or diminished. They have endeavored, for example, as in England, to protect civil liberty by requiring that, with certain exceptions, the officers of the state shall be subject to the ordinary tribunals, and political liberty by insisting that those who make decisions on matters affecting the public shall be responsible to an assembly chosen by it. The precautions may be criticized as inadequate, but the need for precautions is not today disputed. It is recognized that political power must rest ultimately on consent, and that its exercise must be limited by rules of law.

The Dangers of Economic Power

The dangers arising from inequalities of economic power have been less commonly recognized. They exist, however, whether recognized or not. For the excess or abuse of power, and its divorce from responsibility, which results in oppression, are not confined to the relations which arise between men as members of a state. They occur, in the absence of preventive measures, in political associations, because they occur in all forms of association in which large numbers of individuals are massed for collective action. The isolated worker may purchase security against exploitation at the cost of poverty, as the hermit may avoid the corruptions of civilization by foregoing its advantages. But, as soon as he is associated with his fellows in a common undertaking, his duties must be specified and his rights defined; and in so far as they are not, the undertaking is impeded. The problem of securing a livelihood ceases to be merely economic and becomes social and political. The struggle with nature continues, but on a different plane. Its efficiency is heightened by cooperation. Its character is complicated by the emergence of the question of the terms on which cooperation shall take place.

In an industrial civilization, when its first phase is over, most economic activity is corporate activity. It is carried on, not by individuals, but by groups, which are endowed by the state with a legal status and the larger of which, in size, complexity, specialization of functions, and unity of control, resemble less the private enterprise of the past than a public department. As far as certain great industries are concerned, employment must be found in the service of these corporations, or not at all. Hence the mass of mankind pass their working lives under the direction of a hierarchy, whose heads define, as they think most profitable, the lines on which the common enterprise is to proceed, and determine, subject to the intervention of the state and voluntary organizations, the economic and, to a considerable, though diminishing, extent, the social environment of their employees. This business oligarchy is the effective aristocracy of industrial nations. In such conditions, authority over human beings is exercised, not only through political, but through economic, organs. The problem of liberty, therefore, is necessarily concerned, not only with political, but also with economic, relations.

It is true, of course, that the problems are different. But to suppose that the abuses of economic power are trivial, or that they are automatically prevented by political democracy, is to be deceived by words. Freedom is always, no doubt, a matter of degree; no man enjoys all the requirements of full personal development, and all men possess some of them. It is not only compatible with conditions in which all men are fellow-servants, but would find in such conditions its most perfect expression. What it excludes is a society where only some are servants, while others are masters.

The Negative Meaning of Freedom

For, whatever else the idea involves, it implies at least that no man shall be amenable to an authority which is arbitrary in its proceedings, exorbitant in its demands, or incapable of being called to account when it abuses its office for personal advantage. In so far as his livelihood is at the mercy of an irresponsible superior, whether political or economic, who can compel his reluctant obedience by *force majeure,* whose actions he is unable to modify or resist, save at the cost of grave personal injury to himself and his dependents, and whose favor he must court, even when he despises it, he may possess a profusion of more tangible blessings, from beer to motor-bicycles, but he cannot be said to be in possession of freedom. In so far as an economic system grades mankind into groups, of which some can wield, if unconsciously, the force of economic duress for their own profit or convenience, while others must submit to it, its effect is that freedom itself is similarly graded. Society is divided, in its economic and social relations, into classes which are ends and classes which are instruments. Like property, with which in the past it has been closely connected, liberty becomes the privilege of a class, not the possession of a nation.

Political principles resemble military tactics; they are usually designed for a war which is over. Freedom is commonly interpreted in political terms, because it was in the political arena that the most resounding of its recent victories were won. It is regarded as belonging to human beings as citizens, rather than to citizens as human beings; so that it is possible for a nation, the majority of whose members have as little influence on the decisions that determine their economic destinies as on the motions of the planets, to applaud the idea with self-congratulatory gestures of decorous enthusiasm, as though history were of the past but not of the present. If the attitude of the ages from which it inherits a belief in liberty had been equally ladylike, there would have been, it is probable, little liberty to applaud.

The Need for Economic Liberty

For freedom is always relative to power, and the kind of freedom which at any moment it is most urgent to affirm depends on the nature of the power which is prevalent and established. Since political arrangements may be such as to check excesses of power, while economic arrangements permit or encourage them, a society, or a large part of it, may be both politically free and economically the opposite. It may be protected against arbitrary action by the agents of government, and be without the security against economic oppression which corresponds to civil liberty. It may possess the political institutions of an advanced democracy and lack the will and ability to control the conduct of those powerful in its economic affairs, which is the economic analogy of political freedom.

The extension of liberty from the political to the economic sphere is evidently among the most urgent tasks of industrial societies. It is evident also, however, that, in so far as this extension takes place, the traditional antithesis between liberty and equality will no longer be valid. As long as liberty is interpreted as consisting exclusively in security against oppression by the agents of the state, or as a share in its government, it is plausible, perhaps, to dissociate it from equality; for, though experience suggests that, even in this meager and restricted sense, it is not easily maintained in the presence of extreme disparities of wealth and influence, it is possible for it to be enjoyed, in form at least, by pauper and millionaire. Such disparities, however, though they do not enable one group to become the political master of another, necessarily cause it to exercise a preponderant influence on the economic life of the rest of society.

Hence, when liberty is construed realistically, or implying not merely a minimum of civil and political rights, but securities that the economically weak will not be at the mercy of the economically strong, and that the control of those aspects of economic life by which all are affected will be amenable, in the last resort, to the will of all, a large measure of equality, so far from being inimical to liberty, is essential to it. In conditions which impose cooperative, rather than merely individual, effort, liberty is, in fact, equality in action, in the sense, not that all men perform identical functions or wield the same degree of power, but that all men are equally protected against the abuse of power and equally entitled to insist that power shall be used, not for personal ends, but for the general advantage. Civil and political liberty obviously imply, not that all men shall be members of parliament, cabinet ministers, or civil servants, but the absence of such civil and political inequalities as enable one class to impose its will on another by legal coercion. It should be not less obvious that economic liberty implies, not that all men shall initiate, plan, direct, manage, or administer, but the absence of such economic inequalities as can be used as a means of economic constraint.

The Effect of Economic Autocracy

The danger to liberty which is caused by inequality varies with differences of economic organization and public policy. When the mass of the population are independent producers, or when, if they are dependent on great undertakings, the latter are subject to strict public control, it may be absent or remote. It is seen at its height when important departments of economic activity are the province of large organizations, which if they do not themselves, as sometimes occurs, control the state, are sufficiently powerful to resist control by it. Among the numerous interesting phenomena which impress the foreign observer of American economic life, not the least interesting is the occasional emergence of industrial enterprises which appear to him, and, indeed, to some Americans, to have developed the characteristics, not merely of an economic undertaking, but of a kind of polity. Their rule may be a mild and benevolent paternalism, lavishing rest rooms, schools, gymnasia, and guarantees for constitutional behavior on carefree employees; or it may be a harsh and suspicious tyranny. But whether as amiable as Solon or as ferocious as Lycurgus, their features are cast in a heroic mold. Their gestures are those of the sovereigns of little commonwealths rather than of mere mundane employers.

American official documents have, on occasion, called attention to the tendency of the bare stem of business to burgeon, in a favorable environment, with almost tropical exuberance, so that it clothes itself with functions that elsewhere are regarded as belonging to political authorities. The corporations controlled by six financial groups, stated the Report of the United States Commission on Industrial Relations some twenty years ago, employ 2,651,684 wage earners, or 440,000 per group. Some of these companies own, not merely the plant and equipment of industry, but the homes of the workers, the streets through which they pass to work, and the halls in which, if they are allowed to meet, their meetings must be held. They employ private spies and detectives, private police, and, sometimes, it appears, private troops, and engage, when they deem it expedient, in private war. While organized themselves, they forbid organization among their employees and enforce their will by evicting malcontents from their homes and even, on occasion, by the use of armed force. In such conditions business may continue in its modesty, since its object is money, to describe itself as business; but, in fact, it is a tyranny. "The main objection to the large corporation," remarks Mr. Justice Brandeis, who, as a judge of the Supreme Court, should know the facts, "is that it makes possible—and in many cases makes inevitable—the exercise of industrial absolutism." Property in capital, thus inflated and emancipated, acquires attributes analogous to those of property in land in a feudal society. It carries with it the disposal, in fact, if not in law, of an authority which is quasi-governmental. Its owners possess what would have been called in the ages of darkness a private jurisdiction, and their relations to their dependents, though contractual in form, resemble rather those of ruler and subject than of equal parties to a commercial venture. The liberty which they defend against the encroachments of trade unionism and the state is most properly to be regarded, not as freedom, but as a franchise.[6]

---

[6] For evidence on these points see U.S.A., *Final Report of Commission on Industrial Relations,* 1916; *Report of the Steel Strike of 1919* and *Public Opinion and the Steel Strike* (Reports of the Commission of Inquiry, Interchurch World Movement), New York, 1920 and 1921); H. C. Butler, *Industrial Relations in the United States* (I.L.O., *Studies and Reports,* Series A, No. 27, 1927). The quotation from Mr. Brandeis occurs in the *Final Report on Industrial Relations,* p. 63.

The conventional assertion that inequality is inseparable from liberty is obviously, in such circumstances, unreal and unconvincing; for the existence of the former is a menace to the latter, and the latter is most likely to be secured by curtailing the former. It is true that in England, where three generations of trade unionism and state intervention have done something to tame it, the exercise of economic power is, at ordinary times, less tyrannical than it once was. It still remains, nevertheless, a formidable menace to the freedom of common men. The pressure of such power is felt by the consumer when he purchases necessaries which, directly or indirectly, are controlled by a monopoly. It is felt in the workshop, where, within the limits set by industrial legislation and collective agreements, the comfort and amenity of the wage earners' surroundings, the discipline and tone of factory life, the security of employment and methods of promotion, the recruitment and dismissal of workers, the degree to which successive relays of cheap juvenile labor are employed, and the opportunity to secure consideration for grievances depend ultimately upon the policy pursued by a board of directors who may have little love, indeed, for their shareholders but who represent, in the last resort, their financial interests and who, in so far as they are shareholders themselves, are necessarily judges in their own cause.

The Neglect of the Public Interest

The effects of such autocracy are even graver in the sphere of economic strategy, which settles the ground upon which these tactical issues are fought out and, in practice, not infrequently determines their decision before they arise. In such matters as the changes in organization most likely to restore prosperity to an embarrassed industry and, therefore, to secure a tolerable livelihood to the workers engaged in it; methods of averting or meeting a depression; rationalization, the closing of plants, and the concentration of production; the sale of a business on which a whole community depends or its amalgamation with a rival—not to mention the critical field of financial policy, with its possibilities, not merely of watered capital and of the squandering in dividends of resources which should be held as reserves, but of a sensational redistribution of wealth and widespread unemployment as a result of decisions made by bankers—the diplomacy of business, like that of governments before 1914, is still commonly conducted over the heads of those most affected by it. The interests of the public, as workers and consumers, may receive consideration when these matters are determined; but the normal organization of economic life does not offer reliable guarantee that they will be considered. Nor can it plausibly be asserted that, if they are not, those aggrieved can be certain of any redress.

Power over the public is public power. It does not cease to be public merely because private persons are permitted to buy and sell, own and bequeath it, as they deem most profitable. To retort that its masters are themselves little more than half-conscious instruments, whose decisions register and transmit the impact of forces that they can neither anticipate nor control, though not wholly unveracious, is, nevertheless, superficial.[7] The question is not whether there are economic movements which elude human control, for obviously there are. It is whether the public possesses adequate guarantees that those which are controllable are controlled in the general interest, not in that of a minority. Like the gods of Homer, who were subject themselves to a fate behind the fates, but were not thereby precluded from interfering at their pleasure in the affairs of men, the potentates of the economic world exercise discretion, not, indeed, as to the situation which they will meet, but as to the manner in which they will meet it. They hold the initiative, have such freedom to maneuver as circumstances allow, can force an issue or postpone it, and, if open conflict seems inevitable or expedient, can choose, as best suits themselves, the ground where it shall take place.

---

[7] [The reference to the idea, held by certain minor classical economists and by the Marxists, that economic forces are beyond the control and usually the understanding of those whom they affect.]

Selection 11

Income Distribution and Poverty

ROBERT J. LAMPMAN

From Margaret S. Gordon (ed.), Poverty in America *(San Francisco: Chandler Publishing Co., 1965), pp. 102–114. Reprinted by permission of Chandler Publishing Co.*

Currently the lowest fifth of consumer units in the United States in terms of income, with personal income under $2,900, receive only 4.6 per cent of total family personal income. At the same time, 9 million families with less than $3,000 of total money income and 5 million unrelated individuals with less than $1,500 of total money income—or a total of almost 35 million persons—are classified as "poor."

What is the difference between these two statements? Do they refer to the same people? Is concern with inequality of the size distribution of income the same as that with poverty? Do similar policy considerations come to the fore regardless of which set of facts one examines? Is the anti-poverty emphasis of the Johnson Administration either based upon or entangled with the inequality issue?

In approaching these questions, I suggest that we first take a look at the process by which income is distributed and redistributed in the economy; second, that we ask whether inequality has been changing; and third, that we consider the way in which poverty has been changing and can be changed and how that change relates to income distribution.

How "Income" Is Distributed and Redistributed

The gross national product of the American economy, currently running at the rate of $640 billion, is divided among consumers, governments, and business firms on the basis of 65, 20, and 15 per cent for each, respectively. The division is effected by purchases, which are made out of the incomes of households and business firms and the tax revenues of governments. These incomes and tax revenues in turn, are paid out by governments, business firms, and households, thus creating a circular flow.

Incomes take the form of labor income, property income, and transfer payments (payments made on a basis other than for current production). Of income payments for current production, about 75 per cent are for labor and 25 per cent are for use of property. About six per cent of total income is transferred by governments from one set of businesses and households to another. Further transfers are accomplished privately. The most notable institution making such transfers is the family, which combines and transmutes producer-contribution incomes into consumer incomes for or on behalf of individuals. However, other institutions can perform this "transfer" function; employing firms or insurance companies, as two examples, can be used to modify the conversion of producer income to consumer income. Finally, governments and employers serve as collective consumers or transferors of goods and services, some of which add directly to individual consumer welfare and hence may be considered as alternative to money income.

This highly simplified account of the income distribution process is depicted in Figure 1. Figure 2 shows the same process with the family at the center and emphasizes that an individual, if he is to survive, must either earn income or tie into a public or private transferring institution. It is a corollary of this that an individual may have a low income if he or another member of his family supplies little salable labor or property service and if he has only a limited claim on the secondary distribution.

Has Inequality Been Increasing?

Over time the lines on these charts that have been increasing in relative importance are the labor income and public transfer lines. These changes have been associated with changes in the structure of the economy and in the scope of the family redistribution. It can be argued that increased reliance upon labor income and the breakdown of the extended family have given rise to new problems of income insecurity and irregularity which have called forth new arrangements for secondary redistribution. The problems of income management also, no doubt, influence decisions about family formation, relative responsibility, labor force participation, savings, insurance, and provision for extraordinary needs at various stages in the life cycle. Hence it may be that intrafamily distribution and redistribution of income over time are changing in such a way as to offset the apparent meaning of the rise in public transfers. But the general impression one gets is that the functional income shares have moved to accommodate a decline in the inequality of the size distribution of income, that is, in the distribution of the total of all functional income types among consumer units of all types.

Size distribution data are hard to compare over time because what is comprehended in the key definitions of income, income period, and income-receiving unit changes over time. Careful working and reworking of all available data by

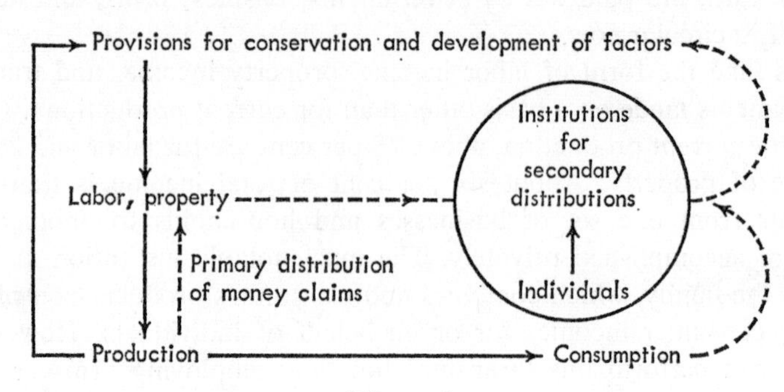

Figure 1

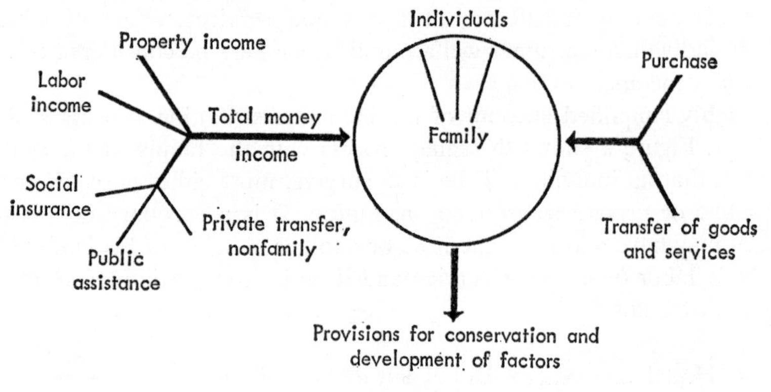

Figure 2

numerous scholars have produced a consensus that there was indeed a lessening of inequality in the 1938–1948 period and no clear trend one way or another since 1948. The lessening of inequality seems to be confined to those groups within the top half of the income distribution, with no great change in the income share of, and no change in inequality within, the bottom half. The lowest one-fifth of the consumer units (families and unattached individuals) got 4.1 per cent of the total family personal income in 1935, 5.0 per cent in 1947, and 4.6 per cent in 1962.

Over the period from the prewar to the postwar years, so many variables have been in the picture that one needs to be cautious about any easy generalization on changes in income inequality. For example, size of family moved into closer positive association with level of income (there was undoubling of middle- and lower-income families, earlier marriage, and a rise in number of children for upper-income families), thus suggesting that the decline in inequality is understated by a simple consumer-unit distribution. On the other hand, home-produced services fell in importance and capital gains and expense-account living increased, suggesting that the decline in inequality is overstated.

If one were trying to find an explanation or justification for the current interest in poverty from sharp changes in the over-all size distribution, I'm afraid he would be disappointed. I suppose it is possible that there is some significance for the lowest fifth in the compression of the distribution within the top half, but it seems rather remote. However, there are a few straws in the wind which suggest that 1949–1950 was a turning point toward more economic inequality among persons. These straws include the following:

(1) In my study of top wealth-holders, I found that the share of wealth held by the top two per cent of families fell steadily from 1929 to 1949 but then rose between 1949 and 1956. This finding is confirmed and extended by data from the Survey of Consumer Finances which show that, between 1953 and 1962, the share of net worth of the top decile of wealth-holders rose from 58 to 61 per cent and that of the bottom fifth of income receivers fell from 11 to 7 per cent.
(2) The narrowing trend in the Negro-white differential was halted and reversed about 1950, in spite of a continued closing of the education difference between the two groups.
(3) There seems to be an increasing association between extremely large families and very low incomes.
(4) Fringe benefits won by organized and highly paid workers have not been extended to lower-income workers.
(5) Earnings of young men aged 20–24 years were more unequal in distribution in 1961 than they were in 1951 or 1941, according to an unpublished study by Dorothy S. Brady and F. G. Adams. However, this is not reflected in over-all income for the younger age groups as reported by Herman Miller.[1]
(6) Increasing numbers of highly educated married women are adding to middle or higher incomes of their husbands.
(7) Early retirement of low-income men seems to be increasing.
(8) It may be that inequality in the distribution of skill and of educational attainment is increasing.
(9) Progressivity of federal, state, and local taxes combined has been decreased.

I would emphasize that these facts and surmises about facts are only straws which have not yet been reflected in income data—and may not be. I would conclude that we have not had and are not currently experiencing an increase in income inequality. However, concern over the halting of the narrowing of inequality and over the possibility that inequality may increase again may have contributed to thinking about poverty issues. It is also possible that increased knowledge about changes in the composition of the lowest fifth of consumer units may have aroused sympathy. Between 1947 and 1960, the unattached individuals, the aged, the female heads, and the heads who were out of the labor force increased in relative importance in this bottom group. This led some to observe that low income was not so much the product of class or economic problems as a sign of social or political failure. The fact that the low-income group included so many who were without influence or even without families

[1] Herman P. Miller, *Trends in the Income of Families and Persons in the United States: 1947 to 1960,* U.S. Bureau of the Census, Technical Paper No. 8, Table 3.

and who were out of the main stream of the economy made the inequality seem different, even if it wasn't quantitatively very different.

Has Poverty Been Increasing?

Here we can leave the change in equality and turn to the matter of poverty. Size distribution data of the standard kind do not tell us who the poor are, primarily because they do not show income in relation to need. Family size and composition and other variables need to be taken into account. The consumer units in the bottom fifth of the size distribution are not, in all cases, the ones in the poverty group if we use a $3,000-per-family and $1,500-per-unattached-individual income cutoff. This is even more markedly the case if the income cutoffs are given further variation for family size and composition and residence. I think it is fair to say that the human interest in income distribution progressively rises as we shift attention from functional shares to size distribution to the poverty-line and level-of-distinctions. This is the shift from concern with Ricardian factors of production and Marxian abstract masses in the grip of abstract forces to concern with ordinary people in trouble. At least a third of these people in trouble are children; almost half of the family heads are not in the labor force, and two-thirds of them have only an elementary education. Most of them are involuntarily poor because of events, social barriers, or personal limitations.

It is plausible to conclude from the poverty information that we are approaching a time when further reduction in the per cent of the population in poverty will be harder to achieve. But that is not to say that poverty is increasing. The percentage of poor has been falling at about one point per year and is now at 19 per cent. The poverty-income gap (the amount by which the total income of the poor falls short of $3,000 per family) is now $12 billion and is declining. Instead of getting worse, as some have alleged, poverty is getting "less worse," particularly in relation to our national resources for dealing with it.

The Process of Change in Poverty

Reduction of poverty and the filling of the poverty-income gap have been proceeding in recent years at the same time as, and partly because of, the fulfillment of other economic and social goals. Further, the rate of advance out of poverty can be sustained only if other rates of increase are sustained, for example, the rate of economic growth, the rate of increase in educational attainment by the poor, and the rate of increase of social welfare expenditures in behalf of the poor. While assisting people to get out of the lowest fifth of the income distribution would be a never-ending proposition, it is conceivable that, by helping some to rise above a fixed, constant-dollar poverty-income line and, at the same time, helping others to stay above the line we could achieve the end of involuntary poverty in the nation.

It is, I think, helpful to consider the process by which the number of poor families is changed from year to year. Some of this year's poor families will rise out of poverty, some will be dissolved by death or otherwise, and some new families and families who were not previously impoverished will start out in or retreat into poverty. So long as the exits from poverty exceed the entrances into poverty, the total poverty population will diminish. Thus, ways to speed the movement out of and to slow the movement into poverty should be sought. (One point deserving emphasis here is that there will soon be a great increase in the rate of family formation, and the poverty rate of these new families will be influential in determining the over-all poverty rate.) But neither should it be overlooked that filling the poverty income gap, and thus perhaps raising the median income of the poor (now $1,800), is of value in itself, even though it is not, in all cases, a way to stimulate further reduction of the poverty rate.

The range of ways to achieve the goals of the anti-poverty movement is to a degree implicit in Figure 2. Public and private resources can help the poor to develop their earning power and more nearly to realize their potential. This can be done either for adults or for children. Where that strategy is not feasible, it may be both possible and desirable to fill part of the poverty income gap by public transfers from the nonpoor to the poor. But it should be pointed out that $12 billion of transfers per year would not be sufficient to fill the gap if such payments induced a reduction of other income to the poor. An income of $3,000 for nine million families would be $27 billion per year, and that might not be enough if those above the $3,000 mark elected to take a grant rather than earn income. Hence, to fill the poverty-income gap with anything short of such massive outlays doubtless requires some care. One program which I would favor as a partial step in this direction is a family allowance system extending out of the income tax, building upon the tax exemptions and deductions for families which are not available to all families except the poor. Hopefully, low marginal rates of reduction in allowances against extra earned income would make this a workable idea for filling some of the poverty-income gap.

SHARING THE COST OF POVERTY AND ANTI-POVERTY EFFORTS

Any and all of these programs are going to cost somebody something, and this takes us back to the income distribution question again. First, however, we should note that it costs us something to have poverty. The poor part of the population contributes very little to the national output. At the same time they consume very little. They produce about three per cent of the total (three per cent of wages and salaries, five per cent of capital income), but they consume about five per cent of the total product. The difference between three and five is largely explained by the fact that the lowest fifth gets 30 per cent of the total of transfer payments, which includes social security, unemployment compensation, public welfare, veterans' benefits, and other transfers.[2]

---

[2] George Katona, Charles A. Lininger, and Richard F. Kosobud, *1962 Survey of Consumer Finances* (Ann Arbor: University of Michigan, Survey Research Center, Monograph No. 32, 1963).

The total income of the lowest fifth is about $25 billion, including $10 billion of transfers ($4 billion of which is public assistance). Only four per cent of families and unrelated individuals (or one-fifth of the poor) receive any public assistance payments. One-half of the poor families receive no transfer payments of any kind.[3]

The "cost of poverty" to the nation is the low productivity of the poor as measured by their earnings and capital income. By definition, poverty would not exist if such incomes were high enough to place all families above the $3,000 line. However, in the short run at least, poverty could be only partially solved by adding to productivity, since a third of poor families do not even have a single earner. If, say, six million poor families and three million poor unrelated individuals were to add enough to their wages and salaries to take them just above the poverty line, about $7 billion would be added to their incomes. This gives what might be called a minimum estimate of the cost of poverty. The figure would need to be somewhat larger, say, $10 billion, to take them out of poverty at the same time that public assistance payments to families with earners were being reduced.

It is plausible to argue that increasing wages and salaries by $7–10 billion dollars is not the end of the story. Wages are 70 per cent of national income; $10 billion divided by 70 per cent equals $14 billion. This adjustment seems necessary, since improving the quality of labor will increase the productivity of capital and land, and hence will raise interest, rent, and profits as well as wages. Moreover, more capital might be formed if taxes were lowered. This approach yields what might be called the high estimate of the cost of poverty.

A proper accounting would adjust the *gross* gain or cost to show the *net* gain, by deducting the cost to the nation of improving the productivity of the poor workers (through increased expenditures on education and health, for example). If such additional expenditures amounted to $1 billion per year, the gross gain of $7–14 billion would represent a net gain of $6–13 billion. A full measure of the "investment" would account for the added effort and forgone income by the poor themselves in improving their productivity.

To the extent that the present poor can raise their incomes by more productive effort, less transfer income will be acquired to alleviate poverty. Hence, a burden can be taken off the nonpoor population. Note, however, that this burden or cost is already accounted for in the estimate of cost in terms of $7–14 billion dollars of added national income. Hence, it would be double-counting to add the savings in transfers to the increase in production. The poor would lose the transfers which the rich save.

One crude estimate of the transfer involved is the total of public assistance payments—$4 billion per year. This $4 billion does not, however, take account of redistributive elements in social insurance, nor does it include the value of public services which are provided free of charge to poor persons but on which

---

[3] James Morgan *et al., Income and Welfare in the United States* (New York: McGraw-Hill Book Co., 1962), 216, 314.

the subsidy is reduced or withdrawn as persons become nonpoor. Examples of this are hospital and medical care, public housing, and family counseling services. Health care is quantitatively most important. Perhaps as much as $1 billion of public funds are involved in this general category of free services. Again, what the nonpoor gain, the poor lose through this conversion of free to nonfree services. Hence, there is no net national gain.

There is another point concerning the burden which the poor place upon the nonpoor, namely, the cost of "nuisance abatement." Presumably the need for police, fire, and public health protection (which presently cost $8 billion per year) would be somewhat reduced by the rise in well-being of the poor. Perhaps because the nonpoor could save as much as $1 billion. This would represent a gain to the nation since it would free resources for other uses.

There is still another point concerning the gain to the nonpoor from reducing poverty. As the poor earn higher incomes, they will be able to pay a larger share of the total tax burden, thereby sharing more fully in the support of governmental services. (This point should not be confused by the fact that the tax burden on the poor is now quite substantial as a share of income that goes to taxes. If we include all taxes of federal, state, and local governments, the poor pay directly and indirectly over 20 per cent of their income in taxes. The over-all tax system is roughly proportional to income through the lowest three-fifths of the income range.) The present poor who would be lifted out of poverty in the future would also be able to carry a larger share of the community's nontax responsibilities. For example, they would contribute more nearly their share of military draftees.

Finally, there would be a qualitative gain to the nonpoor from elimination of poverty, in the form of more complete integration of the population. Rather than having to live in a divided community of poor and nonpoor worlds, they would find themselves in a more open community where all would participate, compete, and cooperate. Everyone (with some exceptions) would benefit from the development of the talents and sense of responsibilities of the submerged poor.

We have been reviewing the question of the cost of poverty and the gain from its elimination. Now, let's turn the question around and ask: what will it cost to reduce poverty? A subsidiary question is: what amount of poverty-reduction can we buy for each billion dollars? This question arises naturally enough out of the debate over the proposed government expenditures of more than a billion dollars for next year. Actually, of course, the total "investment" will be far more than this. It will include state and local as well as federal funds, private as well as public monies, and effort and forgone consumption by the poor as well as the nonpoor.

What will the nation get in return for this outlay? How will the return be divided between the poor and the nonpoor? I suggest in Table 1 a three-part framework for ordering answers to these questions and offer some very rough estimates for Parts I and III based on programs which invest in "productivity raising." The estimates would differ if we considered a transfer-payment ap-

proach, but the method is of general applicability. No estimates are offered fo
Part II. Such estimates should have high priority for research.

Table 1
A THREE-PART FRAMEWORK FOR ESTIMATING COSTS AND GAINS FROM THE ANTI-POVERTY PROGRAM
(billions of dollars)

	Poor	*Nonpoor*	*All people*
Part I. Outlay or Investment Per Year			
Federal funds	.1	.9	1.0
State and local funds	.1	.5	.6
Private funds	—	.1	.1
Foregone income	.2	.1	.3
Total	.4	1.6	2.0
Part II. Gain to Nation Per Year (After Program Has Been in Effect for x Years)			
Added production resulting from higher-quality labor and added capital	—	—	—
Added wages	—	—	—
Added property income	—	—	—
Part III. Redistribution of Taxes and Transfers Per Year			
Reduced public assistance cost	−1.0	+1.0	—
Reduced free services to poor	−1.0	+1.0	—
Reduced cost for abatement of "nuisances"	+0.1	+0.9	+1.0

CONCLUSIONS

This paper opened with some questions about the difference between inequality and poverty. I hope we have conveyed the impression that both terms are
"words of art," but that it is sensible to distinguish between them. Income inequality traditionally has referred to the sharing of arbitrarily defined "income"
among arbitrarily defined "income-receiving units." Poverty, on the other hand
may be defined by relating an absolute real income level to family size and other
indications of need.

Inequality does not seem to have changed dramatically in recent years, or at
least it does not seem to have worsened the income share of the bottom half of
the income distribution. However, there are some straws in the wind that may
presage a future worsening of that kind. Poverty, on the other hand, is retreating
both in terms of reduction of the per cent of people below a poverty-income
line and in terms of a filling of the poverty-income gap. This process has gone
on and can go on without notable changes in inequality of income distribution
However, new attempts to speed up the rate of poverty reduction or the filling
of the poverty-income gap could, depending on what methods are followed

cause changes in the share of total income received by the nonpoor. The costs of poverty and the costs and gains of poverty reduction are shared by both poor and nonpoor.

The emphasis on poverty is a logical extension of social scientists' long concern with inequality. And it will, I hope, be a valuable part of a continuing effort to comprehend and improve the workings of the social and economic systems so that they better serve the needs and aspirations of people.

Selection 12

Public Approaches to Minimize Poverty

THEODORE W. SCHULTZ

From Leo Fishman (ed.), Poverty Amid Affluence *(New Haven, Conn.: Yale University Press, 1966), pp. 165–181. Reprinted by permission of Yale University Press.*

Once upon a time in the good old days before computers and the flood of statistics and theoretical models, there were economists who would appeal to Common Sense to buttress their analysis. It would be ever so convenient if there were a common sense approach to poverty that would be clear, cogent, and useful, but the plain fact of the matter is that poverty is very complicated both socially and economically. Try to convince your fellowman that your definition of poverty is real and relevant and you will see what I mean! Living at subsistences measured in food and shelter is not a meaningful definition. Nor can poverty be defined simply in terms of being below a particular level of income, because some families with relatively little income nevertheless own substantial amounts of wealth. Neither income, nor wealth, nor consumption is a dependable measure. Even when all three are used in combination, the resulting measure will not tell us why and the extent to which our society redefines poverty so as to raise the so-called poverty line over time. Common sense is indeed a rare gift, but it is not sufficient for this task.

Poverty is a complex socioeconomic state that characterizes particular families in a particular society. There can be no doubt that a part of any meaningful concept of poverty is socially determined, because it depends in substantial part upon our class and family structure. Nor is it independent of our social attitudes, for example, with respect to discrimination. The simple fact that people in general in our society hold that poverty is undesirable is a consequence of our social values. But a part of our concept of poverty is also economic, as is clear when we consider the possibilities of reducing the incidence of poverty. The type of economic growth we have had during recent decades reduces poverty; no doubt our types of taxation and public expenditures have also reduced it. It is obvious that poverty can be reduced at some price. What is not so obvious is that there are important aspects of poverty that are akin to economic instability, or to a depression, when there is less than full employment, in the sense that it can be reduced in ways that would leave no one worse off while improving the economic lot of some who would otherwise be in poverty.

The Disutility of Poverty

Thus, I propose to treat poverty as a socioeconomic state in which a part of our families live. I shall take it to be true that the values of our society are such that people generally would prefer to have fewer rather than more families in this state of poverty. From these social values one can straightaway infer the disutility of poverty. What this means is that our preferences are such that a reduction in poverty enhances our satisfactions. The question then arises: What is the price of obtaining such additional satisfactions? How much has to be given up by those who are not in poverty to reduce or eliminate the existing poverty? Since there are a number of ways of reducing or eliminating poverty and since some of them are more costly than others, knowledge about the costs and efficiency of the alternatives is both relevant and important in this area of social choice.

The economics of poverty therefore rests on the preferences and the capability of a people who satisfy these preferences. The application of these two basic concepts may seem elementary and easy; but as we shall see, these concepts are beset with difficulties and there is much confusion in bringing them to bear on the problems of poverty.

Building on Preferences

Here we face a flock of hard questions. How do we specify these preferences? How are they revealed? Should they be changed? Does economic analysis tell us how to alter them? The core of economics takes preferences as they are; they are, as I have already noted, a consequence of the cultural values of a people. Thus, whether we view economics as a kit of tools or as a body of knowledge, it is not designed to change people's preferences. The values and taste of a people may be deemed inferior by some social standard but a cultural reform to improve such preferences goes beyond economics. Once we see clearly that economics takes preferences as they are, a lot of confusion is dispelled with regard to the economics of poverty and the limitations of the contributions of economic analysis.

But this clarification by no means makes it easy to identify the relevant preferences. How do people reveal their preferences with respect to poverty? We turn to their behavior. We can observe private charity—for example, gifts to private agencies that minister to the poor, and gifts to colleges and universities that are in part invested in students, who thereby enhance their subsequent earnings. We observe local, municipal, state, and federal governmental bodies responding to their respective electorates by authorizing programs and appropriating funds to alleviate poverty. But for all that it is very hard to specify and measure the revealed preferences from such behavior.

The Utility-of-poverty Doctrine

There undoubtedly are countries that have pursued policies over many decades which would support the view that their governments were not adverse to poverty for the rank and file of people. There is a century in English history during which the poverty of the lower classes was thought to be desirable, for the then prevailing public view was that such poverty rendered good results. Between 1660 and 1775 the dominant nationalism of England produced an intricate system of foreign and domestic policy that sought to rationalize by all manner of arguments the utility of poverty. Edgar S. Furniss in his prize-winning Hart, Schaffner, and Marx essay devotes a long chapter to "The Doctrine of the Utility of Poverty."[1] The beliefs of illustrious individuals of that period will seem novel to us. Thomas Mun's view was that "penury and want do make a people wise and industrious." Arthur Young asserted that "every one but an idiot knows that the lower classes must be kept poor or they will never be industrious." John Law argued that "laborers were to blame for recurring high prices, because of their 'insufferable' habits of idleness contracted when food was cheap." William Petty joined in this chorus.

Even David Hume was not immune. He supported his belief by stating that in "years of scarcity, if it be not extreme, the poor labor more and really live better than in years of great plenty when they indulge themselves in idleness and riot."[2] Nor did Hume spare farmers. His defamation of them is terse: "A habit of indolence naturally prevails. A greater part of the land lies uncultivated. What is cultivated yields not its utmost for lack of skill and assiduity in the farmers." Hume calls them not only indolent but also squanderers. It follows logically from these beliefs that the real wages of the laboring classes must be held low. One of the ways of doing this, so it was argued, is to increase the price of necessities. When corn becomes plentiful, measures should be taken to subsidize its export. There should be taxes on consumption. Access of the poor to amusements, including strolling players, should be curtailed. The consumption of tea on the part of the poor was viewed as an evil.[3] Charity was thought to be the nursery of idleness. A larger population would keep laborers poor, and the logic of this was to encourage immigration and to be more lenient in naturalization policies. Georke Berkeley, Bishop of Cloyne, proposed to reward parents of large families and to tax families that had no children to attain this objective.

---

[1] Edgar S. Furniss, *The Position of the Laborer in a System of Nationalism* (Boston: Houghton Mifflin Company, 1920). The quotations that follow are from Chap. 6.

[2] See my *Economic Crises in World Agriculture* (Ann Arbor: University of Michigan Press, 1965), pp. 26 and 27.

[3] There was solicitude over the increase in the consumption of tea by the poor; tea drinking was deemed to be "wasteful of time and destructive of industry among the class of people whose duty was to labor continuously." Arthur Young put it thus: "The employment of women and children in drinking tea; . . . an extremity that may surely be called luxury in excess!"

Poverty-prone People

Another variant of the doctrine of the utility of poverty rests on the belief that there are subcultures in our society composed of people who prefer to be poor. Kenneth Boulding states that "a certain amount of the poverty of the hillbilly or of the subsistence farmer, and even of the slumdweller and of the bum involves the rejection of the psychological cost of getting rich and a rejection of the middle-class way of life rather than the inability to find opportunity."[4] Harry Johnson struck the same note in a recent comment.[5]

It is noteworthy that neither Boulding nor Johnson placed professors in this subculture, despite the long-standing myth that professors prefer to be poor. They escaped this particular myth because of what they know about their colleagues! It is undoubtedly true that there are classes of people who are poverty-prone for all manner of reasons other than the state of their preferences. Nor would anyone deny that particular occupations are preferred over others and that some people, for example some farm families, acquire a preference for the work and the way of living to which they have become accustomed. But surely such preferences are not inconsistent with the disutility of poverty.[6]

Approaches to Minimize Poverty

For us to develop a society free of poverty should be fairly easy. By world standards we obviously enjoy very high incomes. New sources of income have been forthcoming not only to support a huge defense establishment, a lot of foreign aid, and a rapidly growing population but to raise personal consumption expenditure on a per capita basis and in real terms about two-fifths since World War II. The economy has produced all this additional income despite the slack in employment during recent years and despite the depression of particular regions, industries, and occupations. Compared to India, where masses of people are in dire poverty, our poverty is minuscule. It is clearly in the realm of economic possibilities for us to be free of poverty.

The choice to have such a society is ours to make. We may of course prefer not to avail ourselves of this choice whatever the social or political reasons may be. The conventional thing to do is to believe in a natural law which will cause poverty to disappear. What remains in the affluent society is pockets of people who because of their preferences or circumstances have not been cleansed by progress.

---

[4] Kenneth E. Boulding, "Reflections on Poverty," *The Social Welfare Forum* (New York: Columbia University Press, 1961).

[5] *Amer. Econ. Rev.*, Vol. 55, No. 2 (May 1965), 543–45.

[6] There are of course many people who prefer to remain poor rather than accept doles or gifts, although much depends on the manner in which such income transfers are legitimatized. But a meaningful opportunity for them to earn additional income avoids this psychological cost. The implication of Boulding's argument that it would be necessary to impose a "middle-class way of life" in order to reduce or eliminate poverty is unwarranted; to attempt to do so would be intolerable.

Proceeding then on the proposition that poverty has for us as a society a disutility, we have at hand an array of approaches to alleviate it or to remove the causes of part of it. I shall restrict my comments to public approaches: first to minimum wages and farm price supports; then to progressive taxation; next to economic growth and employment; and lastly to public investment in poor people.

Raising Wages and Prices by Legislation

This approach, which continues to have a wide appeal politically, involves raising the low wages of unskilled workers and the low prices received by farmers by means of minimum-wage laws and high farm price supports. It rests on the belief that this line of legislative action is a direct and effective way of reducing poverty and that it increases the income streams where it really matters. Labor unions and some farm groups are committed to this approach. However, economists have repeatedly shown that it not only impedes allocative efficiency but as a rule worsens the personal distribution of income among laborers and among farmers. J. E. Meade, in some recent lectures,[7] stresses the marked disadvantages of minimum real wages, whether for a limited class of workers, or for workers in all occupations, or by limiting the amount of work so that the over-all resulting unemployment is shared. Each of these approaches is very inefficient.

As presently administered in the United States, farm price supports predominantly benefit farm families who are well above the poverty line; high price supports impede efficient resource allocation and also confound the income-wealth paradox in agriculture.[8] Consider why "farm families" are so rich in wealth and so poor in income. The facts are (1) the net worth of the assets owned by farm-operator families is on the average twice as large as that of nonfarm families ($44,000 and $21,700, respectively[9]) and yet (2) the proportion of farm families who are below the poverty line of less than $3,000 income is two and a half times that of nonfarm families (43 and 18 per cent, respectively). The value of wealth, which consists mainly of farmland, is subsidized; the value of farm work is depressed by acreage allotments and other measures to contract production. Thus, these programs are strongly biased in favor of farm wealth (income from property) and against income from farm work. The financial benefits in general and the government payments to farmers in particular go predominantly to the more well-to-do farmers, those at the top of the farm ladder, as the estimates in Table 1 show. The over-all effects of the high farm price supports and associated programs upon the size distribution of personal income among farm families are clearly regressive. Could it be that there is here a "war *for* poverty"?

---

[7] J. E. Meade, *Efficiency, Equality and the Ownership of Property* (London: George Allen and Unwin, 1964).

[8] See my "Economic Basis for a New Agricultural Policy Consensus," in *Proceedings of the Fifth Annual Farm Policy Review Conference, Washington, D.C., January 25–27, 1965* (Ames: Iowa State University).

[9] *Federal Reserve Bull.*, March 1964.

Table 1
GOVERNMENT PAYMENTS TO FARMERS IN 1963

Farms with sales of	Distribution of Farms (*per cent*)	Government Payments *Total* (*million dollars*)	*Per farm* (*dollars*)	*Distribution of total* (*per cent*)
$20,000 and over	10.7	918	2,391	54.5
$10,000 to $19,999	16.6	398	670	23.6
$5,000 to $9,999	17.0	213	350	12.6
$2,500 to $4,999	13.0	80	173	4.7
Less than $2,500	42.7	77	51	4.6
Total	100	1,686	472	100

Progressive Taxation

We have come to rely heavily on progressive taxes for revenue and to reduce the economic inequalities between the rich and the poor.[10] Progressive taxation undoubtedly has considerable positive effect in this direction, but it is not free of legislative faults; the tax law is beset with loopholes—for example, special depletion allowances for oil and other minerals and the "swindle sheet" which allows particular personal expenditures to be deducted as business expenses. Much more serious, however, is the fact that the income from business which is not paid out in dividends escapes personal income taxation. To compensate we settle for a poor second best, namely, special large taxes on corporations.

In extending the logic of progressive taxation to alleviate poverty, my colleague Milton Friedman has proposed a *negative income tax*.[11] Under this proposal, when the taxable income of an individual or family falls below a figure set by public policy, the taxpayer "would pay a negative tax, that is, receive a subsidy." There is indeed merit in this approach in alleviating some classes of poverty in our society for reasons cogently presented by Friedman in his book.

Reforms are also long overdue in the domain of federal estate and gift taxation. Douglas Dillon, on retiring as Secretary of the Treasury, called attention to

---

[10] The classic treatment of this subject is by the late Henry C. Simon, *Personal Income Taxation* (Chicago: University of Chicago Press, 1938).

[11] Milton Friedman, *Capitalism and Freedom* (Chicago: University of Chicago Press, 1962), Chap. 12. On pp. 191–192, Friedman states: "First, if the objective is to alleviate poverty, we should have a program directed at helping the poor. There is every reason to help the poor man who happens to be a farmer, not because he is a farmer but because he is poor. The program, that is, should be designed to help people as people not as members of particular occupational groups or age groups or wage-rate groups or labor organizations or industries. This is a defect of farm programs, general old-age benefits, minimum-wage laws, pro-union legislation, tariffs, licensing provisions of crafts or professions, and so on in seemingly endless profusion. Second, so far as possible the program should, while operating through the market, not distort the market or impede its functioning. This is a defect of price supports, minimum-wage laws, tariffs, and the like. The arrangement that recommends itself on purely mechanical grounds is a negative income tax."

the untaxed wealth that is acquired through capital gains. Professor Meade, in the lectures to which I have referred, makes a strong case for radical reforms in death duties and taxes on gifts *inter vivos.* He gives Sweden a good mark on this score: "In Sweden there is (1) a progressive tax on capital gains, (2) a progressive annual tax on total personal wealth, (3) a progressive tax on gifts *inter vivos,* and (4) a progressive tax on individual bequests."[12] The case here does not rest on grounds that income from property is rising relative to total income, or that the personal distribution of wealth is becoming more unequal, or that the incomes of families who are presently in poverty will be lifted appreciably in a decade or two. It rests on the serious defects in the tax treatment of inherited wealth and on the longer-run implications of these defects upon the personal distribution of wealth and income. It will suffice to mention only one of these defects: earnings of business enterprises that are not distributed as dividends escape taxation as current personal income and as capital gains simply by transferring private wealth thus acquired through inheritance.

Growth and Employment

Although they are yoked together by theory and policy, it is useful to distinguish between the rate of economic growth and the rate of unemployment in studying poverty. A searching dialogue is under way in economics to clarify the effects of each upon poverty. I am indebted here to my colleague Harry G. Johnson, whose chapter, "Unemployment and Poverty," deals with a related problem. I shall restrict my comments to three issues: (1) the observed decline in poverty associated with economic growth, (2) the incidences of poverty attributed to unemployment, and (3) the extent of so-called "structural poverty."

As I have pointed out elsewhere,[13] growth in our economy is very pervasive; among other things, it leads to increases in income per family, which in turn leads to a rise in the poverty line because of our social preferences. Even though our concept of poverty measured in terms of real income changes over time, economic growth has reduced substantially the proportion of families that fall below this rising poverty line. For example, since 1935, real income per family has doubled, and we have raised the poverty line about 55 per cent (from $1,950 to $3,000 in 1959 prices), yet the proportion of families below this rising line has fallen from about one-third to one-fifth of all families.[14] To gain perspective historically, let me divide the period since the industrial revolution into two parts: first, economic growth with no appreciable rise in per-family income and second, a fairly recent development, economic growth with increases in per-family income. Classical theory continues to be relevant in investigating poverty

---

[12] Friedman, *op. cit.,* Preface.

[13] See my "Investing in Poor People: An Economist's View," *op. cit.,* pp. 510–520.

[14] I draw here on Eugene Smolensky, "The Past and Present Poor," mimeographed paper, University of Chicago. Also, see Ruth Mack's estimates of (1) a contemporary definition of subsistence and (2) a 1960 definition of subsistence cited in n. 3 of my paper in *Amer. Econ. Rev., op. cit.,* p. 512.

in an economy in which there is growth but no rise in per-family income,[15] but our economy is obviously not of this type. Unfortunately there is no theoretical scaffold in economics that integrates the functional and personal income streams for an economy of our type. I shall advance the hypothesis later that earnings of laborers have been rising as a consequence of the growth of investment in human beings and that this development has been the primary factor in reducing poverty during recent decades.

Lowell E. Gallaway's estimates[16] relating growth and unemployment to poverty bear directly on the first two issues I introduced above. Using the definition of poverty which places families with less than $3,000 of income below the current poverty line, he shows that if the 1947–1956 growth rate and 4 per cent unemployment had been maintained from 1956 to 1963, poverty would have declined by almost 2 percentage points more than it actually did (to 16.6, compared to the actual of 18.5 per cent). When he applies the 1947–1956 growth rate and 4 per cent unemployment, his projected poverty for 1970 declines to 12.6 per cent, but to only 14.2 per cent when he applies the 1957–1963 growth rate and 6 per cent unemployment. The estimates of Gallaway and of the Council of Economic Advisers of the percentage of families in the poverty class are compared in Table 2.

Table 2
PERCENTAGE OF FAMILIES IN THE POVERTY CLASS

	Gallaway's Estimates		Council of Economic Advisers' Estimates	
	1947–1956 growth rate and 4% unemployment	*1957–1963 growth rate and 6% unemployment*	*1947–1956 rate of elimination*	*1957–1962 rate of elimination*
1947 (actual)	31.7		31.7	
1956 (actual)	22.2		22.2	
1963 (actual)		18.5		18.5
1963 (projected)	16.6			
1970 (projected)	12.6	14.2		
1980 (projected)	6.4	8.7	10.0	13.0

The difference between Gallaway's and the Council's projected decline in poverty may be taken as a measure of differing views of the magnitude of structural poverty. I would not, however, take either of these two implicit concepts of structural poverty seriously, because in making these estimates no attempt has been made to specify, identify, and measure the components that cause structural poverty. A simple projection of the observed decline in poverty during recent decades associated with economic growth conceals the components that matter. What we want to know here are the particular new sources of income that have

[15] The magnificent dynamics of Malthus, Ricardo, James Mill, McCulloch, and Senior—the leading classical economists—consists of a model in which earnings per laborer do not rise.

[16] Lowell E. Gallaway, "The Foundations of the 'War on Poverty,'" *Amer. Econ. Rev.*, Vol. 55 (March 1965), 122–131.

accounted for the observed decline in poverty. Once this is known, we can proceed to determine whether further investments in such sources would reduce poverty and by how much. The poverty that would still persist might be called structural, but a large part of it might also be amenable to treatment by other and additional forms of investment.

Investment in Poor People

I now turn to the last of the four public approaches to minimize poverty to be considered here. It is especially relevant in coping with what is commonly concealed under so-called structural poverty. I shall show that much of the poverty of many Negro families and of the poor families in agriculture and in the South is a consequence of long-standing chronic disequilibria rooted in inadequate investment in particular classes of people, who are therefore poor.

Let me begin by calling attention to important shifts in the sources of income that have characterized our type of economic progress. Income streams can be given quantitative dimensions per unit of time—that is, a one-dollar-per-year income stream. Except for income transfers, to obtain possession of an income stream it is necessary to acquire the source of income in that stream. These sources are valuable, and each has a price which may be low or high. The underlying assumptions are quite conventional. The sources of income streams are acquired at particular prices, which change over time; people respond to changes in these prices subject to the restraints of the capital market, their preferences and capacity to save, the effects of taxes and subsidies and of discrimination with respect to employment, and investment in human sources. We can then postulate a dynamic process and derive the following complementary hypotheses that pertain to the process of growth in our economy:[17]

1. The price of the sources of income streams that represent the acquired human capabilities of value in economic endeavor declined during this period relative to the price of other income streams.
2. In responding to this change in the relative prices of these two sources of income, the rate of investment in human sources rose during this period relative to that in material sources.
3. The increase in the investment in human sources of income relative to the investment in nonhuman sources has increased income of persons relative to property income, and the more equal distribution of investment in men has tended to equalize earnings among human agents.

These are testable hypotheses, and they appear to win support from a number of new studies. The private rates of financial return to those who complete more years of schooling support the first. My attempt to test the second, admittedly rough, indicates that, for the period between 1929 and 1957, investment in the stock of reproducible tangible wealth increased at an annual rate of about 2 per cent, while investment in education of the labor force rose at a rate of 4 per cent

[17] I follow closely here, my paper "Investing in Poor People: An Economist's View," *op. cit.*

and investment in on-the-job training of males in the labor force, at over 5 per cent. The marked increase in the proportion of the labor force that has attended high school and college is one of the developments in support of the third hypothesis.[18]

Over the long run both the demand for and the supply of sources of income streams are subject to change, some of which are cumulative and become large over time. Among the factors that alter the demand, three are of major importance.

1. The aggregate demand for goods and services. The level of this demand was obviously far from sufficient during the massive unemployment of the early 1930's, although more nearly adequate during the high employment of the mid-1950's. Since then there has been much slack; idle plants and idle men reduce the demand for the sources of income. Clearly poor people have much at stake in a government policy that will maintain full employment.

2. Advances in knowledge, commonly concealed under "technological change." New knowledge that is useful in economic endeavor requires either new forms of material capital or new skills on the part of labor, or, what is true in general, both are required. This factor, so it appears, has increased the demand for high skills relative to low skills.

3. Changes in restrictions "on the opportunity for individuals to participate in the productive process to the full extent of their potential."[19] What matters here is hiring discrimination against Negroes, against the aged who still are willing and able to do productive work but who are required to quit working or to work only part-time to be eligible for retirement and survivor payments, and against women in the labor force.

The long-run changes in the supply of the sources of income streams may be explored either in terms of adjustments to shifts in the demand, or in terms of factors that are relatively independent of shifts in demand. The adjustment process in which the demand and supply interact is at the core of the economic behavior underlying the formulation of hypothesis 2 above. The major "independent" factors affecting the supply are: research and development activities and dissemination of the resulting useful knowledge from these activities; the mobility (immobility) of particular sources, predominantly labor, in leaving declining industries and occupations; the amount and distribution of public investment in schooling and, closely related, the discrimination against Negroes, rural farm children, and others with respect to schooling.

Thus, the analytical task at hand is to account for the observed decline in

---

[18] During a normal business cycle the supply—the sources of these income streams—does not change substantially. The demand, however, shifts back and forth considerably during recessions and booms and, as a consequence, the income from corporate and some other forms of property fluctuates more over the cycle than national income. The fluctuations in income from wages and salaries are largest for unskilled labor, for workers who are least specific in their training in terms of the labor requirements of employers, and for workers who have the least seniority, with the result that the inequality of the personal distribution of income decreases in years of prosperity and increases in years of depression.

[19] I follow closely here, Harry G. Johnson's "Unemployment and Poverty," Chapter 9.

poverty or, alternatively, to account for the poverty that remains. Although the latter has the appeal of being more direct, it may be less efficient, because the first task is undoubtedly a prerequisite to the second. I shall therefore continue to concentrate on the first task.

Income from Property

By all accounts the functional share of income from property has been declining. The stock of tangible reproducible wealth has not increased at as high a rate as the acquired abilities of workers. Differences in the private rates of return have favored investment in human capital. True, the relative decline in income from material wealth would undoubtedly have been somewhat less during the recent past had the tax on corporate income remained at the prewar level. Meanwhile, what has been happening to the personal distribution of wealth holdings? It is hard to believe that the decline in poverty has been brought about by the fact that poor people have been acquiring a substantially larger share of material wealth. The stock of wealth represented by houses may be an exception in the sense that a house has been an attractive investment for many low-income families while the economy has been adjusting to the favorable tax treatment of home ownership. But houses owned by families with less than $3,000 of income in 1962 had a mean value of only $3,750. Any plausible increase in the net worth of low-income consumers since the mid-1930's could account for only a very small part of the decline in poverty.

Income from Labor

Meanwhile, labor's functional share of national income has been rising. The demand for workers with high skills has been increasing at a higher rate than the demand for low skills. The incentive to increase skills has been strong, and the supply of skills has been responding; for people have been investing much more than formerly to increase their skills. But why has the demand for skills been shifting upward in this manner? In my judgment, it is mainly a consequence of the dynamic process in which the development of skills and growing knowledge have been gradually raising per capita income and changing the pattern of goods and services demanded so as to call for a more rapid rate of increase in the need for high skills relative to the need for low skills. Another factor in this process has undoubtedly been the increase in the demand for producer durables and services by the military establishment.

Implications

The first and most general implication is that the observed large decline in poverty is primarily a consequence of increases in income from labor and not in income from property. The real earnings of workers have been rising because the demand for high skills has been increasing relative to that for low skills and because workers have been acquiring the more valuable skills.

Another implication is that a substantial part of the remaining poverty is a consequence of a number of disequilibria. Although workers have been responding to the changes in the market for skills, the economy in this respect has been in substantial disequilibrium at many points. The reasons why this is so are fairly obvious: namely, unemployment, the adverse incidences of economic growth in some sectors, inadequate knowledge, and a lack of opportunity to invest in acquiring the more valuable skills because of discrimination and the restraints on the capital market in providing funds for this purpose. Let me call attention to three of these imbalances.

1. The market for the skills required in agriculture has been long depressed. Although the labor force devoted to farming has declined by half since 1940, the market for these skills is still in serious disequilibrium. Older members of this labor force have had no real alternative but to settle for the depressed, salvage value of the skills they possess. In many farm areas the quality of elementary and secondary schooling has been and continues to be far below par, and thus the oncoming generation in these areas is ill-prepared to take advantage of the strong market in other parts of the economy for high skills. It should also be repeated here that the vast expenditures by the federal government on behalf of agriculture have not been used to raise the level of these skills; on the contrary, they have been used in ways that enhance the income from some classes of property and that worsen the personal distribution of income among farm families. Thus it should not come as a surprise that, although farm families are presently a very small fraction of all United States families, they account for much of the observed poverty, and in addition many of the families in urban areas who are below the poverty line have recently come from farms.

2. The market for the skills of Negroes has also been long depressed, and the poverty component here is large. This market has been intertwined with that of agriculture and, both on our farms and in our cities, there has been and continues to be much job discrimination. More important still is the low level of skills of Negroes, which is mainly a consequence of the history of discrimination against Negroes in schooling. Not only have Negroes obtained fewer years of schooling but the schooling has been of very low quality; it was especially so for the older Negroes in the labor force.

3. The South is burdened with much more poverty than other regions, basically for three reasons: (1) it is more dependent upon agriculture than the rest of the United States (it accounted for over 45 per cent of all U.S. farms at the time the 1959 census of agriculture was taken); (2) the labor force in the South is more largely Negro than in the North and West and, in terms of marketable skills, the Negroes in the South are even worse off than the Negroes in other regions; and (3) relatively more of the whites in the labor force in the South have low skills than whites in other regions. In short, the South has been lagging seriously behind in providing people the opportunities to invest in acquiring the high skills for which the demand has been increasing at so rapid a rate, predominantly because of social, political, and economic discrimination that continues to work against poor people.

A level of aggregate demand that would make it possible to attain a rate of economic growth which would provide full employment ranks high as an approach for reducing poverty over time. But more than this is clearly warranted. An important complementary public approach calls for investment in poor people. Our so-called structural poverty is to a large extent a result of such investment opportunities in human beings having been thwarted by social, political, and economic discrimination adverse to poor people.

DISCUSSION QUESTIONS

1. Discuss the reasons why R. H. Tawney believes that a more equitable distribution of income and wealth would be desirable.
2. According to traditional economic theory, the price a resource will bring in the market is determined by productivity and scarcity. Discuss other factors that might affect resource prices in particular regions, industries, or professions.
3. With reference to the article by Robert J. Lampman, distinguish between inequality and poverty.
4. Discuss the alternative approaches to minimize poverty suggested by T. W. Schultz. According to Schultz, what is the main factor responsible for the increase in the labor share of income in recent years?

SELECTED REFERENCES

Fishman, Leo (ed.), *Poverty Amid Affluence,* New Haven, Conn.: Yale University Press, 1966.

Friedman, Milton, *Capitalism and Freedom,* Chicago: University of Chicago Press, 1962, Chap. X.

de Jouvenal, Bertrand, *The Ethics of Redistribution,* Cambridge, England: Cambridge University Press, 1951.

Kolko, G., *Wealth and Power in America,* New York: Frederick A. Praeger, Inc., 1962.

Meade, J. E., *Efficiency, Equality and the Ownership of Property,* London: George Allen & Unwin, 1963.

Miller, Herman P., *Rich Man: Poor Man,* New York: Thomas Y. Crowell Co., 1964.

Tawney, R. H., *The Acquisitive Society,* New York: Harcourt, Brace and World, Inc., 1920, 1948.

———, *Equality,* 4th ed., London: George Allen & Unwin, 1952 (1st ed., 1931).

Wallich, Henry, *The Cost of Freedom: A New Look at Capitalism,* New York: Harper & Row, Publishers, 1960, Chap. 4.

PART 6

GOVERNMENT SPENDING

Government spending can be conveniently separated into exhaustive and nonexhaustive expenditures. Exhaustive expenditures absorb goods and services. They consist of purchases by government of goods and services from households and businesses: examples are the purchase of a bomber, the purchase of office supplies, and the hiring of a government employee. They represent a claim by government against the current output of the economy. This output is, therefore, not available for private consumption or investment. Nonexhaustive expenditure is spending that does not absorb output. Instead it redistributes income or assets: examples are interest on the public debt, unemployment compensation, and direct payments to farmers. This type of spending does not represent a claim by government against final output and is not a payment for a current service rendered. It does not greatly affect the volume of output available for private consumption. It does, however, reallocate purchasing power within the private sector.

In 1966 total government spending (federal, state, and local) was 208.7 billion dollars. Of this 153.1 billion dollars represented purchase of goods and services and 55.7 billion dollars consisted of transfers. Federal government purchase of goods and services was 77.0 billion dollars, 60.0 billion of which was for national defense. The major share of nondefense spending was for various government transfers, which do not represent a claim by government on final output.

Government transfer payments raise many ethical questions about the best way to distribute income. They do not involve direct regulation of the market but do indirectly influence the functioning of the market system. Market prices still allocate the goods and services purchased. Also, goods and services purchased by government are purchased from the private sector—government demand is added to private demand. Thus the major share of production is still carried on in the private sector of the economy. Government transfers influence who in the private sector will purchase the output, government taxes reduce the amount that the private sector has to spend, and government spending for goods and services changes the mix of output that will be produced.

What determines the mix between private and public spending, the way in which public spending for goods and services is allocated, and the level and allocation of government transfers? There are no simple answers to these questions. Many public goods are furnished "free" (they are paid for out of general tax revenues) and the public may use them or not use them, as it sees fit: examples would be public parks, the Federal Agricultural Extension Service, and various public health services. Other public agencies furnish their services "free," but the government decides how the services should be used: the prime example is national defense. Other government services are paid for in part by the recipient and in part from general tax revenues: education at a state university is an example. Some government services are sold: examples are postal services and electric power generated by the government.

The allocation of these public goods and services is determined through the political process. In some very general way, the interaction of private and public interest groups through the political process may represent the public interest, but there is no guarantee that this will be the case on any specific issue. The economist can help in the decision-making process by attempting to clarify the facts and values involved and analyzing the economic effects of alternative policy proposals.

With respect to nonexhaustive government expenditure, what can the economist say? He cannot say what is the best distribution of income. He can, however, analyze the effect of various redistribution schemes on consumption, saving, investment, and incentives.

The article by John Kenneth Galbraith argues that the market and the political process do not necessarily give the best balance between private and public goods. Instead, he argues that a balance between the two has not been maintained: there is a wealth of private goods but a great shortage of public goods. Walter Heller discusses budget guidelines for: (1) blending the service, stabilization, and income-transfer functions of government; (2) identifying deficiencies in the private market mechanism; and (3) selecting the most efficient means of carrying out government functions and activities. Alvin Hansen's essay calls for a change in values toward a more intellectually and spiritually satisfying way of life. Government is viewed as an instrument to promote the cultural development of the country.

Selection 13

The Theory of Social Balance

JOHN KENNETH GALBRAITH

From The Affluent Society *by John Kenneth Galbraith. Reprinted by permission of the publisher, Houghton Mifflin Company.*

> *It is not till it is discovered that high individual incomes will not purchase the mass of mankind immunity from cholera, typhus, and ignorance, still less secure them the positive advantages of educational opportunity and economic security, that slowly and reluctantly, amid prophecies of moral degeneration and economic disaster, society begins to make collective provision for needs which no ordinary individual, even if he works overtime all his life, can provide himself.*
>
> —*R. H. Tawney*[1]

The final problem of the productive society is what it produces. This manifests itself in an implacable tendency to provide an opulent supply of some things and a niggardly yield of others. This disparity carries to the point where it is a cause of social discomfort and social unhealth. The line which divides our area of wealth from our area of poverty is roughly that which divides privately produced and marketed goods and services from publicly rendered services. Our wealth in the first is not only in startling contrast with the meagerness of the latter, but our wealth in privately produced goods is, to a marked degree, the cause of crisis in the supply of public services. For we have failed to see the importance, indeed the urgent need, of maintaining a balance between the two.

This disparity between our flow of private and public goods and services is no matter of subjective judgment. On the contrary, it is the source of the most extensive comment which only stops short of the direct contrast being made here. In the years following World War II, the papers of any major city—those of New York were an excellent example—told daily of the shortages and shortcomings in the elementary municipal and metropolitan services. The schools were old and overcrowded. The police force was under strength and underpaid. The parks and playgrounds were insufficient. Streets and empty lots were filthy, and the sanitation staff was underequipped and in need of men. Access to the city by those who

---

[1] *Equality* (4th revised ed.), pp. 134–135.

work there was uncertain and painful and becoming more so. Internal transportation was overcrowded, unhealthful, and dirty. So was the air. Parking on the streets had to be prohibited, and there was no space elsewhere. These deficiencies were not in new and novel services but in old and established ones. Cities have long swept their streets, helped their people move around, educated them, kept order, and provided horse rails for vehicles which sought to pause. That their residents should have a nontoxic supply of air suggests no revolutionary dalliance with socialism.

The discussion of this public poverty competed, on the whole successfully, with the stories of ever-increasing opulence in privately produced goods. The Gross National Product was rising. So were retail sales. So was personal income. Labor productivity had also advanced. The automobiles that could not be parked were being produced at an expanded rate. The children, though without schools, subject in the playgrounds to the affectionate interest of adults with odd tastes, and disposed to increasingly imaginative forms of delinquency, were admirably equipped with television sets. We had difficulty finding storage space for the great surpluses of food despite a national disposition to obesity. Food was grown and packaged under private auspices. The care and refreshment of the mind, in contrast with the stomach, was principally in the public domain. Our colleges and universities were severely overcrowded and underprovided, and the same was true of the mental hospitals.

The contrast was and remains evident not alone to those who read. The family which takes its mauve and cerise, air-conditioned, power-steered, and power-braked automobile out for a tour passes through cities that are badly paved, made hideous by litter, blighted buildings, billboards, and posts for wires that should long since have been put underground. They pass on into a countryside that has been rendered largely invisible by commercial art. (The goods which the latter advertise have an absolute priority in our value system. Such aesthetic considerations as a view of the countryside accordingly come second. On such matters we are consistent.) They picnic on exquisitely packaged food from a portable icebox by a polluted stream and go on to spend the night at a park which is a menace to public health and morals. Just before dozing off on an air mattress, beneath a nylon tent, amid the stench of decaying refuse, they may reflect vaguely on the curious unevenness of their blessings. Is this, indeed, the American genius?

II

In the production of goods within the private economy it has long been recognized that a tolerably close relationship must be maintained between the production of various kinds of products. The output of steel and oil and machine tools is related to the production of automobiles. Investment in transportation must keep abreast of the output of goods to be transported. The supply of power must be abreast of the growth of industries requiring it. The existence of these relationships—coefficients, to the economist—has made possible the construction of the input-output table which shows how changes in the production in one industry will increase or diminish the demands on other industries. To this table, and more especially to its ingenious author, Professor Wassily Leontief, the world is indebted for one of its most important of modern insights into economic relationships. If expansion in one part of the economy were not matched by the requisite expansion in other parts—were the need for balance not respected—then bottlenecks and shortages, speculative hoarding of scarce supplies, and sharply increasing costs would ensue. Fortunately in peacetime the market system operates easily and effectively to maintain this balance, and this, together with the existence of stocks and some flexibility in the coefficients as a result of substitution, insures that no serious difficulties will arise. We are reminded of the existence of the problem only by noticing how serious it is for those countries—Poland or, in a somewhat different form, India—which seek to solve the problem by planned measures and with a much smaller supply of resources.

Just as there must be balance in what a community produces, so there must also be balance in what the community consumes. An increase in the use of one product creates, ineluctably, a requirement for others. If we are to consume more automobiles, we must have more gasoline. There must be more insurance, as well as more space on which to operate the autos. Beyond a certain point more and better food appears to mean increased need for medical services. This is the certain result of the increased consumption of tobacco and alcohol. More vacations require more hotels and more fishing rods. And so forth. With rare exceptions—shortages of doctors are an exception which suggests the rule—this balance is also maintained quite effortlessly so far as goods for private sale and consumption are concerned. The price system plus a rounded condition of opulence is again the agency.

However, the relationships we are here discussing are not confined to the private economy. They operate comprehensively over the whole span of private and public services. As surely as an increase in the output of automobiles puts new demands on the steel industry, so, also, it places new demands on public services. Similarly, every increase in the consumption of private goods will normally mean some facilitating or protective step by the state. In all cases if these services are not forthcoming, the consequences will be in some degree ill. It will be convenient to have a term which suggests a satisfactory relationship between the supply of privately produced goods and services and those of the state, and we may call it "social balance."

The problem of social balance is ubiquitous, and frequently it is obtrusive. As noted, an increase in the consumption of automobiles requires a facilitating supply of streets, highways, traffic control, and parking space. The protective services of the police and the highway patrols must also be available, as must those of the hospitals. Although the need for balance here is extraordinarily clear, our use of privately produced vehicles has, on occasion, got far out of line with the supply of the related public services. The result has been hideous road congestion, an annual massacre of impressive proportions, and chronic colitis in the cities. As on the ground, so also in the air. Planes collide with disquieting consequences for those within when the public provision for air traffic control fails to keep pace with private use of the airways.

But the auto and the airplane, versus the space to use them, are merely an exceptionally visible example of a requirement that is pervasive. The more goods people procure, the more packages they discard and the more trash that must be carried away. If the appropriate sanitation services are not provided, the counterpart of increasing opulence will be deepening filth. The greater the wealth, the thicker will be the dirt. This indubitably describes a tendency of our time. As more goods are produced and owned, the greater are the opportunities for fraud and the more property that must be protected. If the provision of public law-enforcement services do not keep pace, the counterpart of increased well-being will, we may be certain, be increased crime.

The city of Los Angeles, in modern times, is a near-classic study in the problem of social balance. Magnificently efficient factories and oil refineries, a lavish supply of automobiles, a vast consumption of handsomely packaged products, coupled with the absence of a municipal trash collection service which forced the use of home incinerators, made the air nearly unbreathable for an appreciable part of each year. Air pollution could be controlled only by a complex and highly developed set of public services—by better knowledge stemming from more research, better policing, a municipal trash collection service, and possibly the assertion of the priority of clean air over the production of goods. These were long in coming. The agony of a city without usable air was the result.

The issue of social balance can be identified in many other current problems. Thus an aspect of increasing private production is the appearance of an extraordinary number of things which lay claim to the interest of the young. Motion pictures, television, automobiles, and the vast opportunities which go with the mobility, together with such less enchanting merchandise as narcotics, comic books, and pornographia, are all included in an advancing gross national product. The child of a less opulent as well as a technologically more primitive age had far fewer such diversions. The red schoolhouse is remembered mainly because it had a paramount position in the lives of those who attended it that no modern school can hope to attain.

In a well-run and well-regulated community, with a sound school system, good recreational opportunities, and a good police force—in short, a community where public services have kept pace with private production—the diversionary forces operating on the modern juvenile may do no great damange. Television and the violent mores of Hollywood and Madison Avenue must contend with the intellectual discipline of the school. The social, athletic, dramatic, and like attractions of the school also claim the attention of the child. These, together with the other recreational opportunities of the community, minimize the tendency to delinquency. Experiments with violence and immorality are checked by an effective law-enforcement system before they become epidemic.

In a community where public services have failed to keep abreast of private consumption, things are very different. Here, in an atmosphere of private opulence and public squalor, the private goods have full sway. Schools do not compete with television and the movies. The dubious heroes of the latter, not Miss Jones, become the idols of the young. The hot rod and the wild ride take the place of more sedentary sports for which there are inadequate facilities or provision. Comic books, alcohol, narcotics, and switch-blade knives are, as noted, part of the increased flow of goods, and there is nothing to dispute their enjoyment. There is an ample supply of private wealth to be appropriated and not much to be feared from the police. An austere community is free from temptation. It can be austere in its public services. Not so a rich one.

Moreover, in a society which sets large store by production, and which has highly effective machinery for synthesizing private wants, there are strong pressures to have as many wage earners in the family as possible. As always, all social behavior is part of a piece. If both parents are engaged in private production, the burden on the public services is further increased. Children, in effect, become the charge of the community for an appreciable part of the time. If the services of the community do not keep pace, this will be another source of disorder.

Residential housing also illustrates the problem of the social balance, although in a somewhat complex form. Few would wish to contend that, in the lower or even the middle-income brackets, Americans are munificently supplied with housing. A great many families would like better located or merely more houseroom, and no advertising is necessary to persuade them of their wish. And the provision of housing is in the private domain. At first glance at least, the line we draw between private and public seems not to be preventing a satisfactory allocation of resources to housing.

On closer examination, however, the problem turns out to be not greatly different from that of education. It is improbable that the housing industry is greatly more incompetent or inefficient in the United States than in those countries—Scandinavia, Holland, or (for the most part) England—where slums have been largely eliminated and where *minimum* standards of cleanliness and comfort are well above our own. As the experience of these countries shows, and as we have also been learning, the housing industry functions well only in combination with a large, complex, and costly array of public services. These include land purchase and clearance for redevelopment; good neighborhood and city planning, and effective and well-enforced zoning; a variety of financing and other aids to the housebuilder and owner; publicly supported research and architectural services for an industry which, by its nature, is equipped to do little on its own; and a considerable amount of direct or assisted public construction for families in the lowest-income brackets. The quality of the housing depends not on the industry, which is given, but on what is invested in these supplements and supports.

III

The case for social balance has, so far, been put negatively. Failure to keep public services in minimal relation to private production and use of goods is a cause of social disorder or impairs economic performance. The matter may now be put affirmatively. By failing to exploit the opportunity to expand public production we are missing opportunities for enjoyment which otherwise we might have had. Presumably a community can be as well rewarded by buying better schools or better parks as by buying bigger automobiles. By concentrating on the latter rather than the former it is failing to maximize its satisfactions. As with schools in the community, so with public services over the country at large. It is scarcely sensible that we should satisfy our wants in private goods with reckless abundance, while in the case of public goods, on the evidence of the eye, we practice extreme self-denial. So, far from systematically exploiting the opportunities to derive use and pleasure from these services, we do not supply what would keep us out of trouble.

The conventional wisdom holds that the community, large or small, makes a decision as to how much it will devote to its public services. This decision is arrived at by democratic process. Subject to the imperfections and uncertainties of democracy, people decide how much of their private income and goods they will surrender in order to have public services of which they are in greater need. Thus there is a balance, however rough, in the enjoyments to be had from private goods and services and those rendered by public authority.

It will be obvious, however, that this view depends on the notion of independently determined consumer wants. In such a world one could with some reason defend the doctrine that the consumer, as a voter, makes an independent choice between public and private goods. But given the dependence effect—given that consumer wants are created by the process by which they are satisfied—the consumer makes no such choice. He is subject to the forces of advertising and emulation by which production creates its own demand. Advertising operates exclusively, and emulation mainly, on behalf of privately produced goods and services.[2] Since management and emulative effects operate on behalf of private production, public services will have an inherent tendency to lag behind. Automobile demand which is expensively synthesized will inevitably have a much larger claim on income than parks or public health or even roads where no such influence operates. The engines of mass communication, in their highest state of development, assail the eyes and ears of the community on behalf of more beer but not of more schools. Even in the conventional wisdom it will scarcely be contended that this leads to an equal choice between the two.

The competition is especially unequal for new products and services. Every corner of the public psyche is canvassed by some of the nation's most talented citizens to see if the desire for some merchantable product can be cultivated. No similar process operates on behalf of the nonmerchantable services of the state. Indeed, while we take the cultivation of new private wants for granted we would be measurably shocked to see it applied to public services. The scientist or

[2] Emulation does operate between communities. A new school or a new highway in one community does exert pressure on others to remain abreast. However, as compared with the pervasive effects of emulation in extending the demand for privately produced consumer's good there will be agreement, I think, that this intercommunity effect is probably small.

engineer or advertising man who devotes himself to developing a new carburetor, cleanser, or depilatory for which the public recognizes no need and will feel none until an advertising campaign arouses it, is one of the valued members of our society. A politician or a public servant who dreams up a new public service is a wastrel. Few public offenses are more reprehensible.

So much for the influences which operate on the decision between public and private production. The calm decision between public and private consumption pictured by the conventional wisdom is, in fact, a remarkable example of the error which arises from viewing social behavior out of context. The inherent tendency will always be for public services to fall behind private production. We have here the first of the causes of social imbalance.

IV

Social balance is also the victim of two further features of our society—the truce on inequality and the tendency to inflation. Since these are now part of our context, their effect comes quickly into view.

With rare exceptions such as the post office, public services do not carry a price ticket to be paid for by the individual user. By their nature they must, ordinarily, be available to all. As a result, when they are improved or new services are initiated, there is the ancient and troublesome question of who is to pay. This, in turn, provokes to life the collateral but irrelevant debate over inequality. As with the use of taxation as an instrument of fiscal policy, the truce on inequality is broken. Liberals are obliged to argue that the services be paid for by progressive taxation which will reduce inequality. Committed as they are to the urgency of goods (and also, as we shall see in a later chapter,[3] to a somewhat mechanical view of the way in which the level of output can be kept most secure) they must oppose sales and excise taxes. Conservatives rally to the defense of inequality—although without ever quite committing themselves in such uncouth terms—and oppose the use of income taxes. They, in effect, oppose the expenditure not on the merits of the service but on the demerits of the tax system. Since the debate over inequality cannot be resolved, the money is frequently not appropriated and the service not performed. It is a casualty of the economic goals of both liberals and conservatives, for both of whom the questions of social balance are subordinate to those of production and, when it is evoked, of inequality.

In practice matters are better as well as worse than this statement of the basic forces suggests. Given the tax structure, the revenues of all levels of government grow with the growth of the economy. Services can be maintained and sometimes even improved out of this automatic accretion.

However, this effect is highly unequal. The revenues of the federal government, because of its heavy reliance on income taxes, increase more than proportionately with private economic growth. In addition, although the conventional

[3] [Reference is to Galbraith, *The Affluent Society*.]

wisdom greatly deplores the fact, federal appropriations have only an indirect bearing on taxation. Public services are considered and voted on in accordance with their seeming urgency. Initiation or improvement of a particular service is rarely, except for purposes of oratory, set against the specific effect on taxes. Tax policy, in turn, is decided on the basis of the level of economic activity, the resulting revenues, expediency, and other considerations. Among these the total of the thousands of individually considered appropriations is but one factor. In this process the ultimate tax consequence of any individual appropriation is *de minimus,* and the tendency to ignore it reflects the simple mathematics of the situation. Thus it is possible for the Congress to make decisions affecting the social balance without invoking the question of inequality.

Things are made worse, however, by the fact that a large proportion of the federal revenues are preempted by defense. The increase in defense costs has also tended to absorb a large share of the normal increase in tax revenues. The position of the federal government for improving the social balance has also been weakened since World War II by the strong, although receding, conviction that its taxes were at artificial wartime levels and that a tacit commitment exists to reduce taxes at the earliest opportunity.

In the states and localities the problem of social balance is much more severe. Here tax revenues—this is especially true of the General Property Tax—increase less than proportionately with increased private production. Budgeting, too, is far more closely circumscribed than in the case of the federal government—only the monetary authority enjoys the pleasant privilege of underwriting its own loans. Because of this, increased services for states and localities regularly pose the question of more revenues and more taxes. And here, with great regularity, the question of social balance is lost in the rebate over equality and social equity.

Thus we currently find by far the most serious social imbalance in the services performed by local governments. The F.B.I. comes much more easily by funds than does the city police force. The Department of Agriculture can more easily keep its pest control abreast of expanding agricultural output than the average city health service can keep up with the needs of an expanding industrial population. One consequence is that the federal government remains under constant pressure to use its superior revenue position to help redress the imbalance at the lower levels of government.

V

Finally, social imbalance is the natural offspring of persistent inflation. Inflation by its nature strikes different individuals and groups with highly discriminatory effect. The most nearly unrelieved victims, apart from those living on pensions or other fixed provision for personal security, are those who work for the state. In the private economy the firm which sells goods has, in general, an immediate accommodation to the inflationary movement. Its price increases are the inflation. The incomes of its owners and proprietors are automatically accommodated to the upward movement. To the extent that wage increases are part of the inflationary process, this is also true of organized industrial workers. Even unorganized white-collar workers are in a milieu where prices and incomes are moving up. The adaption of their incomes, if less rapid than that of the industrial workers, is still reasonably prompt.

The position of the public employee is at the other extreme. His pay scales are highly formalized, and traditionally they have been subject to revision only at lengthy intervals. In states and localities inflation does not automatically bring added revenues to pay higher salaries and incomes. Pay revision for all public workers is subject to the temptation to wait and see if the inflation isn't coming to an end. There will be some fear—this seems to have been more of a factor in England than in the United States—that advances in public wages will set a bad example for private employers and unions.

Inflation means that employment is pressing on the labor supply and that private wage and salary incomes are rising. Thus the opportunities for moving from public to private employment are especially favorable. Public employment, moreover, once had as a principal attraction a high measure of social security. Industrial workers were subject to the formidable threat of unemployment during depression. Public employees were comparatively secure, and this security was worth an adverse salary differential. But with improving economic security in general this advantage has diminished. Private employment thus has come to provide better protection against inflation and little worse protection against other hazards. Though the dedicated may stay in public posts, the alert go.

The deterioration of the public services in the years of inflation has not gone unremarked. However, there has been a strong tendency to regard it as an adventitious misfortune—something which, like a nasty shower at a picnic, happened to blight a generally good time. Salaries were allowed to lag, which was a pity. This is a very inadequate view. Discrimination against the public services is an organic feature of inflation. Nothing so weakens government as persistent inflation. The public administration of France for many years, of Italy until recent times, and of other European and numerous South American countries has been deeply sapped and eroded by the effects of long-continued inflation. Social imbalance reflects itself in inability to enforce laws, including significantly those which protect and advance basic social justice, and in failure to maintain and improve essential services. One outgrowth of the resulting imbalance has been frustration and pervasive discontent. Over much of the world there is a rough and not entirely accidental correlation between the strength of indigenous communist parties or the frequency of revolutions and the persistence of inflation.

VI

A feature of the years immediately following World War II was a remarkable attack on the notion of expanding and improving public services. During the depression years such services had been elaborated and improved partly in order to fill some small part of the vacuum left by the shrinkage of private production. During the war years the role of government was vastly expanded. After that came the reaction. Much of it, unquestionably, was motivated by a desire to rehabilitate the prestige of private production and therewith of producers. No doubt some who joined the attack hoped, at least tacitly, that it might be possible to sidestep the truce on taxation vis-à-vis equality by having less taxation of all kinds. For a time the notion that our public services had somehow become inflated and excessive was all but axiomatic. Even liberal politicians did not seriously protest. They found it necessary to aver that they were in favor of public economy too.

In this discussion a certain mystique was attributed to the satisfaction of privately supplied wants. A community decision to have a new school means that the individual surrenders the necessary amount, willy-nilly, in his taxes. But if he is left with that income, he is a free man. He can decide between a better car or a television set. This was advanced with some solemnity as an argument for the TV set. The difficulty is that this argument leaves the community with no way of preferring the school. All private wants, where the individual can choose, are inherently superior to all public desires which must be paid for by taxation and with an inevitable component of compulsion.

The cost of public services was also held to be a desolating burden on private production, although this was at a time when the private production was burgeoning. Urgent warnings were issued of the unfavorable effects of taxation on investment—"I don't know of a surer way of killing off the incentive to invest than by imposing taxes which are regarded by people as punitive."[3] This was at a time when the inflationary effect of a very high level of investment was causing concern. The same individuals who were warning about the inimical effects of taxes were strongly advocating a monetary policy designed to reduce investment. However, an understanding of our economic discourse requires an appreciation of one of its basic rules: men of high position are allowed, by a special act of grace, to accommodate their reasoning to the answer they need. Logic is only required in those of lesser rank.

Finally it was argued, with no little vigor, that expanding government posed a grave threat to individual liberties. "Where distinction and rank is achieved almost exclusively by becoming a civil servant of the state . . . it is too much to expect that many will long prefer freedom to security."[4]

With time this attack on public services has somewhat subsided. The disorder associated with social imbalance has become visible even if the need for balance between private and public services is still imperfectly appreciated.

Freedom also seemed to be surviving. Perhaps it was realized that all organized activity requires concessions by the individual to the group. This is true of the policeman who joins the police force, the teacher who gets a job at the high school, and the executive who makes his way up the hierarchy of Du Pont. If there are differences between public and private organization, they are of kind rather than of degree. As this is written the pendulum has in fact swung back.

---

[3] Arthur F. Burns, Chairman of the President's Council of Economic Advisers, *U.S. News & World Report,* May 6, 1955.

[4] F. A. Hayek, *The Road to Serfdom* (London: George Routledge & Sons, 1944), p. 98.

Our liberties are now menaced by the conformity exacted by the large corporation and its impulse to create, for its own purposes, the organization man. This danger we may also survive.

Nonetheless, the postwar onslaught on the public services left a lasting imprint. To suggest that we canvass our public wants to see where happiness can be improved by more and better services has a sharply radical tone. Even public services to avoid disorder must be defended. By contrast the man who devises a nostrum for a nonexistent need and then successfully promotes both remains one of nature's noblemen.

Selection 14

Reflections on Public Expenditure Theory

WALTER W. HELLER

Paper Submitted to the Joint Economic Committee. Reprinted by permission of Walter W. Heller.

What does an economist have to offer a perplexed public and its policymaking representatives on the theory of government functions as they affect the budget? The cynic's offhand answer, "Not much," may be close to the mark if one demands definitive rules of thumb for determining the precise scope of government functions and level of government expenditures. But if, instead, the demand is for economic guidelines to aid the budgetary decision maker (1) in blending rationally the service, stabilization, and income-transfer functions of government, (2) in identifying those deficiencies in the private-market mechanism which call for government budgetary action or, more broadly, those activities where government use or control of resources promises greater returns than private use or control, and (3) in selecting the most efficient means of carrying out government functions and activities (whether by government production, contracts with private producers, transfer payments, loans, guaranties, tax concessions, and so forth)—if this is the nature of the demands on him, the economist is prepared to make a modest offering now and to work along lines that promise a greater contribution in the future.

In a sense, this paper is a progress report designed to show where the economist can already offer some useful counsel, to indicate some of the lines along which promising work is being done, and to suggest certain limitations or constraints within which the economic criteria for dividing resources between public and private use must be applied.

A Basic Framework

As a first step in the search for economic guideposts, we need to disentangle, classify, and define the basic objectives and functions of government that shape its budgetary decisions. Fortunately, Professor Richard A. Musgrave has developed a conceptual framework for this task in his "multiple theory of budget determination."[1]

The component functions of the budget as he brings them into focus are: (1) the service, or want-satisfying, function: to provide for the satisfaction of those individual wants which the market mechanism cannot satisfy effectively (for example, education and conservation) or is incapable of satisfying (for example, defense and justice); (2) the income-transfer or distributional function: to make those corrections in the existing income distribution (by size, by occupational groups, by geographical area, et cetera) which society desires; and (3) the stabilization function: to join with monetary policy and other measures to raise or lower the level of aggregate demand so as to maintain full employment and avoid inflation. The first function is of dominant interest [here] and the succeeding sections of the paper return to it. But several general implications of the Musgrave system as a whole deserve attention before turning to specifics.

Musgrave's formulation helps unclutter our thinking on the component parts of the budget decision. It drives home the significant point that our decisions on how much and what kind of want-satisfying services to provide by government budgets need not be tied to our demands on the budget for correction of either the existing patterns of income distribution or the level of aggregate demand. If we prefer, we can have a small budget for services (financed by taxes levied on the benefit principle) combined with a big budget for redistributive transfers of income (financed by taxes levied on the ability principle), or vice versa; and either combination can be coupled with either a deficit to stimulate demand and employment or a surplus to reduce demand and check inflation. In this respect, it is reminiscent of Samuelson's "daring doctrine" that by appropriate fiscal-monetary policy "a community can have full employment, can at the same time have the rate of capital formation it wants, and can accomplish all this compatibly with the degree of income-redistributing taxation it ethically desires.[2] Musgrave, in turn, points the way to achieving any combination of government services, income redistribution, economic redistribution, and economic stability we set our sights on.

So far, so good. The waters, though deep, are clear and relatively still. They get somewhat muddied and troubled when we move from the clear-cut want-satisfying programs (subject to the benefit principle) and clear-cut distributive programs (subject to the ability principle) into dual-purpose programs, transfers-in-kind in the form of subsidized housing, medical care, vocational education, and so forth. For here we are no longer furnishing services that the majority has voted to meet its own needs (including both selfishly motivated needs like defense

---

[1] See, for example, "A Multiple Theory of Budget Determination," *Finanzarchiv*, 1957, Vol. 13, No. 3, 333–343, and the relevant chapters of his treatise, *The Theory of Public Finance* (New York: McGraw-Hill Book Company, 1959).

[2] Paul A. Samuelson, "The New Look in Tax and Fiscal Policy," in *Federal Tax Policy for Economic Growth and Stability,* Joint Committee on the Economic Report, Washington, November 9, 1955, p. 234.

and police protection and socially motivated needs like foreign aid) via government, but are in effect requiring the minority to accept services which they might or might not have bought had they been handed an equivalent amount of cash. Perhaps they would have preferred to spend it on wine, women, and song, but the majority is apparently saying, "No, we know what's best for you." Can this be justified?

It may be digressing to do so, but let us consider for a moment the provision of free vocational education as a case in point. It might be argued that vocational training results in a direct increase in earning power of the trainee (since employers will be willing to pay him higher wages) and that it should therefore be left in private hands or, if furnished publicly, should be financed under the market principle (by direct charges to the recipient of the service) rather than the budget principle (provided free of charge and financed by general taxation).[3] In terms of the service budget alone, the foregoing conclusion is probably right. But bringing in the redistributive motive puts subsidized vocational training in a different light. The voting majority may feel that income transferred in this form constitutes a more efficient and desirable form of transfer than a direct cash transfer. It insures that the transferred economic power won't be squandered in foolish and dissolute ways. It approaches reduction of economic inequality through greater equality of opportunity. In the process, it strengthens the economy's productive capacity.

The new welfare economics may protest that this is a form of tyranny of the majority of the voters over the minority, that each individual is his own best judge of his welfare. Since the equivalent cash payment would have been spent differently, it is said to be a violation of consumer sovereignty. But it is also quite possible that the recipient of the transfer in kind will vote with the majority to have this kind of program rather than a direct cash payment. The individual may accept and welcome the discipline in such an arrangement which overcomes his own self-deplored lack of will power (a lack which is not restricted to children, aged persons, and imbeciles). How many of us would "prefer" to spend our time quite differently than we do if left to our own devices, yet are willing to accept, or even welcome, the tyranny of a deadline as a condition of participating in a desirable project? Seen in this light, the transfer in kind may interfere more with license than with freedom of consumer choice. I do not mean to dismiss the "tyranny" argument, but its force is certainly softened by the kind of consideration just examined. It may be further softened if we accept the proposition that the responsibility of the voters' representatives goes beyond a mere recording of individual preferences to leadership and education designed to redirect individual preferences along lines which a social consensus deems more constructive.

Even beyond this, the transfer in kind may actually have a large service com-

---

[3] For a discussion of these principles see Gerhard Colm, *Essays in Public Finance and Fiscal Policy* (New York: Oxford University Press, 1955), pp. 8–11.

ponent, that is, secondary benefits which accrue to others than the direct recipient of the service.[4] For example, low-income housing may confer indirect benefits on high-income people in surrounding areas for which they are willing to pay a considerable price. Subsidized housing projects may replace unsightly slums, arrest urban blight which threatens to encroach on better neighborhoods, and reduce fire and police protection costs. To this extent, taxes on high-income people to subsidize low-cost housing may in large part be a payment for the indirect benefits they receive rather than a transfer payment. Clearly identifying and separating the service elements from the redistributive element in this manner suggests that the wants of third-party beneficiaries are being satisfied by using the direct recipient of subsidized housing, medical care, education, and the like as the instrument, willing or unwilling, for this purpose.

This formulation may also shed new light on the theory of progressive taxation. Musgrave suggests that high-income people may be willing to pay proportionately more for a given government service than low-income people (that is, the income elasticity of demand for the service is greater than unity), even in the case of government services like defense and justice, which by their nature must be consumed in equal amounts by all persons. Add to this consideration the important indirect stake which the upper-income groups have in subsidized programs for the lower-income groups (that is, programs not equally consumed by all). The direct beneficiary may put a low value on the service and a high value on money, while the indirect beneficiary (who gets secondary benefits in protection from epidemics, in arresting of urban blight, in a more stable body politic and labor force, and so forth) may put a relatively high value on the service and a low value on money. The tax policy result: progressive taxation on the benefit principle.

Economic Determinants of the Proper Sphere of Government Activity

Given a framework for straight thinking about budget functions, the economist is brought face to face with two questions that come closer to the central problem of the proper sphere of government activity. First, where competitive bidding

---

[4] To the extent that the income-transfer motive is the sole or dominant motive for keeping certain services on the public budget (or at least causing us to supply them on the budget principle rather than the market principle), a rise in average family income and a decline in inequality will eventually bring us to a point where programs such as vocational education and low-cost housing should be moved off the government budget and into the market economy. This point is undoubtedly much more distant for some programs than others. Also, I do not mean to suggest that the main impact of economic growth and prosperity is to reduce government expenditures. Both in the case of intermediate public goods (such as roads), the demand for which typically moves in accord with private goods, and in the case of "end item" services (such as better education and recreation), the demand for which increases with higher standards of living, economic growth and prosperity mean higher rather than lower demands for government services. (See Gerhard Colm, "Comments on Samuelson's Theory of Public Finance," *The Review of Economics and Statistics,* Vol. 38, Nov. 1956, 410.)

via the pricing mechanism is inapplicable, how are the preferences of voters for governmental services to be revealed, measured, and appropriately financed? Second, waiving the question of measurement of preferences, where would the line between public and private control over resources be drawn if economic efficiency were the only criterion to be implied?

On the first question, insofar as it relates to individual preferences for public goods, economists have agreed on the nature and difficulty of the problem, have made some intriguing suggestions as to its solution, and have concluded that it is next to insoluble. The key difficulty is that the voting process, unlike the pricing process, does not force the consumer of public goods to show his hand. The essence of preference measurement is the showing of how much of one good or service the consumer is willing to forgo as the price of acquiring another. But the amount of a public good or service (say, of defense, police protection, or schooling) available to the voter is independent of the amount he pays in taxes or the intensity of his demand for it.[5] Unless and until we devise a reliable and reasonably accurate method of detecting specific voter preferences in some detail, our definition of the proper sphere of government activity will have to rely chiefly on the informed judgment and perception of those whom we vote into legislative and executive office.[6]

This being the case, the economist's task is to contribute what he can to this informed judgment and perception. In effect, the economist's job becomes one of telling the voters and their representatives what their preferences as to governmental activities would be if they were guided by the principle of economic efficiency. In doing so, the economist is not proposing that decisions as to what kinds of activities should be assigned to government—what wants should be satisfied and resources should be redirected through government action—should be made on economic grounds alone. He is fully aware that values such as those of political and economic freedom play a vital role in these decisions. But he can perform the valuable service of identifying those deficiencies in the market mechanism and those inherent economic characteristics of government which make it economically advantageous to have certain services provided by government rather than by private initiative. In other words he can show where government intervention in resource allocation and use promises a greater return per unit of input than untrammeled private use.

The economist recognizes, of course, that there are areas in which he is necessarily mute, or at least should not speak unless spoken to. These are the areas

---

[5] For an illuminating exploration of ways and means to get at a more valid and clear-cut expression of voter preferences for government services, see the pioneering work by Howard R. Bowen, *Toward Social Economy* (New York: Holt, Rinehart & Winston, Inc., 1948), especially chap. 18, "Collective Choice." In this chapter Bowen explores both voting and polling techniques for ascertaining those individual tastes and preferences which cannot find expression in, or be measured by, the market mechanism.

[6] Insofar as voter wants in the public sphere go beyond individualistic preferences to general welfare choices (as Colm, in his article commenting on Samuelson's theory, argues that they not only do, but should), the problem changes form, but the desirability of sharper definition of voter preferences remains undiminished.

of pure public goods, whose benefits are clearly indivisible and nonmarketable, and of which no amount of economic wisdom can determine the appropriate levels of output and expenditure.[7] In the realm of defense, for example, one successful Russian earth satellite or intercontinental ballistics missile will (and should) outweigh 10,000 economists in determining the appropriate level of expenditures. At most, the economist stands ready to offer analysis and judgments as to the critical levels of defense expenditures beyond which they threaten serious inflation in the absence of drastic tax action or curtailment of civilian programs, or, given that action, threaten impairment of producer incentives and essential civilian programs.

A much more fruitful activity for the economist is to demonstrate the economic advantage offered by government intervention, budgetary and otherwise, in those intermediate service areas where benefits are at least partially divisible and marketable. A number of economists have made useful contributions on this front.[8] In what situations does economic logic point to government intervention to correct the market mechanism's allocation of resources in the interests of greater efficiency in their use?

1. Where there are important third-party benefits [usually known as neighborhood effects, external effects, or externalities] which accrue to others than the direct beneficiary of the service as in the case of education, disease prevention, and police and fire protection, the market price and demand schedules underestimate the marginal and total social benefits provided by the service in question. By and large, the direct beneficiaries are the only ones who enter the private market as buyers, with the result that the services would be undervalued, underpriced, and underproduced unless government entered the transaction. Government is the instrument for representing the third-party beneficiaries and correcting the deficiency of the market place (though this is not to deny that private religious and philanthropic organizations, for example, also represent third-party beneficiaries and operate on budget rather than market principles).

2. Just as there may be indirect benefits not reflected in market demand,

---

[7] No attempt is made here to define a public good. Samuelson (in "The Pure Theory of Public Expenditures," *The Review of Economics and Statistics,* Vol. 36, November 1954, 387) has defined "collective consumption goods" as those in which one individual's consumption of the good leads to no diminution of any other individual's consumption of that good. McKenna [in an unpublished paper.—*Editor*] would broaden the definition to include as public goods all those that provide "benefit simultaneously and automatically to more than one member of society." It would seem that while the former definition leaves out many goods provided under the budget principle, McKenna's embraces quite a number provided under the market principle. [For a discussion of public goods see Bator in Selected References at the end of Part VI of this volume.—*Editor.*]

[8] See, for example, O. H. Brownlee and E. D. Allen, "The Role of Government Expenditure," *Economics of Public Finance,* 2nd ed. (Englewood Cliffs, N.J.: Prentice-Hall, Inc. 1954), Chap. 10. See also Max F. Millikan, "Objectives for Economic Policy in a Democracy" (especially pp. 62–68), and Robert Dahl and Charles E. Lindblom, "Variation in Public Expenditure," both in *Income Stabilization for a Developing Democracy,* Max F. Millikan, ed. (New Haven: Yale University Press, 1953).

there may be indirect costs inflicted on society which do not enter the private producer's costs and therefore do not influence market supply. Classic examples are the costs of smog, water pollution, denuding of forests, and the like. In these areas, private output will exceed the optimum level unless government corrects the situation either by regulation or by a combination of expenditure and charge-backs to the private producers involved.

3. Where a service is best provided, for technical reasons, as a monopoly (for example, postal service, electricity, and railroad transportation), the government is expected to step in either by regulation or operation to avoid costly duplication and improve the quality of service. Ideally, its function would also be to guide prices toward levels consistent with optimum output. Involved here is the problem of the decreasing-cost industry, where efficient plant size is so large relative to total demand that average cost decreases as output increases, and the market solution of the output and price problem will not result in best use of the productive assets. To push production to a point representing an ideal use of resources may require, if not government operation, a subsidy financed out of tax revenues.

4. Government may enjoy some advantages in production or distribution which make it an inherently more efficient producer of certain services. Here the classic case is highways, streets, and sidewalks. By providing them free to all comers, government effects substantial savings in costs of distribution since it does not have to meter the service and charge a price for each specific use. In this category we might also fit projects, such as the initial development of atomic energy, which involve such great risks and hugh accumulations of capital that the private market does not have the financial tools to cope with them.

Alternative Means of Carrying Out Government Functions

Given the decisions as to the appropriate sphere of government activity (on the basis not merely of considerations of greatest economic gain but also of value preferences), there remains the problem of choice among alternative methods to implement these decisions, to achieve given aims and satisfy expressed public wants. This choice will affect the budget in different ways. It may increase expenditures, decrease revenues, establish contingent liabilities, or perhaps have no effect on the budget at all (except for a small amount of administrative expenses involved in the supervisory and regulatory activities). Since the operational question is not merely what functions and activities government should carry out but what budgetary principles and expenditure levels these lead to, the problem of implementation must be included in any applied theory of public expenditures.

Here the economist's role is to determine the most efficient method of providing the service or otherwise influencing resource allocation. He is concerned with minimizing costs, that is, achieving the stated objective with a minimum expenditure of resources. Needless to say, other considerations will also influence the selection among alternative means, as even a brief consideration of the types of choices involved in the implementation process will make clear.

What are these choices? Take first the case of direct satisfaction of individuals' public wants. Should the government produce the desired public goods or obtain them from private industry by purchase or contract? To accomplish redistributive ends, should the government provide transfers in cash or transfers in kind?[9] Should government rely on public production of educational services, or should it consider private production combined with earmarked transfers of purchasing power to parents? Thus far, the choices all involve direct budgetary expenditures, the level of which differs, at least marginally, depending on the relative efficiency of the method chosen. But in making his choice, the policy maker must consider not merely the direct costs of providing the service but whether one method involves more or less disturbance of private market incentives and patterns of production than another, whether it involves more or less interference with individual freedom (which is largely a function of the extent of government expenditures and intervention but certainly in part also a function of the form of that intervention), and so on.

Another set of choices may take the item off the expenditure side of the budget entirely, or leave it there only contingently. Should such subsidies as those to promote oil and gas exploration, stimulate foreign investment, expand the merchant marine, promote low-cost housing, and increase the flow of strategic minerals take the form of (1) outright subsidies or above-market-price purchase programs, (2) government loan programs, (3) government guaranties, or (4) tax concessions? The choice will clearly involve quite different impacts on government expenditures.

In many of these cases, the economist can be helpful with his efficiency criterion. But one would be naïve to think that efficiency alone dictates the choice. The economist may show that a direct subsidy could stimulate a given amount of private direct investment abroad or a given amount of exploration for oil and gas, with a much smaller cost to the budget than is implicitly required in the tax-concession method of achieving the same end. Yet, the costlier tax-concession method may be preferred for two simple reasons: (1) it is virtually self-administering, involving no administrative hierarchy to substitute its authority for relatively free private decisions, and (2) it does not involve an increase in the expenditure side of the budget, a fact which has certain attractions to the Executive and Congress.

As yet, no clear boundary lines have been drawn among the various forms of government intervention to mark off those that properly belong within the scope of public expenditure theory. But this illustrative review of the various choices makes clear that some forms of government activity which are not re-

---

[9] One involves so-called resource-using (also called factor-purchase or exhaustive) government expenditures, that is, payments in exchange for current goods and services rendered, with direct control of resources remaining in public hands. The other involves transfer payments, that is, payments made without any provision of current goods and services in return, with direct control over resources passing into private hands.

flected in expenditures at all (tax concessions) or only contingently (guaranties) are an integral part of such expenditure theory. In fact, there may be a stronger case for embracing these in expenditure theory than many government activities which require budgetary outlays but are conducted on the pricing principle, that is, government enterprise activities.

Economists are conducting some provocative inquiries into questions of alternative methods of carrying out government programs in areas where the answers had heretofore been taken for granted. For example, the transfer of schooling to a private-production and government-transfer-payment basis has been urged by Professor Milton Friedman as a more efficient means of providing the desired service.[10] Professor O. H. Brownlee is currently probing further into this question, as well as the possibilities of transferring other publicly produced services into the sphere of private production. Once fairly conclusive findings are devised as to the methods most likely to minimize costs, there remains the vital task of blending these findings with the nonmonetary values that would be gained or lost in the process of transferring from public to private production.

Some Constraints on the Application of Specific Economic Criteria

Repeatedly in this discussion, the note has been sounded that, in determining the level of government activity, the policy maker cannot live by economics alone. More particularly, we need to guard against setting up our economic guides solely in terms of those considerations which lend themselves to sharp economic analysis and definition. In other words, the role of both economic and noneconomic constraints must be given full weight.

The former include a host of considerations relating particularly to economic motivation in government versus private undertakings. Government may, for example, have a decided edge in the efficiency of distribution or be able to achieve a better balancing of social costs and social benefits in a variety of fields. Yet, there may be important offsets to these economic advantages in terms of (1) bureaucracy, (2) lack of profit criterion to gauge the results of government activities, and (3) undesigned or unintended (presumably adverse) economic effects of taxation.[11]

The latter factor, in particular the fact that tax financing of public services

---

[10] See Milton Friedman, "The Role of Government in Education", *Economics and the Public Interest,* Robert A. Solow, ed. (New Brunswick, N.J.: Rutgers University Press, 1965), pp. 123–144. In his prescription, Friedman would, of course, have government regulate the private schools to the extent of insuring that they meet certain minimum standards in their programs and facilities.

[11] These less sharply defined economic effects have to be balanced, of course, against comparable and perhaps offsetting drawbacks in the market mechanism. For an exploration of some of these factors, both in the private and the public sphere, see Robert A. Dahl and Charles E. Lindblom, *Politics, Economics, and Welfare* (New York: Harper & Row, Publishers, 1953), especially pt. V. See also C. Lowell Harriss, "Government Spending: Issues of Theory and Practices," *Public Finance,* Vol. 12, 1957, 7–19.

involves breaking the link between an individual's cost of a given service and his benefit from it, may involve important offsets to economic advantages otherwise gained by government expenditure. Thus far, to be sure, no dire consequences of the disincentive effects of taxation have been firmly proved, but changes in the form of private economic activity to minimize taxes are certainly a cost that must be weighed when netting out the balance of economic advantage in government versus private performance of services.

Beyond the economic factors, one encounters an even more basic and less manageable constraint, namely, that of freedom of choice. Thus, it is quite conceivable that following the kinds of economic criteria discussed earlier in the paper would take us considerably farther in the direction of government spending and control over resource allocation than we would wish to go in terms of possible impairment of economic and political freedom. This consideration enters importantly not merely in decisions as to the proper range of government activity but also in choosing among alternative methods of providing government services.

This is not to imply that all value considerations run counter to the expansion of the government sector of our economy. Such expansion may serve a number of social values, such as greater equality of income and opportunity, a more acceptable social environment, and so on.[12]

To get all of these considerations into the decision-making equation on private versus public provision of a particular service, or on the choice among alternative forms of providing the service, requires a wisdom which goes well beyond the field of economics. Perhaps this explains why so few economists enter politics.

---

[12] This type of consideration is examined in William Vickrey, "An Exchange of Questions Between Economics and Philosophy," in *Goals of Economic Life,* ed. by A. Dudley Ward (New York: Harper & Row, Publishers, 1953), pp. 148–177. See also Max F. Millikan, *op. cit.*

Selection 15

Standards and Values in a Rich Society

ALVIN H. HANSEN

The Eradication of Poverty and the Role of Capital Formation

In this chapter I turn to matters related to but still somewhat beyond the range of the economist. It is not enough to rescue economics, as Keynes sought to do, from the narrow role assigned to it by Marshall—essentially a branch of business cost accounting—and restore it to the loftier plane of Political Economy or, as Adam Smith so aptly put it—the Wealth of Nations. Economics must concern itself with something more than merely maximum output and full employment. It must also concern itself with social priorities. In other words, it must, in a sense, become a branch of moral philosophy, as Adam Smith indeed had it.

In the last half-century the American economy has lifted the standard of living of the mass population to undreamed-of levels of comfort and luxury. Mass poverty has largely been wiped out.

Full employment has been a major factor, perhaps *the* major factor, in overcoming widespread economic distress during the last fifteen years. Serious distress is indeed a function of *low* incomes, but it is also a function of *unstable* income. The periodic complete loss of income, often lasting over prolonged periods of depression, has throughout our history been a leading cause of destitution.

Still, full employment in a poor country will not cure poverty. The eradication of poverty depends basically upon science, technical progress, and capital accumulation. Without a large stock of capital goods, poverty could not be eliminated. Yet this accumulated stock creates not a few of our problems.

The recent literature on growth and rising living standards has had a great deal to say about the ratio of the aggregate capital stock to real income. The comparative stability of this capital-output ratio over the long-run has well-nigh led some economists to forget the law of diminishing marginal productivity. It is just not true that one can continue to build more and more plants and more and more equipment and out of this process grow richer and richer. Historically, the capital-output ratio has been fairly stable,[1] but this is only because, whenever the declining marginal productivity of capital sets in, investment falls off, and so a new balance is reached.

Observing the historical ratio of capital to output, it is very easy to fall into the error which currently we frequently encounter, namely, that *any* desired rate of growth in our standard of living is possible if we but push the rate of investment hard enough. If the historical rate of capital accumulation has made possible an increase in output of, say, 3½ per cent of annum, why then, it is asked, should we not double the rate and thereby obtain an annual rate of growth in living standards of, say, 7 per cent per annum? If output is a function of the rate of capital accumulation, there would be virtually no limit to the rate of long-term growth. We might, it would seem, enjoy any desired rate of growth if we were only prepared to push investment to the limit. Some recent pronouncements from high government officials stem, I suggest, from this philosophy.

For the moment let us concentrate attention on long-term growth. I am here considering this problem in terms of per capita growth. What now are the real bases of long-term growth? The answer, I believe, is not capital accumulation, although this plays a necessary, albeit restricted, role. The answer, I suggest, is rather scientific research and invention. If these can be made to grow at a more rapid rate than in the past, then we shall in the usual case be able to open up deeper and broader outlets for investment and thereby accelerate the rate of long-term growth.[2] These new outlets would probably, but not necessarily, raise the ratio of investment to GNP to a figure higher than the long-term maintainable rate which has been found to be feasible in the past.

Recently, however, we have been talking altogether too much, I feel, not about ways and means of opening investment outlets, but merely about ways and means of artificially stimulating investment. Accelerated depreciation is a case in point. This could, of course, be applied in a cyclically stabilizing manner. But this has not been done. Instead, the measure recently adopted is in effect a subsidy which, made continuously, without regard to cyclical fluctuations, would tend to push investment faster than otherwise beyond the maintainable rate.

It would, of course, be quite possible to carry the process of subsidization of investment very much farther than is contemplated with respect to the accelerated-depreciation device. Indeed, it could be carried to almost any desired point. The rate of obsolescence and replacement would thereby be greatly accelerated.

---

[1] Actually the ratio has apparently declined some from around 3 to 3.5 per cent in 1880–1915 to perhaps 2.8 to 3.0 in 1949–1955.

[2] Public investment can often unlock large private investment opportunities. Power development can never be carried to the full on the narrow principle of a self-liquidating project. Full development requires that cognizance be taken of the *indirect* effect of such programs upon the productivity of the *community as a whole*. Only the government can take this larger view. Even the Public Power people have never fully grasped this principle.

We could, if we wished to, increase the rate of capital replacement to a point at which no house would be more than, say, fifteen years old, no plant more than, say, ten years old, and no machinery more than, say, two years old, or even farther. If we are prepared to restrict our consumption with sufficient severity, we could acquire, at least in the United States, an incredible degree of "newness" or "youth" in our stock of fixed capital goods.

Such a program would, however, clearly involve a highly wasteful use of resources. We would be spending a very high proportion of our productive power merely to scrap useful and comparatively new plant and equipment. We would, indeed, enjoy the possession of a strictly up-to-date stock of fixed capital all around. But the price we would pay for this artificial "newness" would necessarily be a lower output of consumers' goods. Americans love gadgets. Farmers are sometimes so enamored with the sight of expensive and uneconomical machinery that they are prepared to sacrifice their standard of living and that of their families to get it. And many urban families are prepared to sacrifice almost anything to get an expensive new car.

In the United States we have reached a level of productivity so high that we could, if we wanted to, devote perhaps *half* of our resources to a highly accelerated rate of obsolescence and to an extravagantly large accumulation of very new capital goods. But the price would be a severely restricted output of services and of nondurable and semidurable consumers' goods.

Clearly we should not aim at the *maximum* rate of capital accumulation. We should aim at the *optimum* rate. And that optimum rate would be determined, I suggest, first, by the rate of scientific research and invention and, second, by the growth of population.

Scientific research and invention are indeed likely, as I have already indicated, to open up larger investment outlets, but not necessarily so. Scientific research and invention may at times increase productivity yet lessen the need for capital accumulation. Moreover, expenditures in human resources—education, health, et cetera—may not only directly contribute to living standards but may also, no less than capital accumulation, increase the productive capacity of the society. There is far too great a tendency nowadays to plead for policies that encourage investment in material and capital goods—plant and equipment—and to forget that outlays on the improvement of our human resources may be even more productive. We are concerned altogether too much about increased investment in brick and mortar and not enough about investments designed to improve the quality and productivity of our people.

The Rise in Living Standards

Income per family in real terms is now about two and a half times as high as at the beginning of this century. This represents a gain in real purchasing power of 1¾ per cent per annum. At the same time working hours have been reduced from around 60 per week to 40 per week; from a ten-hour day and a six-day week to an eight-hour day and a five-day week. The gain in leisure time is clearly one of the best indices of a higher standard of living.

Still the impressive rise in purchasing-power income requires at least some qualification. A calculation based on money income and price changes is not altogether convincing. In the nineteenth-century rural society many things were free which we now have to pay for. Consider the amount of labor which must be devoted in modern communities, not to positive productive effort, but to neutralizing the disagreeable consequences of dense concentrations of population in large urban communities. Much effort is devoted, not to providing utilities, but to the removal of disutilities, by-products of industrialization and urbanization. Yet the labor expended on the removal of disutilities is counted in our money economy as a part of our Gross National Product.

Industrialized cities with overcrowded tenement districts have made an effort via public parks to recover *some* of the lost sunshine, open fields, and fresh air formerly enjoyed by rural populations. Yet in many communities the parks are not located where people live, where children can have direct access to them. Instead of big and grand parks we need many small neighborhood parks, not for an outing but for daily use, not for an occasional automobile drive but for continuous recreation.

Thus it is that our ugly industrial cities scarcely help to build up a convincing case that our standard of living is as far above that of fifty or a hundred years ago as the figures of money incomes corrected for price changes would indicate. In 1900, 60 per cent of our population lived in rural areas and only 22 per cent in cities of over 25,000. Now only 40 per cent live in rural areas, and 60 million people live in cities of over 25,000. The terrific problems of providing urban transportation involve a vast investment of capital and labor. And while the workweek is far shorter, should we not add back some part of the hours spent in the nerve-racking rush to get to and from work? In these terms there are still many people who have what in fact amounts to a ten-hour day.

In realistic terms, changes in the standard of living can perhaps best be measured in terms of food consumption, housing, health, education, recreation, and leisure.

Changes in the consumption of food disclose clearly a rising living standard. While the consumption of meat per capita was slightly lower in 1950 than in 1900, the consumption of vegetables is nearly 50 per cent higher, fresh fruits 15 per cent higher, cheese 60 per cent higher, and chicken and turkeys 70 per cent higher. These increases, combined with a drastic decline in the consumption of wheat flour—the main item, along with potatoes, in a poor man's diet—disclose a richer and more nutritive diet. In addition to the varied items of diet already referred to, the consumption of such nutrients as vitamin A, thiamine, ascorbic acid, calcium, and riboflavin have increased around 30 per cent per capita. A man is no longer old at fifty, as was the case seventy-five years ago. We have achieved a far healthier diet during the last fifty or seventy-five years. Considerations such as these are useful supplements to mere monetary aggregates.[3]

The American people are certainly better housed now than fifty years ago.

---

[3] *America's Needs and Resources* (New York: Twentieth Century Fund, 1955), chap. 5.

Plumbing, electric lights, and central heating are indicative of this advance. Yet even today we have over 7 million substandard dwelling units which ought at once to be demolished, either because they are without toilet, bath, and running water, or because they are otherwise dilapidated. Kerosene stoves still heat a high proportion of the homes in many working-class sections—a major cause of fires. To complete the task of raising housing standards to the minimum of decency for all would require, it is estimated by the Twentieth Century Fund,[4] around $85 billion. There is still a good deal of unfinished business before we can say that the American people are well housed. Nonetheless, there is a vast difference between the housing facilities available to the American wage-earning family today compared with the situation around 1890, when Jacob Riis gave his lurid description of *How the Other Half Lives*.

So familiar have we become with the widespread use of electrical household appliances that we are prone to think that all Americans are now equipped with these comforts. Yet 50 per cent do not have vacuum cleaners, 30 per cent do not have electric washing machines, and 20 per cent are without electric refrigerators.[5] Still, apart from food and housing and more leisure time, the most conspicuous gains, no doubt, for the great majority are the mechanical gadgets, comforts and luxuries—household appliances, plumbing, the automobile, the motion picture, radio, and television.

Mass Education

The substitution of mechanical power for human power and the consequent gains in productivity have not only reduced the workweek from 60 to 40 hours; they have also made possible a much longer period of education for the whole population. In this respect we have witnessed a truly revolutionary development since 1900, indeed since 1910. As late as 1910 only 5 per cent of the youth of college age (18 to 21) attended college. By 1950 it was 30 per cent.[6] As late as 1910 only a few went on to high school. Then the flood began. Already by 1920 high-school graduations per capita had doubled, and by 1940 the number graduating from high school each year was, per capita, eight times that of 1900. And by 1950 the number of graduations from colleges and universities, on a per capita basis, had reached eight times that of 1900.

This massive increase in high-school and college attendance has come upon us all of a sudden in the last few decades. Indeed, throughout the nineteenth century a high proportion of American children had only four or five years of schooling and often no more than four or five months per year. Today high-school attendance is 6,600,000. Fifty years ago it was only 700,000. Today college and university attendance is 3,000,000; in 1900 it was only 240,000.

Nothing else like it has occurred in any other part of the world. We have not

---

[4] *Ibid.*, p. 512.

[5] *Ibid.*, p. 242.

[6] James B. Conant, *Education and Liberty* (Cambridge, Mass.: Harvard University, 1953), p. 35.

had time to make the proper adjustments. This flood of students into secondary schools and higher institutions has come upon us in a single generation. It is no wonder that our high-school standards are low. No nation could train an adequate number of competent teachers in so short a time. Worse yet, we have miserably failed to give teachers the salary differential needed to draw the best brains into the teaching profession. On the stage we ridicule schoolma'ams, and in the market place we underprice them.

The task of education is, moreover, enormously complicated by the heterogeneity of our population and the difficult problem of immigrant adjustment to American life. Forty-five million immigrants have stormed our shores during the last hundred years. In 1900, 40 per cent of the whole population was foreign-born, or born of foreign parents, and the figure is still 25 per cent today.

The Submerged Tenth in a Rich Society

This mass immigration explains in no small measure the extraordinary spread between the median income in the United States and the income of the lowest decile. And it accounts in considerable degree for many personal and family maladjustments and social dislocations.

What was it that caused this massive movement of people from the Old World to the New? It was primarily the revolutionary increase in population which occurred in Europe throughout the nineteenth century. From 1800 to 1910 the population of the five largest European countries—England, France, Italy, Germany, and Russia—increased from 125 million to 325 million. The chief cause was the sharp decline in the death rate. The struggle for existence grew desperate. Subdivision of the family plots pushed down the subsistence level. Peasants by the millions were forced off the land. In America they crowded, after the 1880's, into our great urban industrial centers. Uprooted from their Old World peasant communities, where human ties were close and moral values were firmly fixed, they were all at sea in a new and strange world. The uprooted immigrant had to readjust his peasant outlook on life.[7] He had to come to terms with an urbanized industrialism.

To make matters still worse, a psychological conflict, placing severe strains on parental discipline, inevitably developed between the immigrant and his children—a conflict born of differences in language and social environment. The restraints and security of the Old World peasant communities were missing. Sheds, shanties, stables, and cellars were drafted for living space in our great industrial centers. The crowded street was the only playground.[8] Out of such conditions have grown psychopathic disorders and social maladjustments. It is true that those endowed with exceptional energy and capacity, both mental and physical, found in the American environment almost boundless opportunities and

---

[7] Oscar Handlin, *The Uprooted* (Boston: Little, Brown & Company, 1952).

[8] I note even today, as I walk around the streets of some of our great cities, that school children in recess time have frequently no place to play except on pavement and adjoining sidewalks.

rose very rapidly to higher social and economic levels. More gradually the great middle group also improved its status and succeeded reasonably well in the difficult process of amalgamation and assimilation. But there was also the submerged tenth or quintile.

The physical and mental deficiencies which we find today among the lower two deciles of our population stem in part at least from the conflicts experienced by the uprooted peasant immigrant unable to find his way about in congested cities amid the uncertainties and insecurity of a laissez-faire industrialism. Against the background of these conditions one can learn a good deal that explains the submerged decile in a rich society.

Our much-heralded high *average* income is indeed the envy of even high-standard countries, but astonishment is often the reaction one gets to the incredibly wide spread between the median income in the United States and the income of the lowest decile. Not only have we been historically the country with the widest cyclical swings; we have also exhibited the widest spread between income classes, especially at the bottom of the scale.

In the United States today there are 800,000,000 families and individual household units with a money income of less than $1,000 per year and an additional 6,500,000 with incomes between $1,000 and $2,000. A considerable proportion live in depressed areas, where unemployment is chronic even when the nation as a whole is enjoying full-employment opportunities. It is a vicious circle. Because the area is depressed, public revenues are limited. Community services, and especially the quality of education, are seriously deficient. Such areas become not merely economically depressed areas; they become also derelict areas, composed of a population with inferior education and lacking in physical and mental vigor. The able, aggressive young people migrate. Those who remain behind constitute, disproportionately, aged persons, remaining members of broken families, and generally persons inadequately equipped to compete successfully in modern industry.

In part it is a rural problem, and in part it is a race problem. Two-thirds of the low-income rural families live in the South. Moreover, the incidence of low incomes among rural families is twice as great among Negroes as among whites.

Lack of education is a primary cause of low income. Low-income families are compelled to spend a disproportionate per cent of their income on food and housing. There is little left for education. Substandard families spend 65 per cent of their income on food and housing, while wage-earning families in general spend only 45 per cent on these two consumption categories. Moreover, as I have already indicated, such families are likely to live in communities where educational facilities are very limited.

The problem of education for the children of low-income families is far more important to the nation as a whole than appears on the surface. An alarmingly high proportion of the nation's children are reared in low-income families. In general there is an inverse correlation between income and size of family. Thus families with five children have a median income of $3,155, while families with two children have a median income of $4,500. The bulk of the nation's children grow up in relatively low-income families with three, four, five, six, or more children. Indeed, of the 55 million children under eighteen years of age, 30 million are reared in families with three or more children. Of these about 16 million, or about 30 per cent of all the nation's children, live in the eighteen lowest-income states. Several of these states have a per capita income less than half that of the richest states.

These poorer states cannot, without substantial federal aid, provide the minimum American standards of education, health, and social welfare. These children are Americans. Yet citizens of New York and Massachusetts are prone to talk and act as though they were foreigners. We are indeed almost immeasurably distant from being *world* citizens. In the present stage of human development this is at least understandable. But is it not incredible that we pretend to be citizens of our separate states and not citizens of the United States when we consider the problem of adequate minimum standards of education for Americans everywhere?

The wide spread between the median income and the lowest decile in our society holds not only with respect to income and education but also with respect to physical fitness. Not only is the rate of illiteracy high in the lower deciles, but the extraordinary high proportion of our total youth physically and mentally unfit for military service is clearly in some part to be explained by the unfavorable economic and social conditions under which the lower deciles of our population live. Our slums persist in the midst of a $400 billion GNP. It is true that the problem of juvenile delinquency is a very complicated one and can by no means be explained simply in terms of income status. Nonetheless, it cannot be denied that our slums contribute not a little to the problem. Slum clearance and a nationwide system of health insurance are high in the agenda of unfinished business.

It is not only the personal incomes and the physical and mental status of the submerged tenth which are seriously deficient. It is also their opportunity to share in the amenities of life which only the community can offer. Our great cities lack adequate parks and playgrounds—Cambridge, Mass., is a notorious example—and they lack community facilities for recreation and social life. The joy of living in a city with beautiful parks within the reach of all and with easy and quick access to the surrounding countryside is something that our lower-income groups do not share in equal measure with comparable income groups in Holland, Switzerland, Denmark, and Sweden.

Joyful living is not simply an individual matter. Among the more important amenities of life are those which only the community can provide. This is a job for government. And if we hide behind the doctrine that all this is no affair of the federal government, we become in practice pure defeatists. I am glad to note, in this connection, the splendid work of the Joint Congressional Committee on the Economic Report with respect to the problems of the low-income families and ways and means of dealing with these problems at the federal level.

The lower-income classes are at a peculiar disadvantage because of the preoccupation of the American society with mechanical gadgets and because of the relatively slight emphasis placed upon social values and community activities. We are increasingly in danger of making our economic system a mere treadmill. We have reached a point in our development where mere emphasis on larger and larger output of mechanical gadgets becomes rather meaningless, if, indeed, not a detriment to truly satisfactory living. We spend billions and billions of dollars on automobiles, of which perhaps half is frittered away on mere size, gadgets, and chrome—all of which add little to the social utility of comfortable transportation. And expenditures on automobiles, not including operation or the vast sums spent on roads, are twice as great as the aggregate expenditure on schools, including school construction and other capital outlays for education.

The average public-school teacher's salary is $3,450, while the average full-time wage for production workers in manufacturing industry is $3,735 and that for railroad production workers (not including supervising employees) is $4,100. A country as rich as ours can and should make the school teacher's profession highly attractive financially. A good rule, and a thoroughly justifiable one, would be an average salary scale twice that of production workers. This means more than a doubling of school teachers' salaries. In ten years we should see a profound change in the quality of our teachers. To say that we can't afford it is nonsense. Eight years hence, by 1965, we can produce a GNP of $550 billion. That is $150 billion more than now. We are spending currently a paltry $3½ billion on public-school teachers' salaries. We can well afford to double or treble that amount out of our rapidly increasing national income.

We shall not solve the problem of education for the submerged tenth or the lowest quintile until we have solved it for all the people. The same holds for youth programs, recreational facilities, and a nationwide system of health insurance.

What Goals Do We Seek?

After ten years of almost incredible *output* performance, we need to assess not merely the speed of our growth and progress but also the direction in which we are going. What *qualitative* goals shall we set up? What kind of country do we wish to build? These are matters that we dare not overlook, lest we perish, as a great nation, in the widst of material plenty.

Now someone will surely say: "What right has this armchair professor to talk about how the American public should use its resources? Leave it to the market to take care of all that." Superficially that sounds good, but in fact that answer will not do. The "market" cannot decide how much we shall spend on schools, on social security, or on national security. We have reached a point in our economic and social evolution where *social-value* judgments, not the market, must control the uses to which we put something like one-fourth of our productive resources. Our economy is no longer wholly a market economy. It is a mixed public-private economy.

And how are these social-value judgments to be determined? Do we leave it to chance, to nature, to the elemental, uneducated instincts of people? That indeed is the rule among savages. But civilized countries follow another rule, and it is this: "Train up a child in the way he should go, and when he is a man he will not depart therefrom." Civilized countries mold their people into civilized ways of thinking, guided by values that experience and knowledge have laid down. We don't leave it to the market. We educate. Only in this way can we achieve the great goals of a civilized society.

Here I come to a critical point. Our schools and churches can no longer be said to constitute the main educational media in this country. Modern technology has largely supplanted these older media. Children, young people, and grownups devote more hours per day the year round to the radio and television and the movies than they do to school, churches, or reading. These mechanical media have become an important, if indeed not the most important, element in our entire educational process. And what worries me is this. These powerful educational media are controlled, not by educators, but by advertisers whose primary purpose is profit, not education. Advertisers do not control the editorials or news columns of our newspapers, though there may be an indirect influence. But they do control our radio and television programs. Is it any wonder that we prefer longer and longer cars with more and more chrome to good schools and well-paid teachers? At the very least, advertisers should not, I suggest, be allowed to sponsor or select the programs other than their own commercials.

We have been brought up with a narrow conception of the functions of public education. Adult education, music, drama, the fine arts, deserve public support. Even our FM fine music programs are painfully encroached upon by advertising.

Thus the problem of social priorities is hard upon us. It is not enough to achieve maximum employment and production. It is not enough to have quantitative goals. We cannot allow full employment to become merely a device to make our economy an efficient treadmill.

America's Needs and Resources discloses (p. 512) that the estimated cost of urban redevelopment in general—including a demolition of our 7 million slum houses—would amount to no more than the equivalent of about two years of defense expenditures at current levels.

In terms of GNP we are spending currently only 40 per cent as much on hospitals today as in 1920–1924 (p. 312). We are spending (including operating and capital expenditures) only 2¼ per cent of our GNP on public schools, elementary and secondary. Indeed, in relation to GNP we are spending 20 per cent less on schools today than we spent twenty-five years ago. A rich country can't afford good schools and good teachers!

This is an area in which economists have been, I feel, neglectful of their duty. We need more study of social priorities.

Yet with all our distorted values there is happily a growing realization that we *have* accumulated a large backlog of long-range public-investment needs. This means larger and larger federal budgets, not only absolutely but also in relation to the GNP. When I say "public investment" I mean not merely public works and resource-development projects. I include investment in human resources as well —schools, scholarship programs, medical research, a nationwide system of health insurance, recreational facilities, et cetera.

The problem of long-range public-investment planning is all the more important in view of our large and now again increasing defense and foreign aid budgets. The national security budgets compete with the growing urgent need for much larger long-range social welfare budgets. I think we should all agree that national security comes first. Indeed, I have never been able to understand why we continually debate the question whether our military strength is more or less equal to that of the Soviet Union when we, in fact, have ample resources to ensure our superiority by a wide margin. Our military program should be adequate to guarantee without question the peace of the world for the visible future. I am not, therefore, suggesting that we should reduce our military program. But I do, nonetheless, say that we should increase *now* by a substantial amount our long-range public welfare budgets. That may involve a reappraisal of tax cuts. We are in a situation in which the marginal *tax* dollar can clearly yield a much higher social utility than the marginal *pay envelope* dollar.

Let it be noted that the growing ratio of government purchases of goods and services—a trend which has been going on throughout our history—does indeed point up the unmistakable *fact* that our economy is becoming more and more a mixed public-private economy. But government ownership and operation of the means of production—the classical definition of socialism—is *not* noticeably on the increase. It is the welfare state that is growing, not the government as owner or operator. The welfare state is primarily a redistributor of income and a colossal purchaser of the products of private enterprise. But private enterprise does the job.

The growth of public budgets means that the public *finance* method of paying for goods and services will grow in relation to the *market-price* method. It does not mean that private enterprise is shrinking or that the tax base is shrinking. The goods are purchased from private enterprise. Thus private enterprise continues to grow in much the same proportion as the GNP. The welfare state does not in any appreciable degree operate to supplant the system of private enterprise. Instead it makes it stronger and more workable.

No one can dispute that we have become a rich society. We have made great advances on the purely economic plane. Unfortunately the progress we have made in many of the noneconomic aspects of life is limited; and in some areas we have, I fear, definitely retrogressed. The economic gains are visible on every hand. And economists, as a professional group, have, I think it is fair to say, contributed in no small measure to this development. Government departments have at long last been staffed with well-trained economists. State papers nowadays are mainly concerned with economic matters, often highly technical. Congressional hearings and legislative programs draw increasingly on the work of economists inside and outside the government. The result is evident in the massive and highly technical messages and reports of the President to Congress.

Would that our colleagues, concerned with noneconomic aspects of American life, could claim equal progress. We are learning, in the midst of material plenty, that man "cannot live by bread alone." How do educators feel when they contemplate the deterioration of our public schools; the social psychologists and pathologists when they observe the increase in mental disorders, crime, and juvenile delinquency, or, on another plane, the current predominance of neurotic art?

We have learned how to make a living; we have still to learn how to live. Until we have eliminated the ugliness of our great industrial cities we cannot claim to have reached as a nation a truly high standard of living. America is long on wealth but short on appreciation of the beautiful. Some years ago I visited, in company with Professor Jørgen Pedersen, a large farm in Jutland, Denmark. It employed eighteen or twenty well-housed farm workers. Two of these devoted full time to beautifying the place, to the flower gardens, the lawns, the trees, the buildings. That farm was a place on which to live, not merely a place to make a living.

Many readers have no doubt visited the famous Town Hall in Stockholm, a noble work of man. Compare this with the city hall in Boston, Mass., to take only one example. The Town Hall in Stockholm is not simply a place where the mayor has his office. It is a community building where citizens of high or low rank can meet in civic-group gatherings amidst an atmosphere of dignity, beauty, and elegance. Such things make for the good life. A higher standard of mere material wealth is no substitute for beauty—for the things of the mind and the spirit.

Few will deny the cultural deficiencies of our cities and towns, and everyone will agree that an adequate program would cost a lot of money. And the answer to that usually is that we can't afford it. We are too poor! Ah, that is it. We have become so gadget-rich that we can't afford to build culturally rich communities. But what does it profit a man if he gains the whole world but loses his own soul?

DISCUSSION QUESTIONS

1. Distinguish between exhaustive and nonexhaustive government expenditures.
2. Discuss the situations mentioned by Professor Heller where government interventions in the market might lead to an improved allocation of resources.
3. The usual argument against transfers in kind is that they restrict individual freedom of choice. How does Professor Heller answer this criticism?
4. Discuss the reasons why Professor Galbraith believes our present economic and political system produces too few public goods relative to private goods.

SELECTED REFERENCES

Bator, Francis M., *The Question of Government Spending,* New York: Harper & Row, Publishers, 1960.

Galbraith, John Kenneth, *The Affluent Society,* Boston: Houghton Mifflin Co., 1958.

Heilbroner, Robert L., and Peter L. Bernstein, *A Primer on Government Spending,* New York: Vintage Books, A Division of Random House, 1963.

Wallich, Henry, *The Cost of Freedom: A New Look at Capitalism,* New York: Harper & Row, Publishers, 1960.

PART 7

BUSINESS, LABOR, AND AGRICULTURE

The influence of government decisions on the economic behavior of business, labor, and agriculture has increased greatly over time. There are two important causes for this increased role of government. First, farm, business, and labor groups have successfully petitioned government to intervene in their behalf. Business firms have been able to secure tariffs, patent and copyright laws, and favorable tax treatment; unions have achieved the right to bargain collectively, exemptions from antitrust laws, and minimum wage legislation; farmers have received price supports, direct governmental payments, and subsidized research, education and extension services. Each group is against government intervention in general but believes that its case is a special case where government action will improve the workings of the market.

The second reason for the increased role of government is that the public and the government have become concerned with the ability of unions and management to tie up large segments of the economy in an attempt to settle wage disputes. Because of the great economic power held by these groups, there is little guarantee that a settlement will be in the public interest and noninflationary. This has meant a major revision of the concept of "free collective bargaining" and in the future may mean that prolonged strikes in major industries will no longer be tolerated. The Council of Economic Advisers has established the following wage-price guidelines:*

---

* *Economic Report of the President, together with the Annual Report of the Council of Economic Advisers* (Washington: U.S. Govt. Printing Office, 1965), p. 108.

1. The general guide for wages is that the percentage increase in total employee compensation per man-hour be equal to the national trend rate of increase in output per man-hour.
2. The general guide for prices calls for stable prices in industries enjoying the same productivity growth as the average for the economy; rising prices in industries with slower that average productivity gains; and declining prices in industries with greater than average productivity gains.

The government has no specific legislative powers to back this up. It acts under the general provision of the Employment Act of 1946. However, considerable pressure can be exerted by the government if it thinks the national interest is at stake. Both unions and management are reluctant to accept such guidelines, and in many cases they have been ignored. Perhaps in time the Congress will pass a law spelling out some form of compulsory arbitration, so that the Secretary of Labor will not have to rush around the country acting as a fireman attempting to put out the fires of labor-management dissatisfaction wherever they break out.

The article by Edward Mason discusses the principal questions for society that are posed by the rise of the giant corporations. With the separation of control from ownership there arises the question of legitimacy: how is management to be selected and to whom are they responsible? The reason that legitimacy is a problem is the existence of power. With an economy of small firms, no one firm had significant economic or political power. But in an economy of relatively few huge corporations, their power becomes a major concern. What assurances are there that this private power will be responsible to the public interest?

The article by Neil Chamberlain discusses the role of the unions in modern society. In the United States we have had business unionism —that is, unions have accepted the private-enterprise setting in which they found themselves and have fought for their share of the pie. Their battlefield has been primarily within the business arena. But if the role of collective bargaining diminishes, unions may seek to maintain their power by moving more into the political arena.

The article by James B. Herendeen discusses government policy for agriculture. Agricultural policy has faced a political stalemate for roughly a decade. This was the result of disagreement among farm interest groups as to what direction policy should move, with each major group being able to veto any effective reform that was not consistent with its interests. In addition, power in the House and Senate Agricultural Committees was in the hands of Southern and Great Plains Congressmen, content with maintaining the status quo for wheat, cotton, and tobacco producers. However, with the 1965 Omnibus Farm Bill, the administration has successfully challenged the present power structure, and more reform seems imminent for the future.

Selection 16

The Corporation in Modern Society: Introduction

EDWARD S. MASON

From Edward S. Mason (ed.), The Corporation in Modern Society *(Cambridge, Mass.: Harvard University Press, 1959), pp. 1–9. Reprinted by permission of Harvard University Press.*

Everyone talks about the corporation, but, in the words of Mark Twain, no one does anything about it. And for this there are some pretty good reasons. In the first place, something very like the modern corporation is the inevitable product of an industrializing society, whether that society follows a capitalist or a socialist trend of development. Lawyers love to describe the corporation as a creature of the law, but law in a major manifestation is simply a device for facilitating and registering the obvious and the inevitable. Given the technologically determined need for a large stock of capital, the managerial requirements set by the problem of administering the efforts of many men, and the area of discretion demanded for the effective conduct of an entrepreneurial function, the corporation, or a reasonable facsimile thereof, is the only answer.

In the second place the business corporation is so much our most important economic institution and it is so thoroughly integrated into our business culture that to suggest a drastic change in the scope or character of corporate activity is to suggest a drastic alteration in the structure of society. If and when this comes about, it will take place not by radical changes in public policy toward the corporation but by radical changes much broader in scope. We are now a nation of wage and salaried employees and, in the main, we work for corporations. The days of Jeffersonian democracy are over and nothing can be done to resurrect them. We look to the corporation for the technical improvements that spark our economic growth. The corporation recruits our youth from college and provides them with pensions in their old age. It is the present support of community chests and other local charities and the future hope of institutions of higher learning. All this is to suggest not that the corporation cannot be touched, but that to touch the corporation deeply is to touch much else.

In the third place, though many people have ideas on what to do about the corporation, there is little evidence of consensus. The "viewers with alarm" are approximately balanced by the "pointers with pride." On the one hand, we hear much talk of "a new feudalism," of "self-perpetuating oligarchies," of "irresponsible private power," and of "the euthanasia of the capitalist owner." But on the other, we are told of "the twentieth-century revolution," the "professionalization of management," the various "public" whose interests are sedulously cared for, and the beneficence of the "corporate conscience." It is not to be wondered that, to date, this cacophony of voices has not produced a very firm view on what to think or what to do about the corporation either in the general public or the minds of legislators.

The problem of what to think and what to do becomes the more difficult when one considers that, despite the fact that the United States has, over the last century, undergone a revolutionary change in which the rise of the corporation has played a dominant role, the rate of economic growth and the shares in which our increasing product has been distributed to the various recipients have remained remarkably stable. Under corporate dispensation the large economic classes in the community seem, over time, to be faring not much better and not much worse than they did before. Yet no one can doubt that the structure of our economy and our society has been profoundly altered. The mid-nineteenth-century nation of farmers, shopkeepers, and small manufacturers has become a highly industrialized economy dominated by organized groups. The percentage of the population in urban areas has continually increased and, despite the fact that it now approaches 60 per cent, the end is not yet in sight. Innovation at the hands of the small-scale inventor and individual enterpriser has given way to organized research. The role of government in the economy persistently increases. The rugged individualist has been supplanted by smoothly efficient corporate executives participating in the group decision. The equity owner is joining the bondholder as a functionless *rentier*.

If these changes had markedly accelerated or markedly diminished the rate of growth of which the economy seems capable, or if they had profoundly changed the distribution between property and labor income, the popular attitude toward the corporation and all its works might be less ambivalent. But this has not happened. To be sure, employment under the combined influence of public policy and the policies of corporations and trade unions seems to be substantially more stable—a stability that may or may not turn out to have been purchased at the expense of persistent inflation. Furthermore, there is no doubt that the class conflicts and acerbities of business conduct of an earlier age have been substantially softened. But, so far as the essential rates and percentages that describe the performance of our economy are concerned, the key word is *stability*. What seems to have happened in our corporate society is that the prime movers of economic growth, the rate of capital formation, and the rate of technological improvement have become institutionally determined. And the political and economic balance among forces in society seems sufficiently resistant to change to prevent any marked redistribution of the fruits of growth. The stock of capital continues to grow at about twice the rate of growth of the labor force. The average yield per unit of capital falls slightly or not at all. The per capita real earnings of labor increase at about 2 per cent a year and the shares of property and labor in the division of the product change with a glacial slowness. *Plus ça change, plus c'est la même chose.*

But if the inevitability of something like the corporate form, the degree of its integration with our culture, and the absence of any markedly adverse influence of the "corporate revolution" on the over-all performance of the economy help to explain the lack of a generally accepted bill of indictment against the corporation, this does not prove that all is well in Eden. Even A. A. Berle, who has done more than most to justify corporate man to his society—and incidentally, has thrown more light than any other man on the questions discussed in this volume—admits that he is afraid.[1] What Mr. Berle and most of the rest of us are afraid of is that this powerful corporate machine, which so successfully grinds out the goods we want, seems to be running without any discernible controls. The young lad mastering the technique of his bicycle may legitimately shout with pride, "Look, Ma, no hands," but is this the appropriate motto for a corporate society?

Almost everyone now agrees that in the large corporation, the owner is, in general, a passive recipient; that, typically, control is in the hands of management; and that management normally selects its own replacements. It is, furthermore, generally recognized that, in the United States, the large corporation undertakes a substantial part of total economic activity, however measured; that the power of corporations to act is by no means so thoroughly circumscribed by the market as was generally thought to be true of nineteenth-century enterprise; and that, in addition to market power, the large corporation exercises a considerable degree of control over nonmarket activities of various sorts. What all this seems to add up to is the existence of important centers of private power in the hands of men whose authority is real but whose responsibilities are vague. At this point a confused medley of voices breaks in to assert the claims of various corporate "publics"—labor, owners, suppliers, customers, creditors, and so on—to whom management is *really* responsible; to point to the ever-widening scope of government jurisdiction and authority which managements must "take into account"; and to extoll the emergence of a code of behavior generally recognized by professional managements, serving for the moment as a "corporate conscience" but in process of becoming a "rule of law."

All this is very interesting but very unsatisfactory, particularly to the intellectual who is bothered by apparent missing links in the chain of authority and by a seeming equilibrium of forces that by every right should be disequilibrating. The nineteenth century produced a social doctrine that not only explained but justified. But the functioning of the corporate system has not to date been adequately explained, or, if certain explanations are accepted as adequate, it seems difficult to justify. The man of action may be content with a system that works. But one who reflects on the properties or characteristics of this system cannot help asking why it works and whether it will continue to work.

---

[1] A. A. Berle, Jr., *Economic Power and the Free Society* (New York: Harcourt, Brace & World, Inc., 1957), p. 15.

The essays that make up this volume are in the main devoted to explaining various legal, economic, political, and social aspects of the corporate system. But they also raise questions of why, whither, and whether. In this introduction, borrowing heavily from the contributors, I shall attempt a brief statement of some of the principal questions that the rise of this modern leviathan is putting to us.

The Problem of Legitimacy

The one hundred-thirty-odd largest manufacturing corporations account for half of manufacturing output in the United States. The five hundred largest business corporations in this country embrace nearly two-thirds of all nonagricultural economic activity. These or similar figures are reiterated with such frequency that they tend to bounce off our heads rather than to penetrate. But by now we are all aware that we live not only in a corporate society but in a society of large corporations. The management—that is, the control—of these corporations is in the hands of, at most, a few thousand men. Who selected these men, if not to rule over us, at least to exercise vast authority, and to whom are they responsible? The answer to the first question is quite clearly: they selected themselves. The answer to the second is, at best, nebulous. This, in a nutshell, constitutes the problem of legitimacy.

In the mid-nineteenth-century economy, corporate management was nothing if not legitimate. The generalizing of the privilege of incorporation was an aspect of a liberal movement that sought to give to all men equal opportunity under law. And the elimination of restrictions on the duration, size, purposes, and powers of corporations represented an attempt to convert the corporation from a special agency of the state into just another form of business enterprise. And indeed in the early stages of manufacturing development the corporation was just another form of enterprise, enjoying, it is true, limited liability, but functioning in essential respects like an individual proprietorship. The owner, if not the manager himself, selected the management, and the management was responsible to the owners. The traditional justification not only of private enterprise but of private property rested on that assumption. But those days are gone forever, and not even the assiduous efforts of the SEC can put ownership back in the saddle.

The phrase "self-perpetuating oligarchy" rings harshly to our democratic ears. But it must be recognized that some of our best people are oligarchs. The Harvard Corporation is self-perpetuating, and no one would deny—at least no one in my position—that this is an able and estimable body of men. The fact of the matter is that in some of the most effective and longest-lived organizations known to man, the management, in effect, is self-selected. So why not in the business corporation?

The answer, I would suppose, depends in part on how effective is self-selection as a method of assuring that the "best people" will continue to be chosen. But it also depends in part on whether good government, if assured, is an adequate substitute for self-government. A lot of people around the world have recently decided that it is not, and are now in process of discovering that self-government is not always an adequate substitute for good government. It would be nice to have both, but it may be necessary to give up a little of the one in order to secure an appropriate measure of the other.

The meaning of self-government within the context of corporate organization depends on who are considered to be "citizens." Some would say they are the salaried and wage employees and would devise plans of "industrial democracy" that lead straight toward syndicalism. But syndicalism has never had much appeal to the Anglo-Saxon mentality. Others consider the citizens to be members of the various corporate "publics"—owners, employees, customers, suppliers, and creditors—and managerial spokesmen assert the responsibility of management to these "publics," without making it clear, however, how divergent interests are to be reconciled. This also is a quasi-syndicalist solution to the problem of legitimacy and one that inevitably assigns different weights to the "votes" of various constituencies. The consumer public, because of lack of organization, is obviously low man on the totem pole.

Legitimacy can ultimately be conferred only by the sovereign, and in the American tradition only the people are sovereign. But the sovereign acts through duly constituted representatives, and this opens the possibility for alternative routes to legitimacy. One possible route leads through court decisions to a rule of law designed to make equitable and tolerable the actions of inevitable private power. Another envisages an extended federalism, with corporations recognized as quasi-political entities properly legitimated. Still other routes move in the direction of public ownership or an expansion of the public-utility concept.

The Problem of Power

Legitimacy is a problem mainly because of the existence of private power. And private power now concerns us because that vision echoing Adam Smith of an atomistic society no longer seems quite relevant to a corporate universe. In that society managerial control was made legitimate by ownership, and ownership was justified in part because of limitations on the power of ownership imposed by the competitive market.

Power, however, is a tricky concept, and it is even trickier to measure. There is a useful distinction between power to do (that is, a capability) and power over, which is anathema. Unfortunately, in any group or society there is little power to do without some power over. This is the dilemma of the philosophical anarchist. He cannot practice his faith, which is concerned with eliminating man's power over man, without becoming in fact a nihilist: one who is against all doing.

Faced with these and other difficulties, the search is directed toward ways of limiting or governing power that may be used against the interests of others while keeping as much as possible of the ability to act in his own or his organization's interest. Economists have been inclined to think of market power which they conceive, and sometimes try to measure, in terms of a departure from its opposite, an impersonal, and hence powerless, purely competitive market. But all markets that have ever existed inevitably contain certain buyers and sellers with some degree of market power. Consequently the search is for that degree of market power which is necessary to an efficient conduct of business but beyond which there is an inevitable divergence between the particular and the general interest. Some call this nirvana "workable competition," others prefer the term "effective competition," and still other draw a distinction between "reasonable" and "unreasonable" market power. Whatever the nomenclature, this concept embraces two ideas worth pondering. The first is that technological and organizational influences inevitably bring about, in a large sector of the economy, markets served by the few rather than the many and that not very much, really, can be done about it. The second is that in a dynamic economy, characterized by product changes, process innovation, advertising, and growth, competition among the few may not be so bad after all. This may be whistling in the dark, but the whistling is going to go on in any case.

But what if technological and organization considerations decree a size and a fewness—a type of competition—that not even a business economist would call workable? Under these circumstances, some would say, break them up even at the cost of some loss of efficiency. Others would turn to public ownership or regulation. And still others, I suspect, despairing of the first and dubious of the second, might prefer the known evil to the unknown consequences of action.

Even if competition among the few is "workable," the problem of private power is not exorcised. Industrializing economies inevitably move away from market relations among firms and toward administrative relations within the firm. Contractual relations between legal equals give way to relations between employer and employee within a bureaucratic hierarchy. This is an aspect of the "power over" that, in our industrialized society, seems inseparably connected with the "power to do." Furthermore, this exercise of power by management and the accompanying loss of freedom by the managed is independent of who does the managing. As Clark Kerr puts it,

> *Some loss of freedom . . . is inevitable in an effective industrial system. It will occur, more or less, whether the system is run by the employers alone, by the State alone, or even by unions alone. Industrial society requires many rules and reasonable conformity to those rules. There must be a wage structure, a work schedule, and so forth, no matter who operates the system. This loss of freedom is one of the prices paid by man for the many benefits in income and leisure that can flow from industrial society.*[2]

Labor has met this problem in part by the organization of trade unions, whose most important function, undoubtedly, has been to assure labor a voice in determining those rules and regulations that affect working conditions. There remains, however, the question: How responsive are union leaders to the wishes

---

[2] Clark Kerr, *Unions and Union Leaders of Their Own Choosing* (New York: Fund for the Republic, 1957).

of their constituents? Economic bureaucracy is not limited to the corporation. For the salaried employee there are all those pressures and subtle influences on the organization man—and his wife—so graphically depicted by W. H. Whyte.

Market power and managerial power reinforce each other in complex ways. In a vertically integrated enterprise, economic processes are subject to managerial control from raw material to finished product, but with market power waxing and waning at different stages depending on the vigor of competition. A large unintegrated firm buying from many small producers sometimes obtains what amounts to managerial control over these enterprises through the leverage of its market position.

Nor do managerial and market aspects exhaust the content of private power in the economy and the society. Large firms and large trade unions exert an influence on wages and prices outside the jurisdictions of their own managers and markets. Key wage and price bargains are made that affect the general level of wages and prices and wage-price relationships. If we are in for "creeping inflation," large corporations and trade unions are the principal creepers.

One is led on from this point to speculations concerning the political influence of large firms and other organized groups. Here we are offered a broad spectrum of choice ranging from "Business as a System of Power"[3] to the iniquities of a "laboristic economy." Does corporate size bring with it political influence or political vulnerability? Probably the first in some contexts and in others the second. Perhaps the safest thing that can be said is that politics inevitably reflects the structure of society and in a society characterized by large organizations, politics will be pressure-group politics.

The Managerial Revolution

Managerial direction is, of course, an aspect of bureaucracy, and its characteristic methods and attitudes have been with us for a long time. Before the rapid technological changes which we call the industrial revolution had confronted business enterprise with the need for complex administrative organization, the state, large municipalities, armies, the church, universities, and indeed all institutions bringing together the efforts of a sizable group of men had developed bureaucracies. Business bureaucracies as we know them, however, date from the industrial revolution, and the first area in which they significantly flowered was railway transportation. As late as 1900, three-quarters of American corporations large enough to have their securities listed on the New York Stock Exchange were railways. But from the Civil War on, this form of organization made progress in other sectors of the economy.

People who talk about a "managerial revolution" usually have in mind, on the one hand, the increasing importance of large corporations on the American scene and, on the other, changes in administrative techniques that have continually in-

---

[3] Cf. Robert Brady, *Business as a System of Power* (New York, Columbia University Press, 1943).

creased the size of the enterprise that can be effectively managed. Those who doubt the significance of this "revolution" point to figures on economic concentration, and indeed it is possible to show that, during the last fifty years, there has been no significant increase, however measured, in the share of economic activity controlled by the largest corporations. The largest corporations have grown mightily, but so has the economy. This, in my view, does not dispose of the matter. In the first place, conclusions on the trend of concentration depend heavily on the date from which one measures the trend. If the date chosen is before the great merger movement of 1897-1903, it can be shown that concentration has, in fact, increased. In the second place, the phenomena we are concerned with are more a product of absolute size than of relative share. And about absolute size, however measured, there is no shadow of doubt. In the third place, there is probably a substantial lag between changes in the size of enterprises and changes in managerial techniques adapted to the new sizes. For these and other reasons, I conclude that, despite the lack of evidence of increased concentration during the last half-century, there may well have occurred a profound change is the way industrial enterprises are managed. It goes without saying that in other broad sectors of the economy small-scale enterprise, managed in a traditional fashion, not only is holding its own but will continue to do so.

These changes in management are commonly grouped under the heading of bureaucracy. And bureaucracy, as the political scientists tell us, is characterized by a hierarchy of function and authority, professionalization of management, formal procedures for recruitment and promotion, and a proliferation of written rules, orders, and record keeping. All this is true of business administration in large corporations, but corporate bureaucracies also exhibit certain differences from typical government bureaucracies that are worth emphasizing. In the first place, corporate managements enjoy a much greater freedom from external influence than do the managements of government bureaucracies. As we have seen, management has pretty much escaped from ownership control; but though private ownership may no longer carry with it control, it does guarantee corporate management against most of the political, ministerial, and legislative interference that commonly besets public management. Perhaps in a corporate society this is becoming one of the primary contributions of private property. Needless to say, this independence of corporate management from any well-defined responsibility to anyone also carries with it the possibilities of abuse we have noted above in our discussion of the problem of legitimacy.

In the second place, corporate managements have traditionally been considered to have as their single-minded objective, in contrast to most government bureaucracies, maximization of business profits. And traditionally the incentives connected with profit maximization have been thought to constitute an essential part of the justification of a private-enterprise system. Now managerial voices are raised to deny this exclusive preoccupation with profits and to assert that corporate managements are really concerned with equitable sharing of corporate gains among owners, workers, suppliers, and customers. If equity rather than profits is the corporate objective, one of the traditional distinctions between the private and public sectors disappears. If equity is the primary desideratum, it may well be asked why duly constituted public authority is not as good an instrument for dispensing equity as self-perpetuating corporate managements? Then there are those, including the editors of *Fortune,* who seek the best of both worlds by equating long-run profit maximization with equitable treatment of all parties at issue.[4] But to date no one has succeeded in working out the logic of this modern rehabilitation of the medieval "just price."

Finally, since corporate managements work exclusively in the business area, which government bureaucracies ordinarily do not, it can be said that the possibility of monetary measurement in the former permits a closer adjustment of rewards to performance, and hence a closer observance of the causes of efficiency than is possible in the latter. This is true, and it is important, but the distinction is not between public and private efficiency but between the efficiency of operations susceptible to the measuring rod of money and the efficiency of those that are not. Furthermore, if equity rather than profits is the desideratum, even this advantage is lost. If equity rather than productivity is to determine the reward, what happens to the canons of efficiency?

One of the leading characteristics of well-ordered bureaucracies, both public and private—a characteristic justly extolled by the devotees of managerialism—is the increasing professionalization of management. This means, among other things, selection and promotion on the basis of merit rather than family connections or social status, the development of a "scientific" attitude toward the problems of the organization, and an expectation of reward in terms of relatively stable salary and professional prestige rather than in fluctuating profits. This professionalization of management has, of course, been characteristic of well-ordered public bureaucracies for a long time. It helps to explain why able young Indians, for example, have in general preferred to cast their lot with a civil service selecting and promoting on the basis of merit rather than with the highly nepotistic business firms of the subcontinent. But it is a relatively new phenomenon in American business and one of increasing importance.

The degree of freedom enjoyed by corporate managements, in contrast to their governmental counterparts, has affected personnel as well as other policies. And no one who has observed at first hand the red-tape inefficiencies of the United States Civil Service can fail to be aware of the superiority of corporate practice. This relative freedom from hampering restrictions on selection plus a high level of monetary rewards has brought the cream of American professional management into business corporations. No one doubts the superiority of American business management. Unwitting testimony, if testimony is needed, is supplied by the care with which Soviet planners examine American management practices.

But the process of managerial self-selection common in large corporations does raise certain questions worth pondering. Granted that we have been vouchsafed good corporate government, is the process of selection likely to assure us continued good government? Is good government enough, or shouldn't

---

[4] Editors of *Fortune,* with Russell W. Davenport, *U.S.A.: The Permanent Revolution* (New York: *Fortune Magazine,* February 1951).

we be permitted a modicum of self-government? Has corporate government, in fact, been as good as all that: aren't certain limitations in this process of recruitment already becoming visible?

If the truth be known, no very coherent account of how corporate executives are in fact chosen is available. This is one of those situations in which those who know don't tell, and those who tell don't know. C. Wright Mills, who, so far as I am aware, has had no experience in choosing corporate executives, asserts that advancement is "definitely mixed up in a 'political' world of corporate cliques."[5] This sounds very much like the process of promotion in a university department. Chester I. Bernard, who has had experience, strongly emphasizes the importance of "compatibility of personnel." Those are chosen who fit, and fitness includes "education, experience, sex, personal distinctions, prestige, race, nationality, faith, politics, sectional antecedents," and "manners, speech, personal appearance."[6] This is a comprehensive list of qualifications and it recalls an alleged selection to a post at All Souls, Oxford, where the varied capacities of the two rival candidates were so evenly matched that the choice finally depended on the relative neatness with which each disposed of his artichoke.

Drawing on experience in other contexts, one would suppose that an able group of men in choosing successors would emphasize ability but that various considerations making for "togetherness" would strongly impinge. In the process of university selection, excessive concern for the old school tie is apt to be discouraged by the possibility of intervention from above and, even more, by active competition from rival institutions. University professors can and do move. So do corporate executives on occasion, but the increasing drag of pension rights and other endowments which ordinarily cannot be transferred seriously handicap movement. Nor is the process of executive selection subject to higher review. Since the managerial elite in our large corporations consists, of a few thousand at most, and since this elite has an influence that far transcends the immediate corporation jurisdiction, it is highly important that the process of selection be kept as competitive as possible even if this requires, as suggested by Brewster, some degree of government intervention.[7]

The Changing Character of Private Property

Berle draws a distinction between "individual possessory holdings" and "power systems" and imaginatively sketches a cyclical development from feudal systems to the seventeenth- and eighteenth-century emphasis on private property, and from that into the modern corporate power system.[8] Certainly owner-

---

[5] C. Wright Mills, *The Power Elite* (New York: Oxford University Press, 1956), p. 133. Cited by Earl Latham, below, p. 229.

[6] Chester I. Barnard, *The Functions of the Executive* (Cambridge, Mass.: Harvard University Press, 1938), p. 224.

[7] Cf. Kingman Brewster, Jr., "The Corporation and Modern Society" (Cambridge: Harvard University Press, 1959) pp. 72–84.

[8] Berle, *Economic Power and the Free Society, op. cit.*, p. 3.

ship of a local grist mill has a different economic significance from the ownership of 100 shares of United States Steel. And issues other than economic are involved. To a Jeffersonian society of small and relatively equal property owners, the "rights of property" was a phrase fraught with social significance. In a nation of wage and salaried employees, even though many are participants in stock ownership plans, the accent is apt to be on "privilege" rather than "right." Schumpeter contrasts the "full-blooded" capitalist owner of the nineteenth century, ready to fight for his property, with the stock-and-bond owner of the twentieth who has only the vaguest idea where "his property" is or of what it consists. The eighteenth-century philosophers considered property ownership as essential to the full development of personality, to the maintenance of individual freedom from the encroachment of those power systems represented by church and state, and to the formation of a citizenry capable of self-government. Corporate ownership is not usually defended in those terms today.

When questions are raised concerning a contemporary justification of private property, the ownership of one's house, its furnishings, and other consumer goods is not an issue. No one except a few communal crackpots and, apparently, the current Chinese Government is concerned with this type of property ownership. Nor are many people this side of the Iron Curtain unwilling to extend the eighteenth-century benediction to private ownership of agricultural land, of corner grocery stores, garages, and gas stations. The problem arises approximately where "individual possessory holdings" give way to "systems of power"—that is, at the point at which corporate size divorces control from ownership and converts owners essentially into *rentiers*. In Berle's terms, "The capital is there, and so is capitalism. The waning figure is the capitalist."

The fact that private property of this sort presents a "problem" does not mean that it is devoid of justification. But it does mean that the doctrines of Locke and Jefferson are no longer quite relevant. And it probably means that the content of the "rights" and "privileges" that may be justified will differ substantially from their eighteenth-century content. After all, it is a little difficult to see in the ownership of corporate securities the source of that invigorating moral, social, and political development that Jefferson saw in private property. And certainly the eighteenth-century economic justifications of private property based on the assumption that ownership carries with it control lack relevance to the corporate universe.

The Corporation and the State

The economies of Western Europe and, increasingly, that of the United States are frequently described as "mixed" economies. This phrase is commonly interpreted to indicate a situation in which the role of government as owner and regulator has become sufficiently large to cast doubt on the validity of "capitalist" and "free enterprise" as appropriate adjectives but not sufficiently large to justify the appellation "socialist." Government ownership and regulation are important ingredients, but they inadequately characterize the "mixture" of public and private that the rise of the large corporation has produced. The growth of the modern corporation has been accompanied by an increasing similarity of public and private business with respect to forms of organization, techniques of management, and the motivations and attitudes of managers. Government has sought increasingly to use the private corporation for the performance of what are essentially public functions. Private corporations in turn, particularly in their foreign operations, continually make decisions which impinge on the public—particularly foreign—policy of government. And government, in pursuit of its current objectives in underdeveloped areas, seeks to use techniques and talents that only the business corporation can provide. Decidedly a *"verwickelte Verwandschaft,"* as our German friends might say. Under these circumstances the classic arguments of the socialism-versus-free-enterprise debate seem a bit sterile, to say the least.

The increasing similarity of public and private enterprise has impressed both liberals and conservatives, though the conclusions drawn therefrom have tended to differ. In an early recognition of this trend, Keynes described it as a "tendency of big enterprise to socialize itself." A point is reached in the growth of big enterprises, he says, at which "the stockholders are almost entirely dissociated from the management, with the result that the direct personal interest of the latter in the making of great profit becomes quite secondary."[9] American managerial spokesmen supplement this thought by emphasizing management's responsibility to workers, customers, suppliers, and others, though they would hardly describe living up to this responsibility—as Keynes probably would—as behaving like civil servants. These and similar considerations have led elements in the British Labour Party to the conclusion that the form of ownership of large enterprise is irrelevant. "The basic fact is the large corporation, facing fundamental similar problems, acts in fundamentally the same way, whether publicly or privately owned."[10]

While large private corporations have been forced by their sheer size, power, and "visibility" to behave with a circumspection unknown to the untrammeled nineteenth century, government, on the other hand, has attempted to give its "business-like" activities a sphere of independence approaching that of the private corporation. Experience with the public corporation in the United States has, it is true, somewhat dampened an earlier enthusiasm for this type of organization. And even Britain, which has sought much longer and harder than we for a workable compromise between independence and accountability in its publicly managed enterprises, has not yet found a satisfactory solution. Nevertheless, it remains true that managerial practices and attitudes in the public and private sectors of most Western economies tend to become more similar.

Private ownership in the United States, however, still confers an immunity from detailed government supervision that a public corporation does not enjoy. And government takes advantage of the independence and flexibility of the

---

[9] J. M. Keynes, "The End of Laissez-Faire" (1926), republished in *Essays in Persuasion* (London: Macmillan & Co., Ltd., 1931), pp. 314–315.

[10] C. A. R. Crosland, *The Future of Socialism* (London, 1957), p. 480.

private corporation to contract out the performance of what are essentially public services. Private firms become official inspectors of aircraft; various types of military "operations analysis" are undertaken by Rand and other privately organized corporations; and substantially more than half of public research and development expenditures go to private rather than public organizations. In commenting on these phenomena, Don Price observes, "If the question (of public versus private) is seen in realistic terms, we shall have to devise some way of calculating whether a particular function can be performed best in the public interest as a completely governmental operation at the one extreme, or a completely private operation at the other extreme, or by some mixture of the nearly infinite possibilities of elements of ownership regulation and management that our variety of precedents suggests. . . ."[11]

If private corporations perform in certain areas services essentially public in character at the request of government, in other areas they perform services essentially public without being asked. It is probably true to say that not since the seventeenth century, when the Levant Company conducted Britain's foreign policy in the Near East as an adjunct to its business operations and the East India Company acquired India for the Empire "in a moment of inadvertence," have the activities of business corporations impinged so closely on foreign policy. Of course, the classic example is that of the oil companies in the Middle East, but in almost every overseas area in which large American corporations operate, their business activities either impede or advance the foreign policy of the United States. This is not because these corporations behave in a manner different from the way they would have behaved in the nineteenth century—although indeed they do—but rather because the foreign policy of the United States has become so comprehensive that it is touched by almost any sizable business activity. This picture of oil companies "making foreign policy" for the United States raises hackles in some quarters and stimulates demands for a bringing of private business activities under public control. But, in the first place, these are not "private business activities" in the nineteenth-century sense of the term, nor are they conducted as if they were. And second, although private and public relations in this area are probably in need of rethinking, further thought is unlikely to lead to a nineteenth-century type of solution in which authority was either private or public, with little or no commingling of the two.

How really mixed—and perhaps mixed up—our economy is these days can be clearly seen by casting one's eye on United States policy and practices in the so-called underdeveloped areas of the world. Our announced policy is to give substantial assistance to the economic development of countries whose economies have long been stagnant. And our preferred means are the stimulation of private enterprise in the underdeveloped areas and the encouragement of United States private investment abroad. But in many of these areas, the opportunities for foreign private investment are negligible, and our grants and loans inevitably

---

[11] Don K. Price, "Creativity in the Public Service," to be published in the yearbook of the Harvard Graduate School of Public Administration, *Public Policy,* Vol. IX.

flow through local government channels. At the same time, in the provision of technical assistance we depend heavily on contracts with American private firms. And we actively encourage mixed enterprise, private and public and foreign and domestic, as a means of getting enterprise moving. The effort is sometimes described as an exercise in government-business cooperation in the promotion of foreign economic development, and perhaps that is as good a description as any. In any case, it is a good example of a mixed economy in motion.

This lack of a clear-cut separation of public and private authority and responsibility offends some people. And indeed, the eighteenth-century political philosophers and political economists provided for their epoch a much more satisfactory intellectual framework than any vouchsafed to us today. The fact seems to be that the rise of the large corporation and attending circumstances have confronted us with a long series of questions concerning rights and duties, privileges and immunities, responsibility and authority, that political and legal philosophy have not yet assimilated. What we need among other things is a twentieth-century Hobbes or Locke to bring some order into our thinking about the corporation and its role in society.

Selection 17

The Corporation and the Trade Union

NEIL CHAMBERLAIN

From Edward S. Mason (ed.), The Corporation in Modern Society *(Cambridge, Mass.: Harvard University Press, 1959), pp. 122–140. Reprinted by permission of Harvard University Press.*

The old symbolism of "capital" and "labor" as two giants engaged in a struggle from which one would emerge as master and the other as servant has become as dusty as the lace valentine. But the notion of management and the unions as rivals in a continuing and irrepressible contest which frequently becomes bitter still persists. This latter view is only partially correct, however. It will be argued here that the contest has become largely a sporting one, for prizes which are as symbolic as the kewpie doll at a carnival sideshow, and that the reminder provided by the parties and the textbooks that management and the unions are engaged in inevitable conflict has the same uninteresting truth and half-truth as the equally frequent reminder that they have interests in common.

The arenas within which management and unions come to grips are first, the business firm, typically the corporation, and second, society at large in its political aspects. The prize for victory in the first arena consists of—or at least takes the form of—immediate economic and psychological satisfactions and a leg up on further rewards of the same kind in the future. The prize for victory in the second arena, society at large, consists of subtler satisfactions in the form of freedom to reconstruct the social structure in the shape of one's own prejudices.

The prize ring which now occupies most of management's attention is the first one: the business firm, the corporation. This is not at all surprising. For one thing, it carries the trophies which management most enjoys—power over economic resources, enabling it to build hard realities in contrast to ideological intangibles—real plants, real products, real organizations. On these its very considerable constructive imagination can be lavished. Even to open a corner grocery store takes a degree of belief in one's organizing abilities which most people lack. To direct the fortunes of a large corporation takes peculiar and unusual combinations of creativeness, self-esteem, daring, and drive, and the very use of these qualities in the business firm creates the conditions which keep them fully utilized.

But equally important in explaining management's greater occupation with the business arena is the fact that it is operating within an ideological framework which it and its predecessors largely created. Business no longer has an ideological initiative, because present institutions still largely reflect a fashioning by its hand—government, schools, churches, civic societies, and the producing units themselves. These have been somewhat altered away from their original conception within the last quarter-century, it is true, but management's reaction has been one of holding the line against further inroads rather than of creating for itself new conceptions of a society it would like to see installed. It lives with the premise that no society can possibly be any better than the recent past, hence to espouse something new is to betray what is (or was) the best and finest. This dictates a holding or, at worst, a retreating action, since the objective is to retain as much of this ideal as is feasible.

The result is that management as a functional group exercises little social *initiative.* The prize which it seeks in the social contest is only a draw, a tie, which will leave things as they are or—even better but not very hopefully—as they were. The disillusion with so-called "Eisenhower liberalism" which spread through the business community following his reelection was indicative of this desire to stand pat, although the degree of the president's "liberal" tendencies was modesty itself.

Obviously, generalizations such as these are necessarily inaccurate in detail, but broad-brush treatment sometimes helps to achieve perspective. Probably the above outline would draw sharp criticism only from members of the group depicted, however. The picture as drawn contains nothing new. Indicative of the persistence of the old perception of the capital-labor struggle, however, is the fact that probably few except students of the labor movement would recognize that a fair amount of management's complacency with the social framework may likewise be imputed to the unions.

Despite all its agitation for "getting out the vote" and despite management's sharp criticism of labor's political activity, the unions have offered their members and the public at large nothing different or special to vote for once the votes have been gotten out. The labor movement in the United States has taken pride in the fact that it is nonideological. It has reveled in its bread-and-butter or pork-chop personality. The unions, like management, have chosen the firm, the corporation, as the preferred tourney field in which to joust. They have made their objective the quick payoff, since their membership demands full value for dues paid, on an annual basis.

The fact that the extra money in the pay envelope which may result from (or, more accurately, coincide with) such negotiations no longer constitutes a badly needed increment to a subsistence wage has not changed the symbolism. The union feels it must continue to play an importunate role to satisfy its members that they are getting their "fair" share.

If union officials are driven to spend their best effort to win the prize in the corporate arena, this does not imply that none of their number has social objectives as well, which can only be won in the larger, political ring. For the most part, however, these are objectives which are quite compatible with the present system—more public-supported housing, federal school subsidies, higher minimum wage, improved social security. None of these objectives, if achieved, would upset any social order or cause many businessmen a sleepless night. There are among union leaders today few who shelter revolutionary or radical designs. The accusing finger is always pointed at one man, Walter Reuther, largely because he has shown himself to be both intellectual and articulate, but Reuther is not only a lonely man among his fellow union leaders but has had little success in selling his ideas to his own membership.

American unionism can hardly be regarded as a labor *movement,* since it betrays no sense of direction and is content to drift. If management provides no initiative in the social field, neither do the unions. If one were to look for political leadership in the United States, the labor movement would be about the last place one would expect to find it. The eyes of the union, no less than management's, are directed to the contest in the corporation—to the struggle over a little more money, a little more job security.

For many years irritated corporate officials have complained that the unions, with their continued importunacy, with their readiness to enlarge the scope of their demands, were gradually taking over management's functions. Some argued that the inevitable consequence would be socialism. In the broader context, however, it is evident how little ground for fear actually exists. The alleged radicalism of the unions was only the mark of their conservatism. The fact that their demands were addressed to management's decisions in the corporation was only evidence of their willingness to join with management in keeping the main contest out of the political gymnasium.

How little political steam there is in the union's boilers was clearly indicated—if indeed there had been any question about it—during the recession of 1957–1958. With unemployment rising to the 7 per cent level, the unions offered nothing but token resistance to the administration's decision that potential inflation deserved more consideration than actual joblessness.

To avoid misinterpretation in an age of suspicion, let it be clear that the point being emphasized is not that the unions *should* engage in political activity for social ends, but simply that they do not, and that their unwillingness to do so has had the effect of confining their energies to the corporate theater. In effect, they have accepted the battleground chosen by management. Satisfied with the social framework within which they operate, they are content to provide an obligato to management's lead. The unions' "challenge" to management control is more apparent than real. It is probable that never before has there existed a labor movement which has voluntarily so well integrated itself with its society. And indeed, where the worker-driven Chevrolet has become almost indistinguishable from the employer-driven Cadillac, why should the worker feel himself divided from a superior class?

The consequences of this confinement of the labor contest to the business field are several. For one thing, it spares the United States from the more divisive political contests encountered in those countries where unionism is allied to socialism or to other blocs with an ideological orientation. If the reduction of social pressures is a desirable objective (as even radicals would have to admit, at least as an ultimate objective), then the absence of any significant ideological struggle from the American scene contributes to the desired end.

But other consequences, too, follow from the unique characteristics of this country's labor movement, some less desirable. The question of leadership in the unions is likely to become more and more difficult of solution. One possible source of future union leaders might be the young politically oriented individuals who see the unions as a vehicle for their political ambitions. But if unions abstain from any significant political activity, they cannot offer attractive futures to ambitious young political careerists. What magnetism does a nonpolitical labor movement hold for the politically sensitive? In other societies, the labor movement has traditionally attracted the political nonconformist: it could look to "radicals" for leadership. But how can conservative unionism expect to attract—or to offer ladders to high position to—the free thinkers and radicals? Here one potential pool of leadership talent, on which the American labor movement drew in the past, offers no future promise. If fresh political leadership is important in order for a society not to stagnate, what institutions will nourish the young nonconformist in the United States? In some countries, the labor unions have traditionally performed that function.

Or can it be expected that the economic plight of the working mass will draw to the unions, as it did in previous decades, idealists who seek some personal part in efforts to better the sorry lot of society's population base? Only to ask the question is to answer it. What idealist can be challenged now by the "plight" of workers struggling to secure an increase in pay so that they may purchase a color television set, a better car, a more up-to-date kitchen appliance?

If the political aspirant, the social reformer, and the young idealist cease to be sources of union leadership, what types can we expect in the future to rise to office in unions whose focus is on the award in the business prize ring? Undoubtedly a number of types could be suggested, but two deserve special mention.

First, there is the individual who would have risen in the business hierarchy itself if he had had the ability or the opportunity. This would include those of potential administrative or leadership caliber who had been unable to secure a college degree, something which has now become almost indispensable to success, at least in the large corporation. Union leadership may yet come to be the mark of success of the formally uneducated man. At the present time it includes those, too, who were victims of the Great Depression of the 1930's, when corporations were doing little recruiting of young executive talent. It seems unlikely, however, that future depressions will have the duration that would make them promising nurseries of union leadership.

For those in this first category, union office comes as a substitute for a management position, which quite likely would have been preferred. It can be expected that union leaders of this type will exhibit most of the same middle-class standards of morality and ambition that characterize their more fortunate business counterparts. Lacking formal education, at least to the same degree, they may not show quite the same polished public image as does the business-man, but beneath the rougher exterior there will be the same desire for respect-ability and acceptance. No applecarts will be upset by these officials, for whom the act of upsetting an applecart could cause only great social embarrassment. Although they will not frequent the social circles dominated by businessmen, they will be members of the same service clubs and will sometimes be cited by businessmen's organizations for their contribution to industrial harmony.

If the United States is fortunate, its unions will be officered by men like these. From them management can expect some hard fighting, but only in the business field, so that no serious advantage will be forfeited even if management oc-casionally or even frequently loses a joust. But there is a second type of union leader, of whom this country has lately become more conscious, whose numbers are likely to increase by virtue of the fact that the industrial encounters in this country are confined to the business area, where the rewards in this affluent society are no longer literally the bread and butter or pork chops which some Robin Hood of a union leader sought to secure for his people, but cash, which, if diverted to some buccaneer's pocket, will harm no one else. Unions now offer prizes of power and money to those who are ruthless or shrewd enough to seize them for themselves. Thus a second class of people from whom unions, in the circumstances they now find themselves, are likely to draw their leaders is the class of adventurers.

Some of these adventurers may be pirates outside the law, carving out their own racket dominion within a gangster empire. Others may seek to stay this side of the law, or at least within some shady area where legal censure is un-certain. Probably most of such adventuring will simply take the form of internal political manipulation for personal advantage. In whatever form, it may be expected to occur principally in industries populated by small businesses rather than in the large corporations, but there is no basis for assuming that this will always be the case. At the same time, it would be unwarranted to expect the class of union buccaneers to overshadow the labor movement as a whole. While piracy will probably increase in importance, middle-class aspirations can be expected to predominate.

This is not to say that all unions will be led by men of one or the other of these types. All that is here argued is that if present characteristics of the Amer-ican labor movement persist, these are two types which are likely to become numerically more significant.

Recent congressional hearings have indeed awakened public consciousness to the existence of the more colorful of these two strata of union leadership. As one unsavory story followed another on the front pages of the daily newspapers, the association between unionism and corruption in our business society seemed more and more confirmed—corruption in the forms of racketeering gangsterism and monopoly position secured by strong-arm methods. But even more interestingly, in marked contrast to the state of affairs preceding World War II, there has been growing acceptance of the view propagated by the public press that unions—under whatever kind of leadership—have gained such strength in the American economy that even the managements of large corporations must knuckle under to them. The attitude has become more generalized that managements have been forced to make major concessions to the insatiable unions and that here lies the principal cause of rising prices. In the new impressionistic abstraction, even General Motors and United States Steel figure as the beleaguered victims, puny figures cringing or dancing before a whip-lashing, grinning monster labeled "Labor." How different from the cartoon versions of even a quarter-century ago, in which the giant figure carried dollar signs over his vest and smoked a fat cigar while trampling with pleasure the little men who vainly tried to escape his iron heel!

If unions have been acquiescent in battling with management in the latter's own chosen ground, the corporate field, has this strategy then been rewarded with greater prizes than if they had forced the conflict into the arena of political action and ideology? Have the unions grown so great in the last quarter-century, feeding on the meat of governmental protection and public indifference, that their power is now beyond the ability of management to resist? To answer this question we must undertake a side excursion to examine the basis of their relative bargaining powers.

Of course, most unions of today are vastly more powerful than their weakling or nonexistent forebears of the early 1930's. There was no automobile union prior to 1933, so technically whatever powers the U.A.W. has since mustered represent an infinite increase. So with many other industrial unions. The A.F.L. craft unions, with a few exceptions, found themselves in 1933 preserving only the forms and panoply of unionism, shadows without substance. The accretions of power since then have thus been—relatively—great. But the ratio in which we are interested is not that of today's union power relative to union power in 1933, but today's union power vis-à-vis today's management power compared with that same power relationship in 1933. For if unions have grown in that time, so may have the corporations.

Indeed, it is not even the comparison of present with past union power relative to management power which occupies us now as much as the question of whether union power relative to management power today—whatever it may have been in the past—is overwhelming. Perhaps the most direct way of approaching that question is by inquiring what restraints, if any, there are on the union's power to bargain concessions from management.

First let us assume we are dealing with pecuniary issues—wages, pensions, holidays, vacations. Obviously there must be some ceiling on the amount which unions can win. No union is likely to be granted a 100 per cent wage increase, for example, and when we ask why not, we are asking at the same time why it may also be unable to obtain a 10 per cent increase.

Suppose the wage bill in a company runs to a million dollars. A 10 per cent increase would require the management to find somewhere an extra $100,000. In some circumstances this may not seem an impossible task. New machinery or improved organization may mean that fewer employees will be needed, so that the sum required is actually less than $100,000. Or sales may have been exceptionally good, so that at the new (and probably more efficient) level of output, the higher wage bill can be tolerated and still permit a higher earnings rate. Or demand for the company's product may be so brisk as to suggest that a slight price increase, perhaps coupled with some change in product design, is warranted. Under the circumstances, management might well prefer to grant a 10 per cent wage advance if it was convinced that the alternative would be a shutdown of its operations. If the union were asking a 25 per cent increase, however, and was serious about it, management's calculation of the effect on its income statement of an added $250,000 charge might be somewhat different.

At other times management's assessment of the consequences of a 10 per cent wage increase might run in other terms. The capital costs of new equipment to raise productivity might constitute a sharp drain on income, so that finding an additional $100,000 for employees would cause trouble. New competitors in one's own line of products, or sharper competition from old rivals, or new product lines which reduce consumer interest in one's own offerings are constant threats to even the large corporation, and the assumption of added costs may seem unthinkable at a time when the struggle is simply to keep up present levels of output, since any decline in production decreases income more than it does costs. Moreover, in such competitive circumstances one hesitates to worsen his market position by increasing the prices of his product line. The net effect of these considerations may be that management refuses the increase demanded by the union, offering some lesser sum instead. And if the union appreciates the firmness of management's position and considers that it may have to ask its members to take a long strike if they are to get more than management offers, and may then not get anything more but only endanger certain of their jobs, the strike call will not be made lightheartedly. Indeed, many leaders of local unions will testify that in such situations it is management that holds all the bargaining cards.

It has frequently been argued that pattern bargaining reduces management's power in these latter situations. National unions press on "follower" firms the same settlement that has been wrested from the larger and more affluent firms. To some extent this argument has validity, but the extent is less than is often imagined. In industries like steel and automobiles, the major firms have formed into *de facto* bargaining associations, in which it is usually the hardship of a given settlement on the least affluent member of the junta which controls what offer will be made by them. In other industries, the ability of a national union to force some pattern on follower firms is limited by the same considerations we have already noted.

The belief is unwarranted that national unions have large treasuries out of which strike benefits can be paid, so that workers feel freer to strike because they will suffer no economic loss. Union treasuries would be quickly bankrupted if they were drawn on so irresponsibly. They must be reserved to provide for the needs of the neediest strikers in relatively few strike situations if they are to be effective at all.

There are instances, to be sure, where national union representatives have pushed local unions into strikes in support of some wage pattern against the will of local union members, and these can always be cited in support of the thesis that national unions can harass small firms almost at will. But the number of such instances is small indeed relative to the total number of bargaining situations, and represents for the most part simply mistakes of judgment, where the union underestimated the cost to a company of paying the increase sought, rather than any malevolent, ruthless, or piratical act.

Finally, the notion that business rivals will pose less of an objection to a wage demand if they all pay equally, since their competitive situation will remain the same, is one which we need not consider here. This view has a close kinship with the belief that union-bargained wage increases are largely responsible for a cost-push inflation, a matter still subject to debate among professional economists. But to the extent that this view is justified, we may ignore it in the context of the present argument, since the union under the circumstances imposes no special hardships on the firms with which it bargains, even if it does on the economy: the producer recoups his position at the expense of the consumer. To the extent this view is unjustified, and the associated employers cannot recover added wage costs from the buyers of their products, we may expect resistance to union wage demands for the reasons already indicated.

The conclusion which emerges from this sketchy analysis is that unions do not possess some irresistible power to extract increases which their greedy and irresponsible leaders dictate to management. Their leaders may be as greedy or irresponsible as other elements in our economy, but the corporate managements facing them across the bargaining table have their own powers of resistance, which are sometimes effective. That the results of negotiations have in the postwar years usually been wage increases for employees is probably far more a consequence of the prosperity of the American economy than of the strength of unions.

Indeed, most labor economists who have undertaken research to establish whether unions have been able to provide differential rewards for their members over the employees of unorganized establishments have concluded either in the negative or in a very much qualified affirmative. In particular industries or localities the union effect may have been much greater, of course, but the impression one gets from the careful and objective studies which have been made is that, in general, an agnosticism as to union influence on wages is warranted.

This is not to imply that some manifestations of union power are not excessive and undesirable and should not be subjected to public control. It is to suggest, however, that the notion that union power is so monolithic that it sweeps all before it is more supportable by prejudice than by impartial analysis.

Unions have, however, without doubt influenced the forms of remuneration. The numerous fringe benefits—added holidays; longer vacations; sickness, accident, and unemployment supplemental benefits; improved pensions; jury pay;

and so on—have been introduced largely in response to union demands and as alternatives to further increases in hourly remuneration. Here the union's bargaining impact has been substantial; at the same time, it seems hardly a matter of moment to management in what form its workers draw their compensation.

Now let us turn to the nonpecuniary concessions which unions have been able to bargain from managements. These include such matters as reliance in whole or in part on seniority for layoffs and promotions, assurances that rates of pay once set will not be changed arbitrarily, guarantees of prior notice in the event of layoffs, compulsory union membership, provisions against discrimination on grounds of race, sex, and color, but, perhaps most importantly, establishment of a jointly administered grievance procedure. This last is designed to permit enforcement by individual employees of any of the provisions of the collective agreement which they interpret in their favor and also to allow protest against unfair disciplinary action by management.

Whatever the unions' effectiveness may be in winning differential wage advantages for their members, there is virtually no dispute that their representation of members in the grievance process provides a major benefit. The helplessness of the individual employee to protect himself from discriminatory actions of a foreman in pre-union days is now generally admitted by management itself. The individual worker has acquired a feeling of independence through the realization that he can protest with impunity a foreman's decision which appears arbitrary and unwarranted, even though he is still obliged to obey that decision while his protest is being heard. If managements—and in particular foremen—sometimes smart under the decree of worker cockiness fostered by the grievance procedure, it is understandable, but from an uninvolved position one may also quite understandably feel pride in an industrial system that permits its most menial member to defend his rights.

The apathetic attitude many members take toward their union has sometimes been regarded by management as expressing a lack of attachment to the organization. In the light of the grievance function, such a conclusion is probably not sustainable. A great many members who never show up at union meetings, never participate in union elections, seldom read the union publication, and feel no emotional loyalties nevertheless regard it as a desirable "insurance policy." Even a respected foreman or supervisor is susceptible to errors of judgment or to decisions based on misinformation or emotion, and sometimes these create hardship. One never expects this to happen to himself, any more than he expects theft or fire, but he has seen it happen to his fellows often enough for protective insurance to seem desirable. His union dues buy that insurance. If he is apathetic toward the union, he is probably no more so than he is toward his other insurance policies.

If the above analysis is correct, the union's economic role has been a relatively modest one, but it has played a major role in providing representation of its members' job interests and insurance against arbitrary actions by management. The more spectacular view that unions have an overweening power to wrest wage increases almost at will from helpless managements appears to have little validity, and the effectiveness of union power seems largely confined to their modest and appealing success in securing equitable treatment for their individual members in shop and office and store.

If this conclusion is sound, however, it raises the question of why all the union-management conflict? If managements have come to accept unions in the grievance procedure—and this is their greatest contribution—why should union members undergo or face the protracted wage negotiations, the costly strikes, the arduous picketing? If these add little to the union's gains, why should they make these sacrifices? Or alternatively, if these, even when successfully resisted, save management relatively little, why should it fight them at such cost?

There are several possible answers. One argument has it that if wage gains come too easily, workers will be restive. There is some emotional satisfaction in believing that one's earnings are what they are because one has driven a good bargain. The story is told of an employer who gave the union the full 10-cent increase which they demanded, without argument, in the first few minutes of negotiations, leaving the union representatives with nothing further to talk about, no reason for pounding the table, no basis for feeling that they had waged a fight on behalf of their constituents. That same union the following year made sure its demands were high enough to evoke employer resistance and a strike, with a resulting settlement that they helped to make.

Dramatizing a factitious worker control over wage settlements is not a very acceptable rationale for collective bargaining, however. A more likely explanation is that, in the area of wage determination no less than in grievance handling, the union is looked on as insurance. It would be hard to convince many workers—and probably hard to convince many economists—that wage increases of the same magnitude would have come so soon without the union. The differential gain may in fact be slight—hardly enough to upset the business firm, whose costs (and returns) are seldom calculated quite so precisely as is sometimes thought. But the average apathetic union member believes firmly that if he had to wait for management to give him an increase he would have to wait an unconscionably lot longer than is the case when his union is on the job. His belief may be in error, the difference in the timing of his wage increase might have been only a matter of months, perhaps at most a year or so, but he has no way of knowing, and the salient consideration to him is that he no longer has to wait for management in its infinite wisdom to make up its mind, since his union has taken the decision on timing out of management's hands.

Economists have often declared themselves in favor of the unions' noneconomic contribution, which, it has been maintained here, is its most important function. At the same time, some have deplored the unions' efforts at wage manipulation. Such an evaluation may be evasive, however. What if the two functions—the economic and the noneconomic—cannot be disentangled? What if the union can remain a viable organization, performing its day-to-day protective functions, only because members believe it also provides them some insurance against "unfair" wage decisions? It then becomes necessary to determine whether the noneconomic function with its favorable effects is sufficiently valuable to more than offset the economic function which is viewed as adverse.

In the light of the above analysis, the answer might well be in the affirmative. But then a more arresting problem intrudes.

Unions have in recent years been allowed to exercise certain legislated privileges and judicial immunities. Picketing has frequently been undisturbed even though it contained more of an element of threat than of persuasion. Restraints on the use of the strike have been approached with caution. The pooling of resources by numerous local labor groups to form a national organization capable of marshaling general support in any threatened location has been pursued even in industries that are substantially local in their operations. Worker violence has sometimes been condoned or blinked at by public officials, even when the law was contravened, on the presumption that when people's emotions are aroused some overflow beyond the confines of peaceful channels is to be expected.

These privileges have been granted or taken on the ground that without them a union's effective power was emasculated. If one believed in unions at all, one was led along to accept the devices by which unions achieved some degree of bargaining power.

But if it can be asserted that the union's chief contribution is in its protective function in the making of shop rules and their application in the grievance process, then this issue is raised: is the bargaining power which unions bring to the grievance process the same bargaining power which they bring to wage negotiations? If the lenient treatment of union excesses is designed to preserve to the unions an effective bargaining power in wage negotiations, but if the unions' role in wage negotiations is at best a modest one, is it then possible to restrict more severely the unions' strong-arm tactics, without thereby endangering their ability to secure individual fair treatment for their members in the grievance process?

We do not yet have the basis for a confident answer to that question. Although the power contest between union and management is most generally associated with negotiation of the agreement, and the subsequent interpretation of the agreement through the grievance process is often described as judicial in nature (with power absent as an influence), the fact is that the power relationship between the parties is never settled, even temporarily. There are at least two types of situation in which it continues to manifest itself.

Ever since collective bargaining became governmentally enforceable in 1935, the question has been debated as to whether a management's obligations to its union are satisfied by its adherence to the terms of the agreement signed by both parties. Managements have almost uniformly contended that their only duty was to live up to their contract, and conversely that the union's only rights were those spelled out in that same contract. All other powers were reserved to management, for it to exercise in its discretion. Unions, on the other hand, have tended to argue that management could make no decision affecting the interests of its employees without consulting the union.

This debate has gone unresolved, although in recent years it has veered more to the "management's reserved rights" end of the spectrum. The chances are this argument will never be settled, however. It would certainly appear that once an agreement was signed, for its lifetime management has preserved a right of initiative in the conduct of the business, without any necessity of prior consultation with the union. Such right of initiative is the essence of management. At the same time, it appears equally certain that there is a shadowland wherein management's decisions so intimately affect the interests of its workers that the process of collective bargaining, if it has any genuineness, requires a good-faith attempt at reaching an understanding with the union, even if, in the absence of agreement, the union has no right to block management's action. This shadowland exists not simply because of any immaturity in the bargaining process but because, even if the parties wished most earnestly to do so, they could never anticipate all the situations which might arise or the decisions which management might feel it desirable to make under unforeseen circumstances.

The existence of such a shadowland—even if denied by management and given undue substance by the unions—provides an area within which power relations can be exercised even after an agreement has been signed. The struggle over the wage issues or other terms of a contract, at recurrent negotiating sessions, by no means settles even temporarily the relative power positions of the two parties. They remain in a bargaining relation from issue to issue throughout the contract period.

A separate but related postcontractual stage on which the power contest is fought out is the grievance procedure itself, as established by the agreement, in which individuals may charge they have been unfairly treated by management. In principle, decisions in the grievance process are presumed to have a judicial quality, constituting determinations of whether the terms of the agreement have been properly applied by management or of whether disciplinary penalties have been in accord with common-law standards of equity. In practice, however, the process reflects the bargaining power relationship, as the union seeks to widen the area of the agreement by interpretation, or management seeks to narrow it. At times one side may concede on one case in exchange for victory in another. Or the employees in a shop may threaten an avalanche of grievances against their foreman unless he sees things their way on some matter vital to them. Or the company may overlook some union or employee violation either to gain goodwill or to invite reciprocity. Or management may make a concession in interpretation in exchange for the union's agreement not to press a particular demand at contract negotiation time. Even the question of how high in the multistage appeals process a case should be carried may be a matter of bargaining strategy—in particular, the decision as to whether the issue should be taken to arbitration.

But even when we grant that bargaining power plays an important role in union-management relations during the lifetime of an agreement, we cannot thereby conclude that unions require the same degree or kinds of power and privilege as they now enjoy in order to represent their members effectively. The question still remains: If unions are given legal immunities on the assumption that these are needed in negotiating for agreements on wages and other monetary benefits, and if these bargained benefits are relatively slight, the real gain for workers coming through union protection against unfair or discriminatory treatment, then do unions need their present privileges to provide this latter function?

That this question will be argued more and more in the future there can be little doubt. Until recently, it was only the foes of the unions who were anxious to clip their wings. It is truly significant that in the post-World War II years it is also economists who regard themselves as friends of unions who have become increasingly willing to reconsider the basis and need for their power. It is to be underscored, however, that this attitude stems less from a belief that unions have been able adversely to affect the wage structure and wage level with their power than from a growing conviction that union power has had a remarkably minor effect, so that the unions' exercises have been largely uneconomic and perhaps, under the circumstances, somewhat unsocial.

If this view becomes more widespread and if it has the effect of diluting the resistance to restrictive legislation on union activities, however, one consequence is almost certain. The unions will be driven more and more into political activity, where, economists are convinced, they can have a more potent influence than at the bargaining table, through legislation dealing with tax distribution, transfer payments, public expenditures, full-employment measures, and so on. The interesting fact is, however, that such a turn of events would be largely anathema to the present contingent of labor leaders. It would thrust them onto a stage on which most of them would feel exposed and uncomfortable.

Let us summarize briefly the above argument. Unions and managements come to grips in two fields of action, the business firm and society at large. Management has preferred to fight its battles with labor principally in the corporate arena, with which it has greatest familiarity and over which it is more capable of maintaining control in a social setting generally congenial to it. The unions have been content to follow this pattern. As a result, they have increasingly tended to breed a strain of leadership suitable to the situation and hence susceptible to the rewards of individual power, prestige, and wealth. As in the larger society within which they operate, these individual rewards may generally be secured within the law, but there are those who have yielded to the temptations of larger rewards in the spreading jungle wilderness of illegal (or at least "less legal") activity.

Within the corporate prize ring, where such individualists most successfully operate, and where they feel most at home, the unions have acquired a reputation for irresistible power. Corporate empires which once brought state and federal governments to heel must now bow before the union bosses, at least in the word pictographs of the popular press. Union members, vassals of their bosses, are content to be ordered to strike or not to strike, at their bosses' pleasure, because of the high wages which such power secures for them. The findings of the objective scholars are quite different, however. It appears that union members enjoy little or no differential wage advantages over their unorganized brethren, and that the unions' chief contribution to their members' welfare has been to free them from the tyranny of arbitrary decision or discriminatory action in the work place. This finding has led such observers, disinterested (and sometimes even partisans of unionism) as they are, to wonder whether alternative forms of union-management relations may not be found which would eliminate the worst aspects of collective bargaining (force, violence, and a privacy which may harbor racketeering) without sacrificing its admirable gains.

Whether an alternative will be thrust upon the unions depends largely on whether the foes of unionism seek to clip a power which they fear and whether the friends of unionism acquiesce in an amputation of power which they regard as unnecessary. If this entirely possible event should take place, however, management would be thrown on the other horn of a dilemma which as yet some of their number have not recognized. For, in that event, the unions would be gradually driven to change their battlefield, and a new breed of leader would be precipitated on the scene. The face of a labor movement led in part by a group which sees it as a means of personal enrichment would fade before the quite different mask of a labor movement led by political reformers, whose objective would be a new social context in which the corporation must operate. Such a metamorphosis may occur in any case, but at a minimum the period of the transition is likely to be affected.

Selection 18

The Farm Income Problem

JAMES B. HERENDEEN

An original article prepared for this publication.

There are many government programs that affect farmers: soil conservation, land reclamation, agricultural extension, agricultural experiment stations, government-sponsored credit cooperatives, and various government price and income supports. This article will be restricted to a discussion of government policies aimed directly at stabilizing or supporting farm prices and incomes.

The farm income problem has existed for at least forty years. It appeared during the 1920's when farmers were burdened with low farm prices and heavy debts incurred during the high-price period caused by World War I. During the 1930's farmers faced even lower prices and incomes, farm foreclosures, and bankruptcy. The present farm programs originated during this period. World War II and the Korean War brought farmers prosperous times. After the Korean War, despite continued prosperity in the nonfarm economy, farm prices fell steadily, farm incomes lagged behind rising nonfarm incomes, the government was plagued with rising surpluses accumulated under its farm price support programs, and the costs of farm programs increased rapidly. Since 1960, the government has gradually reduced its surplus stocks, but government costs of farm programs have remained high.

Income Problems of Commercial and Noncommercial Farms

The average realized net farm income[1] per farm was $4,100 in 1964. However, this figure gives a misleading picture of the economic position of the nation's

[1] Realized net farm income is total cash receipts from farm marketing plus government payments, value of home consumption of food, and rental value of dwellings minus all production expenses. Farm income figures in this article are from James B. Herendeen, "Farm Programs and Income Distribution in Agriculture by Economic Class of Farm and by Area," in *Income Distribution Analysis,* Raleigh, N.C.: North Carolina State University, December 1966, pp. 223–247. They are based, in part, on data from Economic Research Service, *Farm Income Situation,* July 1965, and July Supplement, 1965, U.S. Department of Agriculture, and *United States Census of Agriculture,* 1950, 1954, 1959, U.S. Department of Commerce.

commercial farms—and it is toward these commercial farms that government farm programs have been directed. This article defines commercial farms as those with gross sales over $5,000. All other farms are considered noncommercial.

There were approximately 1.65 million farms with sales under $5,000 in 1964. Their average realized net farm income was about $700. This was much below what might be considered a minimum subsistence income. However, off-farm income keeps many of these farm families from the grips of poverty. The average off-farm income of this group was $3,000 in 1964. In addition to these farm operators, there were approximately 1.5 million hired workers whose average income from farming in 1964 was $1,800. These operators and farm workers are plagued with a chronic low level of income.

In 1964, 1.47 million farms had sales over $5,000. These farms accounted for 91 per cent of all farm-product sales and received 88 per cent of all direct government payments. They comprised 47 per cent of all farm operations. Farms with sales over $10,000 accounted for 78 per cent of farm-product sales and only 26 per cent of all farm operations. In 1964 this group included about 800,000 farms. Farms with sales over $5,000 had an average realized net farm income in 1964 of $7,964. In addition, they had nonfarm income of about $1,700 per farm. They had average productive assets of $108,600 per farm.[2] Allowing a 5½ per cent return on equity capital, the labor income from farming to the operator and his family was $2,947.[3] When nonfarm income was added, the total labor income was $4,647 per operator, or $3,873 per family worker. Because of the substantial increases in land values, if capital were valued at cost, labor returns or net farm income would be somewhat higher. Thus it can be seen that, although returns are low relative to the high investment and high level of skills needed for modern agriculture, the commercial farmers are not a poverty problem. It should be realized that these incomes reflect rather large income transfers to agriculture resulting from government farm programs. Estimates by agricultural economists indicate that total net farm income would fall by at least 30 per cent if farm programs were discontinued.

Government farm programs have been aimed primarily at the resource returns problem of commercial agriculture. There is little doubt that returns to labor and capital in agriculture are much higher than they would be in the absence of such programs. It is a mistake to justify farm programs in terms of poverty in agriculture. There is plenty of poverty, but poor people get little of the benefit of farm programs. Since there is little chance that farmers with sales of under $5,000 will be able to become successful commercial farmers, they can perhaps best be helped by social security, the poverty program, and other such welfare-oriented programs and with programs which aid in their transfer to nonfarm jobs. The rest of this paper will confine itself to a discussion of the commercial farm problem.

---

[2] Productive assets do not include the value of the farm dwelling or 60 per cent of the value of autos.

[3] For these farmers, debts were about 16 per cent of productive assets. Interest on debt has been included as a production expense. Labor income is the return to operator labor, management, and risk. It does not include hired labor.

The Economic Structure of Agriculture

The farm sector consists of many industries. Each industry is composed of many relatively small farms, producing a nearly identical product. Therefore no individual farm has any control over the price of its product but must take price as given by the market (or government).

Much of the nonfarm economy is dominated by industries which produce differentiated products. Because the customers of each firm can distinguish its product from its rival's product, the firm has a certain degree of control over price. In addition, many of these industries are dominated by a relatively small number of large producers. Therefore, each producer must consider the reactions of his rivals in making his price and output decisions. In such a situation price competition is usually destructive and firms recognize the necessity of channeling their competitive energies into product, service, or selling competition. These industries tend to have administered prices that are relatively inflexible. A shift in demand leads to a shift in production and employment in the industry but usually not (at least in the short run) to any significant change in price. If demand falls, the industry reduces production from perhaps 90 per cent of capacity to perhaps 75 per cent of capacity and continues to sell at the same price.

In agriculture, no such mechanism for adjusting plant utilization to demand exists. Since each firm takes price as given, it will always pay to produce at full capacity. Only if all firms restrict output will the individual firm gain from such a policy. With a free market, a fall in demand will lead to falling prices and incomes which will force out of business the marginal farms. Thus total capacity for the industry is adjusted rather than the level of plant utilization.

Also, market demand for farm products is highly price-inelastic at the farm level of marketing. This means that it takes a relatively large change in prices at the farm level to induce only a relatively small change in food consumption. This is true for two main reasons: (1) Food is a necessity which involves a relatively small share of consumer expenditures. Therefore consumers do not change their purchases much in response to small changes in the level of food prices; (2) Marketing margins—the costs of transporting, processing, packaging, and distributing food products—tend to be relatively inflexible for most farm products. For example, let the retail price of potatoes be $3.00, the farm price be $1.00 and marketing margins be fixed at $2.00. If the retail price falls to $2.70, a fall of 10 per cent, the farm price will fall to 70¢ a fall of 30 per cent. Thus, in general, demand is much more inelastic at the farm than at the retail level.

In addition, the income elasticity for food is very low. Income elasticity measures the percentage change in food consumption per unit change in the real incomes of consumers. Thus as real incomes of consumers increase, purchases of food will increase by a much smaller proportion.

Likewise, the supply of farm products is very price-inelastic. This means that farmers will not adjust output very much in response to a change in farm prices. In the short run, supply is almost perfectly inelastic, as it is fixed by past production plans. Once the farmer has committed his resources to a particular crop, he has little choice over what to offer for sale. In the longer run, the same is true for resources committed to farming as a profession. The farmer who has committed his land, labor, and capital to agriculture cannot easily leave the industry as his income falls. The salvage value of his land and physical capital may be much below their acquisition cost. Also the salvage value of his farming skills may be very low in an alternative profession. The labor supply in agriculture is adjusted primarily by the rate at which young people enter the profession. Thus even in a static situation, at least a generation is required to adjust the labor force to changed demand in agriculture.

Rather than a static situation, agriculture has been faced with a revolution in production techniques. This has meant a continued change in production costs and an increase in demand for purchased capital inputs relative to labor inputs. This has been, at least in part, due to public investment in farm technology. Unlike a large industrial firm, the individual farmer cannot afford to invest in his own research. Thus research and development for agriculture has been carried on by government through the United States Department of Agriculture, the Land Grant College System, and the Agriculture Experiment Stations. The Extension Service has disseminated the information to farmers. In addition, farm suppliers—producers of farm machinery, fertilizers, insecticides, and hybrid seed—invested heavily in research and development to increase their sales to farmers.

Most of these new techniques are output-increasing, that is, they allow farmers to grow more output per unit of original input of land and labor and reduce per-unit costs of producing the output. Once a new technique is developed, the competitive nature of the industry forces its rapid adoption. For the individual farmer it pays to adopt the new method, because it reduces his per-unit costs. But when all farmers adopt it, output is increased, price falls, and farmers collectively may be worse off than before the new technique was introduced. This assures that (in the absence of government supports) the productivity gains will be passed on to the consumer in the form of lower food prices. If resources were perfectly mobile, the situation would be corrected by labor and capital leaving agriculture and moving to more profitable employments. However, as was pointed out above, resources in agriculture are not sufficiently mobile to keep up with the rapidly changing resource demands.

The problem has been further aggravated by the relatively high level of unemployment in the nonfarm economy during the past decade. As long as nonfarm incomes are significantly above incomes in agriculture, the rate of labor migration out of agriculture is primarily determined by the availability of nonfarm jobs.

The labor situation is also aggravated by the fact that birth rates are higher in agriculture than in the rest of the economy. The movement out of agriculture has been rapid; farm population has been more than halved in the past twenty years. But this has not been nearly enough to give labor returns in agriculture comparable to returns in other occupations.

Thus the farm income problem continues to persist because the structure of the industry is such that rapid adjustment to change is impossible. Demand for food is highly inelastic and increases over time primarily as a result of population growth. However, rapid productivity gains have continued to increase supply at a faster rate than demand thus depressing prices and incomes. With the new techniques fewer resources, especially labor, are needed to produce the nation's agricultural output. As long as rapid productivity gains continue and many resources remain trapped in agriculture, this sector of the economy will face continued excess capacity and, in the absence of government programs, low resource returns.

Current Government Programs

The philosophy behind government farm programs in the period 1933 to 1960 was that the farm problem was one of temporary maladjustment caused by insufficient demand during the depression, too high price supports during World War II and the Korean War, and rapid increases in productivity in the farm industry. Farm policy consisted of temporary programs aimed at getting agriculture back to the free market. During the Eisenhower years, Secretary of Agriculture Benson tried to move in this direction. He found Congress willing to remove or weaken acreage controls but not willing to reduce price supports drastically enough to force a reduction in output. Small reductions in price supports were offset by falling per-unit costs as a result of productivity gains. Thus the result of the Benson policy was a rapid increase in government purchases of surplus commodities and a deeper involvement of government in agriculture than ever before.

In an attempt to retard the buildup of surpluses, the Soil Bank Program of 1956 was passed. The primary feature of the program was the Conservation Reserve, which allowed farmers to rent whole farms or parts of farms to the government under contracts of from three to ten years. During the contract period the land could not be used for production. By 1960 nearly 30 million acres were in the Conservation Reserve, but the program attracted mainly marginal land and had a small effect on total output. After 1960, Congress allowed the program to lapse by authorizing no new contracts.

Also during the Eisenhower years an attempt was made to move existing surpluses out of the grain bins through a program of subsidized commercial exports and surplus disposal through noncommercial channels. Public Law 480, passed in 1954, allowed surplus commodities to be sold for foreign currencies, given away, or sold for dollars under special loan arrangements.

The Kennedy Administration was the first to view the farm problem as one of permanent maladjustment. Secretary of Agriculture Freeman and his economic adviser, Willard Cochrane, were committed to managed supply for agriculture. However, Freeman, like Benson before him, found Congress less receptive. Attempts to pass enabling legislation for supply control failed in 1961. The Administration was, however, able to pass the voluntary feed grain program.[4]

---

[4] Feed grains are corn, oats, barley, and grain sorghum.

Under this program farmers were offered another alternative for land that had formerly been used for feed grains—they could rent the land to the government. Thus nonproduction had to be made more profitable than production, and the program proved to be quite expensive. The program has been modified somewhat and extended to wheat and cotton. Price supports for wheat, cotton, and feed grains have been lowered to reduce government storage costs, to facilitate movement of farm commodities into export markets, and to keep market prices below prices to participating farmers in order to encourage cooperation with the program. The participating farmer receives a direct payment in addition to this supported price, thus giving a total guaranteed price considerably above market prices. In addition he receives a rental payment for land removed from production. The wheat program now is a two-price program—one for domestic wheat and one for export. Prices of dairy products are supported by a support price on manufacturing milk. Also, milk prices are set administratively by federal milk orders for the major urban centers. Prices and production of other livestock products are indirectly controlled by the control over feed grain prices and production since livestock production tends to adjust to available feed supplies and prices. The 1965 Omnibus Farm Bill included a general land-retirement provision similar to the 1956–1960 Conservation Reserve, which was aimed at retiring 40 million acres over five years.

Despite their rather high cost, the programs have, at least in part, achieved their objectives. Government stocks of wheat, feed grains, and dairy products have been substantially reduced since 1960. Realized net farm income in 1964 was 11 per cent above the 1960 level. This was an increase of $1.3 billion. In the same period direct government payments going to farmers increased by $1.6 billion to a total of $2.2 billion. Total costs of farm income support programs, including costs of storage and surplus disposal programs, were running close to $5 billion per year.

Policy Alternatives

Almost everyone concedes that present farm programs leave much to be desired. They are very costly, they do little for the low-income farmers, and they do little to aid the adjustment of capital and labor out of agriculture. Offsetting this is the fact that we have an abundance of high-quality food, the programs have not greatly retarded the adjustment of labor out of agriculture, and productivity gains have been rapid. Productivity gains would likely have been much slower in the absence of government programs. The expectation of stable prices and incomes encourages rapid adoption of the new techniques. But before passing judgment, what are the alternatives?

1. *A return to the free market.* Many people argue that the farm problem is caused by government intervention and that without government, the industry would adjust by means of the market mechanism so as to allow adequate returns to people in agriculture. No matter what one thinks of current government pro-

grams, this ignores the arguments presented above. Most government intervention is a result, not a cause, of the farm problem. A removal of government programs would mean a fall of at least 30 per cent in net farm incomes. Indications are that farm incomes would remain low for a prolonged period of 5 to 10 years.

2. *Controlling agricultural output by controlling inputs.* One way of controlling production is by controlling the resources used in agriculture.

(a) Controlling the use of land. Acreage controls and land-rental schemes are attempts to control the use of land. With acreage controls, the farmer is asked to restrict his acreage in order to be eligible for a support price on his crops. If acreage controls are used for only a few crops, the excess acres are used to produce other uncontrolled crops, which then become surplus. Thus in the 1950's acreage controls on wheat and cotton led to increased production of feed grains.

General land retirement would allow farmers to rent whole farms or parts of farms to the government with rental rates such that the poorer land would enter first. It is estimated that 60 to 80 million acres would have to be retired to maintain farm incomes in the absence of other government programs. This would cost $1.2 billion to $1.5 billion. This is similar, but on a larger scale, to the Conservation Reserve portion of the Soil Bank Program of 1956–1960. A major advantage of general land retirement is that, where whole farms are rented, labor and capital are also removed from production.

Voluntary land retirement for the major field crops would rent acreage used only for these crops and would not allow whole farms to be retired. This approach is similar to the present feed grain, wheat, and cotton programs and would cost $1.5 billion to $2.0 billion to maintain farm incomes. With a voluntary program, rental rates must be made high enough so that it is more profitable for the farmer not to produce. Thus the programs are expensive and costs increase over time as productivity gains increase the value of output per acre. In addition the surplus disposal program for wheat and some other commodities would have to be continued under this approach or general land retirement. This would probably cost another $1.0 billion per year once the high costs of getting rid of existing surpluses was overcome.

Another method of controlling land use is mandatory acreage control. Here the farmer would be required to reduce output to be eligible for the supported price and would be unable to use the land for other crops. Because of the large amount of farm incomes currently received from production sold to the government or from land rental or other income payments, it would take a substantial production adjustment (12 to 15 per cent reduction of the main crops) just to maintain farm incomes. Farmers are reluctant to accept this much direct government regulation. Also, this type of program would lead to substantial increases in feed prices and, in the short run, to lower incomes for livestock producers.

(b) Another possibility is an active government program to encourage the movement of labor out of agriculture. One such proposal would loan money to farmers to finance their leaving agriculture and finding jobs elsewhere. Three problems arise: farmers have difficulty finding jobs in nonfarm employments because of lack of skills; the land is often taken over by other farmers who are more efficient, and thus output would fall little; and congressmen from rural districts who control the agricultural committees are not likely to vote for a program to move their constituents out of their district. This is why general land retirement programs that retire whole farms have been unpopular with many rural congressmen.

(c) Controlling capital in agriculture. No one has seriously proposed restricting capital inflows to agriculture, but this could be a possible alternative. A strict program of credit rationing would reduce investment in agriculture and thus long-run output. Such direct controls would be highly unpopular with farmers and bankers. An alternative plan would be to restrict government and private funds flowing into agricultural research. Because of the large backlog of technical knowhow that is not yet adopted by farmers, such a program would have little immediate effect on output. Although government funds may start flowing a little less freely, there is little chance that private funds will be restricted.

3. *Controlling the amount of output sold*. Since controlling inputs is a rather inefficient way of controlling production, why not control the amount farmers can market? One such scheme is to give each farmer a marketing quota and make the quotas negotiable. Farmers who wanted to expand output could then buy quotas from those who were willing to give up their right to produce. Thus the gains of operating in a regulated agriculture would tend to be capitalized into the value of the certificates. A major problem with this approach is that it would be difficult to apply the program to production that did not enter the market. Many feed crops are produced and fed on the same farm. For the program to be workable, it must be applied to all major farm products to keep the surplus from spilling from one product to another. One reason for not trying the mandatory approach was the feeling that if feed grain production could be controlled, it would be unnecessary to control livestock production. Livestock production would adjust to available feed supplies. Also, any program which controls directly the amount sold by farmers implies more control over farmers' decisions by the government and thus is unpopular with farmers. Farmers, naturally, want high production without low prices. So far they have had their way.

4. *Direct payments to farmers*. Instead of supporting prices above market clearing levels, why not let prices fall and pay farmers the difference between the market clearing price and the "fair" price determined by the government? Consumer prices could fall and subsidized exports would no longer be necessary. This, essentially, was the plan proposed by Secretary of Agriculture Brannan in 1949. At that time Congress rejected the program. There are two main objections to such a proposal. First, with above-market prices to farmers and no output restrictions, output would continue to expand and depress market prices, making continually larger payments necessary to maintain a given level of farm prices. Therefore government costs would be very high. It would probably require $6 billion to maintain the 1964 level of farm income with no output restrictions. Therefore, to keep costs down, output would have to be restricted or the size of payments going to individual farmers would have to be limited. In addition,

United States surpluses would flood world markets and depress world prices of farm commodities.

The second objection is mainly political. With present programs much of the cost is not apparent when the program is passed. It shows up later when Congress has to appropriate money to pay for storage and surplus disposal costs. With direct payments, the total cost of the programs would be more readily apparent. In addition, the amount going to individual farmers would also be apparent. Farm interest groups realize that, with direct payments, total appropriations and the size of payments to individual farmers would likely be reduced by Congress.

The last two or three years have seen a significant shift in political power away from the rural interests in Congress. Partially as a result of this, recent farm programs have begun to rely more heavily on direct payments in conjunction with land retirement programs.

Future Directions of Farm Policy

With government expenditures on farm income supports running close to $5 billion a year, there is increasing pressure to hold the line on farm program costs. In addition to the direct government costs, consumers pay a higher price for food than they would in the absence of farm programs. In the short run, there is little other employment available for excess resources in agriculture, thus little total output is lost. However, consumption patterns are influenced by shifting income from consumers in general to farmers and other rural people. It should be recognized that farm programs do not support just farmers. Farmers spend most of the additional income they receive. They spend it on farm machinery, fertilizer, hired labor, groceries, television sets, and college educations for their children. Thus the benefits are spread through rural communities and industries that supply agriculture.

In the longer run, given an economy of near-full employment, excess resources from agriculture can be transferred to employment in the nonfarm economy, where they will be more productive and total national income will be increased. Even in the short run, many will argue, there are other areas that need government spending worse than farmers, rural communities, and agriculturally related industries. People interested in spending for education, research, poverty programs, health insurance, and mass transit systems are jealous of the generous budget received by agriculture and critical of rural congressmen for being less generous with spending in other areas.

There is only one way that government costs can be substantially reduced without also reducing farm incomes. This is mandatory production control. But farmers are unwilling to accept this alternative as long as Congress will pass voluntary programs. Such a policy would mean higher food prices as program costs were passed directly to the consumer. Since the money saved by the reduction of government costs would be spent elsewhere, there would likely be no offsetting reduction in taxes.

Any other method of reducing government costs substantially will also lead to a reduction of farm incomes. With a much larger share of farm income support coming in the form of direct payments, the amount going to individual farmers is becoming more apparent to urban congressmen and the nonfarm public. Currently about 74 per cent of the direct payments go to farmers with sales over $10,000. This group of farmers had average realized net farm incomes of about $12,000 per farm in 1964. This included about $2,000 in direct government payments per farm. Thus, as nonfarm interests become more potent in agricultural policy making, it seems highly likely that Congress will set a limit on the amount of payment going to individual farm operators.

The only other way of reducing costs substantially is to return to a free market for agriculture. However, as long as farmers still have substantial political power, it is unlikely that Congress will ask them to face such a harsh choice.

The move to direct payments, lower supports, and general land retirement has set the stage for future agricultural policy changes: general land retirement will increase benefits going to smaller farmers and aid the transfer of labor out of agriculture; political pressure will keep farm-program costs from growing; closer scrutiny from nonfarm congressmen will likely force a reduction of benefits going to the larger farmers; a growing concern over poverty will bring more attention to the problems of chronic low income in agriculture; and a full-employment policy on the part of the government (if it is continued) will also aid the transfer of people out of agriculture. As government spending in other areas increases, farm programs will become a smaller portion of total expenditures and gradually the farm income problem will recede into the background.

Addendum

This article was originally written during the summer of 1965. Cost estimates for alternative farm programs were based on maintaining the 1964 level of net farm income. During 1965 and 1966, the farm income situation was greatly improved. This was primarily the result of increased demand due to the 1964 tax cut and the Vietnam buildup, a favorable export situation, and cyclically low production of cattle and hogs. Aggregate realized net farm income in 1966 was up 26 per cent from the 1964 level. Average realized net farm income per farm was $5,049, and for commercial farms (those with sales over $5,000) was $9,795. Total direct government payments in 1966 had increased to 3.3 billion dollars, or about $2,000 per commercial farm. During 1967, farm prices and incomes have again been falling, and the farm income problem is with us yet.

DISCUSSION QUESTIONS

1. Traditional economic theory was developed to describe an economy of small firms. However, the modern economic system is dominated by giant corporations. Discuss the theoretical and practical economic problems that the large corporation has posed for society.
2. Discuss the reasons why government decisions have come to have much more influence over the economic behavior of business, labor, and agricultrue.

3. If the role of collective bargaining diminishes, labor unions may have to find a new role in order to preserve their power and status. What directions might future labor union policy take?
4. Distinguish between the problems of commercial and noncommercial agriculture. Why have past farm programs dealt primarily with the problems of commercial agriculture? Why has Congress been hesitant to pass farm legislation that has the goal of moving people out of agriculture?
5. Discuss the alternative ways of coping with the commercial-farm problem. Examine each with respect to the level of farm income, government costs, the level of food prices, economic efficiency, and political feasibility.

SELECTED REFERENCES

Berle, Adolf A., Jr., *Power Without Property,* New York: Harcourt, Brace and World, Inc., 1959.

Caves, Richard, *American Industry: Structure, Conduct and Performance,* 2nd ed., Englewood Cliffs, N.J.: Prentice-Hall, Inc., 1957.

Cochrane, Willard D., *The City Man's Guide to the Farm Problem,* Minneapolis: The University of Minnesota Press, 1965.

Galbraith, John Kenneth, *The New Industrial State,* Boston: Houghton Mifflin Co., 1967.

Mason, Edward S. (ed.), *The Corporation in Modern Society,* Cambridge, Mass.: Harvard University Press, 1959.

Rees. Albert, *The Economics of Trade Unions,* Chicago: The University of Chicago Press, 1962.

Schultz, Theodore W., *Economic Crisis in World Agriculture,* Ann Arbor, Mich.: The University of Michigan Press, 1965. See especially Chap. IV.

PART 8

THE BALANCE OF INTERNATIONAL PAYMENTS

During the past decade the United States has been faced with a chronic deficit in its annual balance of international payments. This means that the United States is not earning enough foreign currencies from its exports of goods and services and from the sale of long-term American securities abroad to pay for its imports of goods and services, its purchase of long-term foreign securities, and its military and foreign aid grants and loans to other countries. Or, looked at another way, foreigners have more dollars than they currently wish to spend on American goods and services or on American securities; and therefore they have been trading these dollars for gold which can be spent for other countries' goods and services or which they feel is a safer long-term asset than dollars.

There are two ways that the United States has been able to spend more on its annual international account than it earns. One has been to reduce foreign exchange balances—that is, to pay the difference by exporting gold. The other has been to get foreigners to accept credit —that is, to hold dollars or short-term claims against dollars rather than demanding gold.

The deficits do not result from an inability to sell American goods overseas. United States exports have consistently run ahead of imports. Instead, the deficits arise from the large private and public loans and grants by the United States to the rest of the world. These include investments by American businessmen abroad, loans by American bankers abroad, and loans and grants by the government abroad. Eventually, these investments may generate interest and dividends which will help correct the situation.

Why should the United States be concerned with its annual deficits? After all, this is a rich country that can easily afford its overseas commitments. The problem is not that the United States is in bad financial shape—instead, the international monetary system poorly accommodates large international transfers. The present system relies on gold, United States dollars, and British pounds for international transactions and reserves. International monetary stocks have not expanded in step with the demand for transactions balances. These stocks could be expanded by a general devaluation of currencies in terms of gold. This would make current gold stocks go further but would mean a large subsidy to gold-producing and gold-hoarding countries. An alternative would be to create a new international currency to supplement dollars, pounds, and gold in international exchange.

Adherence to the present system greatly hampers American domestic and foreign policy. High domestic interest rates are required to stem the flow of dollars abroad. During the late 1950's and early 1960's this made monetary policy ineffective as a tool for expanding the domestic economy. This dilemma was resolved by turning to fiscal policy with the 1964 tax cut. In addition, the existence of chronic deficits may force the United States to reduce its military and economic aid and restrict private and public loans to the rest of the world. And, especially in the underdeveloped countries, these funds may be of crucial importance if they are to have a chance of achieving stable governments and economic development.

Selection 19

The Basic Causes of the U.S. Deficits

ALVIN H. HANSEN

From Alvin H. Hansen, The Dollar and the International Monetary System *(New York: McGraw-Hill Book Company, 1956), pp. 35–37 and 147–167. Reprinted by permission of McGraw-Hill Book Company.*

In this chapter I have stressed the difference between the *trading* balance (including both goods and services) and the *transfer* balance and also the difference between the exchange-market balance and the government transfer balance. These distinctions are of the greatest importance. Are the U.S. deficits of the last six years due to basic shifts in trade or are they due to shifts in the transfer of funds? If the deficit were due to a drastic falling off of exports, primary attention should be directed to our export situation. The trouble might lie in our own export industries, or the trouble might be found in restrictive import policies on the part of foreign countries. If the deficit were due to a drastic increase in U.S. imports, the cause might conceivably be located in inefficiency in those American industries that compete with imports. If it is a trade-oriented deficit, that is one thing. But if it is a transfer-oriented deficit, that is quite a different matter. True, in the long run, the trade will respond to established transfer flows. But in the short run transfer shifts cannot be offset by corresponding trade shifts without serious disruption in international trade relations. Transfer shifts can, however, be met without causing dislocations by deliberately offsetting capital flows implemented by adequate institutional arrangements. But in the contemporary world economy it may require international monetary machinery to facilitate the flow of funds across international borders.

Thus the U.S. balance-of-payments deficits emerge basically from two situations, neither of which have to do with the short-run, cyclical, or episodic types of imbalances for which the International Monetary Fund was set up or that central bankers contend with when they make short-term loans to tide a country over a temporary crisis. The two persistent sources of the U.S. balance-of-payments problem are (1) the U.S. program of military and economic foreign aid and (2) the New York capital market, which, on top of the government aid programs, supplies capital to foreign countries. The current U.S. balance-of-payments problem is perhaps unique in all history. Yet many economists and bankers discuss the problem as though it were just the familiar, short-run, cyclical, or episodic case.

What I am saying does not mean that adjustments cannot be made over time which could end the overall U.S. deficits even though the New York market continues its role as major supplier of funds abroad and the United States continues its aid programs. The progressive rise of investment income alone will automatically play an increasing role as a balancing factor. And the feedback effects will gradually show up in the trade balance and perhaps also in the capital account. If, however, a more equitable distribution of foreign aid cannot be achieved, and if European capital markets cannot be substantially improved, it is highly improbable that the goods and services account can fully make the needed adjustments barring policies (tariff increases, exchange control, etc.) that are injurious to a prospering and growing world trade.

Professor Zolotas, governor of the Bank of Greece, has summed up the matter admirably as follows:

> *As a matter of fact, in the last two years the annual outflow of long-term capital alone accounts for more than the corresponding overall deficit in the U.S. balance of payments. The still existing restrictions on capital exports in several industrial countries, and, more significantly, the organizational and institutional shortcomings of capital markets outside the U.S., impose on her, in addition to the responsibilities of a reserve center, the task of satisfying capital requirements in the rest of the world, including the highly developed countries. This situation is incompatible with the smooth functioning of the gold exchange standard, which requires some measure of correspondence in the availability and freedom of movement of capital among major trading countries. The resulting strains from this lopsided operation of the international financial mechanism are being accentuated by the movement of short-term funds, partly in reference to interest rates differentials. Under these conditions one can hardly deny the necessity for the industrial countries of Europe to liberalize and develop their capital markets in accordance with the overall potential of their economies. This, however, is likely to be a gradually evolving process, leaving the main burden of the task at present to the United States. The resistance of the latter to the easy solution of direct capital controls should be generally appreciated.*[1]

"Corrective Measures"

Financial Discipline

As is well known by anyone who has followed the balance-of-payments controversies, proposals to alleviate the pressure on the key currencies often encounter the objection that such panaceas are merely "soothing syrup," pain-killers that fail to reach the seat of the trouble. They give the patient a deceptive feeling of security. The warning signals are covered up. Internal domestic policies are freed from the constraints imposed by external discipline.

---

[1] *Summary Proceedings*, Annual Meeting, IMF, 1963, p. 93.

The problem relates essentially to the control of inflation and the role that external discipline actually plays as a restraining influence. Ask any Western European how he explains the *relatively* moderate increases in wages and prices in a period of great expansion, full employment, and often even over-full employment, and he will almost certainly point to the restraint imposed by international competition.

As a government official or central banker, what he has in mind is almost certainly the threat of a balance-of-payments deficit. If he is an industrialist, he has in mind the fear of losing his export market. His concern is limited to his own business.

Now this is a difference worth noting. In my own thinking, I should like to remove as far as possible the restraints which the external discipline (that is, the balance-of-payments discipline) imposes upon domestic full-employment policies. There will still be plenty of reasons why we should pursue the goal of reasonable price stability, and in particular I do not want to eliminate either domestic or international competition. At first thought this may seem like begging the question, but I do not believe it is. Domestic competition can be vigorous and effective, but here there is no balance-of-payments discipline. International competition is a deep concern for each industry even though these industries are located in a country which never experiences any balance-of-payment problem. Obviously, international competition and the external payments discipline are not one and the same thing. I believe that much confusion arises from the mistaken view that they are identical twins.

How does one explain the fact that the postwar price increases have been kept reasonably under control? Competition, both domestic and international, is certainly a part of the answer. A part of the answer is inertia and lags. A part is an awareness by business concerns that a stable price policy is good public relations. Neither business nor labor likes to face hostile public opinion. I am convinced from President Kennedy's tussle with the steel industry in 1962 that public opinion can be marshaled with sufficient force so that both business and labor become more cautious. The government is something more than a tug-of-war between organized producers. In the United States at any rate there is a very large public that is in no sense a party to any collective wage bargain. In particular, the President, who alone represents the entire nation, can and often does stand out over and above the special-interest groups.

We want and need competition, both domestic and international. But we do not want unfair competition. Domestically we try to suppress unfair competition. Internationally, unfair competition means, for one thing, competitive pressure imposed by a country that is deflating its costs and prices or is engaged in export dumping, export tax remissions, or export subsidies. Discriminatory controls have to be applied against such countries, and indeed this is permitted by the Bretton Woods arrangements. Again, disrupting influences may flow from a country that is experiencing rapid inflation. Once the rate of inflation has really moved into the danger zone, such a country's currency is no longer acceptable as foreign exchange.

These are the extreme cases. They fall outside of the area of reasonable limits.

In economics as well as in law we continually have to apply the "rule of reason," as the United States Supreme Court puts it. Beyond reasonable limits it is contrary to good public policy to permit the external payments balance to control domestic policy. Indeed, this is precisely why countries build up international reserves. These reserves free a country from being *rigorously* controlled, month by month and year by year, by the severe discipline of the external balance. The current debate about the external discipline relates purely and simply to whether we should increase the "international margin" still more to give us greater freedom from the rigorous restraints on domestic policy imposed by this discipline. This is what the current liquidity problem is all about. In the past we have been concerned with episodic and cyclical imbalances. Does this go far enough? Now do we not need to provide time for adjustment of structural imbalances? Greater freedom can be achieved by (1) improving the quality of the foreign exchange component, endowing it with an exchange guarantee and thereby removing the pressure of gold drains, and (2) increasing the aggregate volume of actual or potential reserves. Within reasonable limits this is in the line of progress.

In the 1963 meeting of the IMF a new note was struck. Joseph R. Slevin, reporting for the *New York Herald Tribune,* had this to say:

> *Free-world financial officers are barely hinting at something they used to shout about. The missing subject is financial discipline. It is the painful, orthodox cure for balance-of-payments deficits.*
>
> *Instead of financial discipline the talk now is of liquidity. The stress is upon giving a country generous credit so that it can eliminate its payments deficit gradually.*

Shortly before the conference met, the Brookings Institution published a report on the United States balance of payments by Walter S. Salant, Emile Despres, and others. This report stated unequivocally that "deflationary measures, the classical means of improving the balance-of-payments, reduce employment and real incomes—effects which are neither politically feasible nor economically desirable in a modern industrial country."[1] Deflationary measures, the report said, restrain investment and hamper modernization and innovation. Efficiency increases are more likely to be made in an atmosphere of general expansion and unrestricted foreign competition. Measures which might endanger economic growth and high employment levels should not be adopted for balance-of-payments reasons.

Freedom to Pursue Domestic Goals

It was a cardinal objective of the Bretton Woods Conference to develop, through the IMF and the Bank for Reconstruction and Development, interna-

---

[2] *Report on the U.S. Balance of Payments in 1968,* by Walter S. Salant, Emile Despres, Alice M. Rivlin, Lorie Tarshis, Laurence B. Krause, and William A. Salant (Washington, D.C.: The Brookings Institution, 1963), p. 246.

tional cooperation and collaboration so that balance-of-payments difficulties would not act as a deterrent to domestic full-employment policies. The problem was to find a way to meet payments imbalances without having to resort to deflationary and restrictive measures.

To counteract temporary disequilibria, the IMF was equipped with funds (subscribed by member countries) which could be loaned to members confronted with balance-of-payments difficulties. If a country's exchange rate got structurally out of line (fundamental disequilibrium), it might be helped out of its difficulty by development loans made by the Bank for Reconstruction and Development. Finally the deficit country was permitted unilaterally to alter its exchange rate up to 10 per cent, and if a larger adjustment was necessary the country could ask permission from the Fund. In the case of a fundamental disequilibrium, however, the Fund could not deny the request merely on the ground that the country had followed unorthodox domestic policies. Bretton Woods permitted exchange restrictions on capital movements but not on current transactions. In effect it placed the burden of adjustment on the surplus countries, since it permitted deficit countries to place restrictions on imports if necessary to safeguard their international reserves but only to the extent permitted by GATT agreements and with the advice and consent of the IMF. Bretton Woods expounded the view that full-employment policies are not only good for the country in question but are also beneficial to its neighbors, to world trade, and to international equilibrium.

Throughout the interwar period, Keynes defended the principle of national independence from external influences. To promote this independence he suggested (1) official buying and selling operations in the foreign exchange markets, (2) exchange control when necessary with special reference to capital movements, (3) widening the spread between the official buying and selling price of gold, and (4) adjustment when necessary of the exchange rate. He constantly stressed the point that the burden of adjustment should primarily be assumed by the surplus countries. In his House of Lords speech in support of Bretton Woods he declared: "We are determined that . . . the external value of sterling shall conform to its internal value as set by our own domestic policies."[3]

But Bretton Woods, as events actually turned out, proved to be far short of the resources needed to cope with the herculean task of rebuilding and stabilizing the free world by cooperative financial effort. The Fund's resources, as finally negotiated, had been whittled down to around $8 billion. In reality (considering the postwar collapse in Western Europe) the only asset that could effectively be counted upon was the subscription by the United States of $2,750 million.

Keynes's Clearing Union

This was a far cry from the bold program (politically unacceptable to the United States) which was advocated by Keynes in his clearing union plan.

---

[3] Seymour E. Harris (ed.), *The New Economics* (New York: Kelley & Millman, 1947), p. 374.

Keynes's proposal would have permitted deficit countries to meet the balance-of-payments needs by making overdrafts in the clearing union up to the limit of their assigned quotas. Surplus countries (primarily, and indeed almost exclusively, the United States, as things then looked) would have agreed under the plan to accept payment in the form of bancor, the proposed new international monetary unit to be issued by the clearing union and which was to become the sole means of settling international accounts. And since the aggregate quotas amounted (over and above the United States quota) to around $30 billion, this could have resulted ultimately in the United States being "forced" to extend credit in that amount to deficit countries. In short, the scheme in practice would have implemented an enormous program of foreign aid financed by the United States, not by year-to-year appropriations by Congress, but by advance commitments which could have cumulated to around $30 billion.

Marshall Aid

Considering the magnitude of the task of rehabilitating the postwar world, Keynes's plan was highly realistic in terms of economics but it was politically unacceptable to the United States. Political hurdles are, however, often swept aside by powerful historical forces. The flow of world-wide economic forces could not be dammed up permanently by the severely limited outlook of the United States Congress. As the hard facts of life unfolded it became evident that the Marshall Aid plan, first proposed in June, 1947, made sense. The signal was given by the Communist penetration into Greece, Turkey, Hungary, Romania, and Czechoslovakia. The Marshall Aid program set the pattern for the vast United States foreign aid which by the end of 1963 had cumulated to around $90 billion. The monetary and economic rehabilitation thus financed was essential for the preservation of the Western world.

There was no other way out. The Fund's resources were not intended for long-term rehabilitation. Nor could the Bank for Reconstruction and Development, depending heavily upon funds raised in the private capital markets, cope with the rebuilding of the economic systems of the free world. Indeed, the cumulated total loans made by the World Bank up to the end of 1963 amounted to only about $6.5 billion. Contrast this with the $90 billion poured out in foreign aid, economic and military, by the United States. Thus it was, as events turned out, that the United States became the financial bulwark of the Western world and the dollar became the central pivot—the primary key currency—of the evolving new international monetary structure—the gold-dollar-exchange standard.[4]

Keynes was quite right. The rehabilitation of the free world could only be achieved through vast advances by the United States. But he *underestimated* the amount. Under his plan these advances would have been made through the clear-

[4] Sterling continues to be the key currency for the sterling area, built up around the old British Commonwealth, but the amount of sterling held as official foreign exchange balances has remained frozen at around $7 billion during the last decade.

ing union and financed (at least this is the implication) automatically through an expansion of Federal Reserve credit which would have come into existence as and when American exporters deposited their bancor balances in commercial banks, which, in turn, would send them to a Federal Reserve Bank to be credited to their deposit account. As it turned out, the job was in fact done by the unilateral action of the United States financed, not by expansion of central bank credit, but by appropriations voted by the Congress.

The experience of the last fifteen years clearly reveals a very fundamental fact which has still not been fully grasped, namely, that the modern world cannot function without massive capital transfers. The United States has made gigantic grants and loans, so gigantic indeed that in recent years these outflows (supplemented increasingly by private capital outflow) have resulted in a piling up of excess dollar holdings. These excess dollar holdings are in some measure an indication of the failure of Western Europe to carry its part of the burden of foreign aid and military security. The surplus countries of Western Europe have not been balancing their international accounts by investing these excess dollar holdings abroad. Substantial international payments surpluses have not been offset by long-term international financing.

Spurious comparisons of aid provided by advanced countries have often been made which confuse the financial aspects of a continuing economic colonialism with genuine foreign aid. Properly speaking, aid should be limited to government grants and loans to noncolonial areas and to government contributions to international development institutions like the World Bank. At first the United States was the only significant source of foreign aid so defined. Gradually this has changed and it is estimated that by 1963 the United States provided about 55 per cent of the aid to noncolonial areas.[5]

Experience shows that this matter cannot be left simply to the unilateral action of individual nations. No modern nation has succeeded in providing security for old age by leaving this up to the individual but instead has found it necessary to introduce collective action in the form of social security. So, too, we are learning that the necessary flows of capital offsets to persistent deficits of countries that carry a disproportionate share of the costs of international security requires new programs designed to bolster the gold-exchange standard.

An International Capital Market

No system of fixed exchange rates can survive in a market free from exchange controls, import quotas, and the like without a fluid and effective capital market encompassing the area within which fixed exchange rates persist.[6] Take, for ex-

[5] See *Economic Report of the President,* January 1964, p. 157.

[6] "There is no reason why long-term loans should not be applied for this purpose. The whole idea of the current or the basic balance of a country as an indicator of the 'soundness' of its international position, and of the necessity for keeping the basic balance in equilibrium, ought to break down with rational and deliberate policies of the kind described here. . . . It may be a 'sound' policy to lend and borrow for long periods."—Bent Hansen, Central Bank of Egypt Lectures, 1962.

ample, the twelve Federal Reserve districts in the vast area of the United States. Disequilibrating forces are continually at work making some districts deficit areas in their payments relation to the rest of the country. What holds the whole thing together? By far the most important single factor is the fact that all areas in the United States are integrated into a common capital market. Moreover, the federal government plays a large role in dispensing funds—relief, reconstruction, development aid, social security, unemployment benefits, farm price supports, et cetera. The national unified monetary unit (which means a system of fixed exchange rates) covers the same area as the nationwide capital market and the Federal fiscal system.

Assume that the Ninth Federal Reserve District has a trade deficit with the New York District. The Minneapolis area imports too much and exports too little. A business firm in Mankato sends a $10,000 check to a New York firm from which it has purchased a supply of goods. This check is deposited in a New York bank and sent on to the New York Federal Reserve Bank for collection. The New York Federal sends it on to the Minneapolis Federal. The latter debits it against the Mankato bank's balance. Thus the liabilities of the Minneapolis Federal to the Mankato bank are reduced by $10,000, and offsetting this, it now owes the New York Federal $10,000.[7] The Minneapolis Federal can reimburse the New York Federal by means of a transfer of gold through the Gold Settlement Fund. Both the liabilities and the assets of the Minneapolis Federal will now have declined by $10,000. The Federal Reserve Board may then reallocate the various districts' holdings of gold and government securities so as to restore the gold reserve ratio of the Minneapolis Reserve Bank. For example, United States securities could be transferred from the Minneapolis bank to the New York bank in exchange for gold. Thus the liquidity of the Minneapolis district would be restored. This would permit renewed expansion of Federal Reserve credit in the Minneapolis area and thereby reduce the deflationary pressure. In the meantime, long-run adjustments such as the relocation of labor and industries to more prosperous and expanding areas will gradually be made.

Thus within the boundaries of a sovereign country we do not apply punitive measures and painful disciplines. We fill the trade-balance gap with capital flows.[8]

Bank credit and governmental expansionist measures may facilitate the building up of new industries and the strengthening of old ones. Thus the adjustment is made, not by the process of "going through the wringer" (perverse restraints), but by means of the cooperating expansionist policies and collective action of the nation as a whole, namely, by offsetting capital flows made possible by an ample

---

[7] The figure here used is for convenience only. It is, of course, ridiculously small. It would take far more to cause a gold transfer.

[8] For an excellent discussion of the role of the capital account in the balance of payments see James C. Ingram, *A Proposal for Financial Integration in the Atlantic Community, Materials Prepared for the Subcommittee on International Exchange and Payments,* 87th Cong., 2d Sess., 1962, pp. 177–207.

volume of interregional liquidity. This process of expansion can and should be carried to the point of full employment, but not to the point of inflation.

Keynes had hoped for his clearing union a degree of financial integration akin but not yet equal to that achieved within the domestic economy of a sovereign nation. And Bretton Woods represented a modest effort toward this goal. The point that needs to be stressed is the enormous importance of an adequate flow of equilibrating funds between surplus and deficit areas if the process of going through the wringer—the so-called "corrective measures"—is to be avoided. What is needed is a pool of international compensatory funds adequate not only to offset temporary imbalances but also to hold the line while slow-moving, long-term adjustments are being made.

As long as the credit pool is relatively limited, as is currently the case, the available or potentially available credit reserves need be supplemented by gold. Increasingly, however, as the international compensatory finance structure is built up and strengthened year after year, gold may come to play, bit by bit, a smaller role. Speculation in gold will more and more be brought under control. A larger and larger part of the burden of exchange stabilization will be carried by international compensatory finance. We may then at long last attain an international monetary system which is wholly "managed" and no longer based even partially on gold.

Restrictive Measures

In the nineteenth century, severe self-discipline—meaning, in fact, deflation of wages and prices—was the orthodox remedy (automatically enforced by the gold standard) for balance-of-payments deficits. This policy could indeed, and in fact did, restore balance in the international accounts in the days before World War I, though at the cost of widespread suffering and unemployment. Balance was not achieved without evoking riots and bloodshed. The history of violence in the American labor movement in the last quarter of the nineteenth century attests to that. But through it all, balance was, in fact, restored.[9] The gold standard and the corrective measures it imposed were taken for granted as an inevitable way of life. No one was to blame. It all operated under so-called natural law.

In the interwar period following World War I deliberate action was widely introduced to cope with balance-of-payments maladjustments. Things were no longer allowed to run their course. Government intervention was undertaken on a broad scale. But these "contrived" measures were perhaps even more restrictive in their effect on the international structure than the mechanism of the gold standard had been. In the interwar period deliberate policies were introduced

---

[9] Professor Triffin has long held the view that tight money in the United Kingdom in the nineteenth century reduced capital outflow and cut down the industrial demand for primary products, forcing down the prices of raw material imports. This stimulated domestic consumption and reduced costs. Thus the adjustment was obtained at the expense of the primary producing countries.

which later came to be described as efforts to lift oneself out of the international morass by "beggar my neighbor" devices such as competitive devalulations, prohibitive tariffs, import quotas, exchange control, and other methods of discrimination against foreign countries. Both the prewar automatic constraints and the interwar deliberately contrived policies sought to remedy international imbalances via impoverishment—the former by self-impoverishment, the latter by impoverishing one's neighbors. In contrast Bretton Woods proclaimed boldly the view that international equilibrium can best be won when all member countries are prosperous.

Deflation, low-capacity output with attendant high unit costs, and a low level of public and private investment will not make a country competitive in world markets. To be competitive, a country must be operating at a high level of capacity. To be competitive, a country must be prosperous. To induce home investment and attract foreign capital, it must be a growing, expanding economy. In an atmosphere of growth, innovation can best flourish. Restrictive practices both by labor and by management tend to disappear under conditions of full employment. And finally, a high level of exports requires prosperous neighbors.

This was the optimistic clarion call of Bretton Woods. Countries with short-run, temporary imbalances were to be helped over the hump by the IMF rather than be forced to apply self-flagellation. Once over the hump, a full-employment economy exchanging goods and services in a prosperous world would be in a strong position to adjust to long-run changes and so to cope with the imbalances continually emerging in a dynamic, ever-changing world.

The "Mix" of Monetary and Fiscal Policy

The problem of reconciling domestic full employment and international equilibrium has, however, proved to be far more recalcitrant than was recognized in the Bretton Woods philosophy. In the absence of a world government and a truly international economy, the all-important regulative devices to harmonize domestic full employment with international equilibrium are monetary policy and fiscal policy. If these were properly coordinated internationally, all would be well. In fact, both policies are pursued by individual nations acting for the most part independently. So long as this is the case, what is the proper "mix" of monetary and fiscal policy that deficit and surplus countries should pursue in order to promote as far as possible both full employment and a payments balance?

The rule currently most commonly accepted is that monetary policy should be employed to promote a payments balance and fiscal policy to promote full employment. If a payments-deficit country is also suffering from high unemployment and tries to cure this by means of a low interest rate, capital outflows will create a still greater payments deficit. Higher employment is won at the expense of a payments imbalance. If a country with a surplus in its balance of payments (which is flooding its central bank and its commercial banks with excess liquidity, thereby causing over-full employment and inflationary pressure) tries to restrain the boom by means of higher interest rates, the effect will be to draw funds in from abroad and so increase still more the payments surplus.

The answer for the former country is: Cure the payments deficit with a high interest rate and the unemployment with expansionary fiscal policy. For the latter country the answer is: Cure the surplus by means of a low rate of interest and the boom by means of a restricted fiscal policy.

All this sounds so easy—too easy. The world is neither simple nor logical. Problems are neither white nor black. Higher rates of interest will tend to deter investment, and this militates against efficiency and competitiveness. High interest rates are a deterrent to young and growing businesses and to residential construction and tend to raise the cost of community capital goods such as schools and hospitals.

An ingenious partial way out of this dilemma has been initiated and implemented in the United States. Instead of using a high, long-term interest rate designed to choke off European borrowings in the New York capital market, introduce an interest-equalization tax (an excise tax on American purchases of foreign stocks and bonds) which would have exactly the same effect on foreign sellers as an increase in interest rates,[10] while at the same time it would leave domestic interest rates undisturbed. Another ingenious device, which has been employed with some success, is the following: Let the monetary authorities sell short-term United States government obligations and buy long-terms. This raises the short-term rates and lowers the long-term rates. Raising the short-term rates helps to keep short-term money at home, which helps the payments balance; lowering the long-term rate helps employment.

Unacceptable Expedients

There is no lack of so-called corrective measures which can quickly cure a payments deficit. But most of these expedients are unacceptable "in the sense that they undermine the national and international objectives which it is the very purpose of the international monetary system to promote," as Professor James Tobin has aptly put it. Indeed, "a major sympton of a shortage of international liquidity," he suggests, "would be—and perhaps already is—that countries resort to such expedients."[11]

So long as there is a shortage of liquidity, acceptable policies (policies that are not damaging to the world economy) cannot be applied to correct imbalances. Yet a country may find itself in a tight place. It has to meet its international financial obligations and it has to pay its bills. It can shop around for opportunities to borrow. The United States, as we have seen, has been doing just that. But all this may not be enough to meet *today's* problem. The United States has, to a limited degree, felt compelled to do things it has not liked to do—things that could have been avoided if adequate international liquidity had been available.

[10] The tax, to prevent circumvention, should be applied to bank loans as well.

[11] See *Hearings before the Joint Economic Committee,* November 12–15, 1963, p. 553.

Let us illustrate this concretely. On July 18, 1963, President Kennedy sent to Congress a special message on the balance of payments. In this message he urged the enactment of the interest-equalization tax, referred to above, to become effective as of the day following the message. In addition he suggested a further tying of foreign aid to United States exports, a further reduction in overseas military expenditures, and a further reduction in purchases of strategic materials abroad. The Administration made it clear that it regarded at least some of these measures as temporary. They were emergency expedients designed to buy time for adjustment. The danger always is, as the history of protection shows, that strong special interests will be fostered which tend to entrench themselves in a permanent structure.

Price Stability

Often the most ardent disciplinarians place primary emphasis upon price stability as the means to cure persistent deficits. As a matter of fact price stability presents no conflict between desirable domestic goals and international equilibrium.[12] While a rigidly stable price level is obviously not possible or even desirable, "reasonable" price stability is equally important both from the domestic and international viewpoints.

Leading industrial countries fully recognize this fact. By and large most of the leading countries, at any rate (for a fairly full detailed discussion, see Chapter 11),[13] have on balance pursued a policy of fairly reasonable price stability since around 1953.[14] The decade 1953 to 1963 cannot be labeled one of wild inflation. With respect to the United States there has been no significant inflation since 1958, the year our balance-of-payments crisis began. Wholesale prices stood at 100.4 in 1958 and at 100.3 in December, 1963.

Here a sharp distinction should be made between a program to undo the past and a program to prevent future maladjustments. A program designed to deflate an established level of prices, to break down a cost-price structure by monetary and fiscal measures, is clearly destructive, and no modern country can tolerate it. But an appropriate mix of fiscal and monetary measures designed to prevent a *future* rise in the cost structure is a quite different matter.[15]

Throughout the advanced industrial part of the free world, countries have, in the postwar period, reached a tolerable stability of prices. World trade has been

---

[12] Professor Gottfried Haberler, in an article in *Lloyds Bank Review,* January 1961, expresses the view that for the leading industrial countries the external financial discipline argument does not apply. "Their internal sensitivity to prolonged inflation . . . is a sufficient inducement to financial discipline."

[13] [Refers to Hansen, "The Dollar and the International Monetary System."]

[14] Note the following from the 1962 Annual Report of the IMF, p. 42: "The Fund recognizes that the process of economic growth itself is likely to create pressures on resources that may lead to price increases and that not all price increases are incompatible with sound development."

[15] The cost structure will not rise, in the absence of unjustified increases in administered prices, if money wages rise in line with over-all increases in per-worker productivity. Or at least this is true unless the marginal capital-output ratio is rising, which appears not to be the case in the United States.

expanding rapidly, and international financial relations are subjected to more collaboration and cooperation than ever before. The IMF, together with the supplementary support of the Group of Ten and other arrangements, especially the new Federal Reserve and United States Treasury inventions of recent years—all this has provided reasonable assurance that short-term disequilibrium problems are pretty well under control. The soil is now ready for new approaches with respect to long-term and persistent imbalances, especially those caused by noncommercial transfers and by abnormal capital flows due to the failure of Western Europe to develop adequate capital markets.

The Western world is rich enough in financial resources, if properly marshaled, to wait out the processes of adjustment which are inherent in the very nature of a dynamic, expanding enterprise economy. Looking toward the future, we can devise governmentally contrived methods of international financial integration.

A Concluding Note on the External Discipline

The points of view expressed by the numerous economists who have concerned themselves with current international monetary problems cover so wide a range that any effort to classify may appear to be presumptuous. Such an attempt could easily run into almost endless detail and refinements. Instead I have chosen to cut through endless differences in order to make the simplest possible classification on very broad lines.

Adopting this bold (and no doubt somewhat arbitrary) approach, I divide the sheep from the goats as follows: One flock includes all those who are very much concerned that international monetary imbalances will not defeat the domestic goal of full employment. The other flock includes those whose special concern is the maintenance of price stability and who are therefore loath to weaken the external discipline.

I do not, however, mean to imply that either one of these groups is unconcerned about the matter which is close to the hearts of the other group. I am dealing here with the *predominant* interest of each group. You will notice that I do not even say "primary" interest, I say "special" interest.

Those whose special interest is full employment are very much concerned with improving the international monetary mechanism so as to provide a wide "international margin"—wide enough so that there is ample scope for full-employment policies without continually being confronted with balance-of-payments restraints. They ask for leeway within which to operate. They ask for ample time for the international equilibrating and adjustment processes to work. Those whose special interest is price stability are afraid or at least reluctant to widen the international margin lest this open the door to very strong and perhaps uncontainable inflationary pressure.

This is the gist of the argument. Each side attempts to deny that it is hostile to the goals professed by its opponents. The full-employment adherents stress that they are also concerned about reasonable price stability. They point out that reasonable price stability is a goal that any responsible modern society must seek quite apart from any balance-of-payments problem. The international restraint is not a necessary condition. The external roadblock to full employment is an evil that must be removed. Once it is removed there will still remain plenty of good reasons why the goal of reasonable price stability should be pursued.

The adherents to the gospel of external discipline believe that the goal of price stability is an overriding one and that it is, in the modern "power group" society, extremely difficult to achieve. It needs all the support it can get. A powerful restraining influence is the external discipline. Once this is completely removed, all hell will break loose. Moreover, this group will not accept the view that the goal of reasonable full employment is necessarily rendered impossible of achievement even though the external discipline is retained. Nor is it adamantly opposed to schemes which permit some reasonable widening of the international margin, some enlargement of the area within which one is free to operate.

Thus for some members of each group there is a considerable middle ground. For many it becomes a matter of emphasis rather than clean-cut and sharp opposition. It is like the Republican and Democratic parties in the United States. One can find opponents like Goldwater and Javits in one camp, and Hubert Humphrey and Byrd in the other. But one is more likely to find middle-of-the-roaders on each side.

The external disciplinarians make up a more homogeneous group, on balance, than do the libertarians. The libertarians can quite easily be classified according to the primary method by which they seek to obtain relief from the severe external discipline. Class A wishes to achieve this end by means of an exchange- or gold-value guarantee, partial or complete. Class B wishes to achieve it by means of a greatly increased volume of international liquidity. Class A believes that once the fiduciary component of international reserves is made as good as gold by means of the guarantee, there will be little need for large increases in liquidity. Class B believes (perhaps discounting the political possibility of extensive exchange guarantees) that large increases in liquidity (plus machinery to ensure adequate increases in the future) are urgently needed to provide time for the slow-moving adjustment processes.

Selection 20

Europe and the Dollar

JAMES TOBIN

From Review of Economics and Statistics, *Vol. 46 (May 1964), pp. 123–126. Reprinted by permission of the Review of Economics and Statistics and James Tobin.*

The dollar crisis will no doubt be surmounted. "The dollar" will be saved. Its parity will be successfully maintained, and the world will be spared that ultimate and unmentionable calamity whose consequences are the more dreaded for never being described. The world monetary system will stay afloat, and its captains on both sides of the Atlantic will congratulate themselves on their seamanship in weathering the storm.

But the storm is in good part their own making. And if the financial ship has weathered it, it has done so only by jettisoning much of the valuable cargo it was supposed to deliver. Currency parities have been maintained, but full employment has not been. The economic growth of half the advanced non-Communist world has been hobbled, to the detriment of world trade in general and the exports of the developing countries in particular. Currencies have become technically more convertible, but important and probably irreversible restrictions and discriminations on trade and capital movements have been introduced. Some government transactions of the highest priority for the foreign policy of the United States and the West have been curtailed. Others have been "tied" to a degree that impairs their efficiency and gives aid and comfort to the bizarre principle that practices that are disreputably illiberal when applied to private international transactions are acceptable when government money is involved.

These are the costs. Were, and are, all these hardships necessary? To what end have they been incurred?

They have been incurred in order to slow down and end the accumulations of dollar obligations in the hands of European central banks. It is fair to ask, therefore, whether these accumulations necessarily involved risks and costs serious enough for the countries concerned and for the world at large to justify the heavy costs of stopping them.

Which is easier? Which is less disruptive and less costly, now and in the long run? To stop the private or public transactions that lead one central bank to acquire another's currency? Or to compensate these transactions by official lending in the opposite direction? I do not suggest that the answer is always in favor of compensatory finance. But the issue always needs to be faced, and especially in the present case.

Several courses were open to European countries whose central banks had to purchase dollars in their exchange markets in recent years. (1) They could have built up their dollar holdings quietly and gladly, as they did before 1959. (2) By exercising their right to buy gold at the United States Treasury, they could have forced devaluation of the dollar or suspension of gold payments. (3) They could have taken various measures to correct and reverse chronic European payments surpluses. (4) By occasional withdrawals of gold and by constant complaints they could bring tremendous pressure for "discipline" upon the United States without forcing a change in the dollar parity.

European central banks and governments chose the fourth course, with token admixtures of the third. They have made world opinion, and American opinion, believe there is no other choice. Almost everyone agrees that the pressure of the balance-of-payments deficit upon the United States is inescapable arithmetic rather than the deliberate policy of foreign governments. Yet for almost ten years previously United States deficits were no problem. Clearly it is a change in human attitude and public policy, not inexorable circumstances, that has compelled us to take "corrective" actions.

It is true that the concern of financial officials about "the dollar" was only an echo—and a subdued echo that—of the fears, hopes, anxieties, and speculations that arose in private financial circles in the late 1950's. But financial officials do not have to follow the private exchange markets; they can lead instead. By an equivocal attitude toward private suspicions of the dollar, European officials kept pressure on the United States. Never did they firmly say that they would not force devaluation or suspension of gold payments. Instead, they succeeded in making the maintenance of gold-dollar convertibility at $35 per ounce a unilateral commitment of the United States, under three successive administrations. Once a banker has solemnly assured the world and his depositors that he will never fail, he is at the mercy of those depositors capable of making him fail.

Memories are short, and gratitude is not a consideration respected in international relations, especially when money is involved. But the United States had and has considerable moral claim on European governments and central banks.

The present excess supply of dollars is in many respects an unwinding of the dollar shortage of the immediate postwar period. Capital left Europe because the continent was vulnerable to military attack, its governments were unstable, its industries were prostrate and uncompetitive, and its currencies were inconvertible. Capital has returned to Europe when events have overcome the special advantages which North America seemed to have in these respects. This is, probably the main interpretation of the fact that one of the biggest negative items in our balance-of-payments accounts is the item called "unreported transactions" or "errors and omissions." For years this was a large positive item and was thought to reflect the transfer of European funds here by various devices.

In the past few years it has been a large negative item, amounting to $1.5 billion in 1963. It is therefore relevant to recall the behavior of the United States when the shoe was on the other foot.

During the dollar shortage the United States: gave Western European countries (other than Greece, Turkey, and Spain) $32 billion of military and economic aid; lent them $11 billion additional (in spite of the default of European governments of debts connected with World War I); acquiesced in substantial devaluations of European currencies, without which European exports would still not be competitive; acquiesced in exchange controls, capital controls, quantitative restrictions on imports, and discriminations against the United States and other non-European countries—by no means all of which are liquidated even now. After enabling Europe to overcome the dollar shortage, the United States has been expected to adjust to its reversal *without* the tools that Europe used in its turn. Rightly so, because many of these tools were illiberal expedients—the more reason for replacing them now with compensatory intergovernmental finance.

The United States has undertaken, at considerable cost in real resources and foreign exchange, to defend Western Europe against the Soviet Union. This is in theory a joint effort, but European governments do not even yet fulfill their modest commitments to NATO. While European political leaders solicit constant reassurance that United States military power will remain visibly in Europe, their finance ministers and central bankers complain about the inflow of dollars.

The United States has not only tolerated but encouraged the development of a European customs union that attracts American capital and discriminates against American exports (especially the products of industries, notably agriculture, where North America has a clear comparative advantage).

The United States has borne a disproportionate share of the burden of assistance to uncommitted and underdeveloped nations, in which European countries have a common political and, one might hope, humanitarian interest.

The United States has provided a reserve currency. In the late 1940's no other international and intergovernmental money was available except gold, and the supply of gold was not keeping up with the demand. United States deficits filled the gap with dollars. It is true that this gave the United States a favored position among countries. Anyone who can print money can choose how new money will be first spent. The United States did not seek this privileged role; it arose by accidental evolution rather than conscious design. As it happens, the United States did not exploit it to live beyond our means, to make the American people more affluent. We used it rather for broad international purposes. No doubt in the long run the creation of new international money should be a privilege and responsibility more widely and symmetrically shared. But once the United States and the world are adjusted to the creation of international money via United States deficits, it is scarcely reasonable suddenly to ring a bell announcing that the world's financial experts have now decided that these deficits—past, present, and future—are pernicious.

The United States has not pushed its moral case before world public opinion.

This is because many Americans believe, or prefer to believe, that balance-of-payments deficits, like venereal diseases, betray and punish the sins of those whom they afflict. Others regard them as simply matters of arithmetic and circumstance. Still others are afraid that making a moral argument will indicate to our all-powerful European creditors insufficient resolution to overcome the difficulties. On their side, the Europeans have neatly segregated the contexts. Their financial officials wash their hands of tariff and trade policies, agricultural protection, defense and aid appropriations, and their governments' budgets. Any European failings on these counts are facts of life to which the United States must adjust, rather than reasons for more patience or more credit.

By the narrowest of bankers' criteria—all moral claims aside—the United States is a good credit risk. Its balance sheet vis-à-vis the rest of the world, not to mention its internal productive strength, indicates capacity to service a considerably increased external public debt. The United States has been confined to the types of credit that can be given on the books of central banks. European parliaments cannot be asked to vote long-term loans to Uncle Sam, although the American people voted through the Congress to tax themselves to finance the Marshall Plan when Europe's credit rating was nil.

Meanwhile, European central banks are uneasy holding short-term dollar assets. They prefer gold. Why? Because they might some day force us to give them a capital gain on gold holdings. We compensate them with interest on their dollar holdings when they forgo this speculative possibility. But bygones are bygones; and past interest earnings are irrelevant when future capital gains beckon. On its side, the United States has nothing to lose and much to gain in guaranteeing to maintain the value of official dollar holdings. After stubbornly resisting this suggestion on obscure grounds of principle, the United States Treasury now belatedly and selectively guarantees value in foreign currency.

The only remaining reason to refuse the United States credit is that the United States, like any other deficit country, must be "disciplined."

Disciplined to do what?

To stop an orgy of inflation? The United States has the best price record of any country, except Canada, since 1958—before there was a balance-of-payments problem. The rates of unemployment and excess capacity during the period scarcely suggest that the government has been recklessly overheating the economy with fiscal and monetary fuel.

Nevertheless many Europeans say that when they buy dollars they are importing inflation. It is hard to take this claim seriously. First of all, if acquisitions of dollars are inflationary, so are acquisitions of gold, and Europe shows no signs of saturation with gold. Second, the classic mechanism of international transmission of inflation is certainly not operating. We have not inflated ourselves into an import surplus adding to aggregate demand in Europe. To the contrary, we have maintained a large and secularly growing export surplus. Third, although central bank purchases of foreign exchange have the same expansionary monetary effects at home as other open-market purchases, it is not beyond the wit or experience of man to neutralize these effects by open-market sales or other monetary actions. Fourth, United States farmers and coal producers, and Japanese light manufacturers, among others, stand ready to help European governments reduce their living costs and their payment surpluses at the same time. The truth is that Europe does not really want a solution at the expense of its balance of trade.

Perhaps we are to be disciplined to cut foreign aid. European governments do not attach the same importance as we do to aid programs, especially in the Western Hemisphere. Clearly we need a better understanding on development assistance and "burden-sharing" among the advanced countries.

Should the United States be disciplined to cut off private exports of capital, by controls or by tight monetary policy or both? This has been a major and successful focus of European pressure. The United States authorities have responded by pushing up interest rates, more than a full point at the short end, and by proposing the Interest Equalization Tax. European pressure is motivated in part by nationalistic and protectionist aims—keep the rich Americans from buying up or competing with local industry. This may or may not be a worthy objective, but its worth is the same whether international payments are in balance or not.

Two other issues are involved. The first concerns capital markets and controls. Should the United States move toward poorer and more autarchic capital markets, or should the Europeans move toward more efficient and freer capital markets? Much of United States long-term capital movement to Europe does not represent a transfer of real saving. Instead it is a link in a double transatlantic chain connecting the European saver and the European investor. The saver wants a liquid, safe, short-term asset. The investor needs long-term finance or equity capital and seeks it in the United States. Unfortunately another link in the same chain is official European holding of short-term dollar obligations. But the Europeans themselves could, through institutional reforms, do a great deal to connect their savers and investors more directly and to reduce the spread between their long and short interest rates.

The second issue is the appropriate international level of interest rates. Evidently national rates must be more closely aligned to each other as international money and capital markets improve. But surely the low-rate country should not always do the aligning. This would impart a deflationary bias to the system. In principle easy fiscal policy could overcome this bias, but only at the expense of investment and growth. In the present situation European countries are fighting inflation by tightening their money markets rather than their budgets. They are forcing the United States to fight unemployment with a tight money-easy budget mixture. If interest rates are raised whenever a country faces either inflation or balance-of-payments difficulties, while expansionary fiscal policy is the only measure ever used to combat deflation, a number of swings in business activity and in payments will move the world to a mixture of policies quite unfavorable to long-run growth.

In summary, the adjustments forced on the United States to correct its payments deficit have not served the world economy well. Neither were they essential. European countries have had at their disposal several measures which are desirable in their own right, not just as correctives to the present temporary imbalance in payments. To the extent that they are unprepared to take these measures, they should willingly extend compensatory finance. International financial policy is too important to leave to financiers. There are more important accounts to balance than the records of international transactions, and more important markets to equilibrate than those in foreign exchange.

DISCUSSION QUESTIONS

1. What are the basic causes of the chronic American balance-of-payments deficits?
2. Discuss possible conflicts between a domestic policy of full employment and a stable price level and a policy to eliminate the balance-of-payments deficit.
3. Professor Tobin argues that the dollar crisis is largely the making of the captains of the world's monetary systems. Explain his reasons for this conclusion. What alternative policies could have been followed by the European countries to alleviate the crisis?
4. Discuss the possible "corrective measures" for resolving the balance-of-payments problem.

SELECTED REFERENCES

Committee for Economic Development, *The Dollar and the World Monetary System,* New York: The Committee for Economic Development, December 1966, Chap. 1.

Hansen, Alvin H., *The Dollar and the International Monetary System,* New York: McGraw-Hill Book Co., 1965.

Johnson, Harry G., *The World Economy at the Crossroads: A Survey of Current Problems of Money, Trade and Economic Development,* Oxford: Oxford University Press, 1965.

Kennan, Peter B., *International Economics,* 2nd ed., Englewood Cliffs, N.J.: Prentice-Hall, Inc., 1967.

Salant, Walter S., Emile Despres, Lawrence B. Krause, Alice M. Rivlin, Walter A. Salant, and Lorie Tarshis, *The United States Balance of Payments in 1968,* Washington, D.C.; The Brookings Institution, 1963.

Tobin, James, *National Economic Policy,* New Haven, Conn.: Yale University Press, 1966. See especially Part IV.

Triffin, Robert, *Gold and the Dollar Crisis,* New Haven, Conn.: Yale University Press, 1960.

PART 9

ECONOMICS AND IDEOLOGY

"Any economic system requires a set of rules, an ideology to justify them, and a conscience in the individual which makes him strive to carry them out."* Interwoven with traditional economics is the ideology of capitalism. This includes the belief in private ownership of the means of production, the right of free contract, the idea that government should not intervene in the market or engage in production, and, above all, the idea that, if left to itself, the market economy will produce results in the best interest of all. These are rules of the game of capitalism. They guide the state, the businessman, the worker, and the consumer in making their economic decisions by defining the role of each in the system. Whether the participants defend or attack the system depends on how well satisfied they are with the results of the present set of rules. As people become dissatisfied with the rules of the game, and if they have the economic or political power to make their dissatisfaction felt, the rules of the game are gradually changed and the system, though modified, can survive.

The article by Mrs. Robinson examines the views of three famous economists toward the ideology of capitalism—Marx as a bitter foe who wanted to overthrow the system and establish a new set of rules, Marshall as a sympathetic supporter who wanted to preserve the system, and Keynes as a critic who was sympathetic to capitalism but thought that the system needed to be modified to survive. Each point of view reflects the period in which the author matured: for

* Joan Robinson, *Economic Philosophy, op. cit.*, p. 13.

Marx, the poverty of the 1840's; for Marshall, the prosperity of the 1860's; for Keynes, the discontent of the Great Depression. Each, however, made important contributions to economics that are significant for other times and under other ideologies.

Mrs. Robinson points out contradictions in the theories of Marx, Marshall, and Keynes and indicates that these contradictions were, at least in part, due to their inability to reconcile the real world to their ideological image of the world. The students of these economists have often been so committed to the ideology of the master that they have been unable to separate ideology from economics and unable to sort out what is good in the economics of those whose ideology disagrees with their own.

Professor Schumpeter traces the development of the capitalist ideology and gives a sympathetic treatment of capitalism as an economic system. For him capitalism is a dynamic process continually striving to develop new products and new production techniques. The driving force behind the system is innovation. He does not share the traditional economist's bias for pure competition; rather he feels that large firms are necessary because of the economies of large-scale production and that large firms are able to generate the profits necessary for innovation and change.

With respect to the future of capitalism, Schumpeter points out that Marx's reasoning that increasing poverty and misery would drive the workers to revolution was wrong. However, Marx's conclusion about the demise of capitalism may not be wrong. As capitalism matures, the role of the entrepreneurs fades; and, more and more, industry is run by hired management rather than owners. The success of the system gives political and economic power to the groups that oppose its ideology. The business enterprise becomes increasingly bureaucratic and labor interests become more and more dominant. Thus the system, says Schumpeter, is being transformed from conventional capitalism into a guided capitalism not greatly different from socialism. Capitalism is being supplanted, not because of its failures, but because of its success. It has given power to workers, intellectuals, and professionals who oppose its ideology and has sapped the will of the capitalist to resist change. Whether capitalism survives depends on what we want to call capitalism. Certainly the classical idea of capitalism has already pretty much disappeared.

Selection 21

Marx, Marshall, and Keynes

JOAN ROBINSON

From Collected Economic Papers, *Vol. II (Oxford, England: Basil Blackwell, 1960), pp. 1–17. Reprinted by permission of Basil Blackwell, Publisher.*

THREE VIEWS OF CAPITALISM

These three names are associated with three attitudes towards the capitalist system. Marx represents revolutionary socialism, Marshall the complacent defence of capitalism, and Keynes the disillusioned defence of capitalism. Marx seeks to understand the system in order to hasten its overthrow. Marshall seeks to make it acceptable by showing it in an agreeable light. Keynes seeks to find out what has gone wrong with it in order to devise means to save it from destroying itself.

To summarize in few words a whole complex structure of ideas is necessarily to falsify by oversimplification, but so long as we recognize the danger it may be legitimate to set out in a crude way the essential contrast between the economic theories which are the bases of these three points of view.

The central contention of Marx's scheme as we find it in Volume I of *Capital* is that under capitalism the real wages of the workers tend to be held permanently at a low level while the capitalists receive as profit the excess of product over wages. The capitalists, he maintains, are not much interested in a luxurious standard of life for themselves. Under pressure of competition and the greed for more and more profit they invest the surplus in more and more capital, and they strive with each other to raise the productivity of his own workers, so that the total product is ever increasing. Over the long run, the level of real wages is more likely to fall than to rise. The share of profits in total output grows ever greater as productivity increases and the rate of accumulation rises, until the inner contradictions of the system cause it to explode and a socialist revolution brings a new system into being.

Marshall's view of wages, profits, and accumulation cannot be so clearly seen, partly because he concentrates attention on the details of relative prices, the fortunes of individual firms, and supply and demand of particular commodities, while leaving the main outline into which these details fit extremely hazy. And partly because his whole system is based upon an unresolved conflict. The hard core of logical analysis in the *Principles* is purely static—it applies to an economy in which accumulation has come to an end—while all the problems that he discusses are connected with an economy in which wealth is growing as time goes by. In his view there is a *normal rate of profit* which represents the *supply price of capital,* but it is never clear whether this is the supply price of a certain amount of capital—the rate of profit at which there is neither growth nor decline in the total stock of capital—or whether it is the supply price of a certain rate of accumulation of capital. Profit is the *reward of waiting*—that is, of refraining from present consumption in order to enjoy future wealth—but it is never clear whether *waiting* means maintaining a stock of capital by refraining from consuming it or whether it means saving and adding to capital. It seems to mean sometimes one, sometimes the other, and sometimes both at once, though Marshall is uneasily aware that they are not the same thing. This haziness makes his system impossible to describe in a clear way. But he states definitely enough that *waiting* is a factor of production and that the *real costs* of production are made up of efforts and sacrifices—efforts of the workers and sacrifices of the capitalists. The efforts are rewarded by wages and the sacrifices by profits. Taking the spirit of the argument, which applies to a growing economy, rather than the strict logic, which requires a static economy, the capitalists invest and accumulate because profit is sufficient to counterbalance a sacrifice of present consumption. This causes total wealth to grow; the workers share in the benefit because wages rise with productivity while the supply price of capital remains more or less constant.

Keynes draws a sharp distinction between the two aspects of accumulation: saving—that is, refraining from consumption—and investing—that is, increasing the stock of productive capital. Marx's capitalists automatically save because they want to invest, so as to acquire more means of production in order to employ more labour and gain more profit. Marshall's capitalists automatically invest because they want to save, that is, to own more wealth.

Keynes points out that in a developed capitalist economy the two sides of accumulation are not automatically connected. Saving means spending less on consumption and narrowing the market for commodities, so that it reduces the profitability of investment. Investment means employing labor to produce goods which are not available to be consumed and so increases demand relative to supply. The two sides of the process of accumulation are not linked together in such a way as to keep them in harmony. On the contrary, the very nature of private enterprise causes them to have a chronic tendency to get out of gear. At some time the economy is trying to invest more than it can; the demand for labor for consumption and investment taken together exceeds the available supply and there is inflation. But this is rare apart from wartime. Normally the reverse situation prevails; investment is less than it easily could be and potential wealth is wasted in unemployment.

Each point of view bears the stamp of the period when it was conceived. Marx formed his ideas in the grim poverty of the Forties. Marshall saw capitalism blossoming in peace and prosperity in the Sixties. Keynes had to find an explanation for the morbid condition of "poverty in the midst of plenty" in the period between the wars. But each has significance for other times, for in so far as each theory is valid it throws light upon essential characteristics of the capitalist system which have always been present in it and still have to be reckoned with.

Each, moreover, is bound up with a particular political attitude to the economic system which is highly relevant to the problems that confront us today.

Marx maintained that capitalism is bound to develop in such a way as to bring about its own destruction, and urged the workers to organize themselves to hasten its overthrow. Marshall argued that, in spite of some blemishes, it is a system which promotes the good of all. Keynes shows that it has deep-seated defects which, however, he believed are capable of being remedied. Marx is making propaganda against the system. Marshall is defending it and Keynes is criticizing in order to improve it.

Economic doctrines always come to us as propaganda. This is bound up with the very nature of the subject, and to pretend that it is not so in the name of "pure science" is a very unscientific refusal to accept the facts.

The element of propaganda is inherent in the subject because it is concerned with policy. It would be of no interest if it were not. If you want a subject that is worth pursuing for its intrinsic appeal without any view to consequences you would not be attending a lecture on economics. You would be, say, doing pure mathematics or studying the behavior of birds.

The once orthodox *laissez-faire* theory evaded the issue by trying to show that there is no problem about choosing policies. Let everyone pursue his own self-interest and free competition will ensure the maximum benefit for everyone. This obviously cannot apply where any over-all organization is necessary—the banking system, the railways, the national exchequer. But even where it is technically possible to run the system on a basis of catch-as-catch-can, there is an inconsistency at the very root of the argument. In pursuing self-interest individuals find that it assists them to combine and agree not to compete. Monopolies, trade unions, political parties, arise out of the very process of competition and prevent it from being effective as a mechanism for ensuring the general good. Pure untrammeled individualism is not a practicable system, and the coherence of an economy depends upon the acceptance of limitations upon it. There must be a code of rules of the game, whether established by law or agreed to by common consent. No set of rules of the game can ensure a perfect harmony of interests between all the groups in society, and any set of rules will be defended by those whom it favors and attacked by those whom different rules would suit better.

Economic theory, in its scientific aspect, is concerned with showing how a particular set of rules of the game operates, but in doing so it cannot help but make them appear in a favorable or an unfavorable light to the people who are playing the game. Even if a writer can school himself to perfect detachment, he is still making propaganda, for his readers have interested views. Take, for example, a piece of pure analytical argument, such as that the operation of the gold standard secures stability of the exchanges provided that money-wage rates are flexible. This means that it will not function well where trade unions are strong and prevent wages from falling when the preservation of the exchange rate requires that they should. This is a purely scientific statement and there is not much room for disagreement about it regarded as a description of the way the system works. But to some readers it will appear as strong propaganda against the trade unions, to others as strong propaganda against the gold standard.

This element of propaganda enters into even the most severely technical details of the subject. It cannot fail to be present when the broad issue of the operation of the system as a whole is under discussion.

Each of our three economists is concerned with describing the rules of the capitalist game, and therefore with criticizing or defending them. Marx shows that the rules are unfavorable to the workers, and for that very reason will not be tolerated for long. Marshall argues that the rules are framed in such a way as to produce the greatest possible growth of wealth, and that all classes benefit from sharing in it. Keynes is showing that the rules need to be amended so as to ensure that wealth will continue to grow.

The description and the evaluation cannot be separated, and to pretend that we are not interested in the evaluation is mere self-deception.

Marx is quite clear about his purpose. He is on the side of the workers, and he makes the case against capitalism in order to encourage the workers to overthrow it.

Marshall was not openly and clearly on one side or the other in the clash of interests between workers and capitalists. His case is rather that if everyone will accept the system and not make a fuss about it, all will benefit together.

> *In regard to sectional interests. Nearly all of them are changing their character and becoming increasingly plastic: but the chief change is the assimilation of the training, and consequently the capacity, of the working classes generally to those of the well-to-do. . . .*
>
> *We are indeed approaching rapidly to conditions which have no close precedent in the past, but are perhaps really more natural than those which they are supplanting—conditions under which the relations between the various industrial strata of a civilized nation are being based on reason, rather than tradition. . . . It is becoming clear that this and every other Western country can now afford to make increased sacrifices of material wealth for the purpose of raising the quality of life throughout their whole populations.*[1]

Keynes is against waste and stupidity and unnecessary poverty. He is not so much interested in who gets the benefit of increased production as in making sure that it takes place. He regards a greater equality of income as desirable, but

---

[1] John Maynard Keynes, *Industry and Trade* (New York, Harcourt Brace & World, 1949), pp. 4–5.

his attitude is "moderately conservative"[2] and he holds that if only capitalism could be made to function efficiently, it would be better than any alternative.

The burden of Marx's propaganda is that capitalism is pernicious and should be destroyed; of Marshall's, that it is beneficial and should be preserved; of Keynes's, that it could be made fairly tolerable if people had a little sense.

Each of the three is trying to justify a particular view of the system and so is making propaganda for it. But each has sufficient faith in his own view to believe that the truth will bear him out, and each is trying to make a genuinely scientific approach to economic problems. They cannot help being propagandists, but they are scientists as well. To learn from them we first have to see what it is that they are driving at. Then we can make use of them as scientists while reserving the right to have our own opinion on questions of politics.

Ideas and Ideology

We must admit that every economic doctrine that is not trivial formalism contains political judgments. But it is the greatest possible folly to choose the doctrines that we want to accept by their political content. It is folly to reject a piece of analysis because we do not agree with the political judgment of the economist who puts it forward. Unfortunately, this approach to economics is very prevalent. The orthodox school has been largely stultified by refusing to learn from Marx. Because they do not like his politics they attend to his economics only to point out some errors in it, hoping that by refuting him on some points they will make his political doctrines harmless.

Thus the discussion of Marx has been mainly confined to criticizing the Labor Theory of Value. The Labor theory is an omnibus title used to cover a number of aspects of the Marxian doctrine. One element in it is the theory of what determines the relative prices of commodities in long-run equilibrium. The orthodox economists can easily show that the view that prices are proportional to labor-time required for production is not an adequate theory of relative prices. By concentrating upon this question they succeeded in carrying the argument into a sphere where they could not score a number of superficial points against the Marxists. They were not in the least interested in trying to learn from Marx or in inquiring what the relevance of these points was to the main issue.

In this they were very much helped by the Marxists, who, instead of replying to all the intricate arguments about the theory of prices: so what? allowed themselves to be drawn into a number of sophistries in an endeavor to defend Marx even when he was not defensible.

Under the dust of all this controversy about inessentials the most valuable parts of Marx's theory was lost to sight by both parties.

To take one instance, the schema for expanding reproduction provide a very simple and quite indispensable approach to the problem of saving and invest-

---

[2] John Maynard Keynes, *General Theory of Employment; Interest and Money* (New York, Harcourt Brace & World, 1949), p. 377.

ment and the balance between production of capital goods and demand for consumer goods. It was rediscovered and made the basis for the treatment of Keynes's problem by Kalecki and reinvented by Harrod and Domar as the basis for the theory of long-run development. If Marx had been studied as a serious economist, instead of being treated on the one hand as an infallible oracle and on the other as a butt for cheap epigrams, it would have saved us all a great deal of time.

The Marxists have been just as bad as the orthodox economists in refusing to learn from those whose political views they dislike. Feeling on the defensive, they regard it as a kind of treachery to admit any point made by Marx's critics, and insist upon defending him in every detail, so that they will not even concede to Marshall that the Labor Theory of Value is a crude account of the determination of relative prices which requires to be amended and elaborated in certain respects.

This inflexibility is particularly marked in their reaction to Keynes. Because they reject the idea that capitalism can be rescued from crises by economic measures carried out by governments, they deny the logic of Keynes's argument. They point out that Keynes is subject to an illusion when he appeals to the state as though it were a benevolent impartial arbiter which can be relied upon to do the best for everyone if only it can be made to understand how to set about it. They maintain that the state is an organ of the capitalists and that therefore it is vain to look to it to carry out policies to prevent unemployment for the benefit of the workers.

There is much force in the first part of the argument but the second is a *non sequitur.* Capitalists do not like having crises. Unemployment is accompanied by losses. And nowadays they have a very strong reason to dislike unemployment itself, for it provides dangerous ammunition to their political enemies. In preventing unemployment the governments would be doing for them something that they want done but cannot do for themselves.

Marx in his day had a far more penetrating and subtle insight into the workings of the system than his modern followers do. In discussing the legal limitation of the working day he showed how each individual capitalist had an interest in preventing legislation that would limit his power to exploit his workers. Yet collectively it favored their interests, for excessive exploitation ruins the labor force on which they all depend. Thus, under the guise of resisting the demand for labor legislation put forward by the workers and the humanitarians, they allowed it to be carried out.

In the same way, while declaiming against Keynesian policies as an illegitimate interference with the proper functions of private enterprise, they in fact rely upon it to save them from themselves.

The foolishness of rejecting economic analysis because of the political doctrines with which it is associated is shown by the fact that, as it happens, the aspect of capitalism which each of the great economists illuminates provides the basis for political conclusions the opposite of his own.

The best defense of capitalism as an economic system can be made on the basis of Marx's analysis. This was realized by Schumpeter, and recently carried a stage further by his disciple, Professor Galbraith.[3] They provide a tough, cynical, and intelligent defense of the capitalist rules of the game which is far more effective than the soft, sophistical, special pleading of the orthodox school.

Marx emphasizes the manner in which the capitalist rules of the game foster accumulation and technical progress. His capitalists are not interested in luxurious living. They exploit labor in order to accumulate, and they increase productivity in order to have a greater surplus to invest. "The productiveness of labor is made to ripen as if in a hot-house." They prevent the workers from receiving any share in the increased production, for if the workers consumed more there would be less accumulation and the growth of total wealth would be impeded.

This provides an account of the function of exploitation. It explains, incidentally, why in a socialist economy which is undertaking rapid development the standard of life rises at first very slowly, and why it is necessary, when private profit does not create a gap between wages and prices, for a gap to be created by taxation in order to provide the funds for accumulation.

When Keynes was describing the flourishing capitalism of the pre-1914 world, before he became preoccupied with the problem of unemployment, he set out an analysis which is essentially the same as that of Marx.

> *Europe was so organized socially and economically as to secure the maximum accumulation of capital. While there was some continuous improvement in the daily conditions of life of the mass of the population, Society was so framed as to throw a great part of the increased income into the control of the class least likely to consume it. The new rich of the nineteenth century were not brought up to large expenditures, and preferred the power which investment gave them to the pleasures of immediate consumption. In fact, it was precisely the* inequality *of the distribution of wealth which made possible those vast accumulations of fixed wealth and of capital improvements which distinguished that age from all others. Herein lay, in fact, the main justification of the Capitalist System. If the rich had spent their new wealth on their own enjoyments, the world would long ago have found such a régime intolerable. But like bees they saved and accumulated, not less to the advantage of the whole community because they themselves held narrower ends in prospect.*
>
> *The immense accumulations of fixed capital which, to the great benefit of mankind, were built up during the half-century before the war, could never have come about in a Society where wealth was divided equitably. The railways of the world, which that age built as a monument to posterity, were, not less than the Pyramids of Egypt, the work of labour which was not free to consume in immediate enjoyment the full equivalent of its efforts.*
>
> * * *
>
> *In writing thus I do not necessarily disparage the practices of that generation. In the unconscious recesses of its being Society knew what it was about.*

---

[3] John K. Galbraith, *American Capitalism* (Boston, Houghton Mifflin Company, 1956).

> *The cake was really very small in proportion to the appetites of consumption, and no one, if it were shared all round, would be much the better off by the cutting of it. Society was working not for the small pleasures of to-day but for the future security and improvement of the race—in fact for "progress.*[4]"

There is no disagreement here with Marx's analysis, though the purpose of the argument is to explain why capitalism survived rather than to show why it ought to be overthrown.

In order to make the case against capitalism it is necessary to turn to Marshall's argument. It is true that, in the main, profit is desired for the purpose of accumulation, but that is not the whole truth. Profit is also the basis for consumption by capitalists. They have to be "rewarded for waiting" and they will not save, or even preserve wealth accumulated in the past, unless they are fattened up to a certain point by a high standard of life for themselves. For society to pay for saving by permitting a great inequality in consumption is a very wasteful and expensive method of getting the job done. It would be far more economical to dispossess the capitalists, put past accumulated wealth into the safekeeping of society where no one can get at it, to consume property "in immediate gratification" at the expense of the future, and to decide the rate of accumulation to be carried out on a general view of the development of the economy as a whole rather than according to the whims of individuals.

Marshall's analysis can be used to show why socialism is necessary. According to Marshall's own argument, a greater real benefit is gained from a given income if it is equally distributed than if some individuals are enjoying such a luxurious standard of life that saving is no effort to them while others are struggling to survive. If the object of production is to provide for the welfare of human beings, it is very uneconomic to have the fruits of a given rate of production unequally distributed. But if incomes are equally distributed, there would not be enough saving done to permit development. In order to be able to have a more economic distribution of income, it is necessary for saving to be collective, and if the saving is done collectively, capital must be owned collectively.

If the capitalists fully lived up to Marx's description and really invested the whole surplus, there would be no need for socialism. It is the rentier aspect of profit, as a source of private wealth, which Marshall emphasizes, that makes the strongest case for socialism; and the entrepreneur aspect of profit as the source of accumulation, which Marx emphasizes, that makes the strongest case for capitalism.

Keynes's analysis also provides a case for the opposite political conclusions. He shows, first, that there is a natural tendency for an advanced capitalist economy to run into chronic stagnation, with permanent unemployment, and that it is by its very nature highly unstable. He argues that some measure of interference with the pure private-enterprise system is necessary to keep it running efficiently.

---

[4] John Maynard Keynes, *Economic Consequences of the Peace* (New York: Harcourt Brace & World, Inc., 1954), pp. 18–21.

In particular, governments must undertake a sufficient amount of investment to make up for the failure of private capitalists to keep investment continuously at the desirable level. But so long as a large part of investment is left in private hands it is necessary that the interference must not lead to a state of affairs in which the private section invests less just because governments are investing more. A high rate of accumulation necessarily leads to a decline in the profitability of further investment. It follows that, to keep up the level of demand for labor, wasteful investment is more effective than useful investment. "Two pyramids, two masses for the dead, are twice as good as one; but not so two railways from London to York."[5]

> *In so far as millionaires find their satisfaction in building mighty mansions to contain their bodies when alive and pyramids to shelter them after death, or, repenting of their sins, erect cathedrals and endow monasteries or foreign missions, the day when abundance of capital will interfere with abundance of output may be postponed. "To dig holes in the ground," paid for out of savings, will increase, not only employment, but the real national dividend of useful goods and services.*[6]

Keynes's own purpose was to illustrate the paradoxes of capitalism and to plead for a rational control over investment, but the effect of his argument is to explain why it is that modern capitalism flourishes when governments are making investments in armaments. Instead of being a ruinous burden on a highly developed economy, the apparent economic waste of armaments is really a method of maintaining prosperity. It follows that if there were no need for armaments, it would be necessary to make useful investments and so to encroach upon the power and independence of the capitalists. The capitalists therefore prefer a situation in which armaments do seem necessary. This cure, most of us would agree, is even worse than the disease, and on the basis of Keynes's reasoning it can be argued that capitalism will not save itself from the tendency to unemployment by any other means.

Marx's analysis of capitalism shows its strong points, although his purpose was to attack it. Marshall's argument inadvertently shows the wastefulness of capitalism, although he meant to recommend it. Keynes, in showing the need for remedies to the defects of capitalism, also shows how dangerous the remedies may be.

To learn from the economists regarded as scientists, it is necessary to separate what is valid in their description of the system from the propaganda that they make, overtly or unconsciously, each for his own ideology. The best way to separate out scientific ideas from ideology is to stand the ideology on its head and see how the ideas look the other way up. If they disintegrate with the ideology, they have no validity of their own. If they still make sense as a

---

[5] *General Theory,* p. 131.
[6] *Ibid.,* p. 220.

description of reality, then there is something to be learned from them, whether we like the ideology or not.

The Great Contradictions

It is foolish to refuse to learn from the ideas of an economist whose ideology we dislike. It is equally unwise to rely upon the theories of one whose ideology we approve.

An economic theory at best is only a hypothesis. It does not tell us what is the case. It suggests a possible explanation of some phenomenon, and it cannot be accepted as correct until it has been tested by an appeal to the facts. The business of the disciples of a great economist is not to propagate his doctrines but to test his hypotheses. If the facts turn out not to fit an hypothesis, the hypothesis must be rejected. It is of no use to choose an hypothesis by the color of the economist who puts it forward and then to reject the facts that do not agree with it.

Marx's hypothesis, in the simple form of his theory that he worked out and published in Volume I of *Capital,* is that, taking it by and large, with exceptions and qualifications, it is to be expected that under capitalism real wages will remain more or less constant. He has two grounds for this point of view. One is purely metaphysical. Everything exchanges at its value, that is, for the product of an amount of labor-time equal to that which is required to produce it.

> *The value of labour-power is determined, as in the case of every other commodity, by the labour-time necessary for the production, and consequently also the reproduction, of this special article. So far as it has value, it represents no more than a definite quantity of the average labour of society incorporated in it.*[7]

This is a metaphysical approach to the problem of the determination of wages. When we ask *why* do you believe that labor power exchanges for its value? he replies: Everything that is exchanged is exchanged for its value.

But he also has an analytical answer. The workers are weak and unorganized. Employers can make wages as low as they please subject to the technical necessity to keep the labor force in being. Thus wages are set at the conventional subsistence level. When an excess demand for labor due to rapid accumulation tends to drive them up, or when trade unions face the employers with bargaining power equal to their own and extort concessions from them, the system reacts in such a way as to bring wages down again. First, the mere fact that wages are higher means that there is less accumulation. When population is growing, a slowing up in accumulation causes the demand for labor to lag behind the supply. Secondly, to overcome a threatening scarcity of manpower, labor-saving inventions are made; output per head rises and a given amount of capital employs less labor. The consequent unemployment undermines the bargaining power of the workers. Thus the real-wage rate can never for long be maintained

---

[7] Karl Marx, *Capital* (The Modern Library, 1932), p. 189.

much above the level at which it was first established "when the class of free laborers was formed," that is, when capitalism first took over from peasant and artisan production.

Now, by and large, this hypothesis has failed to be verified. In fact, in the developed capitalist economies the level of wages has risen. The rise in productivity has been sufficient to permit both accumulation *and* a rise in the standard of life of the workers.

Lenin tried to explain this away, and latter-day Marxists have a stock answer which they always produce when challenged on this point. The rise in wages, they say, applies only to the imperialist countries. Profits have been maintained by colonial exploitation and the capitalists could therefore indulge the workers at home by allowing them higher wages. They are pampered "palace slaves" sharing in the exploitation of the colonial workers.

This argument smacks of special pleading—an attempt to force the facts to fit the hypothesis instead of reconsidering the hypothesis in the light of facts. The argument that the high rate of profit obtainable from exploiting low-wage labor in the colonies raises home wages does not seem very plausible. Capitalists expect to get more or less the same rate of profit wherever they invest; if profits abroad are high, they do less investment at home. The demand for labor at home is therefore reduced, not increased, by the existence of cheap labor abroad.

There is no doubt that home labor in the imperialist countries has gained from colonial exploitation, but by a different mechanism. Low colonial wages have helped to make raw materials cheap and so have made the terms of trade favorable to the industrial nations. No doubt also some advantage to the workers spills over from the wealth of capitalists who have made fortunes abroad, through their taxable capacity, charity, and the demand for services. But it would be absurd to suppose that more than a small fraction of the rise in the standard of life of the industrial workers, especially in America, can be accounted for in this way. Wages have risen because of the great technical productivity which has been fostered by capitalism and because the system operates in such a way as to keep the share of wages in the growing total of production more or less constant.

The fact of rising real wages requires a very important modification of the central thesis of Marx's theory. It has turned out not to be the case that increasing misery drives the workers to rebellion. The capitalists have succeeded in buying them off by giving them a share in the product which capitalism brings into being. Moreover, the workers become saturated with capitalist ideology and look at life in terms of capitalist values. They have developed a state of mind in which they do not want the rules of the game to be altered. It is very noticeable today that Marxism flourishes best in countries where capitalism is least successful.

Marx himself became aware that this was going on during his own lifetime.

> *The English proletarian movement in its old traditional Chartist form must perish completely before it can develop itself in a new form, capable of life. And yet one cannot foresee what this new form will look like. For the rest, it seems to me that* [*the new policy*] *is really bound up with the fact*

that the English proletariat is becoming more and more bourgeois, so that this most bourgeois of all nations is apparently aiming ultimately at the possession of a bourgeois aristocracy and a bourgeois proletariat as well as a bourgeoisie.[8]

This is even more true of modern America than it was of England in the Sixties.

Marx never succeeded in completing his great plan. The last two volumes of *Capital* are compilations from his notes, not fully worked out and to some extent confused and inconsistent. It has often been suggested that the reason why Marx was held up was because he could not find a way through the contradiction between his hypothesis and the facts around him.

The contradiction is much more striking today. It is now clear that the revolutionary transition to socialism does not come in the advanced capitalist nations, but in the most backward. It is easy enough to say, being wise after the event, that it is natural to expect "the weakest link in the chain to break." But there is much more in it than that. Current experience suggests that socialism is not a stage beyond capitalism but a substitute for it—a means by which the nations which did not share in the industrial revolution can imitate its technical achievements; a means to achieve rapid accumulation under a different set of rules of the game. This makes a drastic reconsideration of Marx's central hypothesis necessary. There is much to be learned from Marx's analysis of capitalism, but if we simply swallow it whole we are liable to be seriously misled.

On the question of the standard of life, Marshall's theory stands the test of experience better than Marx's. But Marshall's theory also contained a fatal flaw. The unemployment of the interwar period revealed the crack in his system which Keynes penetrated in order to explode it.

Marshall, like Marx, failed to complete the great three-volume work that he projected.[9] Like Marx, he himself saw the weak spot in his own theory. His whole argument depends upon the beneficial effect of accumulation. But abstaining from present consumption in order to save is not the same thing as adding to the stock of capital. Marshall was aware of this flaw in his system and anticipated Keynes's exposure of it.

But though men have the power to purchase they may not choose to use it. For when confidence has been shaken by failures, capital cannot be got to start new companies or extend old ones. . . . Other trades, finding a poor market for their goods, produce less; they earn less, and therefore they buy less: the diminution of the demand for their wares makes them demand less of other trades. Thus commercial disorganization spreads: the disorganization of one trade throws others out of gear, and they react on it and increase its disorganization.

The chief cause of the evil is a want of confidence. The greater part of it

---

[8] Marx-Engels' *Selected Correspondence* (Lawrence & Wishart), p. 115.

[9] He did, indeed, publish *Money, Credit and Commerce,* but it is a pale ghost of the third volume of the *Principles* which he originally intended it to be.

could be removed almost in an instant if confidence could return, touch all industries with her magic wand and make them continue their production and their demand for the wares of others. . . . But the revival of industry comes about through the gradual and often simultaneous growth of confidence among many various trades; it begins as soon as traders think that prices will not continue to fall: and with a revival of industry prices rise.[10]

Here is the germ of the theory to account for crises and chronic stagnation with which Keynes exploded Marshall. Perhaps Marshall, like Marx, was frustrated by seeing the contradiction in his theory without being able to see a way through it.

The inadequacy of Keynes's doctrine does not lie in an inconsistency in the theory but in its narrow range. Keynes is discussing the problem of unemployment in a developed economy where there is productive capacity already in existence and all that is needed is a profitable market for its potential product. He is trying to find a cure for the diseases that beset wealthy nations. His argument throws little direct light on the problems of a country which suffers from a lack of productive capacity or on the kind of unemployment (which Marx deals with) that arises from having too little capital to be able to offer work to all available labor. It is of no use to apply Keynes's prescriptions in situations which they do not suit. Where lack of productive capacity is the problem, merely generating demand only leads to inflation, and expenditure for its own sake—building pyramids instead of railways—is clearly not what the situation demands.

In short, no economic theory gives us ready-made answers. Any theory that we follow blindly will lead us astray. To make good use of an economic theory we must first sort out the relations of the propagandist and the scientific elements in it, then by checking with experience, see how far the scientific element appears convincing, and finally recombine it with our own political views. The purpose of studying economics is not to acquire a set of ready-made answers to economic questions, but to learn how to avoid being deceived by economists.

---

[10] A. Marshall, *Principles of Economics,* 8th ed. (original) (New York: The Macmillan Company, 1949) pp. 710–711.

Selection 22

Capitalism

JOSEPH SCHUMPETER

From Encyclopaedia Britannica, *Vol. 4, 1946 printing, pp. 801–807. Reprinted by permission of Encyclopaedia Britannica, Chicago, Ill.*

A society is called capitalist if it entrusts its economic process to the guidance of the private businessman. This may be said to imply, first, private ownership of nonpersonal means of production, such as land, mines, industrial plant and equipment; and, second, production for private account, that is, production by private initiative for private profit. But, third, the institution of bank credit is so essential to the functioning of the capitalist system that, though not strictly implied in the definition, it should be added to the other two criteria. Common parlance applies the adjective "capitalist" to almost all the phenomena of modern society, particularly when envisaged with reference to the socialist alternative. This article first presents an outline of historical developments (sections 1–4), then a summary of the economics and the sociology of capitalism (sections 5 and 6), followed by a brief survey of some of the principal topics usually discussed in connection with capitalism (sections 7 and 8) and by comments on the problem of the future of the capitalist order (section 9).

1. Early Capitalism

Most of the features that define the capitalist order may be found in the ancient world, and particularly in its Graeco-Roman sector. There were factories producing for markets; there were bankers; and merchants that traded internationally. The upheavals and devastations that accompanied the fall of the western Roman empire never destroyed this capitalist trade and manufacture entirely. The warrior society and warrior civilization that rose from those ruins (feudalism) greatly differed, of course, from the businessman society and businessman civilization of the nineteenth century. But the former also contained elements of, and partly subsisted on, economic activities that differed from those of capitalist times only in technique and importance. Surveying the course of economic history, we find no sharp break anywhere, but only slow and continuous transformation. Need for protection largely accounts for the growth of fortified towns and for the concentration in them of industrial production and trade. The craft guilds—corporations of the arts and trades—that had no facilities for trade at a distance, found their complement in the early trading companies—also primarily the products of the need for protection—and both developed together. The individual of supernormal energy who was irked by the strict regulations of the craft guilds moved out of the towns controlled by them, and either set up a workshop in his home where, with the assistance of apprentices and journeymen, he was able to produce with more freedom and on a somewhat larger scale, or confined himself to furnishing raw materials to such "masters" and specialized in the commercial and financial task (domestic industry).

Interlocal and international trade was, however, by far the most important line of early capitalist endeavor. It was often associated with the business of providing for the financial needs of spiritual and temporal princes—the earliest form of international finance—and with exploitation of the privileges or "concessions" —exclusive rights to mine, to trade, or to produce—that were sometimes granted in return. Fighting its way through the resisting framework of feudal society, this process of economic change slowly evolved greater freedom of property and lending and also the institutions of typically capitalist hue, such as the joint-stock company, the salable share, the bank and the bank deposit, the negotiable paper, the stock exchange. All these institutions and practices, including speculation, were well developed, at least in a number of business centers, by the middle of the sixteenth century, but none of them were then entirely new. Moreover, the public mind then reacted to the phenomena of capitalism in much the same way as it does in our time; it cried out against usury, speculation, commercial and industrial monopolies, cornering of commodities, and other abuses, and the arguments used were, both in their commonsense content and in their one-sidedness, neither much worse nor much better than are the popular arguments of the twentieth century. Governments reacted in sympathy. They dealt with the practical problems that presented themselves by means of regulations, the technical and administrative shortcomings of which must not be allowed to obliterate a fundamental similarity of intention with those of more recent times. This applies also to the extensive labor legislation of that epoch, such as the Elizabethan Statute of Apprentices and Poor Law (*q.v.*) which, on the one hand, continued an old tradition and, on the other hand, embodied ideas so "modern" as index wages and arbitration.

Some economists, among whom it must suffice to mention Max Weber (*q.v.*), have felt the need of explaining the rise of capitalism by means of a special theory. But the problem such theories have been framed to solve is wholly imaginary and owes its existence to the habit of painting unrealistic pictures of a purely feudal and a purely capitalist society, which then raises the question what it was that turned the tradition-bound individual of the one into the alert profit hunter of the other. According to Weber, it was the religious revolution that, changing humanity's attitude toward life, produced a new spirit congenial to capitalist activity. We cannot go into the historical objections that may be raised against this theory. It is more important that the reader should realize that there is no problem. Nothing but proper attention to the details of the social and economic structure of the Middle Ages and of the economic history from the eighth to the sixteenth century is necessary in order to understand that transformation. Far from being stationary or tradition-bound or hostile to economic activity, the medieval world offered plenty of opportunity for rudimentary entrepreneurial venture. Success and failure taught their lessons. And each lesson produced an increment of capitalist practice and capitalist spirit alike. Thus, merely by functioning, the world of Charlemagne developed into the world of Luther and Calvin, of the Chigis (*q.v.*) and Fuggers (*q.v.*), of Charles V and Elizabeth. It still remains necessary, of course, to take into account all the particular events and circumstances that accelerated, retarded, and shaped the process.

2. Mercantilist Capitalism

Of particular interest are those events and circumstances which are extraneous to the logic of the capitalist process and must, from the standpoint of the latter, be considered as accidental. Such an accident was, for instance, the inflow of American silver and gold that superimposed silver and gold inflation on pre-existing inflationary tendencies and accelerated capitalist developments in one very obvious way and retarded them in another less obvious way. Much more important, however, was the circumstance, purely fortuitous though it was, that these capitalist developments impinged upon a social structure of extraordinary vitality whose ruling stratum, the feudal aristocracy headed by the families of sovereign positions, was able to harness the new wealth into the service of its own interests, traditions, and political goals. This symbiosis of two different social worlds was the dominant factor in European history from the sixteenth to the end of the eighteenth century and an important factor even during the nineteenth. In particular, it accounts for the well-known economic policies of the so-called age of mercantilism (see "Mercantile System"),[1] which, roughly speaking, lasted until the end of the eighteenth century.

We behold the struggle of the rising national states. They all fostered domestic industry and supported it in its conquest of foreign markets; they mostly—though not so generally as has been often asserted—sided with employers against the workmen; those of them that were in a position to do so embarked upon careers of rival colonial enterprise and vied with one another in trying to secure the biggest possible share in the slave trade; and all this was geared to the one pivotal purpose of asserting and expanding national power by military force. These traits were indeed blurred and mitigated by many other issues, but on the whole the picture may be summed up in the phrase "doing business sword in hand." The finishing touch is supplied by our impression, though it is not uniformly borne out by such fragments of statistical information as we possess, that, while the wealth of the business class fairly rapidly increased, at least in Western Europe, extreme poverty was widespread among the masses.

---

[1] [Unless otherwise cited, this and similar references are to the *Encyclopaedia Britannica*].

This pattern lends itself to the interpretation that has in fact been put upon it, viz., that the rising business class, or, to use the Marxist term, the *bourgeoisie,* acting on the spur of its economic interest, was the propelling force behind mercantilist policy and, in particular, mercantilist aggressiveness. But the presence, in a position of supremacy, of a nonbourgeois stratum suggests another interpretation; the wars were often, and the incident taxation was always, contrary to the bourgeoisie's interest; the mercantilist state regulated industry and trade with a heavy hand; the rule of a growing bureaucracy was not congenial to the businessman's mind. The bourgeoisie indeed accepted that supremacy. It no doubt endeavored to use to the full the profit possibilities offered by mercantilist policy and itself acquired in doing so something of the prevailing spirit of aggression. But its role is perhaps more truly described as that of a servant than that of a master. The importance of this question of interpretation is obvious: it makes all the difference to our view of the capitalist process whether we attribute observed tendencies toward economic nationalism and political aggression to its very nature or to a distortion of this nature by extracapitalist factors. The history of the subsequent epoch when the business class really enjoyed ascendancy supports the latter view.

3. Intact Capitalism

Accelerated change in technology and organization that revolutionized first agriculture and then industry (see "The Industrial Revolution"; last quarter of the eighteenth, first quarter of the nineteenth centuries) produced a significantly different social pattern which may be termed Intact Capitalism and prevailed substantially from the Napoleonic wars to the end of the nineteenth century. The familiar features of its political complement, liberalism, were laissez faire (*q.v.*), in particular free trade (*q.v.*), and "sound money" (meaning unrestricted gold currency), or at least tendencies toward these goals; a pacific, though far from pacifist, attitude toward foreign nations and, though with many relapses, toward colonies; unprecedented respect for personal freedom not only in economic but in all matters; increasing "democratization," meaning extension of the suffrage and the secret ballot. For a time, the state and its bureaucracy were in full retreat. But nothing is more characteristic of the spirit of that age than its fiscal policy, of which William E. Gladstone (*q.v.*) was the most representative as well as the most brilliant exponent. The principle of leaving individuals to themselves and of trusting their free interaction to produce socially desirable results cannot be better expressed than it was by the three rules which sum up that policy: that public expenditure should be limited to the minimum required for the essential services ("retrenchment"); that budgets should not only balance but display a surplus to be applied to the reduction of the national debt; and that taxation should serve no other purpose than that of raising the necessary revenue, and exert as little effect as possible on the distribution of income and on the channels of trade, from which it followed that it must be light. The income tax was an essential part of this program; but it was not less essential that it should be so low as to constitute a minor item in the taxpayer's total expenditure. We cannot enter into the question whether the social legislation of the period—protection to women and children, hours acts, factory acts, social insurance, the recognition of trade unions and of collective bargaining, et cetera—was in accord with these policies or spelled deviation from them. We merely note that it was not absent.

This system, though well-defined and logically coherent, must of course be understood as a system of tendencies only. The heritage of the past and other obstructions prevented the full realization of its principles except in relatively few cases, of which English free trade is the most important instance. The adverse judgment passed upon these principles by conservative and socialist critics alike must be considered in the light of this fact and, let us add at once, in the light of the further fact that the economic history of that epoch, owing to its brevity, is unduly loaded with records of its childhood diseases, most of which were rapidly passing within its span. Such as they were, however, both tendencies and realizations bear the unmistakable stamp of the businessman's interests and still more of the businessman's type of mind. Moreover, it was not only policy, but the philosophy of national and individual life, the scheme of cultural values, that bore that stamp. Its materialistic utilitarianism (*q.v.*), its naïve confidence in progress of a certain type, its actual achievements in the fields of pure and applied science, the temper of its artistic creations, may all be traced to the spirit of rationalism that emanates from the businessman's office. For much of the time and in many countries the bourgeoisie did not rule politically. But even noncapitalist rulers espoused its interests and adopted its views. They were what they had not been before, its agents.

More definitely than in any other historical case these developments can be explained by purely economic causes. It was the success of capitalist enterprise that raised the bourgeoisie to its position of temporary ascendancy. Economic success produced political power, political power produced policies congenial to the capitalist process, and the latter in turn responded to these policies by further success. Thus the English bourgeoisie obtained free trade, and free trade in turn was a major factor in a spell of unprecedented economic expansion. The same example serves to show that the bourgeoisie was not the only or even the principal beneficiary of these developments. The much-derided "free breakfast table," more accurately, the untaxed exchange of industrial products for the raw materials and foodstuffs of newly opened countries, meant more for labor than did many spectacular reforms of later times. And labor was quite aware of the fact: though many individuals and minority groups challenged the capitalist system, the large majority of the manual workers of all countries accepted it, and was content to improve its position within it, through the period. For the rest, it was the age of steam and steel, of another industrial and agrarian revolution that, following upon the preceding one, once more transformed the economic world and subsided into a period of readjustment, 1873–1897, that is, misleadingly, known as the Great Depression. There is a note of admiration for the performance of the system even in Karl Marx's and Friedrich Engels' (*q.v.*) *Communist Manifesto*. Looking back, however, we should be less impressed by the actual performance of that epoch than by the performance it rendered possible for the future.

4. The Modern Phase (1898 and later)

Upon the Great Depression followed a period of intense prosperity, interspersed with short depressions, that was associated with the new electrical, chemical, automotive, and rubber industries. It lasted until about 1912 and, indeed, amounted to yet another industrial revolution. Like the two preceding ones, this period issued into a period of predominantly depressive character interspersed with spells of prosperity, the longest and most intense of which occurred in the United States, 1923–1929. In order to exclude at least those disturbances that were directly due to actual warfare, this period should be dated 1919–1939. So far there was, except the *absolute* values of statistical figures, nothing new or unprecedented in the sequence of events. On the whole, the behavior of industrial output, price levels, interest rates, profits, monetary and real wage rates, income, and employment repeated the pattern made familiar by previous experience, and peculiar features are amply accounted for by war effects. It is important to note that, contrary to a widespread impression, this also applies to the world crisis, 1929–1932: like every crisis, it was, of course, an historical individual, but its general features did not differ substantially from those of the comparable instances, 1826–1830 and 1873–1878.

Nevertheless, it is undeniable that this epoch witnessed a complete reversal of the attitude toward capitalism and of almost all the tendencies of the liberal epoch. The best method of showing this is to visualize the expectations that an observer might have formed in 1870 and to contrast them with what actually happened. He might have expected steady progress toward universal free trade; more and more peaceful foreign relations; reduction of armaments; decreasing tax burdens; removal of such obstacles to free enterprise as still remained; internationally unrestricted gold currencies; gradual development of security and other labor legislation within the increasing means provided by growing wealth. Instead, we find revival of protectionism from the first; growing antagonism between nations; expansion of armaments; rising public expenditure and taxes; increasing regulation of economic activity; increasing strain in the system of international gold monometallism that eventually resulted in its abandonment in favor of strictly managed national currencies; security and other labor legislations that did indeed develop according to expectation until 1914, but displayed a new spirit and acquired a new significance in Germany during the 1920's and in the United States during the 1930's. Again, all this may be linked with corresponding changes in social structures, philosophies of life, schemes of values. The fundamental explanation, however, is much more complex and difficult than is generally realized, and cannot be attempted here. Instead, we shall briefly notice two important doctrines concerning the change that has come upon, or is supposed to have come upon, the economic process itself, the doctrine of the maturity of capitalism and the doctrine of imperialism.

The first, which may also be called the doctrine of vanishing investment opportunity, is not intended to explain the economic and political pattern of modern capitalist society as a whole. It limits itself to the propositions: (1) that the capitalist system has reached maturity in the sense of having substantially exhausted its possibilities of growth, particularly its opportunities for new investments on a large scale, both for technological reasons and because of the decreasing rate of increase of population; (2) that the whole scheme of capitalist society, particularly its saving habits, being geared to the task of exploiting such opportunities, the permanent depression of anemia will result from their gradual disappearance; (3) that in this state of maturity or stagnation, the capitalist process can be kept going only by incessant injections of purchasing power by means of government deficit spending. This theory, mainly framed to account for the unsatisfactory conditions that prevailed in the United States (and in France) during the 1930's, is unsupported by any facts prior to 1932. Its wide appeal is, however, understandable: the public and the economic profession are equally apt to be more impressed by the real or supposed peculiarities of their own problems and troubles than by any analogies with conditions half a century ago.

The second explanation is the orthodox socialist theory, according to which "imperialism" is the last phase of capitalism. It has been developed, on a Marxist basis, by O. Bauer, R. Hilferding, V. I. U. Lenin, L. D. Trotsky, F. Sternberg, and others. Competition among capitalist firms tends to eliminate all of them except a small number of giant concerns; these find themselves unable to use the productive capacity they have built up owing to the falling, or inadequately increasing, purchasing power of the masses; they are therefore driven to invading foreign markets and to excluding foreign products from their own markets; this state of things produces aggressive colonial and foreign policies and "imperialist" wars, which the proletariat then turns into the civil war of socialist revolution. This doctrine, even if stripped of its most obviously ideological elements, is open to serious objections. Three points, however, must be recorded in its favor: first, it does attempt what no other theory has attempted, viz., to subject the whole of the economic, political, and cultural pattern of the epoch that began in 1898 to comprehensive analysis by means of a clear-cut analytic schema; second, on the surface at least it is strikingly verified by some of the outstanding features of this pattern and some of the greatest events of this epoch; third, whatever may be wrong with its facts and interpretations, it certainly starts from a fact that is beyond challenge, the tendency toward industrial combination (see "Combination in Industry") and the emergence of largest-scale concerns. Though both cartels (*q.v.*) and trusts (*q.v.*) antedate the epoch, the role of what is popularly called big business has so much increased in its course as to constitute one of its outstanding economic characteristics.

5. The Economics of Capitalism

It must be borne in mind that capitalism cannot, any more than any other form of organization, be judged by economic results alone. Account must also be taken of the social and cultural achievements for which the capitalist process provided both the means and the psychological prerequisites. Moreover, as has been pointed out, any final appraisal really involves appraising an attitude toward life, a scheme of life's values, in short, a civilization. It is this fact which precludes agreement even among those who agree about the economic facts and their interpretation.

Not even the purely economic results of the capitalist process, however, are capable of exact measurement, still less of measurement by a single figure. The nearest approaches to such a figure, the various indices of total, agrarian, and industrial output that are available for the leading countries, over varying periods and in varying degrees of perfection, tend to understate actual performance by giving too little weight to new industries, taking insufficient or even no account of improving quality, and are inadequate also for other reasons. However, the often-repeated estimate of a 3 per cent average annual rate of increase of total output, 1850–1910, may serve to give at least a vague idea. For the output of the United States *manufacturing* industries alone, a careful investigation (see Fabricant, *Output of Manufacturing Industry,* National Bureau of Economic Research, 1940) yielded, for 1899–1937, in spite of the world crisis and its aftermath, an increase of 276 per cent (3.5 per cent in the annual average), which, after various corrections, corresponds roughly to a *per capita* increase of 100 per cent in all finished processed goods produced by factories. While appraisal of such figures is not a simple matter, it is safe to assert that a repetition of this performance would eliminate anything that could reasonably be called poverty, *even if no part of capitalist incomes were, by means of taxation, diverted to purposes directly benefiting labor*. This conclusion presupposes, of course, that the relative share of labor in national incomes remains constant. But so far back as our statistical information carries us, this relative share, though fluctuating with cyclical phases, has in fact, contrary to Marxist prediction, displayed remarkable stability. On the absolute share and the course of real wages, see "Wages."

Few observers are in fact inclined to find fault with capitalism considered as an engine of production. Criticism usually proceeds either from moral or cultural disapproval of certain features of the capitalist system (see below, section 7), or from the short-run vicissitudes with which long-run improvement is interspersed (see below, section 8). At the moment, however, we are concerned with the problem of how far the economic achievements of the capitalist *epoch* should be attributed to the capitalist *system*. For instance, it is often argued that observed developments were the fruits, *not* of capitalist enterprise *but* of the technological progress. It is true that the historical increase in output of commodities and services is not only or even primarily due to the increase of capital or of the working population, still less to increased skill or effort of the individual operative, but principally to improvements in technology and organization. But these are not independent of the capitalist system that, on the contrary, tends to call them forth by concentrating human energy upon economic tasks, by creating the rational attitude favorable to technological development, and by setting high prizes upon success in this field. For the rest, owing to the impossibility of experimental variation of conditions, we must look to economic theory in order to derive such answer as we can to the question whether observed results may reasonably be ascribed to the capitalist system.

The first thing to be noticed about the capitalist process is its evolutionary character. Stationary socialism would still be socialism but stationary capitalism is impossible—is, in fact, a contradiction in terms. For the central figure on the capitalist stage, the entrepreneur (*q.v.*), is concerned not with the *administration* of existing industrial plant and equipment but with the incessant *creation* of new plant and equipment, embodying new technologies that revolutionize existing industrial structures. This is the source of his profits (see "Profit"), so far as they exceed interest on owned capital and the remuneration of routine management and salesmanship, as well as the typical source of private capitalist fortunes. The other sources, ownership of appreciating natural resources, especially urban land, speculation, financial piracy, and saving from current income, are of but secondary importance. The financing of this activity is the essential function of bank credit, which removes from the path of the industrial innovator the requirement of ownership of capital. All the typical phenomena of capitalism, all its achievements, problems, and vicissitudes, including the trade cycle (*q.v.*), derive from this process. Nevertheless, traditional theory is primarily a theory of the current management of resources. The points most relevant to our subject may be summed up as follows: If in all markets of products and services sellers and buyers be so numerous that none of them is able to influence price perceptibly by his own individual action (hypothesis of perfect competition [see "Competition in Industry"]), then it can be proved that there will be a tendency toward a determined state of the economic organism, the so-called equilibrium state, in which: (1) all firms will expand their production to the point at which the current price just covers the cost of producing an additional increment of product; (2) all resources including labor are fully employed; and (3) a competitive rate of interest and a competitive rate of earnings of management being counted as costs, all profits above costs vanish. These propositions do not establish, as many nineteenth-century economists believed, that competitive capitalism tends to produced ideal results. But they do serve to dispel certain gross errors, such as that an economic process which is not consciously planned by a central agency must necessarily be chaotic; or that action guided by the profit motive must, because of this fact alone, be less efficient in satisfying consumers' wants than would be action by an agency guided by their interest alone. The fact that a perfectly competitive capitalist system would tend, in the sense defined by proposition (1), to maximize total output, together with certain corollaries concerning distribution, has induced the best theorists among modern socialists not only to drop the Marxist objections but also to frame their own plan for the socialist form of society upon this model and to base their criticism of capitalism, so far as it is not directed against the effects of private thrift (see below, section 8), upon the deviations of capitalist practice from perfect competition. It is indeed obvious that none of those three propositions applies to monopoly (*q.v.*) or even to monopolistic competition, that is, to cases where firms are in a position to fix their prices at will within a certain range instead of being constrained to accept a current market price. In these cases which are, of course, much more frequent than are cases of perfect competition, outputs are not maximized, excess capacity (see below, section 8) and surplus profits appear even in equilibrium, and existing industrial positions are exploited and protected by quasi-monopolistic practices.

Criticism on these scores derives support from the public's impulsive aversion to anything to which the label monopoly can be affixed and has, mainly for this reason, met with considerable political success. But it has no general validity, as distinguished from validity in individual instances. The proposition that monopolists will sell smaller quantities of product at higher prices than will firms in conditions of prefect competition is true only under the proviso that other things—cost structures in particular—be strictly equal, and therefore has but little practical importance. Almost without exception, largest-scale concerns do alter the cost structure of their industry, by introducing new methods of production and in other ways that are beyond the reach of numerous competing concerns of medium size. Therefore it does not follow that their outputs are actually smaller and their prices actually higher than would be the outputs and prices with the methods within the reach of perfectly competitive business. In fact, the behavior of indices of manufacturing output in the era of mergers and big concerns lends some support to the opposite view. Also, it is clear that the potentialities of mass production can be fully realized only by concerns that are beyond the size compatible with perfect competition. Finally, the wages paid in the largest concerns are, more often than not, higher than the wages paid elsewhere for comparable work.

6. The Class Structure of Capitalist Society

The classes of traditional economic theory, such as landowners, capitalists, workmen, are functional categories, not living and acting sociological entities. Classes in the latter sense, and the corresponding concepts of class consciousness, class action, and class war, were introduced by Karl Marx. Choosing ownership of means of production for sole criterion, he recognized two classes only, capitalists and proletarians. But this scheme, though it served his purpose and though it had the further advantage of linking up with the popular distinction between haves and have-nots, rich and poor, is next to valueless for purposes of analysis. On the one hand, even if we disregard the presence of noncapitalist strata—the "symbiosis" emphasized above—and confine ourselves to the classes created by the capitalist process, it still spells distortion and not simplification to reduce them to two. In order to understand the economics and politics of the capitalist epoch, it is essential to see the cooperative and antagonistic interactions of, at least, the classes associated with the control of large, medium, and small business; the farmers, who differ so significantly from the other business classes that there is no point in including them with one of these; the *rentier* class ("capitalists" in a narrower but more useful sense); the professional class; the clerical ("white-collar") class; the skilled workers; the unskilled workers. On the other hand, it is equally essential to realize that these classes, and still more such classes as rich and poor, by virtue of their very nature, do not admit of clearly defined border *lines* but shade off into each other across broad border *zones*.

Class distinctions are perhaps inevitable in any social group of any size and complexity. They have already developed in Soviet Russia. They produce, and are in turn buttressed by, what is usually referred to as "connection." But in capitalist society they are further buttressed by the presence or absence of inherited wealth and therefore present, to the casual observer, a misleading impression of stability: because there are always industrialists, bankers, farmers, laborers, et cetera, and because the corresponding economic and social positions are as a rule passed on from father to son, we are apt to think of these classes as if they consisted of a self-perpetuating set of families and as if rise into a "higher" class, and fall from it into a "lower," were exceptional occurrences. This opinion, although implied in widely accepted social ideologies, is the exact opposite of the truth. It is one of the outstanding characteristics of the social structure of capitalism than its "higher" strata incessantly lose members to, and incessantly recruit themselves from, its "lower" strata and that this incessant rise and fall in general proceeds relatively quickly: the slogan "three generations from overalls to overalls" expresses a great deal of truth.

While this is rarely denied explicitly, no agreement seems possible on another question that is not less important for our general picture of capitalism, viz., whether the kind of business success that spells ascent in capitalist society is causally related to the presence of personal qualities that the observer believes to be socially desirable or undesirable or, to put it differently, whether social ascent and descent through success or failure in business spells positive or negative social selection. Partisans of the capitalist system almost invariably attribute success in business, in the broad average, to superior moral stamina and ability; opponents, not less regularly to either "luck" or absence of moral inhibitions. Although industrial and family history, as well as other sources, afford sufficient material for arriving at an answer, the question has not received from serious scholars all the attention it deserves. In the special case—which is not unimportant quantitatively—where ascent through successful enterprise starts from a working-class environment, it is safe to assert that supernormal will power and intelligence constitute the most important of all ascertainable causal factors. Other cases, while frequently suggesting a similar inference, present greater difficulties of interpretation. Unrealistic ideas about the size and nature of what is commonly called the "leisure class" are another obstacle to arriving at a lifelike picture of capitalist society as it really is.

7. Exploitation and Inequality

As we have seen above (section 5), to evaluate capitalism is to evaluate a civilization in all its aspects. The complexity of such a task is, however, not the only reason why agreement is not to be expected. Another is that moral and cultural *judgments* presuppose moral and cultural *standards* that are matters of individual preference and beyond the range of scientific proof or disproof. All that can be done about them from a scientific standpoint is (1) to establish the truth or falsity of such statements of fact as may enter into those judgments and (2) to point out the economic and cultural consequences to be expected from giving effect to them. The two topics of this section illustrate this truth.

In itself, the statement that capitalism involves exploitation of man by man conveys nothing except ethical disapproval. Recognizing this, Marx tried to give it more definite content by means of his theory of exploitation: starting from the propositions that economic values of commodities tend to be proportional to the number of hours of labor that enter into their production (labor theory of value, derived from David Ricardo [*q.v.*]) and that in capitalist society labor is a commodity, he went on to argue that the workmen will receive wages equal to the value of their labor, which is proportional to the number of hours of labor that enter into the production of their labor force (or of the commodities and services required in order to rear, train, feed, clothe, house . . . the workmen) and, further, that the product of their work will similarly sell at its value, which is proportional to the numbers of hours the workmen are constrained to work. Since workmen can work more hours than it takes to produce their labor force, there is a positive difference between the value of products and the value of the labor force, the surplus value, which goes to the capitalist employer. This is what constitutes exploitation. The argument is open to fatal objections and is no longer upheld by any economists except the Marxists of strictest observance. The other attempt at giving meaning to the term has been made by a group of English theorists. Whereas Marx's theory also applies to the case of perfect competition, there is, according to these theorists, no exploitation in this case; and whereas Marx's theory applies only to labor, any factor of production may suffer exploitation. This will happen whenever, owing to deviations of practice from the competitive model, the share of a factor falls short of what it would receive if perfect competition prevailed. It should be observed that, even if it were possible to agree on what constitutes exploitation, this would not necessarily determine the judgment to be pronounced. For exploitation, even if admitted, might still be the means of providing for economic or cultural needs that we may not be prepared to sacrifice.

The general problem of social inequality cannot be considered in this article. We must confine ourselves to a single type of inequality, the inequality of income (for illustrative figures, see "Wealth and Income, Distribution of"). In capitalist society this inequality is due to the facts (1) that incomes are the result of pricing processes and reflect the market values of products and productive services (this, as is easy to see, also has an important equalizing effect), and (2) that, once acquired, wealth may be transmitted by inheritance. The first fact is essential in the sense that a society from which it were completely eliminated could no longer be called capitalist; the second is not inherent in the logic of the capitalist plan, but so deeply rooted in the structure of capitalist society as to be practically inseparable from it. Again, it should be borne in mind that, in itself, disapproval of this inequality from the standpoint of equalitarian ideals expresses nothing beyond the critic's personal feelings of fitness or justice. These differ widely. The critic may disapprove, on religious or other grounds, of any inequality whatever; or he may reserve disapproval for particular kinds or aspects of inequality, such as "inequality of opportunity," inequalities of income due to inheritance, all inequalities not due to inequality of effort, et cetera. Errors of fact or reasoning may, however, enter into statements of particular reasons for ethical disapproval. One of the most common ones is the belief that the majority of people is poor *because* a minority is rich.

Appraisal of the purely economic effects of inequality depends mainly, though by no means wholly, upon our views (1) on the relation of inequality to economic motives, and (2) on private thrift. Looking back into the past, we can hardly fail to perceive the prime importance of the stimulating atmosphere of inequality. The lure of big prizes coupled with the threat of complete destitution no doubt produced a scheme of motivation of perhaps unique effectiveness. The importance of inequality *within* the highest income brackets should be particularly noticed. A single spectacular success may draw far more brains and means into an industry than would be attracted to it by the same sum if more equally divided. To this extent current views about unnecessarily or even absurdly high rewards and about the total cost to society of entrepreneurial performance should be modified. Under modern circumstances this argument has lost some of its importance, and there is room for difference of opinion on the question what weight should be attached to it for the future. But in any case it should not be forgotten that, whatever its weight, this argument also covers the case of inequality through inheritance: the privileged position of the entrepreneur's family may be more important as a motive than any desire for personal position or enjoyment.

So long as economists were practically unanimous in considering thrift or saving as the principal requisite for the expansion of the physical apparatus of industry (capital formation), or even for all economic progress, the most important, and indeed a decisive, economic argument for inequality was that the bulk of saving is done by the higher incomes and that equalization by share-the-wealth policies would hence paralyze the very process that operates to raise the standard of life of the masses. But that practical unanimity does no longer exist. The classical theory of the role of saving, much too absolutely stated by its sponsors, was bound to lose ground, as it had repeatedly done before, in times of prevalent unemployment. During the 1930's, an increasing number of economists adopted the opposite view, viz., that saving, withholding income elements from being expanded on consumers' goods, has a depressing effect on the economic process and thus impedes, instead of fostering, the expansion of plant and equipment. It ought to have been admitted from the first that the persistence of saving habits during a depression may make things worse than they otherwise would be. Larger claims on behalf of the newer theory are of doubtful validity. The support it lends to prevalent political attitudes toward capitalism should, however, be noticed.

8. Unemployment and Waste

Planning by a central agency, whatever else it may or may not be able to accomplish, can certainly be expected to mitigate the trade cycle. Therefore, so far as involuntary unemployment (*q.v.*) is an inevitable concomitant of cyclical depressions, it may with justice be placed to the debit of capitalism's account. This also covers technological unemployment irrespective of whether or not we include it with cyclical unemployment, on the ground that the investment characteristic of prosperity in part finances labor-saving technologies: in either case, a central agency is in a position to plan technological advance in such a way as to minimize unfavorable effects it may have on employment. However, in order to see this fact in the proper perspective, it must be borne in mind that in many important instances the introduction of new technologies has directly increased employment opportunities; that where it did not, the resulting unemployment has been but temporary, though often severe; and that, so far as we know, the unemployment *percentage* has not, until 1929, displayed any tendency to increase over time, that is to say, that the capitalist process has always absorbed, *at increasing real wage rates,* not only the unemployment it generated but also the increase in population. Interpretation of the persistent unemployment, 1933–1939, that was particularly severe in the United States and France, is the subject of a controversy ("reform versus recovery") greatly influenced by political preferences. No scientifically reliable conclusions can in any case be based on the experience of seven years.

The above argument in favor of a centrally planned economy may be extended, with varying degrees of confidence, to other types of involuntary unemployment as well as to the numerous cases that may be called voluntary or involuntary with equal justice. An example will illustrate the most conspicuous of these. If a trade union succeeds in keeping wage rates abnormally high within its jurisdiction, this will cause unemployment among its members but may nevertheless draw newcomers to its waiting list who will also be unemployed. Both members and newcomers are involuntarily unemployed from the standpoint of the individual workmen, but their unemployment is caused by the voluntary policy of their directing agency. It may be argued that such unemployment would possibly be nonexistent in a perfectly planned society. These cases, however, serve to bring out an aspect of planning which is more or less present in all. In part, unemployment is the price workmen and their organizations pay for the freedom they enjoy in capitalist society. In order to be fully effective in eliminating the one, the planning authority would have also to eliminate the other and to adopt the principle enunciated by Trotsky: who does not obey, that is, undertake the work assigned to him at the wages fixed by the authority, shall not eat.

In the past, criticism of unemployment primarily emphasized the sufferings of the unemployed. For the future this aspect has lost much of its importance, because the capitalist process may be expected to produce adequate means for supporting them. But there still remains the loss to society of the potential products of their services and also of the services of other factors of production that may be unemployed or underemployed along with labor. This loss, largely attributable to the trade cycle, is indeed the most important element in the indictment of capitalism on the score of waste ("poverty in [potential] plenty"). But there are others. Thus, excess capacity is not entirely avoidable in any form of economic organization, but certain types of it are peculiar to monopolistic competition (see above, section 5); even perfect competition does not exclude wasteful multiplication of service; much of the energy of some of a nation's best brains is absorbed by struggles—between concerns and against regulating bureaucracies—that do not serve, or serve only remotely, productive efficiency; in important instances natural resources have been used uneconomically and without regard to the more remote future. Facts may be adduced in support of all these and other headings. The obvious inference, however, should not be drawn without due attention to the following points: (1) against some of those types of waste must be set compensating advantages; for instance, multiplication of service may be the best guarantee of excellence of service; excess or reserve capacity may have its uses in national emergencies; (2) some of the wastes observed are not due to the logic of the capitalist process but to the prevailing hostility to it, which produces protective behavior often harmful to efficiency; (3) *all* those sources of waste must be viewed in connection with the evolutionary character of capitalism; much that appears as unrelieved waste if considered as an incident of a stationary economy ceases to do so when viewed as an incident of a rapidly progressive one; (4) no machine being 100 per cent efficient, appraisals of efficiency are essentially relative to the quality of available substitutes; it is a serious as well as common mistake to overlook the sources of waste that may be inherent in alternative arrangements and, in particular, to compare the *reality* of capitalism with an *ideal* picture of bureaucratic socialism.

9. The Future of Capitalism

This problem, naturally first raised by socialist writers, Karl Marx in particular and, partly under Marxist influence, by the economists of the German historical school, has become a standard topic of popular discussion. This fact greatly increases the difficulty of stating it with precision and of distinguishing the various issues involved. The following comments may, however, assist the reader in forming his opinion.

(a) In most writings on the subject, there is an obvious association between prognosis and preference: there cannot be any doubt but that, in this as in other matters, people are apt to foresee what they desire. This tends not only to vitiate argument and presentation of facts but also to confuse two issues that should be carefully kept distinct. It is one thing to believe that the survival of capitalist institutions is desirable or undesirable; and quite another thing to believe that they will or will not survive. The first is a matter of personal preference; only the second constitutes a problem that may be attacked by scientific methods.

(b) Kark Marx was the first to realize the importance of this distinction and to formulate correctly the fundamental scientific question involved, viz., whether or not there are observable tendencies, inherent in the capitalist process as we know it, which, if allowed to work themselves out fully, will destroy the capitalist and produce the socialist system. Scientific prognosis—medical or other—can never mean more than the assertion or denial of the presence of such tendencies, and it is in this sense only, not in the sense of a prophecy, that the term "inevitable" must be understood. In Marx's affirmative answer to that question, it is necessary to separate the arguments, drawn from his analysis of the capitalist process, by which he supported his answer and the answer itself. *All* his arguments, but in particular the one that asserts that labor will be goaded into revolution by steadily increasing misery, can be proved to be untenable. But this does not dispose of the answer itself, because it is possible to arrive at a correct result by faulty methods. The case for the affirmative answer is, in fact, strong. We observe that, as the capitalist epoch wears on, the individual leadership of the entrepreneur tends to lose in importance and to be increasingly replaced by the mechanized teamwork of specialized employees within large corporations; that the institutions and traditions that sheltered the structure of capitalism tend to wear away; that the capitalist process by its very success tends to raise the economic and political position of groups that are hostile to it; and the capitalist stratum itself, mainly owing to the decay of the bonds of family life that in turn may be traced to the "rationalizing" influence of the capitalist process, tends to lose some of the grip and part of the scheme of motivation which it formerly had. Other arguments, such as the one from exhaustion of the objective possibilities of private enterprise (see above, section 4), may be unconvincing. But the ones just glanced at are quite sufficient. It should be noticed, however, that they establish no more than the presence of a tendency toward the shifting of economic activity from the private to the public sphere, or, as we may also put it, toward increasing *bureaucratization* of economic life, coupled with an increasing dominance of the labor interest. So far as the tendency in question is concerned, transitional states might be in prospect which, while greatly differing from the economic and cultural pattern of intact capitalism, would yet fail to attain full-fledged socialism for an indefinite time. In fact, they might equally well be called the one or the other, according to the requirements of political warfare. The only reason why Marx used to stress sudden transition by revolution was that, as was natural in his time, he greatly overrated the bourgeoisie's power and will to resist gradual changes that are contrary to its interest or uncongenial to its scheme of life.

(c) We have had occasion, however (see above, section 2), to emphasize the importance, for the interpretation of social processes, of circumstances that are extraneous to what may be termed the inherent logic of an economic system. Applying this principle to prognosis, we cannot fail to realize that World War I is an instance in point. Whether or not economically conditioned, if visibly accelerated, In Europe at least, existing tendencies unfavorable to the survival of capitalist institutions. On the one hand, it produced situations of stress that, although due to a chance combination of factors, caused permanent breakdown of social patterns which without such stresses might have persisted indefinitely; this is strikingly exemplified by the case of the U.S.S.R. On the other hand, it caused a permanent change in the distribution of political weights that produced policies which prevented the capitalist engine from working according to design and thus further undermined allegiance to the system; this is exemplified by the case of England. A similar argument, applies, of course, to the war that broke out in 1939: in the 1920's some competent observers used to qualify a prognosis otherwise favorable to the survival of capitalism by the proviso "unless there be another world war."

(d) Much light may be shed (1945) on the *immediate* future by visualizing how far the process of transformation has advanced already. Government control of the capital and labor markets, of price policies, and, by means of taxation, of income distribution is already established and needs only to be complemented systematically by government initiative in indicating the general lines of production (housing programs, foreign investment) in order to transform, even without extensive nationalization of industries, *regulated,* or *fettered,* capitalism into a *guided* capitalism that might, with almost equal justice, be called socialism. Thus, prediction of whether or not the capitalist order will survive is, in part, a matter of terminology. If it is to be more than that, it depends upon the likelihood of a reversal not only of existing tendencies, but also of an established state of things, and therefore upon the answer to the question where the political forces are to come from that will be able and willing to effect such a reversal.

Bibliography

Practically the entire economic literature deals with problems of capitalism. The general reader's best approach to a vivid and realistic view leads through historical works, such as P. Mantoux, *La Révolution Industrielle* (1906, rev. trans. 1928); J. H. Clapham, *Economic History of Modern Britain* (1926–38); V. Clark, *History of Manufactures in U.S.* (1929); H. See, *Les Origines du Capitalisme Moderne* (1926, trans. 1928); W. Sombart, *Der Moderne Kapitalismus* (1924–27); W. Meakin, *The New Industrial Revolution* (1928). For Weber's theory of the rise of capitalism, see R. H. Tawney, *Religion and the Rise of Capitalism* (1926). For the Marxist theory of capitalism, see P. M. Sweezy, *The Theory of Capitalist Development* (1942). On the *"Recruiting of the Employing Classes from the Ranks of the Wage-Earners in the Cotton Industry,"* see the study by Chapman and Marquis, *Journal of the Royal Statistical Society,* vol. 72; on a cognate subject, F. Redlich, *History of American Business Leaders* (1940). Also see E. J. Benn, *Confessions of a Capitalist* (1925); M. H. Dobb, *Capitalist Enterprise and Social Progress* (1925); F. D. Graham, *Social Goals and Economic Institutions* (1942); F. A. V. Hayek, *The Road to Serfdom* (1944); E. M. Queeny, *The Spirit of Enterprise* (1943); J. A. Schumpeter,

Capitalism, Socialism and Democracy (1942); B. and S. Webb, *The Decay of Capitalist Civilization* (1921).

DISCUSSION QUESTIONS

1. Discuss how the ideological differences of Marx, Marshall, and Keynes influenced their theoretical interpretation of the capitalist system.
2. Professor Schumpeter argues that capitalism is being supplanted because of its successes, not because of its failures. Explain his reasons for arriving at this conclusion.
3. Appraise Professor Schumpeter's discussion of exploitation and inequality under capitalism.

SELECTED REFERENCES

Friedman, Milton, "The Relationship Between Economic Freedom and Political Freedom," in *Capitalism and Freedom,* University of Chicago Press, 1963.

Knight, Frank H., *The Ethics of Competition and Other Essays,* New York: Harper & Bros., 1935.

Polanyi, Karl, *The Great Transformation: The Political and Economic Origins of Our Time,* New York: Rinehart and Company, Inc., 1944.

Robinson, Joan, *Economic Philosophy,* London: C. A. Watts & Co. Ltd., 1962. See especially Chap. 1.

Schumpeter, Joseph, *Capitalism, Socialism and Democracy,* London: George Allen & Unwin Ltd., 1943.

PART 10

THE ROLE OF GOVERNMENT

The emphasis in this collection of readings has been on political economy, that is, on the way in which society attempts to achieve its economic ends through its political and economic institutions. Every economic system must face political choices, whether it is a system of laissez-faire capitalism, democratic socialism, or totalitarianism of the left or right. Classical political economists saw the best plan for society in not planning. Each person or firm seeking his own self-interest would, through the "invisible hand" of the market, also achieve the best interest of society. The role of government was to maintain law and order, enforce contracts, define and enforce property rights and other rules of the game, provide a monetary system, and ensure competition. The selection by Milton Friedman provides a modern statement of this view. The critics of the classical view argued that the rules of the game were written by those who had economic and political power—the owners and managers of large business enterprises—to the detriment of those without such power—laborers, farmers, and small businessmen. In addition the critics argued that the laissez-faire system produced recurring periods of inflation and depression. The social costs of such disturbances were great—especially for workers and farmers, who had to suffer the hardships of unemployment and depressed incomes for circumstances beyond their individual control.

The Great Depression produced the *General Theory* by J. M. Keynes, from which much of modern economics derives. The selection by Keynes discusses the social implication of the *General Theory*. Keynes saw the two prime faults of the economic system as its inability to provide full employment and its arbitrary and inequitable distribution of income. The *General Theory* stated that the first problem could be cured by appropriate government fiscal and monetary policies to regulate the level of aggregate demand. This could be achieved within the framework of a capitalist system but it implied an enlarged role for government. With respect to the second problem, the *General Theory* implied that a highly inequitable distribution of income would retard rather than promote the goal of full employment. The problem was not one of inducing saving but rather one of transferring saving into investment. High interest rates and inequitable incomes would tend to reduce both consumption and investment and, therefore, the level of demand.

The selection by Jacob Viner traces the development of the "Welfare State." The "Welfare State" is the result of the dissatisfactions on the part of the rising middle class with the workings of the laissez-faire system. As more and more groups in society gained power through the ballot box, through organizations into political pressure groups, and through rising real incomes, they were able to demand that the rules of the game be rewritten to improve their incomes and increase their power and status in society. The "Welfare State" has evolved from diverse pressures. It has no internally consistent philosophy. But, concludes Viner, ". . . despite its imperfections in theory and practice, in the aggregate it provides more promise of preserving and enlarging human freedoms, temporal prosperity, the extinction of mass misery, and the dignity of man and his moral improvement than any other social system which has previously prevailed, which prevails elsewhere today, or which, outside Utopia, the mind of man has been able to provide a blueprint for."

The modern role of government can be summarized by describing the four economic functions of government:

1. *Regulatory policy*. This involves government regulation of economic activity through compulsory or voluntary controls over private decision making. Included are such activities as antitrust legislation, regulation of private utilities, regulation of the stock market, regulation of output in agriculture, and price-wage guidelines for management and labor.
2. *Stabilization policy*. This pertains to the use of government fiscal and monetary policy to maintain full employment and a stable price level.
3. *Redistribution policy*. Included here are the many government programs aimed at redistributing income or wealth: progressive taxes, minimum wages, direct payments to farmers, unemployment compensation, social security, and many more.
4. *Public service policy*. The government furnishes a myriad of public services: the Federal Agricultural Extension Service, employment services, public parks, national defense, and public education, to mention only a few.

The fact that these functions are performed by government does not guarantee that they will be performed wisely or efficiently or that the result will be in the public interest. Government acts as a result of pressures from various private and public interest groups. A separate power structure is involved with each issue. The programs do not evolve according to a rational philosophy and often are not the result of a strong public consensus. The resulting policies are, instead, compromises between competing pressures and interests within the constraints of the generally accepted rules of the game. This does not mean that the results are bad—only that a democratic system may sacrifice some efficiency in order to gain freedom, security, and equity. As Kenneth E. Boulding has commented with respect to our agricultural policy, "It is quite likely that if we had known better, we would have done worse."*

However, a reliance on ignorance and luck will not guarantee wise economic policy. The purpose of this selection of readings has not been to give final answers to questions regarding economic policy. Instead it has been to give a clearer understanding of the ideas of modern political economy and to review some current policy issues. Only when the public and the policy makers have a high degree of economic literacy can wise economic choices be made.

---

* Kenneth E. Boulding, "The Dimensions of Economic Freedom," in Edgar O. Edwards, ed., *The Nation's Economic Objectives,* Chicago: The University of Chicago Press, 1964, p. 116.

Selection 23

The United States as a "Welfare State"

JACOB VINER

From E. O. Edwards (ed.), The Nation's Economic Objectives *(Chicago, Ill.: University of Chicago Press, 1964), pp. 151–167. Reprinted by permission of the University of Chicago Press.*

I plan in my lecture to compare the pattern or "style" of the present-day American economy with earlier patterns here and elsewhere and with currently prevailing patterns elsewhere. To do so I must make use of abstract and ambiguous labels for different kinds of economic systems, much as I would prefer to be able to dispense with them. There are only three other alternatives that I can conceive of, and none of these is a practicable one. I could make use of a set of labels which are not abstract, which have precise and uniform meaning regardless of time or country, and which have the quality of automatically and accurately communicating that meaning to any audience, whether a sophisticated one like the one that is honoring me at this moment by permitting me to address it or a naïve and simple-minded one. But such a set of labels does not exist in the field of economics or any of the social science disciplines. Or I could dispense with labels and each time that I refer to a particular economic system or pattern repeat the full inventory of its fundamental characteristics. Or could I do so only upon first reference to a particular system, thereafter using such colorless and un-mnemonic symbols as System A, System B, and so forth. Either of these latter procedures would lead to intolerable boredom for you, and perhaps also for myself. There is therefore no escape from the use of labels too simple and uninformative for the ideas they are intended to communicate.

In controversial fields, however, labels in the course of the history of their use inevitably lose some of the objectivity they may have had when originally invented and become carriers of undertones of praise or blame, thus becoming substitutes for rational thought instead of its tools. These undertones, moreover, are liable to be random and undisciplined and to vary with the period, the region, and the persons using them or hearing them used. The greatest of the risks connected with the use of labels is that when a speaker intends one undertone to be caught by his audience, the audience will catch a different one. I know no way whereby these risks and uncertainties can be completely overcome, and no way but continued and disciplined exchange of views conducted in a spirit of cool and mutually tolerant discourse by which they can be reduced to moderate dimensions. I can only affirm that it is not my purpose on this occasion to persuade or to convert anyone to anything, to comfort anyone, or to antagonize anyone, and even if such were my purpose I would do my best to confine myself to logical discourse rather than semantic tricks. But words are treacherous tools, and no matter who is pouring them out on you, eternal vigilance is in the last analysis your only effective defense against being betrayed by them. I have at least put you on your guard.

I choose as a convenient label for the present-day pattern or style of organization of the American economy "the welfare state." The term is of German origin and seems first to have been used in the 1870's by German economists as a term of praise for the social goals of Bismarck and the legislation he was initiating to promote them. With substantial similarity in meaning it is being widely used today to describe the existing or the desired pattern of economic organization in the industrialized countries this side of the Iron Curtain. It is fairly frequently used as a label for the American economic pattern as it has evolved especially since the initiation of the New Deal, although in the United States other labels are sometimes preferred: for example, "people's capitalism," "welfare capitalism," "the mixed economy," and, by critics on the right, the "mixed-up economy," and "cryptosocialism"; by critics on the left, "monopoly capitalism," "decadent capitalism," "Madison Avenue capitalism," and, as the most recent derogatory term to obtain wide currency, the "affluent society." The purport of this last term seems to be to associate with our notions of the quality of our existing system the depressing idea that under it all classes have more income even after taxes than they know how to spend wisely and yet refuse to let the government decide for them the choice between the available range of commodities and services which their incomes shall be used to procure.

It is easier to be precise on what the welfare state is not than on what it is. Like the aristocratic or theocratic societies prior to the industrial revolution, and like socialism, communism, fascism, and naziism, but in lesser degree than all of these, the welfare state is a rejection of the laissez-faire or "liberal" system which substantially prevailed in the Western world in the nineteenth century, and this halfway or partial rejection of laissez-faire is, I think, the most uniform and the most important distinguishing mark of the welfare state. By "laissez faire" is meant, of course, a system under which the intervention of government in economic matters, whether as regulator or operator, is confined to the barest practical minimum consistent with the maintenance of order, the enforcement of contracts, the protection of individuals against direct and overt coercion by other individuals, and the maintenance of the military personnel and facilities necessary for defense against external aggression. In the nineteenth-century liberal society the emphasis was on freedom for the individual from government, not on service to him by government. In the modern forms of authoritarian state the emphasis is on service to the individual, with the character of the service determined from above with statist coercion substituted for the political and civil freedoms of the liberal society. The welfare state tries to find a middle path between service without freedom and freedom without service.

In the liberal nineteenth-century state rich and poor were in principle equally protected from encroachment on their property rights, their rights to follow the occupation of their choice, to live where they pleased, think and say what they pleased, and spend what they had the means to spend on things of their own untrammeled choice. For the organization of the productive process, for the attainment of equilibrium as between what producers chose to produce and what consumers chose to consume, for the determination of the ratio in which income currently produced should be allocated to current consumption or be saved and invested, reliance was on competitive market forces. That competition left to its own devices might lead to private monopoly was either overlooked or denied or believed to be adequately guarded against if government itself refrained from establishing or promoting private monopoly power and enforced the common-law prohibitions of overt conspiracy in restraint of trade.

Wealth always brings to its possessors power and privilege. The privileges which the rich specially enjoyed under laissez faire, however, were not for the most part privileges conferred upon them by government but arose directly or indirectly out of their possession of sufficient wealth to buy such things as education, medical services, gracious mansions, leisure, art, and mistresses. The most ambitious, the most intelligent and gifted, the most lucky of the working classes succeeded in increasing numbers, but for the most part without substantial assistance from the government, in acquiring moderate shares in these material means to the good life, and many of these rose into the ranks of a rapidly growing middle class, which was eventually to impose on most of the Western countries the substitution of democratic political institutions for the absolutist or the aristocratic regimes of the past.

In the nineteenth century average incomes appear to have risen impressively in all of the Western countries, although there is a great scarcity of reliable statistical information. But this increase in average income was in Europe at least in large part and perhaps wholly the result of the relative rise in the size of the middle classes as compared with the working classes. The lower classes gained from the progress of technology some improvement in health and in mortality and some improvement in the lighting and heating of their homes. On the other side of the ledger for them, however, were the increasing congestion and the decreasing access to sun and air and light in their homes, and apparently also deterioration in the quality of the food they ate and the clothes they wore. As best I can determine, it was not until about the 1870's that it can be said with assurance that the standard of living of the bottom 50 per cent of the population of any Western or Northern European country was clearly and substantially higher than it had been in, say, 1820 or 1750 or 1650 or perhaps even 1550. It was not, I think, chiefly political democracy that brought the genuine improvement which did occur from the 1870's on, but largely the cheaper and better food from North America, the Argentine, Australia, and New Zealand, which the application of steam to ocean and land transport made available to Western Europe, and the decline in the working-class birth rate which resulted from the widespread resort to birth-control practices beginning in the 1870's.

Political democracy, laissez faire, and the persistence of mass poverty for the working classes while above them were conspicuous expenditure and growing accumulated wealth—these together constituted an unstable mixture which could not last. It gave rise to socialist movements of several species, and it may be that the fact that the latter failed everywhere before World War I to bring about an explosion of the mixture was largely due to the circumstance that the governments of the time were prudent enough to grant the newly enfranchised masses political platforms from which to voice their complaints and that a foretaste of the welfare state, such as the Bismarckian social legislation in Germany and the Lloyd George death duties in England, as well as the growth in strength of the trade unions, opened up vistas of the possibility of reaching the Promised Land by milder means than revolutionary socialism. In any case, the welfare state of today has its roots in the nineteenth-century dissatisfaction of the working classes with the workings of laissez-faire capitalism. The welfare state also constitutes a partial rejection of the alternatives to laissez faire which nineteenth-century socialist movements proposed. Let me now turn to a more positive description of the characteristics of the welfare state.

In the welfare state the central and subsidiary governments engage in a wide range of economic activities. They accept responsibility for ironing out the business cycle, for relief of the unemployed, and for an extensive program of cradle-to-grave insurance against the normal hazards of life. They encourage and regulate collective bargaining between employer and employee with respect to wages, hours of labor, and working conditions, usually with what by nineteenth-century criteria is an open and systematic bias in favor of labor. Through progressive tax systems and expenditures directed largely to the subsidization of the low-income sections of the country and sectors of the population, they claim to exercise a strong equalizing influence on the distribution of wealth and income.

With respect to free competition in the market, they are torn between two opposite doctrines: on the one hand, the doctrine that free competition is the most effective stimulus to improvement leads to the closest approximation of material rewards to social contribution and maximizes flexibility and adaptability to changes in tastes, processes, and relative abundance of productive factors, the fundamental proposition of nineteenth-century laissez-faire liberalism; on the other hand, the doctrine that free competition leads to duplication of facilities and services, to booms and busts, to the crushing of the weak by the strong, and eventually to private monopoly. They thus embark on extensive and improvised rather than precisely designed programs of governmental intervention. These programs leave a large measure of freedom to market forces and to individual initiative—or lack of it—but they involve a wide range of activities of a regulatory or supervisory character. These programs include also many types of more direct participation by government in economic activity, including even some measure of substitution of government for private operation of industry. Selected industries, especially agriculture, are shielded from the full rigors of competitive forces by subsidization, price supports, preferential tax treatment, and government stockpiling.

The volume and allocation of capital formation are deliberately influenced by subjection of capital issues on the market to licensing, by setting up governmental credit agencies which increase the availability of capital at low rates for selected industries by direct lending of government funds, and by guarantees of repayment to private lenders, the industries so favored being selected on the basis of a variety of social policies and political grounds, but always in response to special concern for the prosperity of particular sectors of the population. In the United States, for example, agriculture, the housing needs of the low-income classes, small business, and ocean shipping are given special favors, and here, as in other welfare-state countries, decaying industries and new pioneer industries are given aid to the recovery of strength or to its new acquisition.

In response to special needs or to political strength, the welfare state typically deals ambivalently with monopolistic practices; in some sectors it combats them by antitrust and anticartel legislation; in other sectors it sanctions and even enforces them, as (to take the United States as an example) in the case of agriculture, in the sanction of price maintenance in the field of retail distribution, and, above all, with respect to labor union practices. "Natural monopolies" such as railroads, urban mass-transportation facilities, electricity and gas generation and distribution, dock facilities, bridges, and roads are either owned and operated by governmental agencies or are closely controlled as to rates and quality of service by government. But this feature of the welfare state is in the main but a moderate extension of the "municipal socialism" which became common from the 1870's on as the working classes won a greater measure of political power. "Nationalization" of industry outside the area of public utilities is not a prominent feature of the welfare state, and its substantial absence from program and practice today is perhaps the most important fact justifying the drawing of a sharp distinction between even the democratic socialism of the nineteenth century and the present-day welfare state. In the welfare state education is made widely available, is overwhelmingly conducted in governmental institutions, and when left in private hands is usually both substantially financed and closely regulated by government.

To finance their activities and also to make taxation serve as an instrument for redistribution of the national income, welfare states collect in taxes up to 30 per cent or more of the national income. Income taxes are invariably steeply progressive and taxes on business are heavy, and in general the total effect of the tax and expenditure activities of the welfare state is probably in a significant degree such as to make the national pattern of income distribution a less unequal one than it would be if all tax revenues were derived from a proportional tax on income and if all governmental expenditures in their immediate impact bestowed benefits on individuals in conformity with the over-all pattern of national distribution of income. But all the welfare states have democratic processes of government, including universal suffrage; in all of them the middle classes and those of the lower-income groups who have absorbed "bourgeois" attitudes are a great and often preponderant portion of the total population, and welfare-state politicians, like all politicians, are highly sensitive to strategically located and well-organized aggregates of voting power. The welfare state is consequently nowhere exclusively and rarely predominantly a "proletarian" state. It is often, at least intermittently, a "bourgeois"- or middle-class-dominated state. In consequence, whatever its proclaimed program of income equalization may be, its tax bite is rarely as strong as its tax bark. Even when income- and inheritance-tax rate schedules are in appearance progressive to the point of near expropriation of the high-bracket incomes or estates, they are invariably accompanied by an elaborate set of loopholes which temper the tax winds for the partially shorn sheep.

Government subsidies, moreover, do not flow exclusively to the very poor, and even though predominantly it is rich Peters who are taxed to pay poor Pauls, to a substantial extent the net outcome of the complex tax-and-subsidy system is that Peter is taxed to pay Peter, after deduction of an appropriate charge to reimburse the government for its services in keeping the taxpayers' money in circulation. In the welfare state instances are even to be found where the very comfortably well-off succeed in one way or another in getting on the dole in forms and dimensions which add to the social status of the recipient instead of, as in the case of poor relief, detracting from it. To a liberal or to an old-fashioned Socialist, this may seem a funny way to run a country, but it is a significant characteristic of the welfare state that it is essentially a democratic response to the whole range of popular interests, values, and aspirations, and that in consequence its general pattern is bound to lack complete internal coherence and to display to the scrutinizing eye instances of gross inconsistency.

To conservatives of the American type, this concern of mine with the selection of an appropriate label for our present-day economic system would probably seem superfluous trifling with the obvious, since the century-old term "socialism" would adequately serve all purposes, or at least all *their* purposes, and a fresh label would not lessen the menace of the poison. I would not only concede but would emphasize that the modern welfare state embodies substantial elements of nineteenth-century democratic socialism. I would even concede the reasonableness of applying to it some such label as "new socialism" or "neosocialism," or even "twentieth-century democratic socialism," provided it were conceded that "new capitalism" or "neocapitalism" would not be an appreciably more misleading term for it and provided it is not claimed that there are no important differences between the programs of nineteenth-century socialist movements and the practices of present-day welfare states.

Nineteenth-century socialism in all of its variants was the doctrine of groups out of power and with no early prospects of power. The orthodox Marxian Socialists had a doctrine of criticism of the capitalism of their time and a program of revolutionary overturn of it by an elite acting on behalf of it, though not itself members of, the proletariat. Marx and his most loyal disciples carefully refrained from spelling out any of the details of social organization that would be introduced "come the Revolution." To what extent this was the result of utopian dreaming, as the proposition that under socialism "the state would wither away" suggests, or was strategic concealment of firm intentions, is still a matter of debate among both friendly and hostile students of the sacred Marxian texts. But from the Marxian critique of nineteenth-century liberal capitalism we have every right to infer that the Marxian aspirations included the complete abolition of private property in the tools of production, a regime under which all able-bodied adults would have to work if they wanted to eat, and suppression of the allegedly sham freedom of political democracy.

The present-day practices of the welfare state do not conform to any of these three goals, and with a minor qualification with respect to nationalization with which I shall deal later, none of these is given a place in any welfare-state program I know anything about. Marxian socialism also had a decided equalitarian bias, and "from each according to his capacity and to each according to his needs" sounds clearly to my ears like an equalitarian slogan even if I don't claim to know what it means or for that matter what "equality" as a rule for distribution of income would mean in precise terms. I am sure of one thing, that in the heaven of original Marxianism or in the present-day Communist version of it as it operates in Russia and elsewhere, the rule of equality closely resembles the leaden Lesbian architectural rule which Aristotle speaks of which adapted itself to every bend or curvature of a wall that appealed to the designing architect's fancy or judgment. In the present-day welfare state there is no doubt a widespread belief in the virtue of "equalization" of income if that is interpreted to mean the gradual elimination of extremes both of wealth and of poverty. Beyond this, I see no clear signs of more ambitious plans or of more radical practice. The welfare state is a threat to the top 10 (or perhaps 5) per cent of its population in terms of the amounts of wealth or disposable income after taxation they will be allowed to retain, and a promise, a realized one in a number of countries, for the lowest 10 or perhaps 20 per cent of the population, in terms of the minimum standard of living that will be guaranteed to them. This may be good or it may be bad, but it is a far cry from Marxian socialism.

Let me now compare the present-day welfare state with non-Marxian nineteenth-century socialist philosophy, although this is to compare a working system without a philosophy with a philosophy which never had the responsibility of application, and whose many and highly changeable programs were therefore more directed toward harvesting votes than drawing up blueprints for whose practicality they had need to worry about. All the nineteenth-century democratic-socialist movements, however, did emphasize "nationalization" of the facilities and instruments of production and a large measure of equalization of income. Such proposals retain a place in the formal programs of some important socialist parties which today operate in welfare states and which are or have been in power. But there is no evidence that outside their minority left wings there is any serious intent on the part of these "socialist" parties actively to pursue these goals, and there is abundant and growing evidence that the present trend of democratic-socialist thought is to abandon these goals as obsolete, as unnecessarily extreme, and as a menace to the political success of the socialist parties in election campaigns.

What seems to have happened is that the socialist party leaders have realized that the middle classes who are terrified by the preaching of such goals are steadily growing in numbers, that political power cannot be maintained or attained unless large numbers can be won over from among the middle classes to their ranks, and that the wage earners themselves are reasonably content with the progress they have made despite the absence of nationalization and of radical equalization; that these latter have not found their status or income or incentives or working conditions appreciably improved when the government has substituted itself for the capitalist as their employer, and indeed that they have in large part absorbed the values and the attitudes of the middle classes and cannot be depended on to continue to give loyal support to parties calling themselves "socialist" or "labor" if these actually and vigorously pursue extreme policies.

Part of the loss of zeal within the socialist parties for fargoing equalization of incomes as a major goal stems from a newly acquired disposition to recognize that in any social system income differentials are essential elements of an adequate set of incentives to effort, to acquisition and exercise of skill, and to assumption of managerial responsibilities. Increasingly also there is belief even among Socialists for whom the idea of "equality" has great moral appeal that as a fact of life the maintenance and expansion of a cultural elite, the promotion of creative art, and the skilled and dedicated diffusion of its fruits do or may require that special material incentives be provided for gifted persons to develop their capacities, and that the conditions of their working life must for such persons be made easier and more removed from discomfort, enforced toil, and responsibilities for family support than for the ordinary run of worker. Important also has been the realization, with the growth and improvement in quality of statistics of income, of how modest the improvement in economic status of the poorer 50 per cent of the population would be in most countries if there were divided equally among it the wealth, or the wealth and income, in excess of the national average of, say, the richer 50 per cent of the population.

While these socialist or labor parties have consequently been moving visibly toward the right in philosophy and in action, all but extreme wings of the parties right of center have been moving toward the center or perhaps even beyond it. Party affiliations are, of course, more closely tied up with class structure in the European welfare states than in the United States or Canada and are emotionally bound to historical traditions of passionate participation in major struggles for principle and for power; interclass mobility is much less free in Europe than in this country, except that in this country racial and religious barriers are important. Party distinctions, therefore, mean more and are more stable in Europe than here, and I am not claiming that because the parties there are moving closer to each other there is no real prospect that the distinctions between them in goals and attitudes will cease to be important. All that I claim is that except for extreme wings of small size and limited range, all the major democratic political parties in Europe operate well within the limits of tolerance of the welfare state and that no threat exists (France perhaps excepted and for other reasons than purely economic issues) of violent social strife in these countries in the absence of subversion by agents of external forces.

The parties of the left which continue to call themselves socialist may or may not be justified in doing so. In most European countries, as in almost all underdeveloped countries, it seems to be good strategy for a political party to carry a "socialist" or "social" label. In the United States and in Canada, on the other hand, it seems clear that it would be political suicide. But whatever labels modern political parties of the left adopt for themselves, all the major parties of the left in the welfare states differ in important respects in programs, in attitudes, in convictions, and in their practice when they gain power from the socialist parties of pre-World War I of which they are the historical heirs. They are not revolutionaries even when political victory by democratic process seems to be beyond their reach, and they are not authoritarians, or prone to engage in large-scale nationalization, or radical equalizers of income, even when they do gain power. They are constitutional parties, and they know, or believe, that their strength would evaporate if they showed signs of losing faith in democratic process and in the adequacy of persuasion by argument and exhortation as the means whereby to retain and to augment their strength.

In the underdeveloped countries many socialist parties are, however, quite close in their programs and doctrines to the European socialist philosophy of the nineteenth century. They lack democratic traditions, and the economic and social problems they face seem more serious and less susceptible of solution or even of palliation than the corresponding problems of Western Europe today, or even fifty or a hundred years ago. The population problem is for them a major and perhaps incurable problem within a space of time short enough to be tolerated. The mild remedies by which the advanced countries succeeded in eliminating all but minor residues of the plague of desperate mass poverty (which a hundred years ago prevailed in most of Europe nearly as virulently as it does today in much of Asia, Africa, and Latin America) to many observers do not seem to be effective or appropriate in the setting of the underdeveloped countries. Middle classes are small and relatively unimportant in a majority of the underdeveloped countries, and the gulf between the very rich and the very poor is emptier and wider than it ever was in Western Europe, to say nothing of the United States and the European-colonized members of the British Commonwealth.

In much of the underdeveloped world violence as an instrument of social change is not held in abhorrence, and democratic processes of making social decisions are either weak and without the backing of long-established traditions and values or are nonexistent. Social change by means of violent revolution, of expropriation and confiscation of the property of the rich, of nationalization of existing industry and establishment under government ownership and management of new industry seem to many in these countries and to some of their friends in welfare-state countries to be their only means of escape from deepening misery and total despair.

For this and other reasons the United States has for about a decade been attempting to nudge them, with the assistance of American financial aid and technical guidance, to adopt welfare-state or "moderate" programs as the remedy for their ills. Their problems, however, may be too deep-rooted and the material and human resources available to them too scanty to make moderate reform either in fact or in appearance sufficient to meet in time and degree the minimum demands which the aroused expectations of their masses lead them to press on their governments. The suppression of human rights, the cruelty, the totalitarianism of the Iron Curtain countries do not deeply shock them, for these are evils which for centuries they have learned to live with. Many in these countries are convinced that some of the Communist programs of social change have been effective for the Communist countries and would be effective for them in providing food, health, education, and status for the masses, in reducing to tolerable proportions the gap between rich and poor, and in endowing them with the mass-production factories which have become for them the outstanding marks of successful economic development.

In guarded fashion high officials and distinguished experts in this and other welfare-state countries are of late revealing in what seems to be a growing tide of opinion that they also are becoming convinced that the methods by which prosperity has been attained in Europe and North America are too mild, too slow, too dependent on a rich foundation of accumulated wealth, of natural resources, and of trained personnel to be adequate to cope with the problems facing the underdeveloped countries. It seems clear that to some extent the American government itself is today trying to convert the better-off classes in some of the underdeveloped countries to acceptance of measures encroaching so drastically on traditional property rights that they would be regarded with horror and apprehension if proposed in this country by any responsible person. If newspaper accounts are to be trusted, the adoption of methods of social change which in their radical character go "beyond the welfare state" with respect to permissible procedures is to some extent being made a condition of continued eligibility for American foreign aid. It may be that this is a sign on our part of maturity and of freedom from excessive doctrinairism and of a willingness to perceive and to face uncomfortable facts. As a believer in the great long-run virtues of patterns of due process and of respect for long-established human rights, including property rights, I am, however, very deeply concerned about this, and I feel that there is urgent need for sober and balanced public discussion of the issue, lest we find ourselves committed, when it is too late to retreat, to pushing the underdeveloped countries down a slippery and perilous slope more rapidly than is safe for us or for their peoples.

This may be too pessimistic a view of the prospects that the underdeveloped countries will seek and find cures for their economic and social ills in programs which can be reconciled with democratic processes and with the preservation of some degree of respect for the long-established rights and the willingness and capacity to render valuable services to the common good of a reformed, enlightened, and self-disciplined, propertied middle class. Financial and technical aid from the richer countries, more generous tariff treatment by these countries of the commodities which are and will long continue to be the staple exports of the underdeveloped countries, breakthroughs through research and experiment in the discovery of successful means of adapting to tropical soils, tropical climates, and tropical and semitropical cultural patterns of the great stock of scientific and technological knowledge which is at their disposal in the advanced countries or can be made available to them—these may yet serve to make the underdeveloped countries safe for democracy and to make democracy seem to them unqualifiedly safe for themselves. Even more important in my perhaps biased opinion would be the discovery of cheap, simple, and effective methods of birth control whose widespread use would not be prevented by ignorance, by cultural prejudices, and by religious dogmas kept in a frozen state of rigidity and immunized from the processes of "progressive revelation" and of "development" of dogma which for both Protestantism and Catholicism have at critical periods in the social history of mankind been invoked to permit religious faith to serve as a powerful aid to social reform rather than operating as a stubborn and irrational barrier to it.

If I may return to the domestic scene, the United States is about as fully a welfare state now as any other of the advanced and democratic countries, including those like the Scandinavian countries and New Zealand, whose regimes, intermittently at least, are in the hands of political parties which bear with pride the socialist label. There are features of the American economic system which are somewhat special to it, but these for the most part do not derive their importance from their relationship to or independence of the philosophies of nineteenth-century non-Marxian socialist movements and their modern heirs. In its ideology the American public, and especially its more conservative sectors, clings more faithfully to the maxims and stereotypes of nineteenth-century laissez faire than do even the European prototypes—if such there be—of the National Association of Manufacturers, the United States Chamber of Commerce, or the American Medical Association. But these are in large part merely semantic loyalties on our part, rather than operative rules for actual behavior. Laissez faire in fact was notoriously not the ruling principle of our captains of industry when it was the tariff that was in issue. This ideological conservatism on our part probably renders us a useful service to some extent, perhaps in preserving for us old elements of policy which deserve to be preserved or to be resuscitated, but most obviously in fostering a scrutinizing and critical inspection by the American public of all proposals for change.

The welfare state is at best a hastily improvised system having characteristics stretching all the way through the range from near-statism to near-anarchy. It is an unplanned response to a host of historical forces and of political pressures which has not yet acquired, and may never acquire, an internally coherent and logically formulated philosophy. It is undergoing constant change, and its movements, forward, backward, and sideways, are not guided by any clear and widely accepted concensus as to where it is going or where it should go from here. It needs critics more than advocates or prophets, and there is applicable to it the saying, "Woe unto Israel if the prophets should ever get the upper hand!" Theodore Roosevelt many years ago thought he perceived a lunatic fringe to every popular movement for reform, but was blind to the fact that there are lunatic fringes on the right as well as the left. But even these fringes, while scarcely ornamental, have some utilitarian services to perform. They press the advocate to seek for good reasons to support the causes he is preaching, and they stimulate the voter to ask the promoter of a new idea to stand up and defend it. Even blind resistance to change increases the probability that the over-all quality of the changes that will be made will be higher than in its absence.

It is not because of a unified and coherent social philosophy that it realized in practice but rather because under it the working classes are reasonably satisfied with their present status and see substantial promise of improvement in it for their children even when not for themselves that the modern welfare state has strength and capacity for survival. In one of his poems, Robert Frost asks:

> *. . . How are we to write*
> *The Russian novel in America*
> *As long as life goes on so unterribly?*
> (*New Hampshire* [1923])

It is not only in America but throughout the free world where the welfare state prevails that there is no prospect and no wish that the "Russian novel" be written. But if in these countries life for the masses was not "unterrible" and if the more fortunate few in these countries showed no compassion for misery and used their power to resist all change, all that would be needed would be the appearance of a demagogic leader to make imminent the danger of a violent social revolution which would make no fine distinctions between the good and the evil in old traditions and institutions and would bring toppling down upon both the well-off and the poor the debris of a social system which through lack of understanding, of sympathy for distress, and of prudence had failed to take the steps necessary if it was to earn and assure its survival.

It is a special characteristic of the American form of welfare state that its political structure makes even more unlikely than for other welfare states close correspondence between a coherent social philosophy and the predominant pattern of social practice. The American system is marked by extreme diffusion of legislative, judicial, and administrative power, and even if consensus of doctrine were almost complete on the part of the public, the machinery for translating this into consistent and coordinated practice would be lacking in large degree. There is, first, the "federal" aspect of our Constitution, which involves a sharing of ultimate sovereignty between the national government and state governments, with the line of demarcation of powers, though shifting in response to technological change and to the processes of change in the social philosophy of our supreme judiciary, persisting as a barrier to effectively centralized national social planning.

There is, second, the constitutional separation of powers between national executive and national legislature, with much less concentration of power except in major emergencies in the hands of the executive than prevails under the parliamentary forms of government which almost all other welfare states follow, and which brings it about that in the United States there is much greater scope than elsewhere for conflict and deadlock between executive and legislative, and need for much greater resort to *ad hoc* compromise in the processes of formulation and execution of the grand strategy and the day-to-day tactics of policy.

There is, third, the division of power between the Senate and the House of Representatives, which makes their relations a close analogue to the "duopoly" of economic theory where for over a century the best minds in the economic profession have utterly failed to discover a formula which describes realistically the mode whereby the inevitable conflicts of interest and of objectives between the two equal powers obtain resolution.

There is, fourth, the almost promiscuous and haphazard dispersal of power within each branch of the legislature, where the weakness of party discipline and the possession of nearly unlimited veto power and delaying power by the committee chairmen, who acquire their posts by seniority regardless of the degree and quality of their ability, of their loyalty to the President, or of their loyalty to their party, result in the processes of legislation being largely subject to the idiosyncracies and the special interests of a small group of men whose qualifications for meeting the heavy responsibilities they bear, whether it be qualities of ability or of character, are even more subject to the hazards of chance than the outcome of a horse race or a football match.

There is, fifth, the substantial power of the run-of-the-mill congressman or senator in initiating, delaying, or modifying specific legislative proposals, which results in making extremely difficult and even impossible the attainment of coherence, timeliness, and self-consistency in the legislative processes as a whole and in making unduly important the role of the lobbyist for special interests, private or regional, who to attain his objectives, good or bad, often needs not the approval of the President or of the administration or of the majority party as a whole or of national public opinion or of the press, but only the dedicated and not necessarily disinterested support of a small handful of freewheeling legislators.

There is, finally, the power of the judiciary, subject to no formal limits except its own standards of judgment and discretion and its own interpretation of its constitutional function and authority, to find *ultra vires* the outcome of the legislative process and even to engage in the equivalent of legislation itself, through its execution of its duty to interpret the intent of Congress and its practice of "filling the gaps" in acts of Congress in the course of its adjudication of specific cases that come before it for decision.

For all these reasons and for additional reasons which limitations of time or of my knowledge and insight prevent me from bringing to your attention, there is in the abstract no reason for making an idol of the welfare state in its American form or for dedicating ourselves unreservedly to its continuance as it is today without qualification or amendment. Given the complex and puzzling problems it is continually facing, the imperfection of the procedures whereby it deals with problems which it cannot evade or defer or with problems which special interests may press upon it for premature resolution, it would be only by the dispensation of a benevolent Providence that it would ever make precisely the right decisions or always avoid major mistakes. It does not have theoretical superiority over all conceivable alternative systems nor ability to register faithfully and accurately the national consensus on every issue that comes before it, on many of which Congress and the President often show that even they had been unaware of just what is wanted and just what should be done until at the termination of the confused and muddled legislative process they examined what they had in fact done. If, therefore, I nevertheless conclude that I believe that the welfare state, like Old Siwash, is really worth fighting for and even dying for as compared to any rival system, it is because, despite its imperfections in theory and in practice, in the aggregate it provides more promise of preserving and enlarging human freedoms, temporal prosperity, the extinction of mass misery, and the dignity of man and his moral improvement than any other social system which has previously prevailed, which prevails elsewhere today, or which, outside Utopia, the mind of man has been able to provide a blueprint for.

A traveler on a main but congested highway said to a local yokel that his map indicated that there were two side roads at that point which were shortcuts to his destination, and asked for advice as to which of the two to shift to. To which the yokel replied: "Whichever of the two you take, mister, you will wish to God that you had taken the other, or neither." That is how I feel about the availability of other paths to the good society than that which the welfare state provides, strewn as that path is with boulders, pitfalls, detours, and unpredictable as is its ultimate terminus.

Selection 24

The Role of Government in a Free Society

MILTON FRIEDMAN

From Milton Friedman, Capitalism and Freedom *(Chicago: Phoenix Books: The University of Chicago Press, © 1963)* [*Clothbound ed., 1962*], *pp. 22–36. Reprinted by permission of the University of Chicago Press.*

A common objection to totalitarian societies is that they regard the end as justifying the means. Taken literally, this objection is clearly illogical. If the end does not justify the means, what does? But this easy answer does not dispose of the objection; it simply shows that the objection is not well put. To deny that the end justifies the means is indirectly to assert that the end in question is not the ultimate end, that the ultimate end is itself the use of the proper means. Desirable or not, any end that can be attained only by the use of bad means must give way to the more basic end of the use of acceptable means.

To the liberal, the appropriate means are free discussion and voluntary cooperation, which implies that any form of coercion is inappropriate. The ideal is unanimity among responsible individuals achieved on the basis of free and full discussion. This is another way of expressing the goal of freedom emphasized in the preceding chapter.

From this standpoint, the role of the market, as already noted, is that it permits unanimity without conformity; that it is a system of effectively proportional representation. On the other hand, the characteristic feature of action through explicitly political channels is that it tends to require or to enforce substantial conformity. The typical issue must be decided "yes" or "no"; at most, provision can be made for a fairly limited number of alternatives. Even the use of proportional representation in its explicitly political form does not alter this conclusion. The number of separate groups that can in fact be represented is narrowly limited, enormously so by comparison with the proportional representation of the market. More important, the fact that the final outcome generally must be a law applicable to all groups, rather than separate legislative enactments for each "party" represented, means that proportional representation in its political version, far from permitting unanimity without conformity, tends toward ineffectiveness and fragmentation. It thereby operates to destroy any consensus on which unanimity with conformity can rest.

There are clearly some matters with respect to which effective proportional representation is impossible. I cannot get the amount of national defense I want and you, a different amount. With respect to such individual matters we can discuss, and argue, and vote. But having decided, we must conform. It is precisely the existence of such indivisible matters—protection of the individual and the nation from coercion are clearly the most basic—that prevents exclusive reliance on individual action through the market. If we are to use some of our resources for such indivisible items, we must employ political channels to reconcile differences.

The use of political channels, while inevitable, tends to strain the social cohesion essential for a stable society. The strain is least if agreement for joint action need be reached only on a limited range of issues on which people in any event have common views. Every extension of the range of issues for which explicit agreement is sought strains further the delicate threads that hold society together. If it goes so far as to touch an issue on which men feel deeply yet differently, it may well disrupt the society. Fundamental differences in basic values can seldom if ever be resolved at the ballot box; ultimately they can only be decided, though not resolved, by conflict. The religious and civil wars of history are a bloody testament to this judgment.

The widespread use of the market reduces the strain on the social fabric by rendering conformity unnecessary with respect to any activities it encompasses. The wider the range of activities covered by the market, the fewer are the issues on which explicitly political decisions are required and hence on which it is necessary to achieve agreement. In turn, the fewer the issues on which agreement is necessary, the greater is the likelihood of getting agreement while maintaining a free society.

Unanimity is, of course, an ideal. In practice, we can afford neither the time nor the effort that would be required to achieve complete unanimity on every issue. We must perforce accept something less. We are thus led to accept majority rule in one form or another as an expedient. That majority rule is an expedient rather than itself a basic principle is clearly shown by the fact that our willingness to resort to majority rule, and the size of the majority we require, themselves depend on the seriousness of the issue involved. If the matter is of little moment and the minority has no strong feelings about being overruled, a bare plurality will suffice. On the other hand, if the minority feels strongly about the issue involved, even a bare majority will not do. Few of us would be willing to have issues of free speech, for example, decided by a bare majority. Our legal structure is full of such distinctions among kinds of issues that require different kinds of majorities. At the extreme are those issues embodied in the Constitution. These are the principles that are so important that we are willing to make minimal concessions to expediency. Something like essential consensus was achieved initially in accepting them, and we require something like essential consensus for a change in them.

The self-denying ordinance to refrain from majority rule on certain kinds of issues that is embodied in our Constitution and in similar written or unwritten constitutions elsewhere, and the specific provisions in these constitutions or their equivalents prohibiting coercion of individuals, are themselves to be regarded as reached by free discussion and as reflecting essential unanimity about means.

I turn now to consider more specifically, though still in very broad terms, what the areas are that cannot be handled through the market at all, or can be handled only at so great a cost that the use of political channels may be preferable.

Government As Rule Maker and Umpire

It is important to distinguish the day-to-day activities of people from the general customary and legal framework within which these take place. The day-to-day activities are like the actions of the participants in a game when they are playing it; the framework, like the rules of the game they play. And just as a good game requires acceptance by the players both of the rules and of the umpire to interpret and enforce them, so a good society requires that its members agree on the general conditions that will govern relations among them, on some means of arbitrating different interpretations of these conditions, and on some device for enforcing compliance with the generally accepted rules. As in games, so also in society, most of the general conditions are the unintended outcome of custom, accepted unthinkingly. At most, we consider explicitly only minor modifications in them, though the cumulative effect of a series of minor modifications may be a drastic alteration in the character of the game or of the society. In both games and society also, no set of rules can prevail unless most participants most of the time conform to them without external sanctions; unless, that is, there is a broad underlying social consensus. But we cannot rely on custom or on this consensus alone to interpret and to enforce the rules; we need an umpire. These then are the basic roles of government in a free society: to provide a means whereby we can modify the rules, to mediate differences among us on the meaning of the rules, and to enforce compliance with the rules on the part of those few who would otherwise not play the game.

The need for government in these respects arises because absolute freedom is impossible. However attractive anarchy may be as a philosophy, it is not feasible in a world of imperfect men. Men's freedoms can conflict, and when they do, one man's freedom must be limited to preserve another's—as a Supreme Court Justice once put it, "My freedom to move my fist must be limited by the proximity of your chin."

The major problem in deciding the appropriate activities of government is how to resolve such conflicts among the freedoms of different individuals. In some cases, the answer is easy. There is little difficulty in attaining near unanimity to the proposition that one man's freedom to murder his neighbor must be sacrificed to preserve the freedom of the other man to live. In other cases, the answer is difficult. In the economic area, a major problem arises in respect of the conflict between freedom to combine and freedom to compete. What meaning is to be attributed to "free" as modifying "enterprise"? In the United States, "free" has been understood to mean that anyone is free to set up an enterprise, which means that existing enterprises are not free to keep out competitors except by selling a better product at the same price or the same product at a lower price. In the continental tradition, on the other hand, the meaning has generally been that enterprises are free to do what they want, including the fixing of prices, division of markets, and the adoption of other techniques to keep out potential competitors. Perhaps the most difficult specific problem in this area arises with respect to combinations among laborers, where the problem of freedom to combine and freedom to compete is particularly acute.

A still more basic economic area in which the answer is both difficult and important is the definition of property rights. The notion of property, as it has developed over centuries and as it is embodied in our legal codes, has become so much a part of us that we tend to take it for granted, and fail to recognize the extent to which just what constitutes property and what rights the ownership of property confers are complex social creations rather than self-evident propositions. Does my having title to land, for example, and my freedom to use my property as I wish permit me to deny someone else the right to fly over my land in his airplane? Or does his right to use his airplane take precedence? Or does this depend on how high he flies? Or how much noise he makes? Does voluntary exchange require that he pay me for the privilege of flying over my land? Or that I must pay him to refrain from flying over it? The mere mention of royalties, copyrights, patents; shares of stock in corporations; riparian rights, and the like, may perhaps emphasize the role of generally accepted social rules in the very definition of property. It may suggest also that, in many cases, the existence of a well-specified and generally accepted definition of property is far more important than just what the definition is.

Another economic area that raises particularly difficult problems is the monetary system. Government responsibility for the monetary system has long been recognized. It is explicitly provided for in the constitutional provision which gives Congress the power "to coin money, regulate the value thereof, and of foreign coin." There is probably no other area of economic activity with respect to which government action has been so uniformly accepted. This habitual and by now almost unthinking acceptance of governmental responsibility makes thorough understanding of the grounds for such responsibility all the more necessary, since it enhances the danger that the scope of government will spread from activities that are, to those that are not, appropriate in a free society, from providing a monetary framework to determining the allocation of resources among individuals.

In summary, the organization of economic activity through voluntary exchange presumes that we have provided, through government, for the maintenance of law and order to prevent coercion of one individual by another, the enforcement of contracts voluntarily entered into, the definition of the meaning of property rights, the interpretation and enforcement of such rights, and the provision of a monetary framework.

Action Through Government on Grounds of Technical Monopoly and Neighborhood Effects

The role of government just considered is to do something that the market cannot do for itself, namely, to determine, arbitrate, and enforce the rules of the game. We may also want to do through government some things that might conceivably be done through the market but that technical or similar conditions render it difficult to do in that way. These all reduce to cases in which strictly voluntary exchange is either exceedingly costly or practically impossible. There are two general classes of such cases: monopoly and similar market imperfections, and neighborhood effects.

Exchange is truly voluntary only when nearly equivalent alternatives exist. Monopoly implies the absence of alternatives and thereby inhibits effective freedom of exchange. In practice, monopoly frequently, if not generally, arises from government support or from collusive agreements among individuals. With respect to these, the problem is either to avoid governmental fostering of monopoly or to stimulate the effective enforcement of rules such as those embodied in our antitrust laws. However, monopoly may also arise because it is technically efficient to have a single producer or enterprise. I venture to suggest that such cases are more limited than is supposed but they unquestionably do arise. A simple example is perhaps the provision of telephone services within a community. I shall refer to such cases as "technical" monopoly.

When technical conditions make a monopoly the natural outcome of competitive market forces, there are only three alternatives that seem available: private monopoly, public monopoly, or public regulation. All three are bad, so we must choose among evils. Henry Simons, observing public regulation of monopoly in the United States, found the results so distasteful that he concluded public monopoly would be a lesser evil. Walter Eucken, a noted German liberal, observing public monopoly in German railroads, found the results so distasteful that he concluded public regulation would be a lesser evil. Having learned from both, I reluctantly conclude that, if tolerable, private monopoly may be the least of the evils.

If society were static so that the conditions which give rise to a technical monopoly were sure to remain, I would have little confidence in this solution. In a rapidly changing society, however, the conditions making for technical monopoly frequently change and I suspect that both public regulation and public monopoly are likely to be less responsive to such changes in conditions, to be less readily capable of elimination, than private monopoly.

Railroads in the United States are an excellent example. A large degree of monopoly in railroads was perhaps inevitable on technical grounds in the nineteenth century. This was the justification for the Interstate Commerce Commission. But conditions have changed. The emergence of road and air transport has reduced the monopoly element in railroads to negligible proportions. Yet we have not eliminated the ICC. On the contrary, the ICC, which started out as an agency to protect the public from exploitation by the railroads, has become an agency to protect railroads from competition by trucks and other means of transport, and more recently even to protect existing truck companies from competition by new entrants. Similarly, in England, when the railroads were nationalized, trucking was at first brought into the state monopoly. If railroads had never been subjected to regulation in the United States, it is nearly certain that by now transportation, including railroads, would be a highly competitive industry with little or no remaining monopoly elements.

The choice between the evils of private monopoly, public monopoly, and public regulation cannot, however, be made once and for all, independently of the factual circumstances. If the technical monopoly is of a service or commodity that is regarded as essential and if its monopoly power is sizable, even the short-run effects of private unregulated monopoly may not be tolerable, and either public regulation or public ownership may be a lesser evil.

Technical monopoly may on occasion justify a *de facto* public monopoly. It cannot by itself justify a public monopoly achieved by making it illegal for anyone else to compete. For example, there is no way to justify our present public monopoly of the post office. It may be argued that the carrying of mail is a technical monopoly and that a government monopoly is the least of evils. Along these lines, one could perhaps justify a government post office but not the present law, which makes it illegal for anybody else to carry mail. If the delivery of mail is a technical monopoly, no one will be able to succeed in competition with the government. If it is not, there is no reason why the government should be engaged in it. The only way to find out is to leave other people free to enter.

The historical reason why we have a post office monopoly is because the Pony Express did such a good job of carrying the mail across the continent that, when the government introduced transcontinental service, it couldn't compete effectively and lost money. The result was a law making it illegal for anybody else to carry the mail. That is why the Adams Express Company is an investment trust today instead of an operating company. I conjecture that if entry into the mail-carrying business were open to all, there would be a large number of firms entering it and this archaic industry would become revolutionized in short order.

A second general class of cases in which strictly voluntary exchange is impossible arises when actions of individuals have effects on other individuals for which it is not feasible to charge or recompense them. This is the problem of "neighborhood effects." An obvious example is the pollution of a stream. The man who pollutes a stream is in effect forcing others to exchange good water for bad. These others might be willing to make the exchange at a price. But it is not feasible for them, acting individually, to avoid the exchange or to enforce appropriate compensation.

A less obvious example is the provision of highways. In this case, it is technically possible to identify and hence charge individuals for their use of the roads and so to have private operation. However, for general access roads, involving many points of entry and exit, the costs of collection would be extremely high if a charge were to be made for the specific services received by each individual, because of the necessity of establishing toll booths or the equivalent at all entrances. The gasoline tax is a much cheaper method of charging individuals roughly in proportion to their use of the roads. This method, however, is one in which the particular payment cannot be identified closely with the particular use. Hence, it is hardly feasible to have private enterprise provide the service and collect the charge without establishing extensive private monopoly.

These considerations do not apply to long-distance turnpikes with high density of traffic and limited access. For these, the costs of collection are small and in many cases are now being paid, and there are often numerous alternatives, so that there is no serious monopoly problem. Hence, there is every reason why these should be privately owned and operated. If so owned and operated, the enterprise running the highway should receive the gasoline taxes paid on account of travel on it.

Parks are an interesting example because they illustrate the difference between cases that can and cases that cannot be justified by neighborhood effects, and because almost everyone at first sight regards the conduct of national parks as obviously a valid function of government. In fact, however, neighborhood effects may justify a city park; they do not justify a national park, like Yellowstone National Park or the Grand Canyon. What is the fundamental difference between the two? For the city park, it is extremely difficult to identify the people who benefit from it and to charge them for the benefits which they receive. If there is a park in the middle of the city, the houses on all sides get the benefit of the open space, and people who walk through it or by it also benefit. To maintain toll collectors at the gates or to impose annual charges per window overlooking the park would be very expensive and difficult. The entrances to a national park like Yellowstone, on the other hand, are few; most of the people who come stay for a considerable period of time and it is perfectly feasible to set up toll gates and collect admission charges. This is indeed now done, although the charges do not cover the whole costs. If the public wants this kind of activity enough to pay for it, private enterprises will have every incentive to provide such parks. And, of course, there are many private enterprises of this nature now in existence. I cannot myself conjure up any neighborhood effects or important monopoly effects that would justify governmental activity in this area.

Considerations like those I have treated under the heading of neighborhood effects have been used to rationalize almost every conceivable intervention. In many instances, however, this rationalization is special pleading rather than a legitimate application of the concept of neighborhood effects. Neighborhood effects cut both ways. They can be a reason for limiting the activities of government as well as for expanding them. Neighborhood effects impede voluntary exchange because it is difficult to identify the effects on third parties and to measure their magnitude; but this difficulty is present in governmental activity as well. It is hard to know when neighborhood effects are sufficiently large to justify particular costs in overcoming them and even harder to distribute the costs in an appropriate fashion. Consequently, when government engages in activities to overcome neighborhood effects, it will in part introduce an additional set of neighborhood effects by failing to charge or to compensate individuals properly. Whether the original or the new neighborhood effects are the more serious can only be judged by the facts of the individual case, and even then, only very approximately. Furthermore, the use of government to overcome neighborhood effects itself has an extremely important neighborhood effect which is unrelated to the particular occasion for government action. Every act of government intervention limits the area of individual freedom directly and threatens the preservation of freedom indirectly for reasons elaborated in the first chapter.[1]

Our principles offer no hard-and-fast line how far it is appropriate to use government to accomplish jointly what it is difficult or impossible for us to accomplish separately through strictly voluntary exchange. In any particular case of proposed intervention, we must make up a balance sheet, listing separately the advantages and disadvantages. Our principles tell us what items to put on the one side and what items on the other and they give us some basis for attaching importance to the different items. In particular, we shall always want to enter on the liability side of any proposed government intervention its neighborhood effect in threatening freedom and give this effect considerable weight. Just how much weight to give to it, as to other items, depends upon the circumstances. If, for example, existing government intervention is minor, we shall attach a smaller weight to the negative effects of additional government intervention. This is an important reason why many earlier liberals, like Henry Simons, writing at a time when government was small by today's standards, were willing to have government undertake activities that today's liberals would not accept now that government has become so overgrown.

Action Through Government on Paternalistic Grounds

Freedom is a tenable objective only for responsible individuals. We do not believe in freedom for madmen or children. The necessity of drawing a line between responsible individuals and others is inescapable, yet it means that there is an essential ambiguity in our ultimate objective of freedom. Paternalism is inescapable for those whom we designate as not responsible.

The clearest case, perhaps, is that of madmen. We are willing neither to permit them freedom nor to shoot them. It would be nice if we could rely on voluntary activities of individuals to house and care for the madmen. But I think we cannot rule out the possibility that such charitable activities will be inadequate, if only because of the neighborhood effect involved in the fact that I benefit if another man contributes to the care of the insane. For this reason, we may be willing to arrange for their care through government.

Children offer a more difficult case. The ultimate operative unit in our society is the family, not the individual. Yet the acceptance of the family as the unit rests in considerable part on expediency rather than principle. We believe that parents

---

[1] [Refers to Friedman, "Capitalism and Freedom"].

are generally best able to protect their children and to provide for their development into responsible individuals for whom freedom is appropriate. But we do not believe in the freedom of parents to do what they will with other people. The children are responsible individuals in embryo, and a believer in freedom believes in protecting their ultimate rights.

To put this in a different and what may seem a more callous way, children are at one and the same time consumer goods and potentially responsible members of society. The freedom of individuals to use their economic resources as they want includes the freedom to use them to have children—to buy, as it were, the services of children as a particular form of consumption. But once this choice is exercised, the children have a value in and of themselves and have a freedom of their own that is not simply an extension of the freedom of the parents.

The paternalistic ground for governmental activity is in many ways the most troublesome to a liberal; for it involves the acceptance of a principle—that some shall decide for others—which he finds objectionable in most applications and which he rightly regards as a hallmark of his chief intellectual opponents, the proponents of collectivism in one or another of its guises, whether it be communism, socialism, or a welfare state. Yet there is no use pretending that problems are simpler than in fact they are. There is no avoiding the need for some measure of paternalism. As Dicey wrote in 1914 about an act for the protection of mental defectives, "The Mental Deficiency Act is the first step along a path on which no sane man can decline to enter, but which, if too far pursued, will bring statesmen across difficulties hard to meet without considerable interference with individual liberty."[1] There is no formula that can tell us where to stop. We must rely on our fallible judgment and, having reached a judgment, on our ability to persuade our fellowmen that it is a correct judgment, or their ability to persuade us to modify our views. We must put our faith, here as elsewhere, in a consensus reached by imperfect and biased men through free discussion and trial and error.

Conclusion

A government which maintained law and order, defined property rights, served as a means whereby we could modify property rights and other rules of the economic game, adjudicated disputes about the interpretation of the rules, enforced contracts, promoted competition, provided a monetary framework, engaged in activities to counter technical monopolies and to overcome neighborhood effects widely regarded as sufficiently important to justify government intervention, and which supplemented private charity and the private family in protecting the irresponsible, whether madman or child—such a government would clearly have important functions to perform. The consistent liberal is not an anarchist.

Yet it is also true that such a government would have clearly limited functions and would refrain from a host of activities that are now undertaken by federal

---

[1] A. V. Dicey, *Lectures on the Relation between Law and Public Opinion in England during the Nineteenth Century* (2nd ed.; London: Macmillan & Co., 1914), p. li.

and state governments in the United States and their counterparts in other Western countries. Succeeding chapters will deal in some detail with some of these activities, and a few have been discussed above, but it may help to give a sense of proportion about the role that a liberal would assign government simply to list, in closing this chapter, some activities currently undertaken by government in the United States that cannot, so far as I can see, validly be justified in terms of the principles outlined above:

1. Parity price support programs for agriculture.
2. Tariffs on imports or restrictions on exports, such as current oil import quotas, sugar quotas, et cetera.
3. Governmental control of output, such as through the farm program, or through proration of oil as is practiced by the Texas Railroad Commission.
4. Rent control, such as is still practiced in New York, or more general price and wage controls such as were imposed during and just after World War II.
5. Legal minimum-wage rates, or legal maximum prices, such as the legal maximum of zero on the rate of interest that can be paid on demand deposits by commercial banks, or the legally fixed maximum rates that can be paid on savings and time deposits.
6. Detailed regulation of industries, such as the regulation of transportation by the Interstate Commerce Commission. This had some justification on technical monopoly grounds when initially introduced for railroads; it has none now for any means of transport. Another example is detailed regulation of banking.
7. A similar example, but one which deserves special mention because of its implicit censorship and violation of free speech, is the control of radio and television by the Federal Communication Commission.
8. Present social security programs, especially the old-age and retirement programs compelling people in effect (a) to spend a specified fraction of their income on the purchase of retirement annuity, (b) to buy the annuity from a publicly operated enterprise.
9. Licensure provisions in various cities and states which restrict particular enterprises or occupations or professions to people who have a license, where the license is more than a receipt for a tax which anyone who wishes to enter the activity may buy.
10. So-called "public housing" and the host of other subsidy programs directed at fostering residential construction, such as FHA and VA guarantee of mortage, and the like.
11. Conscription to man the military services in peacetime. The appropriate free market arrangement is volunteer military forces; which is to say, hiring men to serve. There is no justification for not paying whatever price is necessary to attract the required number of men. Present arrangements are inequitable and arbitrary, seriously interfere with the freedom of young men to shape their lives, and probably are even more costly than the market alternative. (Universal military training to provide a reserve for wartime is a different problem and may be justified on liberal grounds.)
12. National parks, as noted above.
13. The legal prohibition on the carrying of mail for profit.
14. Publicly owned and operated toll roads, as noted above.

This list is far from comprehensive.

Selection 25

Concluding Notes on the Social Philosophy Towards Which the General Theory Might Lead

JOHN MAYNARD KEYNES

From The General Theory of Employment, Interest and Money, *by John Maynard Keynes (New York: Harcourt, Brace & World, Inc., 1965), pp. 372–384. Reprinted by permission of Harcourt, Brace & World, Inc.*

The outstanding faults of the economic society in which we live are its failure to provide for full employment and its arbitrary and inequitable distribution of wealth and incomes. The bearing of the foregoing theory on the first of these is obvious. But there are also two important respects in which it is relevant to the second.

Since the end of the nineteenth century significant progress toward the removal of very great disparities of wealth and income has been achieved through the instrument of direct taxation—income tax and surtax and death duties—especially in Great Britain. Many people would wish to see this process carried much further, but they are deterred by two considerations; partly by the fear of making skillful evasions too much worthwhile and also of diminishing unduly the motive toward risk-taking, but mainly, I think, by the belief that the growth of capital depends upon the strength of the motive toward individual saving and that for a large proportion of this growth we are dependent on the savings of the rich out of their superfluity. Our argument does not affect the first of these considerations. But it may considerably modify our attitude toward the second. For we have seen that, up to the point where full employment prevails the growth of capital depends not at all on a low propensity to consume but is, on the contrary, held back by it; and only in conditions of full employment is a low propensity to consume conducive to the growth of capital. Moreover, experience suggests that in existing conditions saving by institutions and through sinking funds is more than adequate, and that measures for the redistribution of incomes in a way likely to raise the propensity to consume may prove positively favorable to the growth of capital.

The existing confusion of the public mind on the matter is well illustrated by the very common belief that the death duties are responsible for a reduction in the capital wealth of the country. Assuming that the state applies the proceeds of these duties to its ordinary outgoings so that taxes on incomes and consumption are correspondingly reduced or avoided, it is, of course, true that a fiscal policy of heavy death duties has the effect of increasing the community's propensity to consume. But inasmuch as an increase in the habitual propensity to consume will in general (that is, except in conditions of full employment) serve to increase at the same time the inducement to invest, the inference commonly drawn is the exact opposite of the truth.

Thus our argument leads toward the conclusion that in contemporary conditions the growth of wealth, so far from being dependent on the abstinence of the rich, as is commonly supposed, is more likely to be impeded by it. One of the chief social justifications of great inequality of wealth is, therefore, removed. I am not saying that there are no other reasons, unaffected by our theory, capable of justifying some measure of inequality in some circumstances. But it does dispose of the most important of the reasons why hitherto we have thought it prudent to move carefully. This particularly affects our attitude toward death duties; for there are certain justifications for inequality of incomes which do not apply equally to inequality of inheritances.

For my own part, I believe that there is social and psychological justification for significant inequalities of incomes and wealth, but not for such large disparities as exist today. There are valuable human activities which require the motive of money-making and the environment of private wealth-ownership for their full fruition. Moreover, dangerous human proclivities can be canalized into comparatively harmless channels by the existence of opportunities for money-making and private wealth, which, if they cannot be satisfied in this way, may find their outlet in cruelty, the reckless pursuit of personal power and authority, and other forms of self-aggrandizement. It is better that a man should tyrannize over his bank balance than over his fellow-citizens; and whilst the former is sometimes denounced as being but a means to the latter, sometimes at least it is an alternative. But it is not necessary for the stimulation of these activities and the satisfaction of these proclivities that the game should be played for such high sakes as at present. Much lower stakes will serve the purpose equally well, as soon as the players are accustomed to them. The task of transmuting human nature must not be confused with the task of managing it. Though in the ideal commonwealth men may have been taught or inspired or bred to take no interest in the stakes, it may still be wise and prudent statesmanship to allow the game to be played, subject to rules and limitations, so long as the average man, or even a significant section of the community, is in fact strongly addicted to the money-making passion.

II

There is, however, a second, much more fundamental inference from our argument which has a bearing on the future of inequalities of wealth; namely, our theory of the rate of interest. The justification for a moderately high rate of interest has been found hitherto in the necessity of providing a sufficient inducement to save. But we have shown that the extent of effective saving is necessarily determined by the scale of investment and that the scale of investment is promoted by a *low* rate of interest, provided that we do not attempt to stimulate it in this way beyond the point which corresponds to full employment. Thus it is to our best advantage to reduce the rate of interest to that point relatively to the schedule of the marginal efficiency of capital at which there is full employment.

There can be no doubt that this criterion will lead to a much lower rate of interest than has ruled hitherto; and, so far as one can guess at the schedules of the marginal efficiency of capital corresponding to increasing amounts of capital, the rate of interest is likely to fall steadily, if it should be practicable to maintain conditions of more or less continuous full employment—unless, indeed, there is an excessive change in the aggregate propensity to consume (including the state).

I feel sure that the demand for capital is strictly limited in the sense that it would not be difficult to increase the stock of capital up to a point where its marginal efficiency had fallen to a very low figure. This would not mean that the use of capital instruments would cost almost nothing, but only that the return from them would have to cover little more than their exhaustion by wastage and obsolescence together with some margin to cover risk and the exercise of skill and judgment. In short, the aggregate return from durable goods in the course of their life would, as in the case of short-lived goods, just cover their labor costs of production *plus* an allowance for risk and the costs of skill and supervision.

Now, although this state of affairs would be quite compatible with some measure of individualism, yet it would mean the euthanasia of the rentier, and, consequently, the euthanasia of the cumulative oppressive power of the capitalist to exploit the scarcity-value of capital. Interest today rewards no genuine sacrifice, any more than does the rent of land. The owner of capital can obtain interest because capital is scarce, just as the owner of land can obtain rent because land is scarce. But whilst there may be intrinsic reasons for the scarcity of land, there are no intrinsic reasons for the scarcity of capital. An intrinsic reason for such scarcity, in the sense of a genuine sacrifice which could only be called forth by the offer of a reward in the shape of interest, would not exist, in the long run, except in the event of the individual propensity to consume proving to be of such a character that net saving in conditions of full employment comes to an end before capital has become sufficiently abundant. But even so, it will still be possible for communal saving through the agency of the state to be maintained at a level which will allow the growth of capital up to the point where it ceases to be scarce.

I see, therefore, the rentier aspect of capitalism as a transitional phase which will disappear when it has done its work. And with the disappearance of its rentier aspect much else in it besides will suffer a sea-change. It will be, moreover, a great advantage of the order of events which I am advocating, that the euthanasia of the rentier, of the functionless investor, will be nothing sudden—

merely a gradual but prolonged continuance of what we have seen recently in Great Britain, and will need no revolution.

Thus we might aim in practice (there being nothing in this which is unattainable) at an increase in the volume of capital until it ceases to be scarce, so that the functionless investor will no longer receive a bonus; and at a scheme of direct taxation which allows the intelligence and determination and executive skill of the financier, the entrepreneur *et hoc genus omne* (who are certainly so fond of their craft that their labor could be obtained much cheaper than at present), to be harnessed to the service of the community on reasonable terms of reward.

At the same time we must recognize that only experience can show how far the common will, embodied in the policy of the state, ought to be directed to increasing and supplementing the inducement to invest; and how far it is safe to stimulate the average propensity to consume, without forgoing our aim of depriving capital of its scarcity-value within one or two generations. It may turn out that the propensity to consume will be so easily strengthened by the effects of a falling rate of interest, that full employment can be reached with a rate of accumulation little greater than at present. In this event a scheme for the higher taxation of large incomes and inheritances might be open to the objection that it would lead to full employment with a rate of accumulation which was reduced considerably below the current level. I must not be supposed to deny the possibility, or even the probability, of this outcome. For in such matters it is rash to predict how the average man will react to a changed environment. If, however, it should prove easy to secure an approximation to full employment with a rate of accumulation not much greater than at present, an outstanding problem will at least have been solved. And it would remain for separate decision on what scale and by what means it is right and reasonable to call on the living generation to restrict their consumption so as to establish, in course of time, a state of full investment for their successors.

III

In some other respect the foregoing theory is moderately conservative in its implications. For whilst it indicates the vital importance of establishing certain central controls in matters which are now left in the main to individual initiative, there are wide fields of activity which are unaffected. The state will have to exercise a guiding influence on the propensity to consume partly through its scheme of taxation, partly by fixing the rate of interest, and partly, perhaps, in other ways. Furthermore, it seems unlikely that the influence of banking policy on the rate of interest will be sufficient by itself to determine an optimum rate of investment. I conceive, therefore, that a somewhat comprehensive socialization of investment will prove the only means of securing an approximation to full employment, although this need not exclude all manner of compromises and of devices by which public authority will cooperate with private initiative. But beyond this no obvious case is made out for a system of state socialism which would embrace most of the economic life of the community. It is not the ownership of the instruments of production which it is important for the state to assume. If the state is able to determine the aggregate amount of resources devoted to augmenting the instruments and the basic rate of reward to those who own them, it will have accomplished all that is necessary. Moreover, the necessary measures of socialization can be introduced gradually and without a break in the general traditions of society.

Our criticism of the accepted classical theory of economics has consisted not so much in finding logical flaws in its analysis as in pointing out that its tacit assumptions are seldom or never satisfied, with the result that it cannot solve the economic problems of the actual world. But if our central controls succeed in establishing an aggregate volume of output corresponding to full employment as nearly as is practicable, the classical theory comes into its own again from this point onward. If we suppose the volume of output to be given, that is, to be determined by forces outside the classical scheme of thought, then there is no objection to be raised against the classical analysis of the manner in which private self-interest will determine what in particular is produced, in what proportions the factors of production will be combined to produce it, and how the value of the final product will be distributed between them. Again, if we have dealt otherwise with the problem of thrift, there is no objection to be raised against the modern classical theory as to the degree of concilience between private and public advantage in conditions of perfect and imperfect competition, respectively. Thus, apart from the necessity of central controls to bring about an adjustment between the propensity to consume and the inducement to invest, there is no more reason to socialize economic life than there was before.

To put the point concretely, I see no reason to suppose that the existing system seriously misemploys the factors of production which are in use. There are, of course, errors of foresight; but these would not be avoided by centralizing decisions. When 9 million men are employed out of 10 million willing and able to work, there is no evidence that the labor of these 9 million men is misdirected. The complaint against the present system is not that these 9 million men ought to be employed on different tasks, but that tasks should be available for the remaining 1 million men. It is in determining the volume, not the direction, of actual employment that the existing system has broken down.

Thus I agree with Gesell that the result of filling in the gaps in the classical theory is not to dispose of the "Manchester System," but to indicate the nature of the environment which the free play of economic forces requires if it is to realize the full potentialities of production. The central controls necessary to ensure full employment will, of course, involve a large extension of the traditional functions of government. Furthermore, the modern classical theory has itself called attention to various conditions in which the free play of economic forces may need to be curbed or guided. But there will still remain a wide field for the exercise of private initiative and responsibility. Within this field the traditional advantages of individualism will still hold good.

Let us stop for a moment to remind ourselves what these advantages are. They are partly advantages of efficiency—the advantages of decentralization and of the play of self-interest. The advantage to efficiency of the decentralization of decisions and of individual responsibility is even greater, perhaps, than the nineteenth century supposed; and the reaction against the appeal to self-interest may have gone too far. But, above all, individualism, if it can be purged of its defects and its abuses, is the best safeguard of personal liberty in the sense that, compared with any other system, it greatly widens the field for the exercise of personal choice. It is also the best safeguard of the variety of life, which emerges precisely from this extended field of personal choice, and the loss of which is the greatest of all the losses of the homogeneous or totalitarian state. For this variety preserves the traditions which embody the most secure and successful choices of former generations; it colors the present with the diversification of its fancy; and, being the handmaid of experiment as well as of tradition and of fancy, it is the most powerful instrument to better the future.

Whilst, therefore, the enlargement of the functions of government involved in the task of adjusting to one another the propensity to consume and the inducement to invest would seem to a nineteenth-century publicist or to a contemporary American financier to be a terrific encroachment on individualism, I defend it, on the contrary, both as the only practicable means of avoiding the destruction of existing economic forms in their entirety and as the condition of the successful functioning of individual initiative.

For if effective demand is deficient, not only is the public scandal of wasted resources intolerable, but the individual enterpriser who seeks to bring these resources into action is operating with the odds loaded against him. The game of hazard which he plays is furnished with many zeros, so that the players *as a whole* will lose if they have the energy and hope to deal all the cards. Hitherto the increment of the world's wealth has fallen short of the aggregate of positive individual savings; and the difference has been made up by the losses of those whose courage and initiative have not been supplemented by exceptional skill or unusual good fortune. But if effective demand is adequate, average skill and average good fortune will be enough.

The authoritarian state systems of today seem to solve the problem of unemployment at the expense of efficiency and of freedom. It is certain that the world will not much longer tolerate the unemployment which, apart from brief intervals of excitement, is associated—and, in my opinion, inevitably associated—with present-day capitalistic individualism. But it may be possible by a right analysis of the problem to cure the disease whilst preserving efficiency and freedom.

IV

I have mentioned in passing that the new system might be more favorable to peace than the old has been. It is worthwhile to repeat and emphasize that aspect.

War has several causes. Dictators and others such, to whom war offers, in expectation at least, a pleasurable excitement, find it easy to work on the natural bellicosity of their peoples. But, over and above this, facilitating their task of fanning the popular flame, are the economic causes of war, namely, the pressure of population and the competitive struggle for markets. It is the second factor, which probably played a predominant part in the nineteenth century, and might again, that is germane to this discussion.

I have pointed out in the preceding chapter that, under the system of domestic laissez faire and an international gold standard such as was orthodox in the latter half of the nineteenth century, there was no means open to a government whereby to mitigate economic distress at home except through the competitive struggle for markets. For all measures helpful to a state of chronic or intermittent underemployment were ruled out, except measures to improve the balance of trade on income account.

Thus, whilst economists were accustomed to applaud the prevailing international system as furnishing the fruits of the international division of labor and harmonizing at the same time the interests of different nations, there lay concealed a less benign influence; and those statesmen were moved by common sense and a correct apprehension of the true course of events, who believed that if a rich, old country were to neglect the struggle for markets its prosperity would droop and fail. But if nations can learn to provide themselves with full employment by their domestic policy (and, we must add, if they can also attain equilibrium in the trend of their population), there need be no important economic forces calculated to set the interest of one country against that of its neighbors. There would still be room for the international division of labor and for international lending in appropriate conditions. But there would no longer be a pressing motive why one country need force its wares on another or repulse the offerings of its neighbor, not because this was necessary to enable it to pay for what it wished to purchase, but with the express object of upsetting the equilibrium of payments so as to develop a balance of trade in its own favor. International trade would cease to be what it is, namely, a desperate expedient to maintain employment at home by forcing sales on foreign markets and restricting purchases, which, if successful, will merely shift the problem of unemployment to the neighbor which is worsted in the struggle, but a willing and unimpeded exchange of goods and services in conditions of mutual advantage.

V

Is the fulfilment of these ideas a visionary hope? Have they insufficient roots in the motives which govern the evolution of political society? Are the interests which they will thwart stronger and more obvious than those which they will serve?

I do not attempt an answer in this place. It would need a volume of a different character from this one to indicate even in outline the practical measures in which they might be gradually clothed. But if the ideas are correct—an hypothesis on which the author himself must necessarily base what he writes—it would be a mistake, I predict, to dispute their potency over a period of time. At the present moment people are usually expectant of a more fundamental diagnosis; more particularly ready to receive it; eager to try it out, if it should be even plausible. But apart from this contemporary mood, the ideas of economists and political philosophers, both when they are right and when they are wrong, are more powerful than is commonly understood. Indeed, the world is ruled by little else. Practical men, who believe themselves to be quite exempt from any intellectual influences, are usually the slaves of some defunct economist. Madmen in authority, who hear voices in the air, are distilling their frenzy from some academic scribbler of a few years back. I am sure that the power of vested interests is vastly exaggerated compared with the gradual encroachment of ideas. Not, indeed, immediately, but after a certain interval; for in the field of economic and political philosophy there are not many who are influenced by new theories after they are twenty-five or thirty years of age, so that the ideas which civil servants and politicians and even agitators apply to current events are not likely to be the newest. But, soon or late, it is ideas, not vested interests, which are dangerous for good or evil.

DISCUSSION QUESTIONS

1. Professor Friedman lists activities currently undertaken by government which he thinks are unjustified according to his view of the proper role of government. To discontinue these activities would be a revolutionary change in American life. Do you think such a view is likely to prevail? Discuss reasons why the opposite trend, that is, an increased role for government, might be more likely to prevail.
2. Discuss the role of the dominant middle class in the rise of the "welfare state" in the United States and Western Europe.
3. Compare the view of the economic role of government that is implicit in the selection by J. M. Keynes with the view set forth by Milton Friedman.
4. The "welfare state" has not emerged in response to an overriding public or congressional sentiment in favor of an increased role for government. Instead it has emerged in piecemeal fashion in response to pressures of particular interests and demands of specific problems. Government intervention has been a more or less spontaneous response on the part of society to protect itself from the more destructive aspects of a self-regulating market system. Do you agree with this interpretation of the rise of the "welfare state"? What counter arguments might a defender of a self-regulating market system offer?

SELECTED REFERENCES

Boulding, Kenneth E., *Principles of Economic Policy,* Englewood Cliffs, N.J.: Prentice-Hall, Inc., 1958.

Galbraith, John Kenneth, *The Affluent Society,* Boston, Houghton Mifflin Company, 1958.

———, *The New Industrial State,* Boston: Houghton Mifflin Company, 1967.

Johnson, Harry G., "The Political Economy of Opulence" and "The Social Policy of an Opulent Society," in *Money, Trade and Economic Growth,* London: Unwin University Books, 1962, pp. 164–95.

Lerner, Abba P., *The Economics of Employment,* New York: McGraw-Hill Book Co., 1951. See especially Chap. 1.

Myrdal, Gunnar, *Beyond the Welfare State,* New Haven, Conn.: Yale University Press, 1960.

Polanyi, Karl, *The Great Transformation: The Political and Economic Origins of Our Time,* New York: Rinehart & Co., Inc., 1944.

Tawney, R. H., *The Acquisitive Society,* New York: Harcourt, Brace & World, Inc., 1920, 1948.

Wallich, Henry C., *The Cost of Freedom: A New Look at Capitalism,* New York: Harper & Row, Publishers, 1960.